TEAM

Also by Richard Woodley

DEALER

TEAM

A HIGH SCHOOL ODYSSEY

BY

RICHARD WOODLEY

HOLT, RINEHART AND WINSTON

NEW YORK • CHICAGO • SAN FRANCISCO

Published simultaneously in Canada by Holt, Rinehart and Winston of Canada, Limited.

ISBN: 0–03–001061–6
Library of Congress Catalog Card Number: 72–78113

First Edition

Designer: Robert Aulicino

Printed in the United States of America

For Buddy Douds

Author's Note

In accordance with my agreement with the supervisors of the school district involved, I have changed the names of the town, the high school, and of players, parents, coaches and school personnel. Otherwise I have portrayed everything as it was to the best of my ability.

The 1971 Laketown Harvesters

Prentice "Buddy" Fowles, Jr.	head coach
Sandy Branahan	assistant coach
Clifford Albert	offensive guard
Keith Allen	running back
Mike Asher	lineman
Joe Bailey	defensive back
Steve Barker	defensive end, punter
Jim Benning	offensive lineman
Stan Beronski	defensive end
Barry Brill	linebacker
Stan Burn	offensive lineman
Vince Carradino	defensive tackle
John Curtis	offensive tackle
Freddie Delaney	defensive tackle, end
Mark Ferenzi	defensive back
John Finch	defensive back
Jack Forrest	offensive guard
Ken Furst	defensive back
Cary Grimes	offensive end
Don Heidner	flankerback
Tom Kase	offensive tackle
Joe Knowland	lineman
Eddie McArthur	offensive end
Jim Marshall	center, defensive tackle
Bradford McClure	defensive tackle
Bill McCord	lineman
Ray Meister	cornerback
Rich Merrill	utility center
Bob Mills	defensive tackle
Dan Miranda	offensive end
John Mucia	linebacker
Ted O'Neill	offensive end, quarterback, safety

Jonathan Penchak	quarterback
Jim Petrowski	defensive guard
Brian Purcell	offensive end, running back
Stu Rosenman	running back, defensive end
Al Stacey	running back, cornerback
Bruce Stacey	linebacker, running back
Ben Schenkle	running back
Rich Schenkle	linebacker, offensive end
Mike Schultz	lineman
Jerry Spitz	lineman
Paul Treski	lineman
Harry Wallace	lineman
Karl Walsh	cornerback
Jeremy Wendell	lineman

TEAM

1

Laketown High School head coach, Buddy Fowles, fixed his blue eyes on me as he put down his coffee cup. "My idea of football," he said in a disarmingly gentle voice, "is that it is a game. It is rough, but it is only a game. I think it is a good thing for kids if it is taught right. But other things are important—peace, love, honesty, school. I don't think you need to teach hate or viciousness to teach good football. I don't want kids to get hurt. I think you can teach good values for life, *and* produce a good football team—you can do both. I *think* you can. It is what I want to do. If I can't do that, then I don't want to coach. It's that simple."

He turned the coffee cup slowly in his strong, clean hands and looked straight at me. He smiled slightly. "Do you believe me?"

These were football-coaching clichés, nearly. I said, "I don't know. We've only just met."

"It's the way I feel," he said. "But you don't have to believe that. I ask only one thing: You must care first about the boys. That's the only requirement I ask—they come first."

"Sure," I said. "That's the way I feel too."

"I mean it," he said. "I really do. If you mean it too, then you can write anything you want."

Laketown, New York, is a typically sprawling suburban residential town of about 30,000. Only about fifty miles north of midtown Manhattan—an hour's drive on the scenic Taconic State Parkway—Laketown is a largely middle-class community in a county, Westchester, dominated by wealth. It grew up out of the cornfields among idyllic hills, woodlands, and reservoirs which are part of the New York City water supply.

The town population grew nearly 600 percent between 1950 and 1970, and though there is today a local board overseeing the town's growth and architecture, the raw marks of untrammeled expansion are there. The outlying areas of its forty square miles still carry a bucolic flavor, but the interior town is characterized now by development homes interspersed with large old farmhouses, historic mansions, and a new IBM plant. There is no traditional downtown Main Street area, but rather a motley shopping center in the central section called Laketown Heights. Along winding, two-lane, tree-lined highways which follow Revolutionary War routes stand some of the homes and churches from that time, as well as hamburger joints and gas stations from today.

Perhaps 40 percent of the town's workers commute to New York or other nearby cities—not just executives, but others such as factory workers, power company employees, and firemen as well. Despite proximity to the Democratic city of New York, Laketown voters are Republican by a two-to-one majority. A full-time elected mayor, or "supervisor," directs affairs from his office in Town Hall, a neocolonial manse built in 1935. The thirty-three-man police force operates from a new headquarters building. The town is served by two volunteer fire companies and a volunteer ambulance corps with two ambulances.

On the day I came to Laketown in August of 1971, Laketown High was a ten-year-old, two-story, rambling modernistic structure of red brick with inlaid glossy panels of red, blue, and white. A mile out from the main shopping center on Route 202, it was adjoined by athletic fields to the side and rear. Beyond the fields a row of high-tension towers stalked the property line. To the rear rose a densely wooded hill, part of the State Park. The enrollment of 1,500 made it a Class-A school for athletic competition, one class below the largest. The crosstown rival, newer Brushland High, was larger, Double A.

All in all, there was no elite quality in either the town or the school which drew me there to write about the football team. It was ordinariness I wanted, an ordinary football team in an ordinary town. Beyond that, all I needed to find was a coach who would give me complete access to the team. What I actually found, entirely by accident, was a team and coach neither elite nor ordinary, a mix of personalities, styles, and events so captivating that I eventually became convinced I could have scoured the country without finding its superior.

But in the beginning, I was not sure I had picked a fruitful place because so many people thought that the Laketown Harvesters that year would lose most, if not all, of their games.

In late summer, the town had a slumberous, lazy quality. Many families were away on vacation, others swam at the town's Sparkle Lake. Fishermen dotted the shores of the reservoirs, and at night, when they fished from bridges, they set out lanterns to warn off cars passing close by. Occasionally one could see a horse and rider along the road, or off in a field. Fruit stands were being readied for produce of local farms—apples, pears, and pumpkins.

The high school, too, was being quietly readied for students. The athletic fields stood empty, the grass dulled by the sun.

A couple miles from the school, past fruit stands, woods, and Sparkle Lake, was a section of development houses where Coach Fowles lived in a split-level home on a half-acre of land.

It was the evening before the first day of football practice. In the small kitchen, "Squeegy" (Elizabeth) Fowles, a pretty, elfin woman with long red hair, stacked supper dishes in the portable dishwasher. Their son, Jeff, 11, and daughter Laurie, 10, were in the basement den watching color TV. In the living room, pleasantly stocked with modest colonial-style furnishings, soft music of the Ramsey Lewis Trio came from the AR stereo speakers.

In the dining room ell, Coach Fowles sat at the table with his assistant coach, Sandy Branahan, and his two junior varsity coaches. Index cards and notebooks were spread around. A book on the Houston Veer-T offense, and one by Ohio State coach Woody Hayes, lay there for reference.

Coach Fowles outlined policies:

"You will have to correct players. Do it positively, don't tear them down. . . . No swearing, we're not even going to talk about it. . . . Morale is the most important thing. It has won more games than personnel. . . . We say that Laketown always runs, Laketown never walks, not anywhere. . . . They have to have pride in themselves and in the team. They must look and act like Laketown football players. . . . When you talk, they listen. When *they* talk, *you* listen. . . . Give them a break during practices, and then get away from them, let them talk about you, get it out of their system. . . . Football is a game, make it fun. If you've got a joker on the team, encourage him to crack jokes once in a while. . . . Call them by their first names, treat them like a family. . . . Always get outside, no matter what the weather, even if just for five minutes. . . . Make a practice outline every day and stick to the time schedules. Always have a stopwatch on the field. . . . The kids will give you just as much as you give them. If you give 50 percent, they'll give 50 percent."

His assistants nodded and doodled on cards.

"All right. We number our offensive holes from right to left. One is wide right end, nine is wide left end. Our huddle is Notre Dame style, with the quarterback's back to the line of scrimmage.

"I always want us to look razor sharp in the huddle, even if we're losing 50–0. Only the quarterback talks. He calls the play *once*, the set first, then the play and where it's going, then the count it goes on: 'Pro I right, fullback at four, on two.' Then they clap hands and sprint out of the huddle. A sharp huddle, and sprinting out—these are morale factors, and they will drive opponents crazy, to see they can't beat the spirit out of you.

"Our starting count is: 'GO, GO, HUT-ONE, HUT-TWO, HUT-THREE.' I like to go on the first sound when we're passing. For running plays, the linemen like to hold and go on higher numbers, to be able to anticipate the count.

"Our linemen will area-block. Their rule is gap-on-linebacker."

Coach Fowles got up from the table and took a three-point stance in the living room. "First is gap." He straightened part-way up and took a quick blocking step to his left. "Protect that inside gap first if anybody is lined up there, or if a linebacker is stunting through the gap. Second is on." He snapped up and pulled his arms across his chest and took a step straight ahead. "The man in front of you or lined up on your shoulder. Third is linebacker. If nobody is in the gap or on you, go for the nearest linebacker."

He returned to his seat. "Linemen will use a four-point stance, with both hands down—but up on their fingertips, not on their knuckles. Flankers should use a three-point stance. Some people prefer just standing up, but I think that loses you a step when you start.

"Now, defense. Our five-man front with two close linebackers will be very strong against the running game. The cornerbacks don't make many tackles, but mainly turn plays in. Safeties worry about the long pass. Our rule is that we bend but don't break on defense. We won't allow long runs or passes, but will give up some of the shorter ones. The reason for that is that most high school teams cannot grind out eighty yards without making a mistake. We'll play for the mistake."

He sifted through index cards as he spoke. This was largely review. His assistants were quiet.

"Kicking game. Most pro teams spend 25 percent of their practice time on the kicking game. We don't need to spend that much, but kicks are important. Our extra points last year were all two-point plays, running or passing. This year I'd like to find a kicker.

"On punts, we want our punter back thirteen yards, and make sure he *gets* back thirteen yards. Three big boys should be stationed back five yards from the line to act as a second wave of blockers in front of the punter. We were able to center the ball to the punter last year in point eight seconds, and could kick in one point one seconds. The ball hung up in the air an average of three point two seconds. That's a total of five point two seconds. I don't care so much about distance. Everybody on the line takes a blocking step inside, protecting the gaps first, then they sprint downfield, and they should be able to cover the kick in five seconds."

He put the index cards aside.

"Now, practice organization. Next to knowing and caring for the kids, this is the most important thing. Nobody should be standing around. Multiple-skills drills always. That's why, after the mile run on the first day, we don't run laps. Every drill should incorporate more than one skill, because there's not enough time otherwise. We have individuals for sixty minutes, team drills sixty minutes. In the individuals, we start out with cals for maybe ten minutes. Agility drills—where you work on stance and starts, getting off on the count—are about ten minutes. We run the manbuilder—it'll be the hill over in the park again this year—for eight minutes, four of them piggyback. We run tires for six minutes, hang on the bars for two minutes.

"In the team period, we will hit every day but Friday. But we never hit before bars, tires, and manbuilder. I want the boys a little tired when they hit—both to keep them from hurting each other, and because that's the way it is in a game—you are tired from the first play on. At the end of practice we run sixteen forty-yard sprints."

He leaned back and put his hands behind his head and smiled.

"You know, I love music. I *love* it. I even love music in the *locker* room. We have that old stereo in there. I like it on, and turned up loud, every day. I like noise in that locker room. I don't want boys to stand around moaning and groaning and feeling sorry for themselves. *Loud* music, while they shower and dress and get out of there."

He looked over at Coach Branahan who was chewing gum under his mustache and sketching idly on his pad. "I've always been a conservative, ball-control, running coach," Coach Fowles said. "Last year we just ground it out. Now Sandy is changing my mind. We've got a couple of boys who can throw, and we're going to throw all over the place." He leaned forward and stared gaily into the eyes of his assistants. "Gentlemen, we are going to surprise a lot of people with our passing game."

WEDNESDAY, *August 25*

It was a sunny day, but cool for late summer. Bees and bugs drifted in and out of the open classroom windows. School would not open for two more weeks, but this room rustled with the breathing and fidgeting of forty-five boys dressed in gym shorts, tee shirts, and sweat socks. Most of them sat at desks, some sat on the floor, some leaned against the large hinged windows, two sat aloft the cabinets at the rear, gently swinging their stockinged feet.

It was the first day permissible under state law for high school football practice. These were the Laketown High School Harvesters of 1971, in their first hour. They would practice together for ten and a half weeks, and play eight games.

They were listening intently to their head coach.

"Gentlemen," Coach Fowles said, "I believe that everybody who wants to play should be allowed to play, so I have never cut anybody from the squad, and I won't this year. I have only two rules: Give 110 percent always, and look and act like a Laketown football player."

Buddy Fowles, who would soon turn thirty-nine, was, in addition to being head football coach, a guidance counselor at the high school. He had come to Laketown from Pennsylvania eight years ago to teach fifth grade and be assistant high school coach. Six years ago he was named head coach, and three years ago he left the classroom to join the guidance department.

He was six feet tall and trimly built, dressed, as was Assistant Coach Branahan, in tight white football practice pants and beaten-up, ripplesoled coaching shoes. A whistle dangled on a white cord around his neck. His hair curled neatly, tight to his head, except for a lock which encroached on his brow at an angle. His upper teeth protruded some, and he licked them occasionally. He played his blue eyes around the room like a searchlight, fixing upon face after face. He spoke clearly, with precise syllables and careful emphasis.

"What do I mean by 110 percent? I mean to push yourself beyond what *you* think you can do. And what is it to look and act like a Laketown football player? It doesn't mean to dress a certain way, but it *does* mean to be proud of how you look and act, and to tell the truth always. We are a *family*, gentlemen, all of us, together. The family comes first. We must be proud of the family."

Most members of the family had modishly long hair over their ears and down their necks. Two had blond hair spilling over their shoulders. Only a couple had closely trimmed traditional haircuts. Three had mustaches, two had goatees. Even Assistant Coach Branahan, leaning against the blackboard behind Coach Fowles, had bushy hair over his ears and neck, and a mustache. Coach Branahan, the offensive coordinator, was in his first year up from the junior varsity where he had been head coach. In his mid-twenties, he was shorter and heavier than Coach Fowles. He wore thick glasses. On the cord around his neck he had a whistle, keys, and a stopwatch.

Coach Fowles reminded his audience that last year the varsity had won six and lost two, and had bigger, more experienced personnel, most of whom had graduated.

"This year in my humble opinion we have the toughest schedule Laketown has *ever* had. We have *never* played schools as big as we will this year. And you know what? That's *beautiful*. We have only two starters back from last year. A lot of people think we'll do badly. That's because they don't know. We will outwork other teams, we will be in better shape, we will hit harder, and we will have more pride. We will hang on the bars —you guys will have grips like Beowulf; we will run the manbuilder harder than you think it is possible; we will be quick and we will *hit*. And we will surprise a lot of people with this football team when we open up on September 18."

He turned to the blackboard. "We will go into details on all this later. But basically, on offense this year we will use pro splits. Both the flanker, on the 'pro' side, and the opposite end split 10 to 15 yards. We will use both the I formation and the split-backfield." He sketched the offensive formations on the blackboard.

Pro I right:

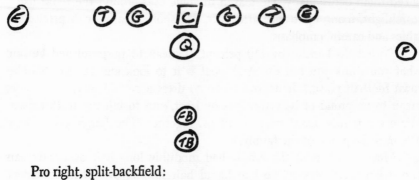

Pro right, split-backfield:

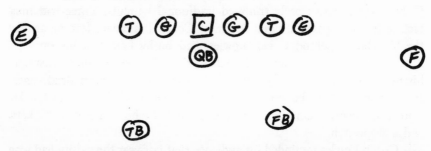

"Splits between linemen will be two and a half feet on each side of the center, three feet between guards and tackles, and tackles and ends. In the split-backfield, the running backs will line up behind the tackles.

"On defense we will feature a five-four, outside-shoulder line-up, with linebackers opposite the guards and about a yard off the line, and corner-backs out about four-by-four yards."

He sketched the five-four:

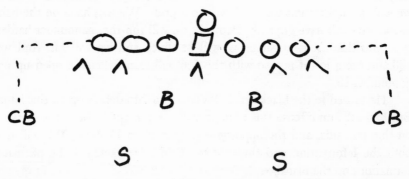

After giving them a minute to study it, he erased the board and said, "Let's go outside."

The team's introduction to ten weeks of football practice was a mile run on the soft, rutted track that surrounded the football field. The Harvesters emerged from the locker room, their mottled white helmets bobbing arrhythmically aboard bodies which, in white shorts and tee shirts, seemed pitifully small. They burst upon the cinders and sand and quickly spread out, in ascending girth from lean to fat, all sweating immediately in the eighty-five-degree heat.

From that time on, the team as a whole would never again during the season be entirely clean, or without pain, or without complaint.

Showered, their hair sticking moistly to their heads, two players sat with Coach Fowles on the gymnasium seats. I knew them only as Bruce and Rich, supposedly two of the toughest on the team. Rich had gently curling dark hair that framed his handsome baby-face and covered his ears. He looked shyly at the floor. He had been a substitute linebacker last year. Bruce was huskier, with short, straight blond hair. He fidgeted at his gym bag with strong, square hands. He was one of the two starters back from last year, at defensive end.

Bruce spoke first, briefly glancing at the coach. "See, well, we want to get a chance to play both ways, because, you know, to get into a college. . . ."

Rich stole a look at the coach and carefully pushed a lock of hair to the side of his forehead with a thumb and two fingers. "We heard," he said, "it was necessary to go both ways in high school to get noticed by a college. . . ."

"Yeah, you know, just we'd like to *try*, and. . . ."

"Mmm-hmm," Coach Fowles said softly, his eyes never leaving their downturned faces. "Playing both offense *and* defense is very, very hard work. I have nothing against anybody playing both ways. But you should know what it means. It means that you will have to pay an even larger price than the others, because it is so demanding. And of course you will have to *make* both the teams to go both ways. Do you understand that?"

"Sure," Bruce said eagerly, "we just wanted you to know. . . ."

"Then there's no problem," Coach Fowles said. "Do your best, and we will see."

At dusk I sat in my Volkswagen bus in the parking lot of the downtown shopping center with a boy whose name was Jonny. He was one of the two on the team with truly long hair, a quarterback. He was lean and tall, with a long face and large hands. He moved with the easy grace of an athlete—not necessarily a football player. He wore dungarees and a denim shirt. He propped his leather boots up on the dash and pushed his loose hair away from the sides of his face with both hands.

"See," he said, turning his palm up in a loose-wristed gesture, "I don't really need football for college. My grades are good, and I've already got lacrosse. Like I tied the school scoring record in lacrosse last year, and some colleges have, you know, been interested in that. Last year I was a third-stringer in football." He showed a toothy grin. "I centered for punts." He pushed his hair away again. "I considered not going out this year—like, some people consider me kind of a clown, not serious—but, you know, when it starts—the competition. I really dig the competition." He smiled broadly. "It's an ego trip."

He spoke with a confidence that seemed not immodest. I asked him about the general attitudes of the team I was to spend these weeks with. He ran them down: Eighty to 90 percent of the guys had smoked marijuana at least once; virtually the entire team was antiwar; enforcement of the drinking laws—eighteen years of age in this state—was a joke, and the guys drank off-season; the sexual revolution was here, and was a good thing.

"But Laketown girls aren't much," he said. "You'll see. My own main concern is that the world be made safe for everybody to coexist in."

I asked him why he wore his hair so long.

"I'm not hung up on it," he said, "I just think I look better with long hair."

Could it be a problem, I asked, on the football field?

"Naw. It doesn't bother me what anybody might say. And if they grab my hair, I'll tuck it under my helmet."

THURSDAY, August 26

The Laketown High School Athletic Department's rules and regulations, besides prescribing gentlemanly behavior and cleanliness, dictated that athletes would be suspended for the season for: drinking or smoking; taking unprescribed drugs; stealing. The team sat on the fold-out bleachers in the gymnasium and listened to the athletic director, Rick Bronson, a lean, broad-shouldered, well-muscled man who had the only crewcut in the room.

"Smoking and drinking, drugs, and stealing—these should be no problem," he said.

"Not if you're careful," somebody said, and they chuckled and snorted. Bronson smiled too, and went on.

"We've got a new item this year." He read it: "Because athletes are expected to set exemplary standards for their peers, they shall never cut any regularly scheduled classes while in attendance at Laketown High School. The first cut will result in suspension from the next scheduled interscholastic contest. The second cut will result in suspension from that team for the remainder of that sports season."

He let the reaction die down, then said, "It means what it says. You all better remember it."

Today was warmer, but still not hot. It was six days before the team could don pads and begin to hit. The boys wore shorts. Some wore cleats, many still wore sneakers.

After calisthenics, the backs went first to the bars—horizontal metal ladders atop a metal scaffolding about eight and a half feet from the ground. The backs leaped up and grabbed the rungs to hang for two minutes. Meanwhile, the linemen pranced in high-step through parallel rows of automobile tires in a more familiar football exercise.

Today, the tires and bars caused agony after thirty seconds. Runners of the tires slowed and stumbled, gasping; those hanging on the bars grimaced and moaned, and many dropped early and massaged their hands. After two minutes, backs and linemen switched exercises.

Then on the whistle they headed through a swampy area to the manbuilder. "LAKETOWN NEVER WALKS!" Coach Fowles yelled to the puffing Harvesters as they ran off toward a deceptively steep hill in the adjacent state park. They paired off, and for four minutes they slogged about 15 yards up the grassy slope alternating in carrying each other piggyback. Coach Fowles blew the whistle. "SPRINT UP!" They lined up in three waves, breathing hard, to sprint up the hill on the count—"GO, GO, HUT-ONE"—for four more minutes.

Another whistle. "TIRES! RUN OFF, RUN OFF! LAKETOWN NEVER WALKS!" And the Harvesters ran off the manbuilder back across the swamp and gathered again at the tires. Several boys were now bent over, heads hanging down, hands on knees. One overweight boy felt sick and was sent to sit in the shade. They ran the tires for another four minutes. "All right, ONE MINUTE LEFT! NOW'S THE TIME, KICK IT IN! LAKETOWN NEVER QUITS!"

They drove themselves, faces contorted, and over the sound of their stomping feet came gasping and grunting.

Whistle. "Okay, Laketown, run it off, take a break."

They went over to the school building and sagged to the turf, hanging their heads or leaning back against the brick to recover with their eyes closed. Players drifted inside for drinks of water. Those who had cleats on removed them before entering the school, as regulations prescribed.

Coach Fowles watched them from a few yards away. "We will be in better shape than anybody we play," he said to me.

After the ten-minute break, the team gathered on the soccer field adjacent to the football field and ran through a few offensive and defensive sets. Then they lined up for the concluding 40-yard sprints.

For a moment, Buddy Fowles stood aside, delaying briefly while the boys caught their breath. He shook his head slightly. "We *are* small," he said quietly. "We're going to *have* to be quick."

Then he strode out, his white football pants tight over his pale white legs. He faced the team, looking slowly up and down the line.

"Who's got more pride?" he asked.

"LAKETOWN!" they yelled at him.

"Who's in better shape?"

"LAKETOWN!"

He paused, then asked quietly, "*Who's* got more pride?"

"LAKETOWN!" came the answer louder than before.

"WHO NEVER QUITS?" he bellowed.

"LAKETOWN!" came the answer louder still.

"All right boys, first quarter, on one. GO, GO, HUT-ONE. . ." They charged out for the first of their sixteen 40-yard sprints.

In the locker room, the players looked definitely like boys, with baby fat and pimply legs. A record of the rock group Led Zeppelin scratched at top volume on the old stereo which gave shocks if you touched it in the wrong place. The shower shooshed over young bodies wandering in and out. The boys were exhausted, and there was little conversation. Just the shower and the scratchy music and the clanking of lockers.

"I personally hope it's ninety-five degrees on the day of the first game," Coach Fowles told his freshly showered players in the classroom. "Because *we* will be in better shape."

On the blackboard he sketched the fullback counterplay.

Pro I right, fullback counter at six:

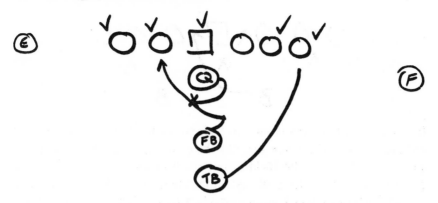

"The fullback takes one quick step to the right, then goes back the other way to receive the ball. The quarterback should give him the ball as deep as possible so the fullback can see the holes better. Our backs are always going to run to daylight. This is a tremendous play. We must have averaged eight yards a carry on this last year."

Laketown would feature a shifting five-four defense called the *laura*. He sketched the shift showing linemen moving to inside shoulders of their opponents.

Laura left:

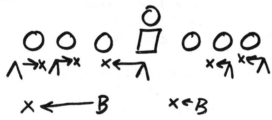

It is especially strong, he told them, against the run, and the shift usually would go toward the wide side of the field. Linebackers, referred to as *barrels* in this case, would stunt—charge through the line into the back-field—in combinations of "left and right barrels in or out." For example, he sketched on the board left barrel out:

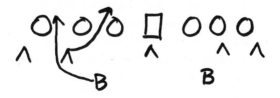

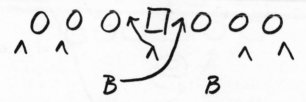

He turned and faced the room. "In high school football, it's not how big you are, it's how *quick* you are. On these stunts, if you linebackers are quick, you'll be in the backfield so fast you'll be amazed. And when you get in there, take the hand-off right from the quarterback if you're quick enough. Otherwise, knock down anybody with a different colored jersey."

FRIDAY, *August 27*

Pouring rain. Led Zeppelin blared in the locker room as the boys put on their shorts. They tramped down the empty hallway either wearing sneakers or carrying football shoes. In the classroom Coach Fowles told them, "It's *beautiful* outside. It never rains on our football team."

On the blackboard he sketched an *inside belly* play. "The quarterback fakes to the first man on a dive, the fullback, then steps deep and hands off to the tailback coming from the other side. We should hit the hole in 0.8 seconds."

Players fondled their helmets and looked out at the heavy rain. Coach Fowles was silent for a few seconds, looking at them. "It's beautiful," he said softly, smiling, and the players instantly turned their heads back to their helmets.

"Out there," he said, "don't stand around for a *minute*. Keep moving. And when you come in, don't sit around and talk. Get into the showers immediately."

They spent forty-eight minutes in the mud. They hung on the bars, ran the tires and the manbuilder.

During the break, a short, strongly built boy with the name "Petrowski" written on tape on his helmet, took off his worn football shoe. His big toe had raw, oozing flesh where the nail should have been. He grimaced as he rubbed his foot. He said that a log had fallen on it, and at the hospital they broke two novocaine needles trying to deaden the pain so as to remove the nail.

"Should you be playing?" I asked.

"Naw," he said, "the doctor said not for a couple of weeks, but I want to play middle guard, and I'm not going to miss all this practice and lose the chance."

Another player held his arm across his chest. He said he fell into a lawnmower and cut some muscles, and that it would take three or four years to regain full strength. "It hurts when I hang on the bars," he said.

During the team period, they rehearsed some of the plays they had been shown over the last couple of days; the straight dives, counters, and the belly series.

After they had run twelve of the sixteen sprints, Coach Fowles stood in front of them. "Boys, I honestly thought you hustled a bit more yesterday. But that's all right. You worked hard today, and you will work harder tomorrow. Okay, start of the fourth quarter. The fourth quarter always belongs to us, because we're in better shape. And you know why? Who works harder?"

"LAKETOWN!"

"Who's got more pride?"

"LAKETOWN!"

"All right, on the second 'go': GO, GO. . . "

After he showered and dressed, Jonny Penchak, the long-haired quarterback, wanted to throw some more passes. Coach Fowles said it would be okay to throw in the cafeteria, still empty of tables and chairs, and went with him to catch the passes and make minor corrections on Jonny's delivery: to have him bring his arm slightly more over his head; get his forward foot planted more precisely in the direction the pass was aimed. He had Jonny throw some while kneeling.

"My Adam's apple is the bull's-eye," Coach Fowles said. Jonny's passes over the few yards of the cafeteria were close to the bull's-eye.

"You've got hands like Goose Tatum," Coach Fowles said, referring to the old Harlem Globetrotters' star whose name was a household word while I was growing up.

"Who's Goose Tatum?" Jonny asked.

SATURDAY, *August 28*

Practice at 8:00 A.M. A tremendous rain and windstorm during the night had blown down trees. Today, however, was a beautiful day, clear except for puffy high clouds, with a nice breeze.

There was a faint new tension in the classroom today, and I suspected it was because this was the first day that both candidates for quarterback would be out—Jonny, and bigger, taller Ted O'Neill. Ted, who last year had led the JVs to a 7–1 record, had been away at a basketball camp until today.

"He won't beat me out," Jonny confided to me. "I don't think he likes to hit. I *love* to hit."

Buddy Fowles moved quickly around the blackboard. He discussed holding blocks for pass protection, and using hands on defense to push blockers away. "Unlike the pros," he said, "we don't use their favorite tactic of slamming hands over the blockers' earholes. First of all, we just don't *do* that. Second, we don't want a 15-yard penalty. We don't want *any* penalties, and we better not *get* any. They are mental mistakes, and there's no excuse for a mental mistake, not in any sport. We don't jump offside, we don't waste time-outs. Physical mistakes are something else, but we're too smart to have mental mistakes. *Aren't* we, Fred?"

Fred had been asleep. His head popped up from his desk.

"Good morning," Coach Fowles said cheerfully. Fred grinned sheepishly.

The coach reviewed defenses, laura right and left, stunts. And he put in a six-man-line, short-yardage defense called the *frankenstein*.

"We will use the six-man frankenstein on third and short," he said. "Our goal-line defense is almost a six-five, with the linemen submarining to cause a pile-up. They will line up with heads down low, cans up in the air, and dive underneath."

He wrote on the blackboard the priority list for defensive linemen:

1. Line up properly
2. Move on the ball
3. Protect your area
4. Locate the ball
5. Pursue
6. Tackle, cause fumble

Coach Branahan introduced a *72 flood pass*, which called for both the end and flanker on one side to slant out to the same area, flooding the zone; and the *56 action pass* which had the quarterback faking to a back into the line, then sprinting to his right to throw.

Coach Fowles snapped his fingers loudly. "How many men do we want in on every tackle, gentlemen?"

"*Eleven!*" the room answered.

"Right!" He snapped his fingers again. "I *want* gang-tackling. I encourage it. All right. Monday we pass out equipment. Tuesday we play football, we hit."

On the muddy practice field, Jonny Penchak quickly asserted his leadership. He led the team through calisthenics, jumped into the first wave to call signals for the sprints up the manbuilder, and moved into the quarterback spot in the huddle to run the plays. The team seemed to respond to Jonny in a more personal way than it did to Ted O'Neill. Somebody told me that Ted was arrogant. Jonny's passes from his smooth, quick overhand delivery, were bullet spirals. Ted threw with a more labored three-quarter-arm motion, and his passes wobbled.

In the pseudoscrimmage, without pads, the team was barely reined in. They were anxious to hit. Helmets whacked together. Defensive end Stan Beronski, with his muscular, tapered torso shirtless and glistening with sweat, slammed with his padded forearms and bumped into the quarterbacks. Coach Fowles cautioned him several times. "Rush them," he said, "but let them pass. Not too much contact now." Stan smiled.

At this point, the coaches were not assigning positions. They let the team sort itself out. Coach Fowles called to them, "Let's have a defensive team over here that wants to play football." And the players scrambled for the huddle, lining up wherever they wanted to play.

Bruce Stacey, one of the two who earlier had asked Coach Fowles if he could play both ways, was trying flankerback on offense. He dropped an easy pass. "They called him 'iron hands' last year," Coach Fowles told me, "because he couldn't catch." But Bruce was so strong and fast that the coaches felt if they could get him into the secondary, no one man could tackle him.

Rich Merrill, small but tough, was trying defensive safety. He stood a bit pigeon-toed aboard spindly legs. He had the wind knocked out of him while trying to break up a pass. Coach Fowles immediately shooed everybody away, then straddled him and lifted his hips and talked to him softly. Rich got up and reluctantly stood aside for a couple of plays.

A big, soft-bellied lineman named Vince Carradino, called Dino by the players, was left face down in the mud after a play. His back had seized up. He was motionless as Coach Fowles looked down at him. He gasped, "Just leave me alone for a minute, I'll be all right."

"Better see the doctor again before we hit, Vince," Coach Fowles said.

"Dino is really putting out this year," Coach Branahan said.

Jonny threw two long bombs to a lean, hard-muscled flanker named Don Heidner, and smiled briefly at the compliments. Stan Beronski slammed into him as he threw the third time, hooking his finger in Jonny's tee shirt and spinning him around. They both laughed.

In the sprints, Coach Fowles called off the quarters, four sprints to a quarter. "Okay, last quarter. Who owns the last quarter?"

"LAKETOWN!"

"That's right, because we're in better shape. The last quarter is OURS!"

In the locker room, the stereo blared out Beatles music: "Lovely Rita Meter Maid," and "When I'm Sixty-four." Everybody showered and left quickly, except Jonny, who was always last.

Coach Branahan mentioned to Coach Fowles that he had happened to see one of their opponents working out for about fifteen minutes. The unwritten rule was that you didn't scout other teams' practices. "Probably 98 percent of the coaches I know wouldn't spy on practices," Coach Fowles said. "I wouldn't."

"I just *happened* to see them," Coach Branahan said, smiling.

MONDAY, *August 30*

A hot day, in the mid-eighties, with a nice breeze. Stan Beronski's Yamaha 350 motorcycle was parked outside the locker room beside a Suzuki and a Triumph. In the locker room there was the plastic clatter of pads being passed out: hip pads, rib pads, shoulder pads, thigh pads. Coach Fowles was especially proud of the shoulder pads, similar to the pros', costing thirty-five dollars a pair. Jonny searched for a small, light pair that would allow him to throw easily. Center Jim Marshall, a 220-pounder, said he wouldn't wear rib pads, or at least wouldn't buckle them, because they bind when you breathe heavily. The hip pads were heavy elastic girdles, with pads embedded in them. They were a dull, sick brown from years of use.

Suddenly much larger, the players sat in their classroom seats, shoulders bulging. Some wore tee shirts over and under their shoulder pads, some just under, and some wore no shirts at all. The pads creaked when the boys moved.

"Today take a little longer to loosen up," Coach Fowles told them. "It's a hot day. Watch your diets on days like this. You'll perspire a lot more, you need more salt. If you get nauseous or dizzy, don't be a hero, take a rest. No sweat shirts tomorrow when we hit—not one. I know it's hard on tee shirts, but wear them tomorrow over your pads. With shoulder pads, blocking pads, hip pads, pants, forearm pads, tape—there's no place for the heat to go.

"After practice today, there'll be a meeting for seniors only, to talk about captains. Remember, this is *your* team, not *our* team. Every team has its own personality. This team is no exception.

"Mouthpieces tomorrow. Bring in two dollars. If you're in for *one* play without your mouthpiece, it's a 15-yard penalty."

"You clip it on your faceguard?" somebody asked.

"Or you can clip it on your bicycle," Jonny Penchak answered.

Sandy Branahan went to the blackboard to diagram the *stomp*, a quick pitch to the fullback running wide, with guard and tackle pulling to lead the play.

Pro I right, Stomp at One:

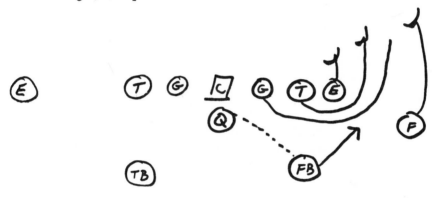

"You linemen that are pulling on that side have to get outside *quick*," he said.

He then sketched a *look-in pass* which called for the split-end or flanker to take one step forward and then turn around to take a quick pass.

"If we have a flanker," Coach Branahan said, "say Bruce Stacey at 180, and the defensive cornerback over there is 140, we think he can run right over him, if we get the ball out to him right away."

"On passes," Coach Fowles said, "you can't let the defensive linemen raise their hands. So block them low and they'll keep their hands down. And watch out for those passes thrown to the side. If they're laterals, they're free balls, if they're dropped, they're fumbles, not just incomplete passes. So if there's any doubt, fall on it."

He erased the board and then, as the players began rustling to get up, raised his hand as if in benediction. "The Jets and Kansas City are on TV tonight. Watch for specific things, try to call out the sets. Don't just watch the ball-carrier. Learn something."

He looked out the window, then down at the floor, then up at his boys, slowly sweeping the room with his blue eyes, and smiling a little. "Boys, for about ten minutes on Saturday morning we looked like a football team. It was like a shooting star. It's coming. Today on the field it will be better. And get a good night's sleep. Because tomorrow—we start to hit."

The team trooped out through the locker room and sat down outside to put on football shoes—Adidas, Pumas, many light soccer-style shoes with molded rubber cleats, rather than heavier football shoes with steel-shanked cleats. Only one player wore the old-style high football shoes. There were still a few sneakers. The boys were gradually getting new shoes, which at Laketown they bought for themselves.

In their pads and tight white practice pants, the team was suddenly transformed from young boys to real live football players.

"They look like a football team," I said to Coach Fowles.

"Hmm–mmm, not yet," he said shaking his head.

They danced through jumping-jacks and the carioca—which is a running cross-step first to one side and then to the other. They flopped onto their bellies and did eight pseudo-push-ups, then to their backs and did eight pseudo-sit-ups. They went to the bars and tires, then to the man-builder, then back to the tires, then to the manbuilder again.

After the break, the backs went down to the playing field to run plays and pass patterns, while the linemen stayed up by the school for drills with Coach Fowles.

The linemen moved their feet in a blur, running in place. Coach Fowles held the ball out in front of him. He swung the ball to the right, and they danced that way, then back to the left, and they went with him. He moved the ball down and they flopped forward on their bellies. He blew the whistle and they reacted in a series of forward rolls. They got down in a four-point stance as their coach barked the cadence:

"GO, GO. . . . Get off on the count, on the COUNT. . . . GO, GO. . . . QUICKER. . . . GO, GO, HUT-ONE. . . quicker, quicker. . . . GO, GO. . . ."

He drove them hard, up, down, running in place, flopping on their bellies, back, forth, "GO, GO, HUT-ONE. . . . " Finally he let them stand and pant for a few seconds. "There are two types of drills, boys, quickness and conditioning. A quickness drill lasts about fifteen seconds. When we tell you this is for quickness, you should practically throw a fit out here. Okay, move on the ball. GO, GO, HUT-ONE. . . . "

Vince Carradino, whose back seized up yesterday, stood nearby dressed in civvies, watching the linemen. The chiropracter had told him it was a spasm in the lower back. He would hit tomorrow with the rest.

"I'm gonna die," he said.

During the break, Jim Petrowski, who had lost a toenail, sat on the grass with head bowed, by himself. His toe had started bleeding because the tip of his shoe collapsed and rubbed on it. He would play anyway. He still wouldn't tell anybody about the toe. He wouldn't limp.

"I gotta get a *job* on this team," he said, with a smile which showed he was missing a front tooth.

I asked Coach Fowles about Jack Forrest. Jack was short, but muscled and strong, about 160, with a sweet face and sloping eyes and long curly hair which made him look even younger than seventeen. He worked hard and smiled often. He had been a guard last year, but hardly played. He had gone to a football camp for a week in the summer and had come back ready to try again as a blocker. Coach Fowles had been watching him too.

"Since he's too small to be a guard," I said, "why don't you have him try halfback?"

Coach Fowles rubbed the back of his neck and didn't smile. "There are three types of players," he said. "There are those who have no ability. There are those who work hard and have ability. And then there are those who work hard and just don't have ability. It's the last group that breaks your heart."

"What about Jack?" I asked.

His smile showed that he was not heartbroken about Jack. "The way it looks now, Jack will definitely *start* at guard. I wouldn't have believed it, how much he has improved from last year. Wow, is he quick!"

The seniors gathered and sat on the grass. Coach Fowles stood talking with last year's all-league fullback, swarthy, 205-pound Art Bellino. Then he addressed the seniors.

"Boys, you have to decide about selecting captains. We have three permanent ones for the season, and then you elect one honorary game captain each week. When do you want to select them, tomorrow? Next week?"

"When did they do it last year?"

"Let's wait until we *hit* for a week."

"I think Stan is right, we should hit for a week and see what happens."

Coach Fowles listened, then said, "You people are the heart of the family, right here. There have to be sacrifices to make a good team. The sacrifices begin with yourselves. Leadership has to come from within. Captains can be very important to you. . . "

"How do we straighten people out who are violating rules?" somebody asked.

Coach Fowles looked at the questioner, and then at the others, as if absorbing something broader than the question. Then he looked over at last year's fullback and asked, "How did you do it last year?"

Art Bellino stood with arms folded. "We just beat 'em over the head," he said, unsmiling.

"I have to agree," said Bruce Stacey, this year's tough linebacker. "I don't agree at all."

Heads turned toward the center of the group of seniors, toward Bradford McClure, whose long, curly dark hair was held away from his brooding, handsome face by a blue headband. His voice was a bit high-pitched, but assertive. "I don't agree at all," he repeated, looking at Coach Fowles. "Each team has its own personality, like Coach said. I don't think we can copy last year. Look at these freaks around here. I mean, we're just different this year."

Others chimed in agreement or disagreement. Coach Fowles followed the words of each closely with his eyes, letting the talk gradually die. Seniors looked at the ground, and pulled up blades of grass.

"I think you boys should have a private meeting tomorrow to discuss things," Coach Fowles said, "without the coaches."

2

The team would hit today. In the locker room, there was little conversation as they strapped on their MacGregor and Rawlings Armor-Flex shoulder pads. Tee shirts were stretched irrevocably over them.

As I watched, I suddenly became aware that the haze of unfamiliarity through which I had viewed these boys a few days before was fading, and, as when a camera lens is focused, they were becoming distinct.

There was playful, willowy Jonny Penchak, with his long hair and big hands; and his competitor for quarterback, Ted O'Neill, big, strong but less lithe, vocally flamboyant, with curly brown hair beginning to cover his ears.

There were two sets of dissimilar brothers, Al and Bruce Stacey, and Ben and Rich Schenkle. Bruce, the linebacker who hoped to play also in the offensive backfield, a squarely built, muscular, hard-running blond; his younger brother Al, the halfback, taller, slimmer, faster, quieter, with light, very curly blond hair.

Rich Schenkle, the other tough linebacker, who also wanted to play offensive end, taller and a year older than Ben, shy, dark, quiet; Ben, a compact running back with long, straight dark hair that sometimes hung over his innocent eyes, more outgoing and devilish than his older brother.

There was Stan Beronski, the strong, aggressive, sculpted defensive end with blond hair over his shoulders; and Bradford McClure, a dark, brooding, independent back of moderate size and speed.

There was Jim Petrowski, the gutsy defensive lineman who wore strong glasses off the field and lacked a toenail and a tooth; and Jim Marshall, the lumbering 220-pound center with straight blond hair and a modest smile.

There was Jack Forrest, the hustling little offensive guard who had improved at football camp; and Vince Carradino, ponderous, dark, mournful-looking lineman with a bad back.

There was Ken Furst, a wiry, quick-footed, slender-hipped back with straight blond hair down to his shoulders; and Don Heidner, the solid, sure-handed, speedy flanker who wore glasses on and off the field.

There was Rich Merrill, the tenacious but undersized safetyman with Prince Valiant hair and a demure smile; and Tom Kase, a tall, broad-shouldered, sharp-nosed offensive tackle with straight brown hair, who might be the fastest lineman on the team.

To this list of my first acquaintances on the team was now added another. In the little coaches' room, Buddy Fowles sat with one haunch on the desk next to the telephone and listened to a big gentle-looking boy with bushy, curly hair and an innocent, soft face. He was John Curtis, and his arms were folded and he looked uncomfortably at the floor and spoke hesitantly.

"It's been the toughest week of my life," he told the coach. "I couldn't sleep."

Coach Fowles gazed at him directly and nodded. "What finally caused you to decide to come back?"

John scuffed a foot. "I thought I'd miss it too much, that's all. When fall comes, I knew when Saturday would come, you'd all be down here playing football. . . ."

Coach Fowles smiled. "You had a rough year last year, with all those seniors."

John smiled at the floor, and nodded. "So anyway, I'm back. I'm sorry I let you down."

A large smile burst from Coach Fowles. "Not at *all!* You didn't let me down. I'm glad you're back. And if at any time you feel you want to leave, just come in and tell me about it."

They shook hands, and John went out to get dressed for practice.

There was increased fidgeting today in the classroom, rattling of helmets on desks, sliding of stockinged feet on the floor. Coach Fowles passed out mouthpieces, opaque plastic tooth-guards with long tails which were to loop around the helmet facemasks and clip on. The directions on the packages said to stick the mouthpieces briefly in boiling water, then dip in cold, then clamp your teeth down hard on them to make a perfect impression for your mouth.

"Don't forget to bring your two dollars," Coach Fowles said, with a hopeful smile. "If you're wearing this during a game, the company guarantees $1,000 coverage."

Coach Branahan diagramed a *motion pass* to the tailback.

"The flanker goes in motion, then runs a shallow flag pattern. The tailback sets up as if to pass-block, then goes out and circles for the pass."

He sketched a tailback draw, a fake pass with a delayed hand-off to the tailback up the middle.

Coach Fowles described the line technique for the play. "The center and left guard should yell 'Pass!' to confuse the defense. The linemen come up just like it was for pass blocking. Turn your men out. The hole opens wherever, depending upon their pass rush. The back will find daylight if the linemen give him two seconds or so. But it's not a good idea against a team that loafs. The whole idea is to draw them into a hard, fast pass-rush, then run by them."

He erased the board, then turned to the players and dusted off his hands. "Tomorrow you're going to be stiff. We won't scrimmage today, but we will have a 'thud' period—blocking in the line but no tackling. *No tackling.* Two-hand touch only. Everything stops on the whistle. But don't let up until the whistle. That's when you get hurt."

He paused, his eyes panned across the room. "Gentlemen, there are going to be bumps and bruises. I don't want to hear about bumps and bruises. Injuries are different. I want to know about injuries. If you don't know your plays, don't worry about it. Do the best you can, and try to learn them. Okay, let's go."

"What did you think of the meeting?" Coach Fowles asked me as we followed the team out to the field.

"I thought it stank," I said. "They weren't really paying attention."

"I thought it was fine," he said, smiling. "They want to play football."

The machines were out today: the seven-man blocking sled, a contraption of seven yellow dummies affixed to blue steel supports, the whole thing aboard runners; and the blaster, a steel framework in which heavy rubber protuberances crisscross the middle at knee and chest level. The backs charge into the blaster one at a time and are slowed, tripped, enmeshed by the insidious flexible rubber arms. When they run it right, with the proper lean, balance, power, they rip through it cleanly.

At the blocking sled, the linemen got down in a four-point stance and charged, driving the sled backwards. Coach Fowles rode the sled, behind the dummies, on a long wooden plank. He barked the signals, and there were no pauses. Linemen hit harder and harder. Mouthguards flew off, a finger was cut and ignored. Seven men hit the sled, spun off and went to the rear of the lines, to be replaced immediately by a new row. "GO, GO. . . . " Seven more rammed the sled, driving it over the grass with a violent clanking, the dummies recoiling at each charge. You could hear the signals and the collisions down on the football field, 300 yards away. "GO, GO. . . . Move on the COUNT. We should be CONCENTRATING more."

Coach Fowles jumped off the sled and sprinted 20 yards away, calling over his shoulder, "Okay, boys, over here—quick, quick! Laketown never walks. All right, on the first whistle, bunny-hop forward. On the second whistle do a forward roll and run in the direction I move the ball."

He blew the whistle and the first wave hopped forward, rolled, and then sprinted to the right when he feinted that way with the football. "QUICKER, QUICKER!" The practice lawn was alive with their panting and sweating.

The linemen paired off and lay on their backs, in opposing directions with the tops of their helmets abutting each other. "This will teach agility," Coach Fowles said as he walked briskly among them to check their positions. "Stay low. We'll have more pride in the family. We'll see how much love we have out here. Don't run around anybody. That doesn't help a man practice."

At the whistle they spun over and sprang up and charged low at each other. The pads and helmets whacked like a dozen typewriters. It was the first solid man-to-man contact of the 1971 season.

"It's a good drill," Coach Fowles said to me, "because it makes them quick, and lets them hit. But they're so close when they get up that they don't get up too much steam. That equalizes it so nobody gets run over."

"All right, boys, take a ten-second break. Okay, MANBUILDER! RUN OVER! LAKETOWN NEVER WALKS!"

The backs, who had been running plays and pass patterns on the football field, responded to his loud call, and sprinted over to join the linemen in the rush to the hill.

After running the manbuilder, they ran the tires. The coaches were quiet. "Notice that Sandy and I are not yelling at them today," Coach Fowles said. "They're too dependent upon us to push them along. Motivation has to come from within. They'll feel that after a while, and they'll begin to yell at themselves."

In the scrimmage, linemen grunted and groaned through their first heavy hitting. Tee shirts were ripped to shreds. A boy stuck a thumb in his mouth to feel for a broken tooth; another rubbed an eye where somebody stuck a finger; "Man, is my heart pumping," said another, holding his chest. Guard Jack Forrest picked himself up slowly after making a block. He wore no tee shirt, and his bare arms showed slight burns from contact with shoulderpads.

"How do you feel?" I asked.

"Like garbage," he said.

The team had only a few pairs of old, tattered hand pads.

A chubby defensive tackle clutched one hand with the other to his belly. His unpadded hand had been stepped on. Coach Fowles took him aside and gently spread the fingers on the injured hand and traced the bone lines of his fingers, comparing them to the uninjured hand. He was suspicious about a bone, and sent the lineman in to take a shower and put ice on his hand. He discreetly directed another boy to go in with him.

"I never want a boy who is hurt to go in by himself," Coach Fowles said to me, "even if it doesn't seem serious. You never know."

The team ran the belly series, the draws, the passes, using both the I formation and the split-backfield.

Bruce Stacey dropped two passes in a row, then stood dejectedly aside as somebody else slipped into his huddle spot. Players alternated in and out of offense and defense on their own. Nobody was assigned a position, or told to give it up. Nobody argued or complained.

Coach Branahan leaned into the offensive huddle. "Jonny, try the action pass." Jonny faked to a back and started to roll out to his right. Defensive end Stan Beronski, grabbed him by the shirt. Jonny tried to duck away. "Come on, Stan, let me throw," he said. But Stan twisted his hand up in the shirt and spun Jonny around until the whistle blew.

On the way back to the huddle, Jonny said, "Did you see what Coach was wearing in school today? *Flares.* Herringbone too."

Freshly showered and dressed, the team's seniors gathered in the school cafeteria. They sat casually on chairs and tables. Coaches were not present. In the middle of the group sat Bruce Stacey, the linebacker.

"Well," he said tentatively, "uh, five of us met last night and talked about what to do about training rules." He spoke slowly, and looked mainly at the floor. "We were just, uh, thinking of suggestions. The best we could think of was an honor system, like the type West Point has, where if you see a violation, you have to report it. If you see it and don't report it, you're just as guilty as the person who makes the violation."

Stan Beronski sat a few feet behind Bruce, leaning back in a chair, his arms folded, his long blond hair hanging damp and straight over his shoulders. "That's absurd," he said. "I'm not going to tell anybody about violations, and I'm not going to get kicked off the team *either*."

"Who says you five guys are the boss?" somebody asked.

"We aren't the boss," Bruce answered. "We are just five concerned guys."

"Five guys don't decide anymore," said Bradford McClure.

"It's just the best idea we could come up with," Bruce said plaintively, his face flushed. "We're not deciding anything, just suggesting." He didn't look up at Bradford.

"Look guys," said a brawny, dark, curly haired fullback named Stu Rosenman, "I admit I've been smoking. . . . "

Jonny leaned forward. "How did it *feel?*" he asked, wide-eyed.

"No really," Stu continued seriously, "I really *did* feel it today. I couldn't sprint. So I admit I've been smoking. . . . "

"Let's hear it for Stu. . . . "

"I don't care *what* a guy does if it doesn't hurt him on the field. . . . "

". . . If you don't get caught. . . . "

Voices were mixing together in a growing current of chuckles, sneers, one-liners. Bruce continued looking at the floor. The room gradually became quiet again, then still, as Bruce sat.

Keith Allen, a fast, broad-shouldered halfback whom some called a greaser because of his slicked-back hair, thin mustache, and interest in fast cars, sighed. "What do we do now fellows?" he asked, "Sit and stare at each other?"

A couple of mothers wandered up the hall toward the cafeteria, and were discreetly waved away by their sons. They disappeared, in the nick of time as it were, because Jonny said, "So long as we play well, I don't give a FUCK!"

The only thing decided at the meeting was to assign the job of cleaning the locker room to three boys each week. After the meeting Bruce Stacey gloomily wielded a mop.

"I feel I let the Coach down," he said. "I thought I had influence in there. Drinking? Yup. Bradford was one of them." He leaned on his mop and held out an open palm. "You *know* it slows you down, that's just body chemistry. Coach said he didn't want to hear about it. He said, 'You guys handle it, and if *you* can't, then I will.' Last year the seniors thumped a guy who wouldn't stop drinking. Really rocked him in practice, and in two weeks he quit. Last year we wouldn't tolerate anything."

He resumed mopping. "I guess you can tell I'm pretty straight, right down the line."

I asked him who the five guys were who met last night.

"Me and my bother Al, Jim Marshall, Rich Schenkle, and Jonny."

"Jonny was with you?"

"Yeah—I know it didn't seem that way just now. That's just the way he is, a joker. He said he'd be with us, then he deserted."

"If you had your way," I said, "what would you have done?"

"I would have kicked Stu Rosenman off the team, because he admitted smoking. And I would have kicked Stan and Bradford and some others off for drinking."

WEDNESDAY, *September 1*

In the coaches' room, Sandy Branahan had a foot upon a chair and was tying his ripple-soled shoe. "Buddy," he said, "a senior called me last night."

Coach Fowles stripped off his tie and hung it in the locker. Sandy straightened up and looked at him.

"He said they had a meeting, some of them," Sandy went on, "and they talked about telling on another player for breaking some rules. Maybe we should remind them it's *one* family."

"All right, boys," Coach Fowles said, striding quickly into the classroom. They settled into their seats, their helmets on desk tops in front of them. "Boys, every team is different. Every year, every team, is different." He looked around the room. "This is the only sport where a team has a meeting before every play, where the family can get together. When I was in high school in western Pennsylvania we had a running back who broke a couple rules. Now, the coach didn't have a crystal ball. So a couple of boys had a friendly talk with the other boy."

There were a few chuckles.

"I *mean* friendly. They didn't run to the coach first. They went to the boy. Sometimes that works, sometimes it doesn't. It's always best to try to work it out within the family. The family comes first."

He looked slowly from face to face. "Boys, if the family doesn't stick together, we've *had* it. You seniors remember, this is the last time around. In college, football is different, less personal, not so much fun. And in the pros it is business, you get paid . . ."

"We're not gettin *paid?*" Jonny Penchak said from his seat on the floor, palms up.

Coach Fowles paused, smiled, and turned to the blackboard. He diagramed a screen pass.

Pro right, split-backfield, screen pass at nine:

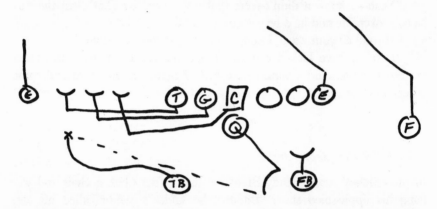

"The quarterback drops back, fakes a draw to the fullback, then drops farther back. Meanwhile the tailback has drifted outside and is behind a blocking wall when he takes the pass. You know who's dangerous against the screen pass? The defensive lineman with the big gut, who's loafing, who's not really rushing the passer—that's the guy who intercepts screen passes. The whole idea here is to draw them into a hard pass-rush.

"Quarterbacks, on *any* pass, when you're in doubt about receivers being free, eat the ball, or throw it into the tuba. All right, we will thud again today. I want *no* quarterback tackled. Let's go."

Coach Fowles watched the team struggle up the manbuilder piggyback. The ground was soggy and stank of sewage, the grass had turned to mud. He was not encouraged by the way the line had been hitting the blocking sled. "Boy, do we need work!" he said, shaking his head. "We've got to be quicker. This line is so small it's got to be quicker than everybody, and we're a long way from it yet."

"Do you think they can do it?" I asked.

"Of course," he said with a broad smile, looking over his shoulder at me as he stepped closer to the team. He blew the whistle. "OKAY, SPRINTS!"

Jonny lined up the first wave at the bottom of the hill. He called the play. "Pro right, split-backfield, 72 flood pass, on the second go. GO, GO. . . ." And they churned up the hill.

The team started through the tires without waiting for the whistle. "Shows they want to play," Coach Fowles said. "COME ON, ONE MORE MINUTE!" he shouted to them. "EVERYBODY'S TIRED. LAKETOWN NEVER QUITS!"

He turned to me. "This is such a small team," he said, "that a good game plan against us should be to run right over us. Just overpower us. But mark my words, when a team sees us they'll try to score in a hurry, try to throw. That will be a mistake."

He cupped his hands over his mouth. "ALL RIGHT, LAKETOWN, KICK IT IN! LAST QUARTER'S ALWAYS OURS. RIGHT NOW! DRIVE YOURSELVES! FIVE SECONDS, FOUR. . . ." He blew the whistle. "NOW RUN IT OFF, RUN IT OFF. GOOD JOB, BOYS, GOOD JOB."

The team slumped down for the break. Players took off their cleats and went in for water. Suddenly there was a yell, and the double-doors to the hallway burst open and two players stumbled out, belting each other. They tripped to the ground and arms and legs sliced the air. Other players grabbed at them. Coach Fowles ran up and pulled them apart. They were yelling incoherently, and still trying to swing.

One was Barry Brill, his dark hair wet and mussed, his aquiline nose running and wet with tears, his strong arms quivering. The other was Ted O'Neill. Barry was yelling something about not fighting fair, about pulling hair. Ted, the larger, just breathed heavily, fists clenched, face impassive.

Coach Fowles moved Barry away, but for a moment he broke free and he and Ted leaped at each other again. At last they were separated, and Coach Fowles stood between them.

"You fucking *pig!*" Barry said

"I don't have to take shit from you," Ted said.

"Okay, boys," Coach Fowles said, "okay, take it easy now." He looked from one to the other. "All right, just calm down."

" No shit at *all!*" Ted said.

"*All right*, Ted!" Coach Fowles said. Tears still streamed down Barry's face, and his breath came choked. Ted stood with feet apart, fists clenched, face blank.

"All right," Coach Fowles said, "okay. Now, I'm going to listen to both of you, but you're going to take it easy. You're not going to fight *any more!* Okay? Okay? All right. Now Barry, what happened?"

Barry's words came in moist spurts. "Fucking O'Neill—can you imagine? A pig thing like that? Right in the hallway he comes up—where people DRINK." He looked at Coach Fowles, his face set in appeal. "I mean, can you imagine that? I mean, shit. . . "

Barry pointed at Ted. "He was going to *piss in the fountain!*"

Ted listened, tense and silent.

"Go on," Coach Fowles said.

"So I told him to stop, and I pushed him away from the fountain. I mean, you can't just—well, and then he pushed me back and started calling me names, like 'dirty Jew' and 'kike'—I mean, how much do I have to take? And then he punches me and we fight, and the fucking coward doesn't even fight fair. He grabs my hair. . . "

Coach Fowles had a hand on Barry's shoulder. Now he put it on Ted O'Neill's shoulder. Barry then stepped forward.

"Go ahead, ask him! Ask him if that isn't just the way it happened," Barry said, pointing at Ted.

Coach Fowles held up his hand. "Okay, Barry. Ted, your side now."

"That's about what happened," Ted said calmly. "I admit I was wrong at the fountain, and I was wrong to call him those names. I didn't mean anything, you know, you just get excited. He's always putting me down, you know, always talking me down, and I just got tired of his shit."

"All right," Coach Fowles said. "Ted, you were wrong twice, for what happened in there, and for fighting. Barry, you were wrong for fighting. . . "

Barry stepped forward boldly, still on the other side of Coach Fowles. "And he doesn't even fight *fair*. I'll fight him anytime, anywhere—*ask him!* With boxing gloves." He pointed at Ted, who clenched his fists again. "You know what he is? He's *chicken*. He won't fight me in a fair. . ."

Ted hit him with a roundhouse right, swinging over Coach Fowles's shoulder and crunching his forearm across Barry's face. Barry put his hands to his face and stumbled back.

"TED O'NEILL!" Coach Fowles yelled, "What are you *doing*, Ted?" He looked behind him quickly to see that Barry was not badly hurt, and then grabbed Ted O'Neill's arms and looked directly into his eyes. "Ted, that was a sucker punch. Never, never do that, Ted, to anybody. I don't believe what I just saw you do, Ted. Never do another thing like that, ever in *life!*"

He stood with the two boys. Barry had a red welt under his eye. There were now small tears on Ted's face. Coach Fowles walked away with Barry. Barry rubbed his face.

Barry told Coach Fowles that they had had minor fights before, that Ted had called him a kike before. "I don't fight," he said, holding his palms out to Coach Fowles. "I don't fight, but how much do I have to take?" Tears came again.

"Barry," Coach Fowles said, "you guys will have to work it out. You *have* to. Now, you have to be aggressive to play football. But fighting is not the answer. And if fighting is not the answer, you have to work it out."

"But Coach," Barry said, "I can't get back at him on the field. He's got seven guys blocking for him, and then you don't allow the quarterback to get hit. There's no way I can fight back."

"Barry, we have the pit drill. Maybe you can work it out there."

He left Barry and went over to Ted. "Ted, I know you're hoping to get a college scholarship for athletics. But you know what? College scholarships are not for hotheads. They won't even look at you if they think you can't keep your head under pressure. I told you you were wrong twice, and Barry once. And then that sucker punch! Ted, you were wrong *three times*. You guys are going to have to work this out."

He brought the two boys together. "All right, this is over. Now I want you guys to go down there and rejoin the family. We are going to play football now. It's going to take guts to go down there, but you've both got guts. This scene is over."

Coach Fowles directed the scrimmage, but was preoccupied by what had happened. "I just can't believe it," he said. "There has never been a fight in the six years I've been head coach. It's like a nightmare, what happened up there."

Barry was playing linebacker when Ted was at quarterback. Quietly, Coach Fowles moved Barry to offensive tackle. Barry threw a hard pass-block for Ted. A couple of plays later, Coach Fowles leaned into the huddle. He patted Barry and Ted on their butts and said, smiling broadly, "Okay! This is a *team*. Everybody is together."

And later, when the team was lined up for sprints, he told them all, "We're *together*, the whole team. This is a new start, right today. I saw a lineman throw a tremendous block for a quarterback, and both guys showed guts and class."

He said privately to Jonny Penchak and Bruce Stacey, "You seniors have a lot of responsibility. Barry and Ted are both juniors. We have to love each other. We've got to work it out."

In the coaches' locker room, Buddy Fowles sighed as he pulled off a sock. "I'm really whipped now," he said, "tired. I couldn't believe what happened. You know, it reminds me of the world. No communication, and then a fight."

"Why not just let them fight it out," I suggested, "with boxing gloves like Barry said?"

"Oh no, no!" he said, snapping up straight. "Fighting is not the answer. It's just the symptom of something. Just like swearing. Swearing's not the problem by itself, just a symptom." He sighed again. "It's a shame about sensitive kids, how they get discouraged from expressing themselves. I guess maybe all kids are sensitive. I have a friend who had a football scholarship to Notre Dame, and he said they *encouraged* you to fight. I think that's wacky. What values are we trying to teach, anyway?"

He stood vulnerably in jockey shorts. He was in good shape, except for scarred knees.

"You're not considering disciplining Ted or Barry?" I asked.

"Oh no," he said. "Really I'm not much for rules. I know we *have* training rules and school rules and so on, and I am bound to enforce them I guess. But things aren't black and white. I guess I try to understand the problem."

"What would you do if you walked into a place and caught a player drinking?" I asked.

He winced fleetingly. "Well, the rules. . . . "

"What would you do?"

"I guess it would depend on the problem, what I could do to help. The easiest way is to go by the rules sometimes, and then not face the problem. I really don't like to kick anybody out of anything, because it may be the best thing they have going for them. *Reinforcement*, that's the way to teach. That's why I always try to be positive, say they're doing well— the things they *are* doing well, not lie about it. Like with game films. By what he says, a coach can make a game film look as good or as bad as he wants. For me it's a question of accentuating the positive. Reinforcement."

"As opposed to Vince Lombardi's style?"

"Well, he had many fine qualities as a coach." He mused for a few seconds. "You really have to be alert to what people are actually saying. Conversations—and fights—are on so many different levels at the same time. Barry Brill is maybe an average football player, but he is very, very smart, a top student. Ted O'Neill is a fine athlete, but not as smart as Barry, an average student. So maybe Barry has to be careful about attacking Ted in his weak spots, and Ted has to be careful about lording it over somebody because he's a superior athlete."

He looked at the wall. "Last year I had a black kid who was on drugs. The captains thought he should be kicked off the team. I tried to keep him on the team, but then he left. I felt that somehow I had let that boy down, failed him."

"You think somebody else could have succeeded?"

"That's not the point. I don't make those value judgments, whether anybody else could have done better. Hunh-unh. All I know is *I* didn't succeed."

I stood next to Bruce Stacey in the shower. Water gushed over his un-marred young skin and blond hair.

"That fight would never have happened last year," he said, soaping under his arms so that foam spilled down his sides like clouds in a brisk wind. "Isn't Coach Fowles great though? He taught me in fifth grade. He helped me with a lot of little things. My grades were bad, but they went right up with him. Then after him, they went down again."

Parents and students alike recalled coach Fowles's fifth grade classes with admiration. This year's high school seniors are the first of his earlier fifth-grade classes to come through, so he had a special feeling about this team.

THURSDAY, *September 2*

Barry Brill and Ted O'Neill sat in Coach Fowles's guidance office. They sat at right angles to each other, their knees almost touching. Barry had a black eye, and he looked often at Ted. Ted's face was stone, and he looked only directly at Coach Fowles.

Barry said that his father's initial reaction to the fight was, an eye for an eye. "But I can't do that," he said, "just hit a guy when he's not look-ing. But it's hard going around with this eye. It's embarrassing. If a guy hits me, I can't just walk away."

Ted spoke matter-of-factly. "He's always looking down at me, talks destructive. I hit him when he said I'm afraid to get hit. I just lost control. I called him names in frustration."

Coach Fowles leaned toward them on his swivel chair and listened intently. He talked softly and carefully. "It takes more guts to walk away from a fight. It really does. Boys, this is the first time there has been a fight in my six years as head coach, and it is going to be the last. That is the way it is during games—you will walk away if somebody punches you. That takes real guts. But that has to be our goal."

He fastened his gaze on Ted, and continued softly, but with clear firmness. "Will you do your best, Ted? That's all I ask. Will you try?"

"Yes."

"Okay, I *believe* you, Ted. I trust you, I really do. It's like signing a contract with me. You're honest, Ted. You and I have signed a contract. Barry?"

Barry nodded and his mouth formed a soundless yes.

Coach Fowles leaned back a bit. "You know, a lot of adults are down on kids. They're wrong. Kids are better than ever. I really wish lots of adults could coach a football team. They'd see kids giving their *all* down there, day after day, for the good of the team." He paused and pursed his lips. He narrowed his eyes slightly and looked first at Barry, then at Ted.

"Boys, I can tell you that you would be kicked right off many teams for fighting. That's the truth. And I'll tell you this: The team comes *first*. I don't want it to happen again. I *mean* that. Don't back me into a corner. Do you understand?"

Mrs. Forrest and Mrs. Allen, Jack's and Keith's mothers, came into the classroom to remind the boys that the oven mitts, being sold to raise money for new capes, had not all been sold, and that the money had not been turned in. They were greeted with chuckles and assurances. Coach Fowles stood aside without expression, and made no comment.

The running backs were sent off to a corner of the playing field to run the gauntlet. A back carrying the ball was to run between two rows of players who slapped at the ball and tried to make him fumble. It started off as a serious drill. Then a tee shirt was ripped by mistake. In quick succession, all the other tee shirts were ripped off as backs came through. Finally, no back made it through the gauntlet because the drill became trip-the-back-and-sit-on-him.

Later, in the scrimmage, the running backs were lax in their pass-blocking. Jonny was grabbed twice in a row before he could throw. He kicked the grass in disgust. "Come ON, guys!"

Coach Fowles stalked over to the huddle. "You guys better do a better job! You couldn't beat Vomit Tech with that blocking."

"When is *that* game?" somebody said.

Coach Fowles chuckled, and then said, "I'll tell you what, boys. You better give Jonny time to throw, or you'll wish you were in the band."

A small, hard, quick, black boy named Bennett, who had been trying out for flanker, was at practice in street clothes. He told Coach Fowles his parents had made him quit the team because of his grades.

"I'm sorry you have to leave the team," Coach Fowles said, pawing the ground with his shoe, "but whatever your parents say to do, you *do*, Bennett."

Coach Branahan told me that the school has no special academic requirements for athletic eligibility. "The idea is that for the kid with a seventy average, sports might be the best thing in the world."

John Finch, who wanted to play cornerback, and often mocked the sport's violence by swishing his hips gaily, was out with a badly bruised thigh. Guard Jack Forrest and running back Keith Allen were out with swollen knees. Bradford McClure was also missing, but nobody seemed to know why.

A regular observer at practices was a slim boy with thick glasses, prominent teeth, and a ready smile. He jogged with the team from one drill area to another, and threw a football with any player willing. Players asked him how he was.

Coach Fowles explained to me that he had some cerebral difficulties, "But what a beautiful boy. He wanted so badly to play football last year, and I don't ever cut anybody. But I really didn't know what to do with him. He would work out and so on. Finally I told him to suit up for the last game. I told his parents that I couldn't promise anything, but I would try to put him in for the last play.

"Well, we got a good lead, and I was hoping we would have the ball on offense, so we could split him way out and run the play in the other direction. But we were on defense. I decided to put him in anyway. I told him to stay way over here near the sidelines near me. But he was so excited he went in and got in the middle of the field. I was scared to death the play would go at him. I didn't know whether to run out and get him or not. He didn't hear me yelling. Anyway, they ran the play and it was all right. People in the stands cried, they were so thrilled to see him out there. Hey Billy, come over here and meet somebody."

Billy came over. Coach Fowles introduced us and then said, "How'd you feel getting into that game?"

Billy smiled brightly and rubbed his hands together and shifted his weight rapidly from one foot to the other. "Pretty shakey. But it was still great. My moves are getting better. I'm keeping in shape." He got down in a three-point stance and rammed a dummy with his shoulder as Coach Fowles watched.

In the locker room, Jonny Penchak pulled up his knee pad and massaged his chafed, red knee. "These pads are like canvas," he said. "You slide on them, then it gets infected. It happens every year."

FRIDAY, September 3

Coach Branahan addressed the team in the classroom. "Yesterday several times receivers broke free 15 to 20 yards deep. That means that the defensive secondary is not really trying. It doesn't help the team practice when you make things easy for the offense. Another thing: Passers need 2.5 seconds at least. Several times linemen were in on the quarterback in 2.2 seconds. Pass-blocking has got to be better."

Coach Fowles looked around the room. "Anybody know what happened to Bradford?"

There was no answer.

"Nobody?" Coach Branahan said. "Maybe if anybody knows he can speak to us afterwards."

"All right," Coach Fowles said, "Coach Branahan and I agree that the offense is really starting to come. But the pass-blocking—I never want to see our quarterback blindsided, *ever!* Yesterday an end came in on Ted O'Neill's blind side, and if he'd have wanted to he could have put him out of the game. You backs should be quick enough to pick up the weak-side end."

It was very humid and hot, the most uncomfortable day so far. Mosquitoes and bugs were thick. Coach Fowles watched players hanging from bars and running the tires. "Look at those kids," he said. "How can anybody say the kids today aren't dedicated? And they are learning a lot about themselves by going through this. But I always tell them after their first loss, 'Now's the time you're *really* going to learn a lot about yourself."

The scrimmage was lethargic. Jonny wiped his sweaty palms on his tee shirt. "Nobody feels like practicing," he said. "They're dragging. You watch, somebody'll get hurt today."

The offense huddled and then jogged lazily up to the line.

"Back in the huddle!" Coach Fowles yelled. "Back in the huddle! You look like VOMIT HIGH SCHOOL! Look like LAKETOWN coming out of that huddle!"

They huddled again, and this time broke smartly.

"You got to let em know they're not putting out," he said to me, "just a little more criticism. But they're getting bored with this. We have our first scrimmage next Saturday, a three-way thing against Port Chester—they're Double A—and Cardinal Spellman from New York City. Two big, tough teams. They'll feel more like working as we get closer to that. I don't want to start getting them excited now."

He watched Jonny hand off to a back. "He's not carrying out his fakes, Sandy," he said to Coach Branahan. He said nothing to Jonny. "I never like to criticize a quarterback in front of the others," he said, "because the quarterback is their leader. You've got to treat a leader *like* a leader."

Jonny stood aside to let Ted O'Neill take over. Jonny always seemed loose and relaxed. I asked him if he ever got uptight for a game.

"Naw, I never worry about *my* job," he said.

"You don't seem to be carrying out your fakes," I said.

"Yeah, I know. There are just certain things I can't take seriously unless it's in a game—like carrying out fakes."

Rich Merrill, still trying it at safety, made a hard, diving tackle at Bruce Stacey's powerful legs. He was left motionless on his back. Coach Fowles ran over and immediately chased everybody else away.

"Just the wind, Coach," Rich said, gasping.

Coach Fowles chuckled as he lifted Rich's hips. "I know. It's a great feeling, isn't it?" He continued the slow, methodical lifting motion that would restore Rich's wind. "Not only that," he said, nodding his head toward the sidelines, "but your father's here watching practice."

Parents and other adults often drifted down to watch practice. Coach Fowles always went over to greet them and ask how things were and to answer their questions. If it was somebody he didn't know, he asked if he could do something for them—gently checking whether they just might be from an opposing school.

He introduced me to the father of one of last year's players.

"How's the new electric scoreboard coming?" the man asked.

"Well, we've got it," Coach Fowles said. "It cost $4,000. Now I guess they've found out it's going to cost another $3,000 to install it because they have to dig a trench from the school to lay the electric cables."

The man scoffed. "You know what I'd do? I'd get that scoreboard up by getting five or six local contractors to donate the work."

"Well, you may have a point. . . ."

After the sprints, some of the players took off their helmets and shoes and sprawled in the grass. The locker room was too cramped for everybody comfortably to take off equipment at once.

Suddenly there was a roar. A motorcycle churned away from the building and across the practice fields. The rider bobbing on it had his white helmet on and blond hair streaming out behind. Opening it up, he was quickly in the distance, turning, sliding, bouncing over ruts.

"Is that Jonny?" Coach Fowles said, slapping his forehead.

Jonny was roaring around on Stan's Yahama 350.

"HEY, JONNY!" Coach Fowles yelled. He rubbed his eyes.

Jonny slid onto the running track and began circling the football field. Then he jumped the curb and for a split second the wheels were out of line in the air. He crashed to the ground, the wheels slithered, then straightened out. He headed straight for Coach Fowles, who took a deep breath and blew his whistle and waved his arms. Jonny had his chin tucked down and roared past, trailing a roostertail of mud. He buzzed around the corner of the school. In a few seconds, he came putting slowly back and stopped in front of Coach Fowles, grinning widely.

"You want me, Coach?"

"Hey, Jonny," he said almost wistfully, "how fast were you going?"

"Who, me? Seventy-five or eighty."

"Jonny, you're going to kill yourself."

"Naw. Hey, Coach, you see me almost lose it coming off that track?"

Coach Fowles slowly shook his head as Jonny drove away to park the bike.

"He's crazy," I said.

"He's fantastic," Coach Fowles said, laughing.

SATURDAY, *September 4*

"How many saw the Colts against the Cowboys last night?" Coach Fowles asked in the classroom. It was 8:00 A.M. "Plays last only about five to seven seconds—that's as long as you have to work. The Dallas defense is so quick. On the football field, if you're not quick, it doesn't matter how big you are. Quick is not necessarily fast. In a 100-yard dash, some of you could beat some of the Cowboys. But in covering an area the size of this room—forget it! They can really *move!*"

"I watched the game with pencil and paper," Coach Branahan said. "I was looking for *anything* that might help us. I just let the baby cry, so I could watch every play. Like there was a quick wingback screen . . ."

"What's the toughest thing to teach in football?" Coach Fowles continued. "Pass defense. Now you ends on offense, when you go out, you study the cornerback, get as close to him as possible. What do we tell our defensive backs? Never let the receiver get within five yards. If a receiver can get close enough to him to almost step on his toes, a quick move and he's *got* him. Sure, you cornerbacks are giving away the short pass, but you can't cover everything.

"We're going to start working on our six-five goal-line defense. Now, that defense is weak against a pass. But what do most teams do inside the five? They *run*. Now get this: A running play shouldn't gain an *inch* against our six-man line. You just can't run on that defense, not if you linemen line up properly and submarine and cause pile-ups. If they do run on that line, you should do something else, like join the band."

There was some laughter.

"Hey, I have nothing against the band, I really *like* the band."

The laughter spread.

"And I'll tell you something, we're going to have a good band this year."

"Is it too late to join?" somebody asked from the back.

"All right, the football field is 53⅓-yards wide. The hashmarks are 17 yards in. The first thing you should know on defense is where the hashmarks are. Most teams prefer, number one, the wide side of the field; number two, to go to the right. Now on the laura defense—L stands for long side of the field, the wide side. Usually you will want to shift that way. But depending upon your opponents' tendencies, you might want to shift to the short side of the field if they have a tendency to run that way. So with a right-handed team, you might want to shift to the left—their right.

"Couple other things on defense. You linemen, watch out for traps. If nobody blocks you head-on, look out for a trap-block coming from the side. How many of you linemen have ever been trapped? It's like running into a tree with your head turned. Also, watch out for backs sneaking through the line to go out for a pass. If you ever see a back sneaking through, tackle him.

"Misdirection." He stopped and panned his eyes slowly around the room. Then he ambled down the aisle between the desks, tipping his head up to look at the ceiling. Forty pairs of eyes followed his gaze and looked at the ceiling. He snapped his fingers, and the heads dropped.

"How many of you *didn't* look up? That's misdirection, fakes. Eyes can fool you. That's why running backs should look the ball right into their hands on fakes, because the defense will be fooled by where you are looking.

"Today we're going to work on some specialties. I'd just as soon kick the extra points—boys, there are going to be a lot of them this year. So you people who want to, try kicking. Same for punts. We won't crack the whip. The desire to improve yourself must come from *within*. Motivation doesn't start with Coach Branahan and myself. It starts with *you*. If it doesn't come from within you, we won't have a football team.

"Okay, couple things when we're watching the clock. *White defense*. Time is running out and all we care about is not giving up a last-second touchdown. When we call 'White!', linebackers drop back about eight yards, corners about fifteen yards, safeties about twenty yards. If they call off-tackle, so what? They gain eight or nine yards, and the clock keeps running. We don't care if they get ninety-nine yards if they don't score a touchdown.

"Now, on offense. Time is running out, and we are trying to beat the clock to score. If you hear 'Stop the clock!' we go into a special last-minute offense. You will automatically line up in a pro-right, with a split backfield, and the play will be a 72 flood pass, on the first 'GO.' That's it, that will be it for the whole year, automatically."

Jonny threw several times deep to Don Heidner, the fast flanker who wore glasses. Don was getting behind the defense on fly patterns. Jonny had a satisfied smile after laying one right in Don's arms 35 yards away.

He also threw to Cary Grimes, a tall, stick-lean end who was the only black player left on the team. Three had been out on the first day. One quit shortly and gave no reason; the other had been forced to quit by his parents. Cary was fast, but couldn't hold Jonny's stinging passes over the middle.

It was another hot, buggy practice, the hottest so far. They were anxious to finish. Players waiting to get into the scrimmage made plans for the afternoon. A bunch would go swimming. Several talked about going to a Kris Kristoffersen concert Sunday night.

"Goddamned *oaf!*" said Jim Petrowski, doing an Indian dance on one leg. "Stepped on my *toe!*" It was the first time anybody had caught Jim's nailless big toe squarely. He hopped around, then got down in his four-point stance for another play at defense.

Several boys tried kicking. Ted O'Neill and a strong, quiet defensive end, Steve Barker, worked on punts. Jim Marshall, the big center, tried kickoffs and extra points. His kicks were long, but not accurate.

"Hey, Coach, am I going to center for punts this year?" Jonny asked.

"Nope."

"Aw." Jonny picked up a stray ball and booted it and danced around with a wrenched knee. "Last year when nobody cared what happened to me," he said, "I got to center for punts."

Nobody else, however, seemed able to hike the ball back the necessary 13 yards. A succession of pretenders, including center Jim Marshall, rolled the ball back to the punter. Jonny jumped into the competition and centered it perfectly, then walked away smiling, holding his palms up.

Jonny's father was waiting for him after practice. He was standing in the sun immaculately clad in plaid Bermudas, a blue short-sleeved shirt, blue socks, and black shoes. Jonny stood in front of him drenched in sweat and stained with grass and dirt.

"I just don't wanna go, Dad," he whined, slapping his helmet against his thigh pads. "I told you yesterday, I want to go swimming with the guys. I just don't wanna go."

Jonny's father, a chemist, was quiet, polite, and firm. A few minutes later Jonny stalked up the incline toward the locker room entrance. In disgust he hurled a football at the door. It hit the ground, took a crazy bounce straight up, and smashed a lightbulb.

SUNDAY, September 5

Jonny and Jim Marshall stopped by Coach Fowles's house to tell him that a lot of people were going to be amazed at how good a team they were going to have.

MONDAY, September 6, Labor Day

A voluntary practice, and twenty-seven showed up. It was so hot and humid that practice was agony. Coach Fowles worried about boys getting sick. Several were dizzy. His rule was that you never took off your helmet, even on the sidelines. Today he let them take them off, along with their shoulderpads, and they ran just eight sprints rather than sixteen.

TUESDAY, *September* 7

Stiflingly hot again. More and more players were wearing no tee shirts, just bare shoulder pads on bare skin. They sweated even in the classroom.
Coach Branahan diagramed the *outside belly play*.
Pro right, split-backfield, outside belly at one:

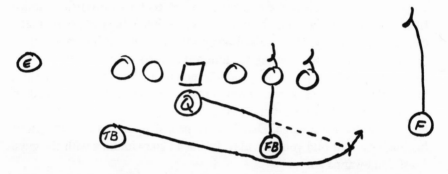

"From a split-backfield you fake to the fullback, and then pitch out to the tailback going wide. Quarterbacks make sure you really seem to tuck the ball into the fullback, to draw those linebackers in. And fullbacks, really carry out that fake."

Coach Fowles let the players absorb what was on the blackboard for a few seconds. "Okay, boys, you know we have our first game scrimmage on Saturday morning. Today I exchanged information with the Port Chester coach. They run a type of triple option. He said they have a quarterback who is not big. He didn't tell me much. They are strong. He asked about our team. I was honest. I said we have two starters back, we are not a big team, we will throw the ball.

"Now the point of the scrimmage is not to get all psyched up. It is not important to 'win' a scrimmage. The point is to learn something. Saturday morning we will dress here, except for shoulder pads. Carry those and your helmets. We will get on the bus at quarter to eight. It will take about an hour to get there."

He paused and looked slowly around the room. He raised his voice a bit. "Now there are a few things I want to talk about. Number one is school. School starts tomorrow. You know about cutting classes. It doesn't matter how *I* feel about it, it's a *rule*, and that's *it*. The point is, you walk into school tomorrow and get into trouble then or anytime, cut a class— that's *it!* Think about it *now*. If you don't like it, then quit if you want to. Use my name as a reference. I'm not kidding. Because you had the guts to stick it out this long. Even if you *feel* like you're going to get into trouble, come and see Coach Branahan or me.

"Publicity. You're going to get fantastic publicity around school. Prepare for it and don't let it take your head. Don't make a lot of noise in the halls. The spotlight will be on you. Let's stay out of trouble with this school, gentlemen."

As we watched the team run the tires, I asked Coach Fowles how he expected to do against Port Chester and Cardinal Spellman.

"I really expect us to get pushed around physically," he said.

"Oh?"

"Yeah, I really do. They're big schools, they play really rough, hard-nosed football. They'll push us around. But that's fine. I don't mind that at all. We'll learn a lot about ourselves."

"Should there be a pit drill today?" Coach Branahan asked.

"I think we're ready," Coach Fowles said.

He blew the whistle to conclude the tire-run. "All right boys, over here, form a circle. Let's have two guys in the pit."

The team milled into a rough circle forming a kind of enclosure about five yards across. Jim Marshall and Rich Schenkle emerged silently from the circle and came to the center, each looking at the other's feet. Jim straightened his helmet, and Rich tugged on his arm pads. Then they got down in four-point stances facing each other, almost nose to nose. Jim moved his hips in anticipation. Rich chopped the ground with his right foot. Their fingers, supporting the forward weight of their bodies, were white with tension.

Coach Fowles put a hand on the back of each. "Jim, you're offense. Rich, defense. Set?"

Now there was some movement in the circle, some crowding forward.

"Come on Jim. . . . Stay low, Rich, stay low. . . . Drive him out of there, Rich, use your hands. . . . Hit guys, hit!"

Coach Fowles bent over and put his hands on his knees, keeping his whistle in his mouth. "go!"

Rich and Jim lunged into a heavy collision, the initial dull thud of their bodies followed instantly by the sharper whack of Rich's forearms driving under Jim's chin. They grunted and wheezed. Again and again Rich slammed his padded arms under Jim's bent body, trying to straighten him up. Jim, head down, using his fifty-pound weight advantage, plowed forward. For a second Rich's body was arched back, his mouth twisted behind his face mask, as he strained to hold his position. Then he gave, and Jim drove him over backward into the howling circle of teammates.

"Don't let him do that, Rich! . . . Come on Rich, straighten him up! . . . Take his head off, Sugarbear! . . . Way to drive, Jim!"

Coach Fowles stepped in. "Rich, this time offense. Jim, defense. go!"

Rich shot forward, burying his shoulder into Jim's broad midsection. Jim clamped down with his forearms and fists across Rich's shoulders and pushed him off to the side. Then he drove down on him with his weight and bulled him out of the circle.

"Good work, boys! . . . Way to be, Jim! . . . Good hit, Rich! . . ."

Hands reached out to tap the combatants' helmets and rears as they rejoined the circle.

Next it was Stan Beronski and Jim Petrowski. Stan was five inches taller, but Jim, a wrestler, was quick. Stan slammed his forearms into Jim, but the little lineman stayed low, growling, churning his legs, until Stan overpowered him. Jim slipped to the ground with Stan on top.

Then the two offensive guards, Clifford Albert and Jack Forrest, faced each other. Clifford, fifteen pounds heavier than Jack, felt the rivalry especially strongly, although he played left guard and Jack right. They collided, and Clifford swung his forearms, then his fists. Coach Fowles blew the whistle.

"Fifteen yards, Cliff!" he yelled. "That's a punch. All right, boys, good work. Take a break."

"They don't like the pit," Coach Fowles told me. "You're performing in front of everybody. Peer pressure is incredible. I don't know what skills they learn in there, but the psychology is amazing. I like it because it actually gives people confidence. It doesn't matter how good you are, or how big. If you just go in there and do your best, and stay low, you won't be humiliated. And you find out you can take it."

Coach Fowles slapped his forehead. "Oh, man, you can really tell we haven't worked on defense. Harry! Harry! What are you doin?" He stalked angrily in between the offensive and defensive lines. The players stood nervously. He stood before Harry Wallace, a huge, blubbery defensive guard wearing a red "Friendship Farm Basketball Camp" tee shirt over his shoulder pads.

"Harry, where do you line up on the laura?"

Harry muttered something, and his legs moved up and down involuntarily.

"OUTSIDE SHOULDER, HARRY! Okay Harry, you get outta there. Somebody get in here who will line up properly."

Coach Fowles installed Ted O'Neill at defensive safety, and was impressed by his pass coverage. "This is just like basketball for you, Ted, this is *cake*."

WEDNESDAY, *September 8*

First day of school. The building and grounds were transformed by buses, cars, motorcycles; long hair and dungarees; short skirts and tall boots; droopy shirts and clogs; pressed chinos and neat sport shirts open at the neck to show the clean white triangle of a tee shirt; wide-eyed, short-haired kids with shined shoes, who could be twelve; girls with glazed, eye-shadowed faces, and boys with mustaches, who could be twenty-five. It was difficult to assess the age of these people, although one knew that from this fluorescent sea came the Laketown football team, and they were sixteen through eighteen.

The senior players had a meeting and picked as season's captains Jim Marshall, Stan Beronski, and Rich Schenkle. Coach Fowles was surprised and seemed disturbed by the news. Usually, he said, he had a chance to talk first to the team about what leadership qualities are important for captains.

Ben Schenkle, Rich's younger brother, was out indefinitely because he had a tooth knocked out in a tussle with his brother. The tooth was wired back in and would take a while to set. Coach Fowles asked him how it happened.

"Aw, I don't know," Ben said. "We were just messin around and I fell and hit the ground and the tooth just came out and was layin there."

"What were you tussling about?" Coach Fowles asked.

"Oh, nothin I guess. Over a shirt or something."

"But you weren't fighting."

"Naw."

Ben would try to kick extra points at least until his mouth healed. Jonny Penchak predicted to me that when Ben was able to run, he would start at fullback. He was only five-seven, and chunky, and seemed an unlikely candidate to me.

Linemen banged into each other, offense to defense, working on their technique.

"All right, let's go. Left-shoulder block," Coach Fowles said. "Hit the knee, move up to the waist, turn him laterally. Imagine how you're going to look in the movies."

"What bullshit," a linesman said quietly aside. "I just hit my man and drive him out."

A fellow named Freddie Delaney came out for practice; he had missed up to now because he had to work. He was of average size, strong, freckled, and smiled a lot. He hit like a tank, and could probably play in the defensive line. Much of the time he didn't know where he was supposed to line up or what he was supposed to do. "You don't teach Delaney," one of his friends said, "you aim him."

There was a rule that a player must practice at least fifteen days before being eligible for games. With only ten days left before the season began, Freddie would miss the first game.

The two coaches stood together watching the team slog up the manbuilder. "Hey, Buddy," Coach Branahan said, smiling, "I hope we don't run up against a receiver like Don Heidner."

"Really?"

"Hey, he is something. Some *hands* that guy's got, and speed and moves. Man, if we can get him deep. . . ."

Players were beginning to steal looks over at the coaches, anticipating the whistle.

"They can really feel it when their time is almost up," Coach Fowles said.

In the pit drill, Barry Brill, who always wore orange and black sweat socks, drove out Tom Kase. Tom, the tackle, was a wrestler, strong and quick. "Wow!" Coach Fowles said under his breath. "It's not often you see Tom beat in here."

Coach Fowles was informed that the football team could no longer practice on the soccer field. He didn't argue about it, but told me later, "Our playing field is all torn up because the lacrosse team practices on it. That bare spot around the 10- or 20-yard line is from lacrosse. I can understand how other coaches feel, but we've got to practice somewhere, and the playing field is already in bad shape."

He told the team, "Today we have a better place to practice—right field of the baseball field."

The team lined up for a play. Coach Fowles came walking toward me with a purposeful stride. "You know what I'm thinking about?" he asked. "About taking my wife to dinner, and having some Chinese food on Master Charge. What a day at school with all the schedule changes."

Bruce Stacey, playing middle linebacker, picked himself up from a hard tackle and walked away with a thinly disguised limp. Coach Fowles went over to him and told him that he was not to practice for a couple of days. Bruce walked slowly, head down, toward the locker room.

"Those are the guys you have to watch," Coach Fowles told me. "They won't tell you they're hurt. They'll keep on playing until they really damage something. Bruce bruised his hip a couple of days ago, and he's been trying to play with it. He just hit it again. These guys have such pride."

Stu Rosenman, a fullback, said, "Coach, when I cut, my knee went in and out."

"Take it easy on it and see how it feels," Coach Fowles said.

Jack Forrest, the little guard, took himself out for a few plays. He was breathing heavily. "I've got no strength out there," he said. "I don't understand it. I'm down from 168 to 154 in five days. I can't figure it out, coach, I just have no strength at all. I'm getting eleven hours sleep a night. I drink two quarts of orange juice every day, get lots of salt."

Coach Fowles was puzzled, because it was unlike Jack to complain or loaf. "There's such a thing as sleeping *too* much," he said. Jack walked away. "So much is in the *mind,*" Coach Fowles said.

He yelled at a stocky, slow boy playing in the defensive secondary. "Wake *up,* Reuben! Come on, help the family!" Reuben couldn't keep up with the pass receivers. "This is the first time he has stayed out this long," Coach Fowles said. "He sleeps. He tries to play safety but he can't. I mean, he's a nice kid and I like him, but . . ."

There was a fumble, and the scramble for it was sluggish.

"Hey, come ON!" Coach Fowles yelled. "Any time the family jewel is on the ground, get ON it!"

During the specialty period, Coach Branahan asked, "How fast should extra points get off?"

"About 1.1," Coach Fowles said.

"We're doing it in about 1.6," Coach Branahan said.

Ben Schenkle kicked in both straight-ahead style and soccer style. His kicks did not carry deep, but were fairly accurate. Jim Marshall kicked them deeper, but still with less accuracy. They used a kicking block, an oblong piece of wood about six inches long and two tall, with a rubber slab on top. Rich Merrill centered with one hand, nice, slow, looping spirals which took forever to get there, but, unlike those tried by other players, did finally arrive at the holder.

Coach Fowles was interested in psychocybernetics. "I was reading an article last night," he said while changing into street clothes, "and studies show that kids who cry adjust better to kindergarten than kids who don't cry. Did you know that? They did some studies once with foul shooting in basketball. And they showed that kids who just practiced foul shooting before the actual shooting test didn't do as well as kids who were told beforehand they were going to do well. In other words, it seems to show that having your confidence built up may be actually *more* important than practice. So much is in the *mind!*"

THURSDAY, *September 9*

The seventh straight sizzling hot day, and it was taking a toll on the players. They dragged and loafed. Coach Fowles was not out for calisthenics and bars and tires. He was held up in his office making schedule changes for students. Finally he came running out and immediately took the linemen up to the practice field behind the school. Running backs went to the far end of the playing field with Coach Branahan. Jonny stayed at the near end with receivers—flankers, split ends, and tight ends.

Jonny threw hard, but the receivers were loafing. They dropped passes and joked around. Jonny was disgusted. "Come on guys, cut out the shit," he told them. He yelled at them several times. Finally he kicked the ground angrily. "Christ! You know what, guys? We're gonna get our ass kicked. We're not that big and we're not that tough."

He said to me, "Everybody fucks around just because there's no coach here. That's really bush."

Bradford McClure was back today. He had been on Cape Cod and his VW van broke down. He had to get a new engine put in. He shrugged at the question of what his absence would mean. "I just probably won't play," he said. He was out for flanker, and he ran his patterns hard, didn't shirk.

Coach Branahan started the running backs up toward the manbuilder. "Okay, manbuilder," Jonny said to the receivers. Bradford didn't move.

"I didn't hear anybody yell 'manbuilder,'" he said, sneering. "Practice on a day like this sucks."

Jonny came over. "Hey Brad, why do you always act like you don't care?"

Bradford smiled. "I just haven't got any balls," he said.

After the break, Coach Fowles gathered the team in the shade of the huge elm tree near the school end of the playing field. "All right boys, get down on one knee and take your hats off."

Some sat down, some lay down, all took their helmets off.

"Boys, our first football game is September 18, against Our Lady of Lourdes, from upstate. We have never played them before. Today I talked to their coach, and I learned a few things. Now, I don't want to scare you, but you wouldn't be here if you were easily scared. I don't want you psyched up. But there are a few things I would like to share with you.

"Our Lady of Lourdes won their league championship last year. They lost only once. Their entire starting backfield is back this year. Lourdes has five varsity coaches, compared with our two, so you can assume they will be well coached. They run a multiple-option wishbone offense, which is a very difficult offense to run, and a very difficult offense to stop. Oklahoma and Texas run the wishbone.

"Now, their coach told me—and I have to trust him because I can't imagine why he would lie about it—they are so good that if they put their eleven best men on the field, without two-platooning, they can beat anybody from Albany on down to New York City."

There were some sighs from the reclining Harvesters.

"That's what he said. And then he said an interesting thing. He said that they would two-platoon against us. Now of course you can decide for yourselves whether that means he respects us or not. They will two-platoon against Laketown. He also said that their really big game was their second game, the week after they play us. I think that is an interesting thing to say.

"Boys, they are a big, tough football team. Anybody here who thinks that we are playing Little Sisters of the Poor is in for a very difficult Saturday afternoon. None of this means we should change anything we are doing on the practice field—except to work harder. We still have a long way to go. When the time comes, we will be ready. Meanwhile, we know a little bit about their football team, and they know a little bit about us. I told him we were not big, and not experienced, and that we *probably* would throw the football from time to time."

There were some chuckles at the understatement.

"We have a scrimmage on Saturday, and that is only a learning situation. So for right now, let's just get out there and work on what *we* intend to do, and not worry about what any teams plan to do against us."

The cheerleaders were out today for the first time, bouncing, flailing, flicking out dungareed legs, scooping silent cheers with their hands as they swooped toward the earth. From this distance, up on the practice field, they clapped soundlessly in a nubile pantomime before empty stands. Overhead were ponderous thunderheads, made elegant by the sun which outlined them in gold.

Jonny Penchak jumped out of the circle and got down to face tough, defensive end Steve Barker in the pit. Coach Branahan gave a protective start toward the quarterback, then said quickly and quietly to Coach Fowles, "I don't think. . . ."

"Yeah, but I think we'll let it go," Coach Fowles said under his breath.

Jonny drove his bare forearms up under Barker, but was no match for the end's strength, and was pushed over backward with a leg bent under him. There was a quick whistle.

"Ooooh," said Coach Branahan softly.

The maintenance men had mowed the right field of the baseball diamond, and chalked it off in football lines for the team to practice on. Coach Fowles said he wanted to send them a note of thanks. "They didn't have to do that," he said.

Jim Marshall, lined up at defensive left tackle, watched the offensive huddle break, then said quickly to me behind him, "They're comin right at me."

Jonny handed off to fullback Stu Rosenman who started at Marshall, hesitated, and was tackled by Jim and others.

"Okay, Jim, good job," Coach Fowles said. "What did you see?"

"I caught their eyes coming out of the huddle," Jim said.

"Okay boys, always watch the eyes, because they give away a lot. You offensive players, be careful not to tip."

Coach Fowles said to me, "Jim Marshall is big and strong, the only trouble is he stands up straight on defense, gets up too high."

Safetymen Rich Merrill and Ken Furst got knocked woozy making tackles. "It's the first time I ever saw stars like this," Ken told Coach Fowles who was bending over him.

Ken also ran tailback on offense. He broke one run all the way, zigzagging sharply through the secondary. "I love to see him run," Coach Fowles said, "just like a rabbit."

Coach Fowles asked me if I had noticed anything different since the fight between Barry Brill and Ted O'Neill.

"I guess some of the tension is off," I said, "they just don't seem to have anything to do with each other."

He shook his head. "I just can't believe that ever happened. It's like a nightmare to me."

Jonny and I stood in the shower. "I just don't take school very seriously," he said. "Like going to school every day seems silly, you know what I mean? During football and lacrosse I have to, but after lacrosse, in the spring, I just sort of stop going. There are a lot of things I just can't take seriously."

Reuben, the boy Coach Fowles had yelled at yesterday for sleeping in the defensive secondary, quit today. He came in and told Coach Fowles that he loved football, but just wasn't any good at it. Coach Fowles told him it took a lot of guts to come in and speak to him, and that he wished he would stay with the team because it helped just to stick it out. But he said he understood, and he thanked Reuben and shook hands with him.

FRIDAY, September 10

The day before the first real game-scrimmage, it was still hot. The team went through a light workout in shorts. Jack Forrest just ran the track, still feeling weak. Jonny's arm stiffened up some. Coach Fowles said that Bruce Stacey wouldn't play in the scrimmage tomorrow because of his bruised hip. Barry Brill would start in that linebacker spot, with Rich Schenkle as the other linebacker.

Coach Fowles asked the captains to decide whether they wanted to have clean uniforms for tomorrow. Stan Beronski said it didn't matter, "They get dirty anyway." Jim Marshall said he wanted them clean, "Because otherwise they really stink in the bus." Rich Schenkle agreed. So the word went out for everybody to wash practice uniforms for tomorrow.

"Washing them is easy," Jack Forrest said, "but they're a pain in the neck to dry."

Coach Fowles poured me a glass of cream sherry and put a record of Barbra Streisand on the stereo. The athletic director had told me a few days before practice started that Laketown would be lucky to win one game this year, and that he saw a one-and-seven season. I asked Coach Fowles for a prediction.

"Well, I'll know a little more after tomorrow," he said. "Some people think four and four would be a good season. Some think we'll do worse. I think with our new open offense we could go four and four, or better. It could be seven and one. The kids are working hard. So much is a question of mental attitude."

Prentice "Buddy" Fowles, Jr. grew up in western Pennsylvania, the oldest of two brothers and two sisters, and the son of "Jap" Fowles, a former all-American college player and briefly coach of the professional Pittsburgh Steelers of the National Football League. He felt he never quite measured up to his father's hopes for him as a football player, but did manage to play as a reserve end at Juniata College, a small Pennsylvania school.

"I hurt my knee playing football," he said. "They took out the meniscus and cartilage. Sometimes it goes out when I'm running, but I can just fiddle with it and get it back in." He bent his knee and I listened to it crackle and snap. "My wrist too. I got flipped upside down by a blocker in a game and landed on it. I never had it x-rayed." The wrist crackled also. "I never was a very good football player, but I'll tell you what: Hurting my knee like that made me a better person. I'm not kidding. Because it made me have more empathy for others who have misfortunes. It really did."

Buddy and Squeegy earned their B.A. degrees from Juniata College (where Squeegy was voted the senior woman who most typified the spirit of the school) and then married. They went through economically lean years during which Buddy was an elementary school teacher and assistant high school football coach, and they had their two children.

"I had to have three jobs for a while," he said. "One thing I did was I sold encyclopedias. You know what that taught me? I could have been a great salesman. I think I could sell anything. I could be a good recruiter for a college football team. But I really love high school football. I really love kids. A lot of people think that being a high school guidance counselor is more important than teaching elementary school. It's interesting how we look at education. As parents we try to do right by our kids when they are small, and then we turn them over for several hours a day to people many of whom really hate kids and hate teaching. But I loved teaching fifth grade. I miss it. It was one of the most rewarding and important things I ever did."

I asked him how much money he made now, and he told me without hesitation: about $21,000 altogether, of which $1,150 was for coaching, and about $1,500 was for having a master's degree (in administration, from Columbia University). Squeegy was a master teacher supervising nontenure teachers in an elementary school.

"I make good money," he said. "I wouldn't kid anybody about that. You know what I made when I taught in Pennsylvania? Forty-five hundred dollars. When I came here I almost doubled my salary right away."

His won-lost record in five years as head coach has been modestly good: 3-5, 4-2-2, 4-4, 4-3-1, and 6-2.

I was beginning to find his interests a befuddling mix of cliché and imagination. He was an avid reader of Dale Carnegie—"I've read *How to Win Friends and Influence People* over and over"—and of the poets Byron, Keats, and Shelley. "I was at best an average student in high school, and not then interested in anything like poetry. Then later I had this one great teacher who made these things exciting to me. That's why I think teaching is so important."

He was raised a Catholic, and is a firm believer in God's love, but is not a regular church-goer. He was a foe of our involvement in Vietnam nearly from the beginning. I told him I was having trouble sorting out the paradoxes of football and peace and love.

"I know you are," he said, smiling. "You know what the most important accomplishment is for me in coaching? I think I've given the kids a little more confidence in themselves. That's more important than won-lost records. But I still think we can do both."

He put a Dionne Warwick album on the stereo and carefully adjusted the volume and tone. "I love to have music on all the time," he said. "Music is for the soul, it really is." He listened for a few moments. "Man, am I anxious to see what the team's got tomorrow."

3

SATURDAY, *September 11*

It was dark and drizzling at 7:15 A.M. when players began showing up in the locker room. Other than having clean practice uniforms, the team made almost no style concessions for its first game-scrimmage. Tee shirts were still worn rather than jerseys, some players would still wear no shirts over their shoulder pads. Clifford Albert, the small left guard with short curly hair, was more gung-ho. His high-topped shoes were polished and had new white laces—the required style later for regular game days.

At 8:00 A.M. they started boarding the yellow school bus. Coach Fowles asked them to check their equipment: make sure their helmet screws were tight, that they had shoelaces that wouldn't break, and that they had all their pads. Paul Treski, a smiling, silent, broad-shouldered, knock-kneed reserve lineman who was teased a lot, had forgotten his hip pads and ran back to get them.

The bus rolled a few blocks and then pulled over, because Clifford Albert's mother was waiting alongside the road with the Gatorade. It took fifty minutes to get to Port Chester, but no one knew how to find the school. Twice we stopped at gas stations and Coach Branahan, his ample rear shivering in his white football pants, sprinted across the cement to ask the attendants for directions.

At last we were there, at the old fortress of a school which overlooked the football field and permanent bleachers. Nobody else was in sight. Coach Fowles went into the school to find the Port Chester coach. The Harvesters milled around and put on their shoulder pads.

Bradford McClure was wearing a red, white, and blue necktie as a headband. Later he would substitute his purple "game band." It was Bradford who first spotted the pretty long-legged, long-haired maiden in dungarees sitting by herself at the top of the stands.

"You don't have to cut your hair for football?" the girl asked. Bradford shook his head. "They do at Port Chester," she said.

Minutes later Bradford, seated several rows down, developed an urgent itch, and began swishing his rump on the seat. He stopped abruptly and turned his head part-way around. "Uh, is that girl still here?" he asked softly. He closed his eyes as he spotted her. He sprinted down the steps and crouched while he was bombarded with sticks, stones, leaves and other debris by his teammates.

The Cardinal Spellman team arrived from New York City, and the players spilled out of the bus, growling, snapping, clapping, cheering, hopping, slamming shoulder-to-shoulder. They were wearing game uniforms and looked slick in red jerseys and white helmets. Then Port Chester came out of the school, also dressed in game attire, also yelling, clenching fists and teeth, cheering themselves on. They raced over the top of the stands and down the steps and onto the field and commenced high-speed calisthenics, just as the Cardinal Spellman team was doing. Port Chester had five coaches, dressed alike in blue baseball caps, gray jerseys, and blue shorts.

Laketown players, wearing tee shirts, torn pants, dilapidated shoes, helmets with peeling paint, stood with folded arms watching this display of spirit.

"Whatever that is," Bradford said, sneering down at the field, "sucks."

For Laketown, the scrimmage was a disaster. Jonny's first pass against Port Chester was intercepted and run back for a touchdown. After his first plunge into the line, Stu Rosenman came back to the huddle shaking his head and muttering, "I never been hit *that* hard." Laketown punted once. The pass from center bounced back to Steve Barker, and then his kick was blocked.

On defense, the small Harvester line shifted around uncertainly. Big Port Chester backs banged in and through it.

The host team scored on the ground, and then on a long pass when the two safeties, Ted O'Neill and Ken Furst, confused assignments. Laketown spirits were lifted briefly when Don Heidner went all the way on a flanker reverse, and Ken Furst zigzagged for a touchdown up the middle on a draw.

Against Cardinal Spellman, it was worse. Spellman, using the wishbone offense with the quarterback running wide and either pitching to a back or keeping the ball himself, scored three quick touchdowns.

"Right now," Coach Fowles said to me, "you are witnessing our team being eaten alive."

Coach Branahan shook his head wearily and chewed his gum hard.

A Laketown play was supposed to go over right guard, but Jonny and two running backs all collided. "What in the world was THAT?" Coach Fowles yelled, striding in among the dejected players. "That looked like a debacle at the three hole! COME ON!"

Several girls, standing along the sidelines, tittered.

Cardinal Spellman went in again from the four, right over big weak-backed tackle Vince Carradino. "Goddamn it!" Dino said.

"Vince!" Coach Fowles hollered, "You get outta there and sit on the sidelines until you decide you can play football without that language."

Don Heidner was also banished when he dropped a pass and said, "Shit!"

Noting that the opposing players and coaches were using the same language, I asked coach Fowles why he was so tough. "Are you a puritan?" I asked.

He put his fingers to his temples. "It's a question of mental attitude. I don't want them wandering around worrying about mistakes. I want them thinking about the next play."

Cornerback Al Stacey, the hard-working sixteen-year-old senior, was suckered in on a wishbone play and the pitchout beat him to the outside.

Coach Fowles moaned. "Come on, Al! Your job is the outside. THINK!"

Jonny hurried his passes, threw them into the ground. Ted O'Neill was similarly unsuccessful at quarterback. Jonny was put back in and immediately was slammed down by the pass-rush. He strolled to the sidelines rubbing his neck. "You know what football does?" he said. "Football gives you a headache."

Rich Schenkle, playing offensive end, caught a pass up the middle and was dumped hard. He hobbled to the sideline with a severely bruised knee. A minute later Rich tried to sneak back in, and was restrained by Coach Fowles. "No more today, Rich," he said.

That meant that both tough linebackers, Bruce Stacey and Rich, were out. Bruce paced the sidelines in frustration, criticizing the team's play.

Coach Fowles went up to Bradford McClure on the sideline and told him to go in at offensive tight end.

"No," Bradford said, his arms folded across his chest.

"No?"

"I'm a flankerback," Bradford said, "I'm not playing end."

Coach Fowles stared into Bradford's eyes for a few seconds, then walked back onto the field.

There was a half-time break for Laketown, while the other two teams played. The Harvesters stood around and drank Gatorade and soda. Some ate sandwiches. For many of them it was the first time they had seen Mrs. Fowles, who was seated on the grass nearby with a picnic lunch and their two children.

Squeegy shook her head and said in her little girl voice, "I have never seen Laketown like they are on the sidelines today. They have their helmets off, they're messing around laughing, not paying attention. That's not like Laketown."

Buddy Fowles told the team to sit down on the grass. He told them: "Don't be intimidated out there. Otherwise you'll sit on the bench. Another thing. I have seen some punches out there. I asked the official if any of our boys did anything, and he said no. This is not a Mickey Mouse situation. If somebody pops you, you turn around and walk away."

He said that just before the big fight, which was the only bright spot of the day, and in which the Harvesters did not participate. All of a sudden the two teams on the field were battling, spread out in a free-for-all. The only Harvester to get involved was Rich Merrill, who went out to try to break up two combatants and was roughly pulled off by Coach Fowles. "STAY OUT OF IT!" Coach Fowles yelled.

In the middle of the field a Port Chester coach punched a Cardinal Spellman coach. "Don't you ever push one of my kids!" he hollered.

Coach Fowles and his team watched it all from the sidelines. "See why I'm proud of our boys," he said. "That will never happen with our team." He turned to the Harvesters and said loudly, "We're too grown up for that, Laketown."

Finally the fight was over, and then the scrimmage. Coach Fowles walked over to congratulate the Port Chester head coach. "I'm really impressed by how well your defense pursues," he said, shaking hands.

The Port Chester coach eyed him suspiciously. "What are you setting me up for?" he said.

"I mean it, I thought they moved real well."

"Hmmm," said the Port Chester coach, walking away.

"Why can't people ever believe you when you compliment them?" Coach Fowles said to me. "You know what? I'll tell you exactly what those coaches think of me. Number one, they think I'm a nice polite guy who is not really tough enough as a coach. Or, number two, they think I am a con man."

"Were you conning him?" I asked.

"Hey, I really thought his line was very quick. I didn't say they were quicker than we will be when the season starts. I meant what I said."

We joined the straggling Harvesters headed up the hill toward the bus. He yelled, as he began to trot, "Laketown NEVER walks! RUN UP!"

As we neared the bus, he turned to Coach Branahan. "Sandy, I heard my *peers* out there say we *stank*. If we play that way we will be zero and eight, or one and seven." Coach Branahan nodded.

It had started to rain, and the rain mixed with the dense sweat in the uniforms as the team struggled out of shoulder pads and clacked aboard the bus. They were not particularly somber. "The team's a bunch of freaks anyway," Jonny Penchak said.

Bottles of Gatorade started around. There were also number-ten cans of fruit juice, but no opener. Somebody whacked holes in the tops of cans with football cleats.

Jim Marshall, the center and co-captain, stood up and announced dolefully, "We made some mistakes today. Go home and think about them, write them down, bring them in Monday."

Stan Beronski chuckled as he slurped ginger ale. Some boys put their heads down on the seatbacks in front of them. Rich Schenkle was one. Jonny pulled small bits of foam rubber from the ripped seatback and tossed them into Rich's dark hair. Somebody pulled Paul Treski's pants down. Gradually the jokes and chatter died down, and the bus became quiet except for the droning engine and the rain driving against the windows.

Jonny was tired, and he stretched as he got off the bus in Laketown. "Man," he said. "I miss the regular summer days when you could sleep until eleven or twelve, and then somebody would call and say, 'What are you doin?' Then go out for some burgers. Come back about four. Maybe cruise around for some chicks . . ."

It felt as if a whole day had passed, but in fact it was only noon. Jonny and I went to his house for lunch. He lived in a quiet neighborhood of rather new homes in a pleasant two-storey brick house with a small yard in front and a patio in back. His parents were away. We fried steaks and then had graham crackers and tea, and orange juice.

He did not want to dwell on the scrimmage, other than to acknowledge that the team, and he in particular, had had a bad day. "We scrimmage JFK on Tuesday," he said nonchalantly. "I'll be ready. I know I'll be able to throw."

He got out his cheap steel guitar and fingered some rock and accompanied it with his soft whine of a voice. He played the music of The Byrds, and Crosby, Stills and Nash which he learned on his guitar from records. He got very absorbed in his guitar, so when I asked him if he smoked grass he finished several bars of his song before he answered.

"Naw. I don't get stoned. I'm not really into drugs, you know. Some of the guys on the team are. But I'd really just rather drink if I want to get high." He strummed some more. "With my long hair I'm, you know, kind of established as a freak anyway. So I don't have to do anything."

"Do your parents hassle you about your hair?" I asked.

"Naw. They're really good people. Some people assume that my father might, because he looks so straight, you know? My father is the smartest guy I've ever known, I guess. He's not as straight as you would think. In fact he told my mother that as long as I kept my hair clean, I could have it as long as I wanted. They're very liberal, you know, tolerant."

I asked him if he was worried about the injury today to Rich Schenkle.

"Sugarbear?" He grinned toothily. "He'll be okay. He's really tough. Like you know, with his sweet baby-face and smile, he's really got a malevolent character. He's really a mean, tough kid, loves to hit, loves to fight. He has fights mainly about old girl friends." He whined a few bars of a song. "I really dig Rich, you know? He's not a very usual dude. I dig Ben, too. Ben will start at fullback pretty soon."

"You told me that before. It's hard to imagine."

"He will, if he can play with that tooth. You'll see. Like, Ben doesn't really look like a runner, you know? But you watch. He'll start. Want some more grahams? I could eat a box of these every day."

Later that evening I went to the Fowleses' house, and we had some Scotch. "Buddy," I said, "they killed us."

He smiled. "Do you realize that's the first time you've said 'us' about this team?"

"I just meant Laketown," I said.

"I know what you meant," he said, still smiling. "You know what? If they had a panel of impartial observers at that scrimmage, they would have given us an A for class. That fight was disgraceful. Our kids didn't do that. That is not what football is all about. Did you notice that Ted

O'Neill and Barry Brill sat together on the bus? I thought that was beautiful. That means more to me than the scrimmage. That is what this is all about."

It was true that I was stunned by my own partisan attitude. It had quickly become *my* team. I was embarrassed by their shabby uniforms and their humiliation in the scrimmage. That concerned me more than two guys sitting together. I was worried about the season.

Coach Fowles looked at me. "I have never seen a Laketown football team look as bad as this one did today," he said, making me wince. "We *could* lose all our games, And you know what? You are going to see a miracle take place. Up until today they have been an interesting bunch of beautiful individuals, but not a team. There is no way I and Sandy Branahan can make them a team. They have to do it themselves. Now you will see a miracle. Maybe this week, maybe next, they will become a team, and you will be amazed at how good they will be." He clinked his glass to mine.

"Then you will have to get rid of some guys," I said.

"Why?"

"I have never seen a kid defy a coach and stay on a team," I said.

He smiled. "You mean Bradford. I'm not going to kick him off the team, and I don't think he'll quit either. See, that's just the way society reacts to sensitive individuals with minds of their own, the people with real imagination. The minute such a person goes against the grain, society tries to ostracize him. Those are the people we *need*. We need to find a way to include the very best people, to work together toward a common goal. I'll tell you what: Bradford McClure will stay on the team, and he will be the key to this team coming together. Do you believe that?"

"No."

"Hey," he said, clinking our glasses again, "this is going to be a very interesting season."

SUNDAY, *September 12*

"You expected to get pushed around physically yesterday, right?"

Buddy Fowles stirred his coffee and looked into the cup. "Yeah, I did."

"Did it turn out anything like you expected?"

"Two things on defense disappointed me. Number one, we did not pursue as well as we should have, we didn't move laterally. I really thought we had worked hard on quickness. And number two, I didn't think our gang-tackling was very good. You saw the way Port Chester gang-tackled? That's the kind of tackling we usually get. It's a tremendous morale booster for the team doing it, and you cause a lot of fumbles. The kid carrying the football, if he's been hit by four or five people time after time, well, after a while he gets discouraged.

"And truthfully I expected more from our offense. I had the feeling we were completely handcuffed. We've got to work harder on our running game. You can't throw if you're not hitting on passes. A couple of times, with the screen pass and the flanker-around, we looked great. But that's not an offense. If we want to go 50 percent with passing, we have to be able to run. We have totally concentrated on our passing game, and so I think we are out of balance. I was always taught, you run for the dough, you pass for the show. So, okay, I like throwing the ball this year. But with a running attack you get field position, you physically wear down the other team, and you eat up the clock. Last year there were times we were sitting on the ball six or seven minutes at a time, grinding out 60, 70 yards. We beat teams physically. So, okay, we're not as big and strong as last year. We can still have good balance." He poured another cup of instant coffee.

"Did you think the kids were intimidated?" I asked.

"Well, our kids got confused. They didn't know how to block that Port Chester defense. They used a four-four, and we worked on that, but they did it a little differently. They had their tackles out on our tackles, but pointed in. And they fired inside. The theory is, that forces two men to block you. That doesn't bother me too much, because with good preparation during the week you can prepare for that.

"I *am* worried about the fact that they were beating us across the line of scrimmage. Size doesn't have too much to do with that. If a back can hit the hole in 0.8 seconds—well, I never felt our backs really went at that hole. Like Stu Rosenman. Stu's a great kid. But he's a fullback, and he knew he was going to be hit before he ever got his physical. And you remember he came back to the huddle the first time and said he was surprised how hard he got hit.

"Now, Stu's got a choice to make. Is he going to be in awe of a defensive line? Or does he have enough confidence in himself to run a little harder? Remember, the very next play was a pass to him, and he dropped it because he heard footsteps behind him. Football is one of the few sports where you can be directly intimidated. Physically. Yes sir. Tom Kase is a good offensive tackle, awfully quick. But Tom Kase was intimidated yesterday by that big defensive tackle. He did not want to play football against that man.

"Football's a game, but what do you do in life? If you're not successful the first time with something do you say, 'Gee, I didn't realize that life was this difficult?' Or do you pull your guts back into your stomach and say 'I'm going to try harder.' "

"Jonny didn't like getting pushed around yesterday," I said.

"No, he didn't. Jonny did not have a good day. He took a couple of real good shots. They really popped him. He's not afraid, that's for sure. But you know what? You always say that he has so much confidence. Well, yesterday you saw. He needs more. He is not as cool as you think. We wonder whether our throwing game can be the bread and butter of our offense. I don't know. Yesterday we got in trouble with it, and Jonny got a little excited."

"Ted O'Neill really wants that job," I said.

"Yeah, well, I thought Ted wasn't as accurate as he should be either. And in all honesty, it wasn't because he and Jonny got rushed so bad. Our pass protection was pretty good. On the JVs last year, the passing game was tremendous. So now, coming back on the bus I asked Don Heidner about it. How many passes has he caught in practice would you say? Maybe 100 passes. How many passes did he catch at Port Chester? I don't think one. So I asked Don what's the difference between JV and varsity football. He said the difference is that in JVs they ignore you on a pass pattern, and you know you're going to get open. But in varsity you can't get open.

"I thought a few of the boys did pretty well. Jim Petrowski was in on a lot of tackles. He's not a big boy, but he has a lot of courage. I thought Barry Brill made one real good tackle. I thought Ken Furst ran well, got away from a lot of people."

He leaned back and took a deep breath and sighed. "It's really the little things that bother me, the morale things. On Labor Day, twenty-seven people showed up for the voluntary practice. That's the lowest number ever. That showed there was something wrong. And then, when you start to get walloped and pushed around like we did yesterday, watch what happens. Kids don't have their hands folded behind their backs in the huddle, or they take their helmets off on the sidelines—little things. Everybody starts to move their goals down just a notch. You don't see that unless you're really looking for it. You see them walk off the field instead of run. We say Laketown *never* walks. That's because those little things . . . nothing else will get you through at a time like that.

"Did we communicate with each other on defense? Hunh-unh. They all want a team—Bruce, Jonny, Rich, Bradford—but we're not a team yet."

"You're disturbed," I said, "about the captains."

He sighed again, and spoke a bit reluctantly. "Well, at some point they've got to come together, and that hasn't happened. Captains could help that. I think they made a mistake. I hope I'm wrong, but that's my feeling. They've got three great kids as captains. But we're talking football now, getting a group of people ready to play a very rough game. Now we have Stan Beronski, a great kid, highly intelligent, sensitive. He and I have some great conversations about a lot of things, but he doesn't communicate with most of the kids. Rich Schenkle—he's a good football player, a great hitter, but he doesn't talk to the kids. And Jim Marshall doesn't say that much either. Now these three kids are going to play good football regardless. But what about the kids on the fringe, what about the kids that need to be patted on the back? Nothing!

"You know who the real leader on that football team is? Bruce Stacey. Or Jonny. And I handpicked those two as chairmen of our morale committee. Jonny the intelligent one, you know, sensitive; Bruce the brawn, yet not completely out of it sensitivity-wise. One reason Bruce didn't get elected is that some of the kids feel he comes on too strong with his attitudes.

"This is the first year that I haven't counted the ballots, and I didn't even have a chance to talk to the team about it. It was a personality contest. It's not that these kids aren't looked up to by the other players, but we're talking about bringing everybody together in a team. And Bruce Stacey, with Jonny's help, and the help of the other three, and the help of the coaching staff, could have done that."

"Are you going to do anything about it?"

"There's nothing I can do. They've made their choice, and for the coaches to, say, name a couple more boys as captains or something, that would show the kids that the coaches lacked confidence in their judgment."

He leaned back and folded his arms behind his head. "Well, football's a funny game, a great game, and a lot of values can be learned from it. We all saw different things out there yesterday. I think it was a good learning situation, we learned a lot about ourselves. We learned that we have to work harder. This week we have to learn to move the ball consistently.

"Now, just what was the purpose of the scrimmage? To make the other teams look bad? Or get our offense going? We're all flesh and blood, and we all get hung up on how we want our team to look good."

"Were you embarrassed?"

"Well, those other teams didn't get a true picture of Laketown, but that doesn't bother me. What kind of tone are the coaches setting for a scrimmage? I wanted them loose, not all fired up. One reason our kids weren't very depressed coming home on the bus is that they weren't all psyched up in the first place. We had scrimmages in western Pennsylvania where we had the kids all psyched up, like fantastically. Over in New Jersey, at the school where Vince Lombardi once coached, they're literally afraid to lose over there, *afraid* to lose! Okay, now, what's the priority? Is it putting so much pressure on the kids to win?

"Hey, we open up with three real tough teams. Boy, we could be zero and three like *that*, you know, and then we've really got problems."

He rose and picked up the coffee cups. "Anyway, these are some of the questions we've got to answer before we start practice Monday. Because if we go into that football game next Saturday with the team this way, we're going to get taken apart."

The two coaches sat huddled in the dark dining room watching on the wall the flickering foot-long rectangle of light which was a color film of one of last year's games of Our Lady of Lourdes.

Coach Fowles used one hand to point out aspects of the action six feet away, and the other hand to switch gears on the projector. The projector clacked with slow motion, freeze-frame, reverse, forward. Back and forth went the players on the wall. He and Coach Branahan chattered and nodded and fretted. The film was stopped and started and reversed so fast that it made me dizzy to watch. I could not detect most of the things which to them were important elements to watch for in their first game: nuances of movement in the line, subtle movements by the quarterback, missed or completed blocking assignments, how hard they hit.

Buddy Fowles turned on the lights and leaned back. Sandy Branahan got up and went into the living room and picked up his baby and paced with her.

"They like the option and inside belly best," Coach Fowles said. "That wishbone is tough."

"Do you think the quarterback is running a true option?" Sandy asked.

"Hmmm, hard to tell. It looked like sometimes he was reading the second man in. Sometimes it looked like the pitchout was called in the huddle. We sure had trouble defensing the wishbone yesterday."

"I'll say," Sandy said, chortling.

"Out of twenty-two last year, they have eleven back," Buddy said. "The whole backfield is back. The quarterback is really going to know his job."

"Hmmm," Sandy said, pacing with his baby.

"How to stop Lourdes? The laura's okay. A gap-eight might stop it. I think they're beatable. They made some mistakes. But we're going to have a heck of a time stopping them. They'll eat the clock up."

"Hey, Buddy, how about Steve Barker at defensive tackle and Barry Brill at defensive end?"

"Hmmm," Buddy said.

MONDAY, September 13

The rain beat against the classroom windows. Nobody inside smiled. Boys looked down at their desktops and fingered their helmets.

"I've got to be honest with you," Coach Fowles said at the front of the room. "There's just one word that sums up what happened Saturday: *debacle*. It was a disgrace, a nightmare. I couldn't believe that a team from Laketown could be pushed around like that. I had a lump in my throat the last five minutes."

He shook his head deliberately, but his eyes were not sad. They were clear, and they focused hard on the boys around the room.

"Boys, if you want to play football, fine." His voice now was soft and slow. "Then let's play—football. If you don't want to play football, don't —play—football. It's that simple." His voice rose a bit. "Football is a rough game, so rough that not everybody can play it. Not everybody *should* play it. Not everybody should be a doctor. But it's so rough that girls are not *allowed* to play it. Just men. It's so rough that we spend a ton of money outfitting people so that they don't get hurt. We pay about twenty dollars for the helmet to protect your head. We pay about thirty-five dollars for shoulder pads. It's *rough!* And that's the way it's gotta be played, gentlemen. Not with viciousness, not with meanness, not trying to hurt anybody intentionally. But if you don't play it rough, you're going to get hurt.

"Now we've got some kids in here right now who will hit as hard as anybody I've ever known—I mean *legally*. You're allowed to block and tackle. And I did not see too many good blocks and tackles on Saturday. I saw some. I saw some things happen that made me proud I was from Laketown. An impartial panel of judges would have given us an A-plus on behavior. But we can do that and still have a good football team. We can do both.

"But I'll tell you what bothered me. Rule number one: Do your best. We did not do our best Saturday. We did not play very well. That's a fact. But it was a learning experience. Hey, I hate excuses. I know that Bruce Stacey didn't play, and I know that Rich Schenkle only played a little bit. But I didn't run to those other coaches and say, 'Hey, we got two tough boys that didn't play.' That's for the birds. If you have to lose, lose like a man. Don't lose with a ton of excuses, because that doesn't change anything.

"And if you come back to a huddle and you say, 'Oooh, man, they really hit me,' if you feel that way, do me a favor, do the family a favor, do the dedicated kids in this room a favor, and say quietly to me that you don't think football's your thing. Because it starts *here.*" He tapped his head. "It starts in the mind.

"You know what boys like to do? Boys like to go out and play in the mud and get dirty. And that's beautiful. Because today we're going to be boys, and we're going to get dirty in the mud. And you'll love it. And on this coming Saturday I want to see a different football team. Last Saturday is gone. It's a state of mind."

He stopped and looked slowly around the room, his gaze shifting from face to face.

"Eight weeks from now, this is all a memory, gone forever. You can't bring it back. You won't believe how fast it's going to go by. Forty-eight days of football. Forty days of practice and eight games. Then it's all over. Be fair to yourselves. You'll never know how good you could have been, unless you try. Rule number one: Do your best. Eight weeks from now, have—no—regrets."

He looked out the window at the rain, and players took the opportunity to shift in their seats.

"Boys, we did not schedule a cake-eating high school for our first game. We scheduled a real good football team. And they better be good. Our Lady of Lourdes was nice enough to schedule us before their *big* game. They are already thinking about their *next* game, against what their coach believes is the best team in the state. They'll loosen up against us.

"Now, their coach didn't say that. He said they don't expect a runaway against Laketown. That's nice of him. I was glad he said that to me. I've heard a lot of whining around here: 'Oh boy, our Lady of Lourdes is so tough. . . .' Well I hope their coach gets some phone calls so that he finds out how atrocious we were last Saturday. I hope he does. Because today is our *first* day of football practice.

"Positions are open on this football team. If you want to play football on Saturday you're going to hit today. Tomorrow at three o'clock we go over to John F. Kennedy High School and scrimmage them. And you're going to hit over there. And believe it or not—it's like a dream come true—they're going to run the wishbone triple-option offense against us. And we are going to have a defense to stop it. They will help us. We are not going to try to make JFK look bad tomorrow. They will help us be ready to play a football game at 2:00 P.M. next Saturday. And boy, I want to see some sweat fly on Saturday."

He stood silent and nodded his head slowly as he looked at his team. Several boys squirmed. "Gentlemen, I want to make this statement now, at twenty minutes after three on Monday: No matter what happens, I know I will be proud of you on Saturday afternoon."

As if that were a signal, the tension in the room popped into questions: "Do they have a preference on the option? . . . Will you get the names of their backfield? . . . Do they counter a lot? . . . Do they really pop, Coach? . . ."

Coach Fowles smiled and turned to the blackboard and picked up the pace of his talk.

"All right, we know a lot about Lourdes. Coach Branahan and I spent about six hours yesterday looking at films. First of all. . . ."

The special defense to stop the Lourdes triple-option was introduced today on the mud sea which was the practice field. It was called the *laura-center*:

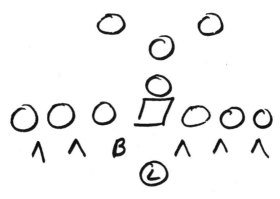

"The middle linebacker," Coach Fowles said, "will be Rich Schenkle, if he can play, or Jim Petrowski. L, the laura man, is Bruce Stacey. He has one job—the quarterback. He will go wherever the quarterback goes. And there's going to be a terrible collision. After Bruce hits him a couple of times, the quarterback's leg is gonna hurt, his hand will hurt, even his fingernails will hurt. And then he's not going to want to run with the football any more. He'll pitch out to a back. But then our cornermen are going to come up fast, and they will hit too. What is the object? The object is to force them to pass. They don't like to pass."

What exactly caused the team to jell? Perhaps the pep talk, perhaps the dark memory of the scrimmage disaster, perhaps anticipation finally of opening game. Whatever it was, the Harvesters hit each other with devastating power in the mud. The defense slashed into the offense so hard that it brought smiles of pained joy to the faces of the running backs.

Perhaps it was Bradford McClure. Bradford, who had sulkily refused to play end last Saturday, had met Coach Fowles in the hall before practice. "You guys didn't look very good on Saturday," Bradford had said.

"What do you mean, *you* guys?" Coach Fowles had asked, prodding. "You're part of the team."

Bradford had shrugged and kept his hands in his pockets and scowled slightly. "I got in for four plays. How can I be part of the team?"

So now on the practice field, coach Fowles spoke to Bradford among the other players. "Bradford," he said matter-of-factly, "which do you want to play, defensive tackle or defensive end?"

Bradford shrugged. "It doesn't make any difference," he said.

Coach Fowles smiled broadly and put his arm around Bradford's shoulder and guided him to the defensive tackle spot. "I know it doesn't make any difference," he said, "because I know that you want to play football and I know you're tough."

Bradford shrugged again and got down in the four-point stance in a line position he had never played before. On the first play he hit halfback Ken Furst head-on and slammed him over backwards. "That's the first time I've seen Bradford smile this season," Coach Fowles said to me.

Coach Fowles was not through with him. "Okay, Bradford. Bruce is still out. You call defensive signals."

"I don't know anything about defensive signals," Bradford said.

Coach Fowles had not stopped smiling. He maneuvered Bradford to his place facing the defensive huddle. "You're going to learn very fast, because you're smart."

Bradford scoffed.

"Aren't you?" Coach Fowles asked, staring hard and intimately into Bradford's eyes.

"Sh-i-i," Bradford said under his breath as he faced his teammates and announced: "All right, Laketown five-four laura center. Let's go."

The defense was impregnable. Jonny directed the "Lourdes" wishbone offense. Al Stacey, playing cornerback, made a series of jarring tackles on pitchouts. Jim Petrowski was a dervish at middle linebacker. Barry Brill made a driving tackle on Jonny, then limped into the locker room with a jammed knee.

Coach Fowles watched the ferocious hitting. "Sandy," he said to Coach Branahan, "I think we've accomplished what we set out to do. We've got 'em hitting and feeling like a football team." The coaches exchanged grins.

Bruce Stacey and Rich Schenkle, the tough linebackers, looked on with a blend of frustration and satisfaction. Bruce would have x-rays tomorrow of his hip, so he wouldn't scrimmage against JFK, but he hoped to play Saturday. Rich thought he could hit tomorrow. Jim Marshall, the center, also watched from the side, with the chipped bone in his hand protected by an Ace bandage. He would be ready Saturday.

The locker room scene was mostly playful. But Jonny Penchak had his head down as he pulled off his sweat socks.

"The team looked tough today," I said.

Jonny had not forgotten last Saturday. "I really don't like to play bad," he said, slapping a sock down on the tile floor. "It really bothers me to play bad."

Jim Marshall came into the coaches' room, smiling. "Coach, you really turned them around today."

"We've got a long way to go, Jim," Coach Fowles said.

When Jim left, Coach Fowles said to me, "*Perhaps* you've witnessed the turn-around of a football team today. *Maybe.* We'll have to see."

"Do you think Bradford McClure can play defensive tackle?" I said.

"H-e-y," he said, chuckling. "Bradford will *start* at defensive tackle on Saturday. And you know what? He'll be tremendous."

Out on the school driveway, Jim Marshall drove his old Dodge convertible, loaded with cheering players, back and forth through a deep puddle, tossing water up over the car hood. And then the car stopped running and we all pushed it to get it started, slogging through the puddle in the rain and laughing at how silly it all was.

The scrimmage at JFK High School, in the alternating rain and sun, was unexciting. Laketown dominated it, and neither team seemed psyched up. The laura-center defense, with the linebacker *monster man* keying the quarterback, was effective against JFK's triple-option wishbone. But even that was inconclusive, for JFK did not execute the options fluently, and the man chosen especially for the monster position, Bruce Stacey, was unable to play because of his bruised hip. Laketown's three best linebackers were out—Bruce, and both Rich Schenkle and Barry Brill with bruised knees.

Players talked among themselves about how tough they would be when those three came back. "You can't wait for injured stars to solve your problems," Coach Fowles told them. "You go with what you have, and no excuses."

Offensive guard Jack Forrest was tried in the monster, or laura, position; so was Jim Petrowski; so was fullback Stu Rosenman. But none of them was impressive. There was a lot of gang-tackling, which had been missing in the earlier scrimmage. Alternating left cornerbacks Al Stacey and John Finch made stinging tackles on wide plays.

Bradford McClure impressed the coaches at left defensive tackle. When he got confused and pushed around at his new position, he was razzed by his teammates on the sidelines, and once as he picked himself up from the ground, he straightened his helmet with middle fingers demonstratively extended over the earholes. "I can't move around fast enough for this position," Bradford said.

On offense, Jonny still couldn't get his passing game going. In the mud, he had trouble setting up, and the receivers had trouble cutting and holding onto the ball.

The running game improved, especially the inside-belly series, with a fake to a back running wide, and a hand-off inside. Tailback Ken Furst went all the way on that, cutting behind Jack Forrest's block at the four hole. Al Stacey, Stu Rosenman, and Keith Allen—who was down all week because he wasn't playing much—also went up the middle for the distance.

Freddie Delaney, who joined the team late and would not be able to play in the first game, got in for a few plays at middle guard on defense. Guys on the sidelines said that there was always a fight when Freddie got in. After two plays, JFK players were swinging at him, but he kept an innocent expression.

At the end, Laketown ran off the field, past a pond and some weeping willows, and boarded the bus. While they were waiting to start, Coach Fowles told the players that it was "the beginning of a football team today. The thing I liked best was the gang-tackling." Cornerback John Finch said the thing he liked best was a girl with long black hair who had been on the sidelines. The bus was waiting because Stu Rosenman and Stan Beronski had detoured and jumped into the pond by the weeping willows.

WEDNESDAY, September 15

The coaches had decided to break tradition. In previous years, uniforms had been handed out to seniors first, then juniors. This year, uniforms would be passed out in order of players' presumed ability.

Words from today's English class were on the blackboard:

EMOLLIENT	MUNDANE
NOSTALGIC	PALLIATIVE
EXPIATE	FOMENT
PARADOX	PREDACIOUS
ARCHETYPE	STARK

Coach Fowles erased them and wrote "TEAM" in large letters and underlined it.

"I don't want to sound like a philosopher," he said, "but when you play football, you have a football *team*. Get a thesaurus and look up 'team'. For us, the team comes first. My wife knows that. I spent ten hours with football on Sunday, looking at films and going over offenses and defenses and scouting reports. She didn't argue with that. She knows that's it. Lourdes is not coming down here Saturday to play our juniors or seniors. They're coming to play our football—*team*.

"Now I know we've only got thirty-four jerseys. There are a lot of guys on the team—more than forty. What do some coaches do? They *cut*. It would be easy to cut. But I've never cut a player in my life. I want everybody who wants to play to play. Now, you're all *great*. But I have no crystal ball. If you don't hit in practice, I can't see into your brains to see if you're going to hit in a game. If somebody doesn't get a jersey, and he feels bad about it, we've got practices out there to do something about it."

Coach Branahan took a step forward. "I remember the honor the first time I put on a varsity jersey," he said. "There are 1,500 people in this school, and thirty-four varsity jerseys. So it's an honor. Our twenty-two best players are getting uniforms first. Coach Fowles and I talked about it a long time."

So the jerseys—white with green numerals for home games, green with white numerals for away, each worth $14.95—were passed out. First choices went to the three captains, Jim Marshall, who took 51, Stan Beronski who took 84, and Rich Schenkle who took 63. Then came Bruce and Al Stacey and Jonny Penchak; next Bradford McClure, Jack Forrest, and Clifford Albert; and so on. One of those who didn't get a regular varsity jersey was senior Cary Grimes, the popular, lanky black end. Junior Jim Petrowski was angry at that.

"See *that!*" he said to me. "It's not fair Cary didn't get a jersey. He works hard. Some guys work their hearts out and don't have talent. And then they don't get a jersey. Other guys are just good. They have it easy."

"You know what's happening right now?" Coach Fowles said to the team. "Coach Branahan is going through your lockers. There are freshmen who don't have any equipment. We have a feeling there's some extra equipment in your lockers."

There was some moaning. Coach Fowles smiled. "They're just looking for equipment," he said. Which was fortunate. It was rumored that one starting lineman had an ounce of marijuana stashed there.

Cornerback John Finch said the search would be rewarding. "I got three pairs of football pants in my locker," he said.

Coach Branahan came back in, shaking his head in a smile. "We found some equipment," he said, "and *you* Penchak, you baboon, you had your combination written on the outside of your lock."

"I always forget it," Jonny said.

"Okay, pay attention," Coach Fowles said. "The laura-center defense did give JFK some problems yesterday. But you have to line up *exactly*. Nose on *inside shoulder*, not in the gap. The regular laura is *outside* shoulder, and the only change for the front five when they switch into laura center is to go to inside shoulder.

Coach Fowles thumbed through some index cards. "The Lourdes starting count is 'DOWN, GO.' Remember that. If the quarterback takes the ball on the same count most of the time, anticipate it. We feel their most dangerous play is the inside belly. Their second most dangerous play is the quarterback-option around end. Third most dangerous is the wishbone counter. We have covered all these with our defenses, by lining up on inside shoulder, with the laura man on the quarterback, and the cornerbacks coming up quick. Remember, our whole theory is to force them to *pass.*"

He lay the index cards aside.

"When we go out for practice today they will be videotaping you as you run out of the building."

Bradford McClure's head popped up. "What? When? What for?"

Coach Fowles raised his hand in peace. "They want to use it for 'Meet the Team Night' tomorrow. Don't worry. Just do what they say."

Bradford sneered. "Video-fucking-tape," he said under his breath, "sucks."

"For 'Meet the Team Night'," Coach Fowles went on, "you will dress in shorts. I want a couple of you to dress in full football gear. I know you don't like it, but I don't want to hear any complaints. Be sure to bring your aunts, uncles, and friends."

The team lined up casually in the hallway, prodded into something like alphabetical order by students from the audiovisual department. They pranced out toward the camera one at a time, to make a tape that would coincide with one of the cheerleaders jumping up and down and yelling brightly that if this Harvester couldn't do it, that Harvester could. After they had gone out, the camera was discovered not to be working, and it had to be done all over.

The humidity was high, and the practice dragged. Fullback Stu Rosenman was in street clothes. He had a severe contusion on his upper right arm. "The doctor said it would be a week and a half," Stu said, "but I'm going to try to play Saturday."

Little fullback Ben Schenkle was dressed, despite his wired-in tooth. He was ignoring the admonitions of his doctor. "My parents said I could play, and Coach said okay."

His older brother, linebacker-end Rich, came out dressed and ready, and lined up to hit with the team.

"Get *outta* there, Rich," Coach Fowles said.

"My leg's okay, Coach, it's okay, it's. . . ."

"Get outta there!" Then he added as an afterthought, "Go in and take your shoulder pads off right now."

Rich hung his head and kicked the ground and headed in.

"He doesn't know *how* to hit half-way," Coach Fowles said to me. "If he still had his shoulder pads on, he'd get in there somehow."

Guard Jack Forrest was kicked in the funnybone of his arm, and hopped around in agony. Cornerback John Finch staggered out of the scrimmage after being poked in the eye. Defensive end Stan Beronski picked himself up slowly after a tackle. Coach Fowles was on him like a cat.

"What's wrong, Stan?"

"What do you mean, Coach?" Stan said, smiling and turning his palms up. "Nothing's wrong."

"Okay, stay out for a while."

"What for?"

Coach Fowles aimed him for the sidelines. Stan shrugged and stood aside with the others and told them he didn't know why he'd been taken out.

"Do you really think he's hurt?" I asked Coach Fowles.

"Yup."

"Where's he hurt?"

"I don't know. He'll never admit it."

Linebacker Bruce Stacey, still out with a bruised hip, paced the sidelines and hollered criticisms, except once when his brother, running back Al, was blamed for not carrying out a fake.

"Hey, Coach," Bruce called, "they tackled him, so he *had* to be carrying out the fake."

Coach Fowles chuckled. "We know he's your brother, Bruce, but he still didn't hold the fake."

Then he said to me. "I love to see that, between brothers. One of my favorite pictures is that one from Father Flanagan's Boys Town, you know the one, where one boy is carrying another on his shoulders, and he says, 'He ain't heavy, Father, he's my brother.' If everybody thought like that, they could send all the soldiers and policemen home."

I suggested that maybe it wasn't love for humanity that Bruce was expressing, but more a kind of in-group family intolerance, something related to blind nationalism.

Coach Fowles turned away from the practice and pondered that. "Mmm," he said, "maybe." He thought for a while and worked the ground with his foot as they played on. "What do you think causes most wars?" he asked.

I tried to think of the answer he wanted.

"Nationalism," he said.

"You confuse me sometimes," I said.

"No, I don't," he said, smiling and turning back to his team.

Somebody missed a block and a running play lost yardage. "Hey!"

Coach Fowles hollered. "You let us down. Ten guys pour out their guts and one guy lets them down. Do your JOB!"

He pursed his lips and turned away. "It doesn't seem fair, does it, that one guy can ruin it for all eleven on a team."

"That's the way the world is," I commented, still thinking grandly.

"*Is* it?" he said, smiling wryly. "That boy won't let us down on Saturday."

They tried the punting game. Two punts in all. Ted O'Neill sent one off the left side of his foot for 15 yards. The offensive linesmen scurrying downfield tipped their heads back and searched the sky vainly for the punt which was meant to accompany them. Steve Barker sent one similarly off the right side of his foot. The two abominable punts followed a brief time during which various players scattered around the field and bent over to try to center the ball back 13 yards. Again, only Rich Merrill could, sending his slow, looping spirals back to the general area of the kicker.

I told coach Fowles I thought it was a little late to still have no punting game.

"There's only so much time every day," he said. "Kickers have to work out on their own."

THURSDAY, *September 16*

There was a roundup story about area teams in the twice-weekly newspaper *The Patent-Trader*. It read:

LAKETOWN

"We are inexperienced, lack good size, and face a real tough schedule," said Laketown head football coach Bud Fowles. "But the team attitude is tremendous and we are working to develop quickness and agility."

Coach Fowles and his multiple-offense Harvesters are out to better last year's 6–2 mark. The going may get tough because Laketown lost 23 seniors to graduation, 20 of which were starters.

Sharing the quarterbacking chores during summer drills have been Jon Penchak, a senior with limited playing experience, and Ted O'Neill, a junior who led the JV to a 7–1 record last fall. Fowles said that it is too early to make a decision on who will start, adding that both throw well. He believes performances during scrimmages will tell who gets the starting nod.

Fowles stated that all positions in the backfield area are "up for grabs" and that the battle is among Al Stacey and his brother, Bruce, Don Heidner, Ken Furst, Brian Purcell, and Stu Rosenman. All of the names are new with the exception of the Stacey brothers who have seen action and are both seniors.

The line is a strong point for the Harvesters, with tri-captains Jim Marshall, Rich Schenkle, and Stan Bernski leading the defense. Fowles will play several of the linemen two ways. Others who will see action will be Clifford Albert and Jack Forrist the two senior offensive guards.

Coach Fowles said that most of the defensive positions are wide open and that the players are battling for the starting job.

Fowles plans on using two kickers with O'Neill and Steve Barker sharing the booting chores.

The article was accompanied by a picture of last year's Harvester line hitting the seven-man sled with Coach Fowles looking on. Someone had clipped the article and posted it on the locker room bulletin board. The players remarked mainly that nobody ever spelled their names right.

It was a hot, sunny day. There was no team meeting. The players began calisthenics by themselves, and the captains led them through bars and tires. The team seemed quiet today, the last day of contact before their first game.

"The kids are beginning to sense that it's getting close," Coach Fowles said.

The practice fields were busy. The freshman football team was out. So was the girls' field hockey team. A big yellow back-hoe operated beyond the far corner of the football field, digging holes for the foundations of the new electric scoreboard. Last weekend several players went out and sold $500 worth of oven mitts to help pay for it and for the new capes which had been ordered.

The football team practiced behind the goal of the main soccer field. The athletic director came out and took Coach Fowles aside. The soccer coach, he said, has been complaining bitterly about the football team encroaching on his turf.

"I just spent a half hour with him," the AD said plaintively. "What can I do?"

"Rick," Coach Fowles said, "we haven't run a single play on that field, I swear it." Still, he ordered the football Harvesters back another five yards from the soccer Harvesters' field.

It was to be a *thud* practice, with blocking but no real tackling. Rich Schenkle asked if he and Bruce Stacey could hit with the rest.

"Sure," Coach Fowles said, "you can hit the sled."

"Thanks," Rich said ironically.

Coach Fowles talked to Coach Branahan. "He'll go out there and really *hit* people," he said, "and get hurt again." But they decided that the two injured players needed the psychological lift of being able to hit after the long layoff.

"If you hurt that leg," Coach Fowles told Rich, "I'm going to throw you in the swimming pool."

Rich smiled and danced into the defensive lineup, at linebacker with Bruce. On the first play, running back Keith Allen went over left tackle, and Bruce Stacey smashed him straight up with his forearms. Keith came back to the huddle holding his shoulder.

"Supposed to be thud," he muttered.

On the next play Jonny ran right on an option, and Bruce sliced through and rammed him, knocking Jonny's helmet off and cutting his mouth. He helped Jonny up and Jonny smiled and said it was okay.

With the thudding getting harder, and Rich jumping in and out of the line threatening to blitz the quarterback, offensive linemen jumped offside on two successive plays.

Jonny slammed the ball down. "How we gonna play a game on Saturday if we can't even run a play!" he hollered at the offensive linemen, who looked at the ground sheepishly. With Jonny in control, the coaches looked on silently.

Jonny was suffering another minor woe. Two days ago he had finally run completely out of his treasured old soccer shoes, which he always wore for lacrosse. They had simply disintegrated, and no amount of taping could hold them on. Yesterday he showed up with new Pumas. Today he left them at home, and had to borrow a pair. They had given him blisters.

Keith Allen was wearing forearm pads, and the coaches were opposed to offensive ends and backs wearing them because it made it harder for them to handle the ball. Coach Fowles told Keith to take them off. Keith ran a play and banged his arm, and put the pads back on. The next time he carried the ball he fumbled. The coaches didn't say anything.

Ted O'Neill, at quarterback, sprinted right to pass. Stan Beronski grabbed his jersey with one hand, whirled him around and sent him rolling. As Ted got slowly up, Stan and Bradford grinned devilishly at each other. Ted was often treated roughly by Jonny's friends.

The team went in early. John Finch, whose eye was poked yesterday, had just returned from the doctor. His eye was still watering heavily, but he was all right. He watched the team go in, and then stood outside, looking across the playing field at the hillside, where the trees were turning orange and red for fall.

"I really dig it," he said. "In the fall during the season this whole hill is covered with color. The air is clear. It's cool. It's beautiful. I really dig the fall."

Then he got on his battered old Triumph motorcycle, spun the rear wheel on the asphalt, and took off.

"Meet the Team Night": In the locker room the players put on tee shirts and white shorts and sneakers. Jonny was putting on all his pads to show the parents how well protected their kids were. "I hate this," he said, "this is bush."

In the gray gymnasium, 300 parents and friends sat on the bleacher seats which pulled out from the wall. The floor was brightly polished. A huge American flag hung on one wall. Orange beams rose under the ceiling. Six closed-circuit TV monitors aimed toward the bleachers.

Coach Fowles told the parents, "We're not the Dallas Cowboys, you know, we're just a high school football team. . . . Fathers, take time to talk to your boys. . . . I know the mothers are worried about injuries. . . . I have only two rules, Do your best, and. . . ."

Cheerleaders, the varsity in green sweaters, the JV in white, yelled and jumped to "Laketown Fight. . . ."

Jonny came out with Coach Branahan and calmly stripped down to his hip-pad girdle to show the parents.

The players trotted out in their white shorts. They were introduced on the videotape produced the day before, with the cheerleaders yelling, ". . . If *he* can't do it . . ." and the film showing them running out of the building. On a large screen in the center, color stills were projected, with names and positions. There were varying levels of cheers from parents and friends for each of the players. Coach Fowles, shown last on the screen, got the biggest cheer of all.

The audiovisual instructor, a long-haired man from the television world, leaned against a far wall with his hand on his forehead as he watched the crowd and listened to the cheerleaders. "I don't believe this," he said.

The team set up in the I formation, and ran the inside belly, tailback at six.

Bradford McClure stood nearby with arms folded over his chest. "This sucks," he said. "I wish we could get out of here." He hooked a finger at the refreshment table which was along a wall to the parents' right. "Fucking football players cleaned out all the cookies and shit before the *parents* even had a chance."

Many parents hung around after the show, talking to the coaches and players, drinking coffee. Short-haired fathers stood beside long-haired sons, disguising the blood line to some degree. Bradford's father was shorter than his son, with thinning hair and glasses.

"Hey, John," Coach Fowles said to him, shaking hands, "Bradford tell you he was starting Saturday?"

"No," Mr. McClure said, glancing at his son. Bradford stood with arms folded and eyes rolled toward the ceiling.

"Bradford, you didn't tell your father? Did you tell your brother?"

"Nope," Bradford said, looking away. Bradford was the third brother to play football for Laketown, and his older brothers were considered to be better athletes.

Stu Rosenman was edging away from his father. "I told you I'm gonna hang around for a while," he said irritably. His father, much smaller than Stu, with a raspy voice and bushy eyebrows, said, "You didn't tell anybody."

"Oh for Christsake," Stu said, "I'm staying, that's all."

Stu went over and picked up tiny Kelly Branahan from Mrs. Branahan's arms. He sat down and cooed to the baby, surrounded by an admiring gaggle of cheerleaders clasping their hands.

"Get Stu near a baby," said pretty, slender Mrs. Branahan, "and that's what happens. I never saw a boy who loved babies so much."

Barry Brill's mother came up to Coach Fowles and said she felt Ted O'Neill should be disciplined for hitting her son. Coach Fowles nimbly told her that he thought it was beautiful how the two boys had sat together on the bus going to Port Chester.

Coach Fowles went over to Cary Grimes's father, a tall, strong black man who walked with a slight limp from an old college-football injury. Coach Fowles explained why Cary didn't have a varsity jersey yet.

Mr. Grimes nodded. "Hey, listen," he said. "You're exactly right. Make him earn it. That's the best thing that can happen to Cary. He needs that. Don't just *give* him anything."

Rich Schenkle walked over to me with a pleasant dark-haired woman. They stood beside me and said nothing. Rich looked around the gym and up at the ceiling. Then he ambled away.

The woman promptly stuck out her hand. "Hi, I'm Mrs. Schenkle,

Rich's and Ben's mother. Rich brought me over to meet you, but he just couldn't bring himself to introduce us."

Ben came shuffling up, his bell-bottomed dungarees dragging on the floor, his long, straight dark hair slanting over one eye. "Hi, Richard. Mom, you meet Richard yet?" She nodded, then waved good-bye. Ben and I walked across the floor toward the refreshment table. "What do you think of the cheerleaders?" he asked.

"They have fat legs," I said.

Parents drifted out of the gym, and the remaining players dropped their inhibitions and strutted and laughed and spoke loudly and teased the girls.

As we were leaving, Coach Fowles said to me, "I got a recruiting inquiry from Notre Dame today, just a form where they ask you to fill in a couple of names of players they should watch. You know who I put down?"

"Rich Schenkle and Bruce Stacey," I said.

"Right. It's interesting, but it's not important. Nobody from here is going to play football for Notre Dame. I don't even know if I'd want them to. Big-time football involves some attitudes I don't like."

"Is the soccer coach a jerk?" I asked, recalling his protesting the football team's being on the soccer field.

"No," Coach Fowles said. "I can understand his concern. He's an interesting person."

"Everybody you don't like you call 'interesting,' " I said.

"I just think all people are interesting," he said. "That doesn't mean I don't like them."

FRIDAY, *September 17*

At school today, the players wore ties and jackets, a requirement of Coach Fowles for every pregame school day.

Now the team was seated in the classroom, dressed in shoulder pads and gym shorts. There was no contact practice the day before a game. They elected their honorary game captain, to go with the three permanent season captains.

"I consider it an honor for any boy selected," Coach Fowles told them. "Bruce Stacey will be our honorary captain for tomorrow."

He turned to the blackboard. "All right, Our Lady of Lourdes. Starting with offense. . ."

There was some whispering and chuckling in the room.

"Hey!" Coach Fowles said, abruptly turning from the blackboard. "This isn't really funny now. We can have all the fun we want after we beat Lourdes. Now, offensively they run a wishbone. We watched movies of them in a game last year for about fifteen hours, Coach Branahan and myself. Number 11, a halfback, is not a very big kid, but he runs hard and looks very good. However, he is hurt and may not play. Their right halfback is what I would call a vicious runner, but their coach tells me he is a doubtful starter also because he injured his thumb severely. I don't think the coach is trying to fool me. Whether or not these two boys play will probably depend on how *we* do.

"Their last year's JV team was undefeated, so they have some good people up this year who we didn't see in the movies. Their coach tells me his big question mark is going to be his line. We will stunt our linebackers against them. The whole idea is to try to confuse their blocking rules. If you're quick enough firing through there, linebackers, you will get the quarterback before he turns around. Or you will be there to take his hand-off from him before his own backs get there. Just fire in and grab arms and legs. Cause fumbles. You're going to be in there so fast that the jewel's going to be falling on the ground all day.

"Defensive ends, make sure on every play you hit their ends and slow them up before you release. Hit them every play. Then your job is to protect off-tackle. Once you've shut that off, then you can join the party slamming into their option plays to the outside.

"Cornerbacks: Come up and take on a blocker, force the runner inside. Otherwise those options are touchdowns.

"Now, defense, this is very important: Let's be alert to little things. Let's really watch their eyes when they come out of the huddle, watch their stance, get the rhythm of when the quarterback gets the ball snapped. Let's try to *mentally* defeat this team, as well as physically. Yes, Jonny?"

"Coach, looking at their roster, it looks like they're not any bigger than we are. Their average is about 160, 170."

"According to the sheet," Coach Fowles said, "I agree."

"But you can't go by a sheet of paper," Freddie Delaney said soberly.

"That's right, Freddie," Jonny said, waving his index finger over his head. "Don't go by no paper." The others in the room laughed and Freddie smiled. "Also," Jonny went on, pointing to the symbols in the play diagrams on the blackboard, "the object of the game is for the seagulls to get the eggs."

Freddie put his head down.

Coach Fowles put his foot up on a chairseat and leaned forward with his hands on his knees. "Boys, remember: Life's battles don't always go to the bigger or faster man. In the end, the man who wins is the man who thinks he can."

There were some groans.

"The weight thing is baloney," he continued. "A kid that weighs ninety-five pounds is gonna play tackle if he really wants to. I saw one of our big kids driven back five yards last Saturday at Port Chester. I see a defensive lineman pushed around like that tomorrow and he's gonna be right over there with the cheerleaders. Because that's a *mental* mistake, and we don't make mental mistakes."

He pursed his lips and slowly shook his head and looked from face to face. "All right. Defensively they like a five-four, and they appear to stay in it and play nose-up football. They might offset to one side. We saw a couple of six-threes. And that's it. We didn't see any stunts, except occasionally the two inside linebackers when they got right up in the line and showed it.

"One thing: They like to try to block punts. They come up the middle. So you people on that punting team—we've said it before and we'll say it again: That is a very important job you have tomorrow. On kickoffs, they seem to like to run them back to their right."

He paused and looked around. "Gentlemen, we are quicker than they are. And they've never seen this laura-center defense before in life. They cannot run against this defense, believe me, not if we play it well. We are not playing a fancy football team, we really aren't. They just stay in there and play hardnosed football. We are just going to out-hit them, that's all. That's the name of the game tomorrow. I want you to play as rough as you can—not dirty, *rough!* No more questions?

"All right boys, the pep rally tonight. Report at 7:15 in ties and jackets. The team will be introduced outside in the parking lot. The band will be there, so . . ." He raised his voice over the chuckles, "So you will *love* it. The dance afterward is fine. Be home by 9:30 because phone calls begin at 9:45 or 10:00. I can't wait to hear your beautiful voices on the telephone. I love to hear the musical pitches in your voices *so much* I might call twice.

"Tomorrow, people who are getting taped report at 12:15. Specialists can be on the practice field behind the school to warm up at 1:10. If quarterbacks or others want to work a little sooner than that, you may. Everybody will start warming up at 1:25. And at 2:00 P.M., gentlemen, we will play football."

Football players sat around the cafeteria, on tables and chairs, looking out the windows down at the parking lot. Under floodlights, the band played and the cheerleaders jumped. The players wore ties, mostly brightly colored on brightly colored shirts, and sport jackets. Some wore dungarees. Bradford McClure sat on a table, gazing out the window and frowning.

"What is all this shit about the family?" he said. "Last year as juniors we got kicked around all the time, and this year as seniors we don't even get the advantages—all this shit about jerseys going to the best players instead of the seniors. How come we don't do it like last year?"

"Because of the way we're playing this year, Bradford," Stan Beronski said, smiling.

The team was called, and trotted out the door in single file down into the parking lot where they were introduced by name. Nearby was a huge stack of lumber. After the band played a couple of numbers, the stack was touched off explosively, roaring into a giant bonfire for the celebrants.

"What juvenile shit," said a player standing near me, his hands jammed into his dungaree pockets. "It sucks," said another as we watched the fire.

I pointed out that sparks shooting high off the summit of the blaze made beautiful arcs against the night sky.

"Yeah, *that's* cool," said a player, nodding. "Let's go get stoned. Somebody else drive. My license isn't good for night."

Three players and I got into a VW van and drove away. We drove deep into a nearby woods. One of the players put a piece of cinnamon incense into the ashtray and lit it. Then he took out a huge joint of marijuana. The paper had a nude girl on it, and was colored red, white, and blue. He passed it around. I declined, and asked if they were up for the game tomorrow.

"Naw," said one, "not now."

"It's too early," said another. "I won't get up for it until a few hours before the game."

The lights of another car came up behind us on the rutted trail. The driver got out and leaned in our window to say that he had half a keg stashed nearby. "Come on," he said.

"Naw," said one of the players. "We gotta get out of here."

He closed the window. "Let's go. Fucking greasers are nothing but trouble."

The dance cost $1.50, except that football players got in free because they had to leave early. We strolled through. The rock band played with intolerable volume. Coach Branahan was there, and his wife was wearing a long gown. Coach Branahan spent most of his time telling people to put out their cigarettes.

"Hello, Barry Brill."

"Hello."

"Ready for tomorrow?"

"Yeah."

"Okay, get a good night's sleep."

"I will."

". . . Hello, Mr. Stacey."

"How are you, Bud? Checkin up on the lads?" (chuckle).

"Well, I'm just tuning in."

"Well, they're both in bed. I picked them up at the dance at 9:30, and they went right up."

"Good. Tell them I called."

"Sure will. Good luck tomorrow."

". . . How's your hand, Tom Kase?"

"Oh, not bad. I'll wear that Ace bandage with the arm pad over it."

"Okay. You let us know if it starts to bother you. And don't forget: Anticipate that count, Tom."

"Yeah, that's what I been workin on."

"I know, and you're looking much better. Get a good night's sleep."

". . . Hello, Rich Merrill. All set to get that ball back in eight-tenths of a second?"

"Sure."

"Good. Listen, on that kickoff team you get down there in a hurry, Rich."

"Okay."

". . . Jim Benning?"

"Yeah, Coach, how are you?"

"Good. How'd you like the dance?"

"Pretty good. What time you want me down there tomorrow, Coach?"

"Are you going to watch the JV game?"

"Yeah, to watch my brother."

"Okay, then about eleven, if you want tape."

"I'd like to have some on my hands so they don't slip."

"Well, we can see. Officials don't like tape like that on hands, unless it's covering an injury. Get a good sleep."

". . . Hello, Mrs. Forrest."

"Hi, Coach," said Mrs. Forrest, who was chairman of the Laketown Athletes Parents' Club. "Hey, you hear about our latest one? We *might* get the concession stand."

"You're kidding."

"No. I dropped by the principal's office this week, had a little chat. If we get that concession stand, oh wow! Right off the bat going to paint it white, fix it all up. How about balloons with 'Laketown' on them, right? And on our car raffle we're offering twenty-five dollars to the person who sells the most tickets, and fifteen for second and ten for third."

"I think that's a great idea, Mrs. Forrest. Listen, just as an aside, is your son home?"

"Yeah," (chuckle) "he's in bed, went up maybe three minutes before you called."

"Three minutes, huh? Okay, fine, tell him I called."

". . . Ted O'Neill."

"Hi, Coach."

"Ted, listen: Every play is what, when you're on defense?"

"Pass."

"Right. Just key your man and you'll be fine. And when you do make that interception, cut to the near sideline, okay?"

"Okay."

". . . I'm calling Clifford Albert now. He was so excited at his first physical that he couldn't pass it because his blood pressure was too high. Hello, Clifford? All set for tomorrow?"

"Yes, Coach."

"Any questions on the blocking rules?"

"No, coach, I feel good."

". . . Hello, Stu Rosenman."

"Hello, Coach."

"How's your arm?"

"Uh, okay."

"Good. Tell your father and your mother, thanks very much for their help. They'll know what I mean."

"Okay."

". . . This will be Bradford McClure. Compare him with Clifford Albert and some of the other kids, like night and day. Even over the phone he will sound passive. Hello, Bradford McClure."

"Hi."

"How are you, Brad?"

"All right, I guess."

"What do you mean, you guess?"

"Tired."

"You are? What are you tired from? Did you go to the dance tonight?"

"Uh, I was there for a little while."

"Well, you should be a little excited—I don't know if you are or not."

"Oh, I will be tomorrow."

"Good."

". . . This is the Petrowskis'. A real football family, both from western Pennsylvania not too far from where I'm from. But they don't bug me on that. Hello, Jim? Line up on the inside shoulder of those guards, right?"

"Yeah."

"And be just as quick as you've been every day in practice. And protect your area, find the football, and gang-tackle. You'll be fine, Jim."

"I hope so."

". . . Hello, Mrs. Schenkle."

"Hi, Coach. The boys were both in bed by ten o'clock, and I wish that had happened all summer long. You on there, Ben?"

"Yeah. Hi, Coach."

"Hey, Ben. On those extra points tomorrow, just concentrate on kicking the ball and you'll be fine. You're on the receiving team too, right?"

"Yeah, and the kickoff."

"Good. Two good spots."

". . . Hello, Ken Furst. Listen, you ramble when you catch those punts tomorrow, right?"

"Okay."

"Just keep those feet moving. Where'd you get such quick feet, at that football camp?"

"I don't know," (chuckle) "probably."

". . . You know, Paul Treski takes a lot of kidding. But he's strong. You know what he bench-presses? I couldn't believe it. Hello, Paul Treski? Hey, Paul, what can you bench-press?"

"Oh, about 185."

"That's pretty good."

"Thanks."

"Get a good sleep, be ready tomorrow."

". . . Is this Stan Beronski?"

"Hello, Coach. Jonny tried to call you a while ago, cause it was getting late. He figured you weren't around maybe you were in an accident or something."

"No such luck. Get a good night's sleep."

". . . Hello, Don Heidner. Listen, Don, after you catch those passes, take off for the sideline and go all the way. You know you're not allowed to spike the football this year. You can just drop it in the end zone or hand it to the official. Okay?"

"Right. I'll remember."

". . . Keith Allen is probably down in the dumps. He's been upset. Hey, Keith Allen. You know what? I've been calling the wrong number. Had the numbers reversed."

"I was wondering what happened."

"How do you feel?"

"Aw, I don't know."

"What's the matter?"

"Aw, tonight I was just thinking, I guess, kind of in a daze."

"Well, last time I saw you in a daze, the next day you looked really good."

"Yeah, I know. That's one of the things I was thinking about."

"Good."

"I think I'm really psyched for tomorrow."

"That's really good, Keith."

"Boy, when I get in there . . . boy, I just hope that I do as good as I . . ."

"You'll do fine. You're going to wear those forearm pads though, right?"

(Chuckle) "Well, I intend to take 'em off."

"You know, I think you love those things. It's like Count Dracula's cape."

"Yeah, ha-ha, kind of."

". . . Hello, is Freddie Delaney there?"

"He's in bed, went to bed about an hour ago. What's the problem?"

"No problem. I just always call the boys on Friday nights."

"Oh, oh, oh, he's fine. In bed. No problem with him."

"Fine, just tell him the coach called."

". . . Hi, Vince Carradino, how are you, Dino? How's your back feel?"

"Good."

"All set to go tomorrow?"

"Ready."

". . . Hello, Jonny Penchak."

"I was beginning to wonder what happened."

"You just found your way down to the end of the list this year. How'd you like the dance?"

"Aw, not too much."

"All set to go tomorrow?"

"Yeah, don't worry."

"Hey, Jonny, you knew our offense seven years ago."

"I hope I know it tomorrow."

"No question you will know it tomorrow. You'll be fine. The team is in good hands, Jonny."

"I hope so."

"I *know* so."

"Well, I think we'll give 'em a good game."

"No, I don't *think* we'll give 'em a good game. We're going to *beat* them. There's no doubt in *my* mind. You can do anything when you're prepared, and we're prepared, Jonny. You just relax right now and get a good sleep, and be ready to go to work at two o'clock tomorrow."

"Right, Coach. Thanks for calling."

"Some people see the phone calls as checking up on the boys," Coach Fowles said over a Tom Collins. "I don't really think of it that way. To me, it's one time during the week, just before the game, when I can have a direct word with every player on the team, some personal contact. I think it helps a little in bringing the family together. People who think the boys need checking on just don't understand. They have worked too hard, paid too big a price, to screw up. They want to play football on Saturday. I *know* they will be home, whether I call them or not."

"Will you make a prediction on tomorrow?" I asked.

"Well, I don't like to make predictions. But okay. I'll tell you, as football players, Lourdes has got a better football team. But I think we will beat them."

"Do you ever admit to yourself before a game that you'll probably lose?"

"Oh sure. And sometimes I'll also say to myself we're going to win this game with no problem at all. I think we'll win tomorrow. But it will be a tough football game. Anyway, I'm not hung up on winning."

I chuckled, and he chuckled back, competitively.

"You're having trouble believing that," he said.

"Football is football," I said.

"No, football can be many different things."

SATURDAY, *September 18*

It rained in the morning, and was humid and cloudy an hour before game time. But the field was firm. An occasional breeze blew away from the school down across the playing field, ruffling the grass.

The opening day crowd, which would reach about 3,000, drifted toward the main bleachers on the Laketown side and the smaller section on the visitors' side. Some stood by the rickety red snow fence which enclosed the field.

The Harvesters loosened up on the practice field behind the school. They wore their white home uniforms and white helmets with new black-bordered green stripes down the center. The stripes were tape, which the players had applied yesterday.

Around the corner of the school, on the asphalt sidewalk outside the locker room, the team captains met for the coin toss. The four Laketown captains, completely dressed—with helmets on, mouthpieces dangling from face masks, and black antiglare greasepaint under their eyes—stood menacingly. The two Lourdes captains were dressed in tee shirts, hip pads, and sweat socks.

Coach Fowles stood a few yards away, watching intently as the referee greeted the captains and everybody shook hands.

The referee flipped a 1923 silver dollar, Lourdes called heads and lost.

Rich Schenkle said Laketown would receive, and the referee asked the Lourdes captains which goal they would like to defend. The larger captain looked out toward the playing field and shrugged.

"Guess it doesn't make any difference," he said. "We'll take the goal on this end."

The Lourdes captains returned to their locker room, and the Laketown captains trotted back around the corner of the school to the practice field to rejoin their teammates.

"They were big," Rich Schenkle said.

"They looked old," Jim Marshall said.

Coach Fowles walked behind them. "Wow!" he said to me, "I would never have allowed that coin toss like that if I had been the Lourdes coach. Send my captains out there like that, not dressed? And without knowing all the conditions, how the field was, which way the wind was blowing? They weren't ready at all. It's like they aren't taking us very seriously."

Several players sprayed sticky, pine-scented Firm Grip onto their hands. Jonny sprayed it all over the front of his jersey. " 'Cause it smells good," he said. Rich Schenkle tugged on new seven-dollar hand pads that he had bought himself. Linemen banged shoulders into each other. Ted O'Neill punted. Jonny Penchak threw passes to his backs and ends. Then the team came together for calisthenics. The captains stood in front, facing them to lead.

"Who we gonna beat?" Jim Marshall shouted.

"LOURDES!"

"Five weeks for ONE AFTERNOON!" Bruce Stacey yelled.

"All right, PUSH-UPS!" said Jim, "One, two, three. . . . "

"SIT-UPS!" said Stan Beronski, "One, two. . . ."

After cals Jonny lined up the offense to run a series against the defense. He had Stu Rosenman at fullback, Al Stacey at tailback, Don Heidner at flanker. Brian Purcell, sturdy, quiet, curly haired, was at right end, Dan Miranda at left end. John Curtis and Tom Kase were at tackles, Clifford Albert and Jack Forrest at guards, and Jim Marshall over the ball at center.

Lined up against them were Stan Beronski and Steve Barker at ends. Bradford McClure was at left tackle; Vince Carradino, filling in for Jim Marshall who would play there, at the other tackle. Middle guard was Jim Petrowski. Rich Schenkle and Bruce Stacey were the linebackers. Karl Walsh, lean, bespectacled, was at one corner; Ray Meister, small, with long curly hair and a helmet that seemed about to cover his eyes, filled in for Al Stacey at the other corner. Ken Furst and Ted O'Neill were at safeties.

Jonny pushed his hair back over his shoulders and directed the team through four running plays. The linemen banged into each other and tapped the ball carriers as they came through the holes.

"Come on, come on, come ON!" Coach Fowles yelled at them. "Be QUICK, Laketown, gotta be QUICKER off the ball."

The team was snarling and ready. Coach Fowles picked up the football. "Okay boys," he said to them. "You've got four minutes in the locker room, all by yourselves. Say whatever you want. Just be ready to play football when you come out."

The team charged into the building, cursing the bottleneck in the doorway.

The locker room was like a compression chamber. Every noise—breathing and cursing, clattering of cleats—was suddenly loud. Players ripped off their helmets and banged them on lockers and the floor. The team was packed together in the small room, fidgeting and milling like cattle.

Jim Marshall's voice, lame and hoarse with tension, rose first above the noise. "You know what they're saying out there?" He banged his helmet against a locker. "They're saying we SUCK! THEY'RE SAYING LAKETOWN SUCKS! We don't play Horace Greeley for THREE WEEKS YET, and there are people out there from GREELEY, and they're laughing and saying we're FOOLS, THAT WE CAN'T PLAY FOOTBALL, that we SUCK! THEY CAME TO LAUGH AT US!" He banged his helmet again and spun part-way around. "And Lourdes is saying we're PATSIES, because they're already planning their SECOND GAME! THEY THINK THEY'RE GONNA PUSH US ALL OVER THE FIELD!"

Jim Petrowski, his hands clenched and as white as his bared teeth, seemed near tears. "They think they're gonna beat the SHIT out of us, and it ain't gonna HAPPEN! WE AIN'T GONNA LET IT HAPPEN!"

There were snarls and curses. Jim Marshall turned his back and looked at the floor, breathing heavily. Rich Schenkle took a step forward. "No reason we have to lose out there," Rich said, his voice halting as he searched for words. "Why do we—why should—WHY SHOULD WE LOSE? WHY? Lot of people think we're going to lose out there. I DON'T THINK WE'RE GONNA LOSE, LAKETOWN!"

"We can win this," said Bradford McClure, more quietly. "Come on, we're a TEAM!"

"Come on, Laketown," Jonny Penchak said softly, looking at the floor and clenching and unclenching his throwing hand.

Coach Fowles walked briskly in, followed by Coach Branahan. "All right boys," he said, his gentle voice contrasting with the harsh mood of the room. "Let's go. We'll line up single file and walk down to the field, and then when we get to the track, we'll run on. Time to play football, let's go."

The team lined up silently and walked slowly out and down the slope toward the field. Little boys ran and jumped and yelled beside them. Parents snapped pictures. Stan Beronski led the somber line, and no one spoke. Then at the running track, they broke into a brisk trot, between the double rows of clapping cheerleaders, along the sideline, in front of the folding chairs on which the band would sit, down to the Laketown bench.

Across the way, the red-jerseyed Lourdes players assembled. The captains went to the center of the field for the mock toss of the coin. When they came back, the public-address announcer said Laketown won the toss and would receive.

The team stood along the sideline for the National Anthem. They held their helmets under their arms. John Finch did not take his helmet off. He left it on as a protest, and looked at the ground. His brother had been killed in Vietnam last year.

Then Coach Fowles called his team together. They gathered around him and leaned in, extending their hands to clasp as nearly as possible all the others. Together they looked like a huge human tulip yet to bloom. In the very center the noise of the crowd was nearly shut out. A score of hands reached out to touch the coach, and he seized several of them hard. For a few seconds in the huddle Coach Fowles closed his eyes and it was silent. Then he said softly:

"Boys, this is it. A brand new season, a brand new team. We can do whatever we want to do, because we are together. Because we are a family. Boys, who we gonna beat?"

"LOURDES!"

His voice rose a notch. "Who we gonna beat?"

"LOURDES!"

Bodies were now bouncing up and down rhythmically as the chant grew, "LOURDES, LOURDES, LOURDES!" And the huddle exploded with yells and raised fists. The kickoff-receiving team trotted out to its positions to start the season.

Laketown returned the kickoff to its 25. Jonny Penchak brought his team out smartly into the I. Center Jim Marshall, first to the line, bent over the ball, propping it up at an angle with both hands. Jonny set his feet close behind Jim, bending his knees and dipping his shoulders to place the heels of his hands together, fingers spread wide to receive the ball, under

Jim's butt. Two steps directly behind Jonny, fullback Stu Rosenman dropped down into a three-point stance, leaning forward on one hand. A half-step behind Stu, tailback Al Stacey crouched with his hands on his knees. Ten yards out to the right, flankerback Don Heidner rested on his right hand, his right toe dug in slightly behind his left. Linemen Purcell, Kase, Forrest, Albert, and Curtis spread along the line of scrimmage in the four-point stance, on toes and fingertips. Split 15 yards to the left of them was end Dan Miranda, down on one hand. All eleven Harvesters had their heads up, their eyes straight ahead. Despite the long hair fluttering under the backs of their helmets, the team looked sharp, alert, disciplined, as Jonny barked the first official "GO, GO. . ." of the season.

But they couldn't move the ball. Neither Al Stacey nor Kent Furst, alternating at tailback for the first two plays, could penetrate the Lourdes line. On third down, Jonny overthrew Ken at the left sideline. Finally, Steve Barker's punt went off the side of his foot and rolled forward only 15 yards. Lourdes quickly had the ball on the Laketown 40.

Lourdes came out in their worrisome wishbone formation, their linemen down in the four-point stance like Laketown's, but with surprisingly wide splits between them. Rich Schenkle, standing upright at linebacker, danced in and out of the line to fake a stunt. A step behind him, crouched and still, was Bruce Stacey, the "laura man," his eyes fixed on the quarterback.

On their first play, Lourdes ran in tight on their right side, at Jim Petrowski and Bradford McClure, for three yards. On second down, the quarterback rolled to his left. As Bruce Stacey banged into him, he tried to pitch out to his trailing back, and the ball went wild to be recovered for Laketown by cornerback Karl Walsh, who had come up fast, on the 38.

Once again, Laketown could not move. Coach Branahan sent in the flanker-reverse play. Don Heidner, swinging left from his flanker position out on the right, was trapped for a seven-yard loss by the defensive end who had come across the line untouched. Another short punt gave Lourdes the ball on their 30.

They ran a sweep to the left, chopping down end Steve Barker, for 12 yards. Then they faked an option the other way, the quarterback drawing Bruce Stacey with him, and instead handed off on a counter up the middle at the very spot Bruce had just left. The halfback faked cornerback Karl Walsh in, and then swung outside, stringing the sideline all the way to the Laketown 21 where safetyman Ted O'Neill hauled him out of bounds.

Then the quarterback rolled to his right, and Bruce Stacey knifed through to drive a shoulder into him and jar the ball loose. Cornerback Al Stacey dove for it, but Lourdes recovered, for a loss to the 24.

Lourdes tried a third-down pass on the right side, but Bruce and Al Stacey, Bradford McClure, and Ted O'Neill all converged to knock it away at the Laketown 10.

A fourth-down sweep to the left gained only two yards, and Laketown took over.

Alternating Al Stacey and Ken Furst on the belly series, Laketown got its first first down on the 36. Jonny overthrew tight end Brian Purcell at the Lourdes 45, then came right back with the same play, hitting Brian on the Lourdes 38. Jonny dropped back again to complete a pass in the left flat to Al Stacey, who leaped over one man along the sideline to reach the Lourdes 20.

There Lourdes held.

Jonny came off the field with his head down, but he was congratulated by the coaches for the brief show of offense. The performance had so roused the bench that the reserves had to be pushed back away from the sidelines continually.

The second quarter began. After an exchange of punts, Laketown had the ball on its own 25. On third down, Jonny dropped back, looked, rolled to his right, and finally rifled the ball over the middle. But it sailed over Don Heidner's fingertips and into the arms of a Lourdes halfback, who returned it to the Laketown 35.

On Lourdes' second play, Bruce Stacey dove to make a tackle, then sprang from the pile-up waving his arm forward to signal Laketown possession. Lourdes had fumbled for the third time.

On first down, Jonny again tried to deep pass to Brian Purcell, but overthrew him. Jonny dropped back again, but this time was hit hard by two Lourdes linemen. The ball dribbled out of his hands. The official ruled that he had been throwing, and that it was an incomplete pass, not a fumble.

Jonny went back for the third straight time, took a hop-step forward, and hurled one deep, 35 yards, to Don Heidner who had a step on two defenders. The ball came down perfectly on his fingertips and Don raced the rest of the way for a 64-yard scoring play. Laketown had its first touchdown of the season.

With the crowd screaming, and the Lourdes players dejectedly lining up to defend against the extra-point try, Jonny came to the sidelines.

"Quick-out to Don on the right?" he asked.

"Call it, Jonny," Coach Fowles said, patting him on the rear.

Jonny put a bullet pass in Heidner's gut just over the goal line to the right, and Laketown led, 8–0.

The half ended with the Harvesters in their surprising lead.

The team sat on benches and on the floor swilling Gatorade and water. They were not the same team that had left the locker room an hour ago to start the game. They were bloodied, bruised, and dirty. They breathed hard.

"Those guys are going to be really fired up," Bruce Stacey said, stepping over legs to get to the water fountain. "We just better stay on top of 'em."

"They're gonna come back," Jonny Penchak said, knocking dirt off his new Puma shoes.

"Their coach is in there *now* telling them all their *mistakes*," Bruce said. "He's gonna *fire those guys up*. We got to *just keep popping them*. He's telling them, those five fumbles they made could have lost them *five touchdowns!*"

Jim Petrowski still had his pregame tension. "THEY GOT FIVE COACHES IN THERE TELLIN THEM!" he hollered. "FIVE COACHES screaming at them RIGHT NOW. They're going to be SO PISSED OFF when they come out, they're gonna want to RIP OUR HEADS OFF! We can't say we were ahead 8–0 at the half and then they killed us—THAT'S NOTHIN TO BRAG ABOUT!"

"At least four more touchdowns," Bruce said. "We can get 'em."

"They're just CAKE," Jonny said, "that's what they are. You know something?" He got to his feet. "Just watch the way the quarterback pitches the ball—that's CAKE! If we had a quarterback who did that, he'd be on the bench."

"We *do* have a quarterback like that," somebody said, and somebody else laughed.

"Heh, heh, heh," Jonny said. "Remember, the second half is always Laketown's half."

"Who's in better shape?" Bruce called. "Anybody tired? Who's tired?"

"Nobody's tired," Jonny said. "We worked *too hard*, Laketown. Eight and 0, seniors, 8 *and* 0 *this year!*" He raised his fist.

The coaches came in.

"Boys, I'll tell you what," Coach Fowles said, stepping over sprawled players to get to the center of the room. "There's no doubt about it, we are out-hitting this other football team. We are hitting harder than they ever dreamed we could hit. I think that football team came down here overconfident, cocky, and they thought all they had to do was throw their helmets on the field and they'd beat us. Well, now they know that's not the story. There are twenty-four minutes left. They're not playing football the way they can. So this half expect them to come back. But before they *can* come back we'll go right down their throats."

He paused briefly and looked over his team. "Boys, I'll tell you what: I am so proud to be able to say I am associated with you. You have displayed guts, determination, 100 percent desire. That was beautiful. And this half we're gonna do better.

"All right, let's start with the most important part of the game, defense. Don't let those wide gaps bother you. The principle of this defense is to force them to run wide, and to pass. Maybe we could use a little more coverage inside, but that's no sweat. Our linebackers still cannot be blocked. Ask Bruce Stacey."

"Way to go, Bruce," Jonny said.

"Nobody can get to our laura man, right Bruce? But our laura man can get to a lot of people. Defensively keep doing exactly what you are doing, use your hands and get rid of those blockers and gang-tackle. When you run off that field twenty-four minutes from now, you shouldn't have any strength left, cause you play your guts out every second. Let's really work, wear them down. Coach Branahan, tell them what you feel we are doing offensively."

Coach Branahan took a step away from the wall. "All right. On defense their tackle is looping outside, their end is coming inside. So there is just one man to beat if we run the inside belly *wide*, all right? So tailbacks, run it wide, between the two and three holes."

"Jonny," Coach Fowles interjected, "you might have to make that hand-off a little bit deeper than normal."

"Okay, Coach."

"Linemen," Coach Fowles continued, "*fire out!* Stay with your blocks. It looks like we're beating them off the ball, is that correct?"

"Yeah, yeah."

"All right, good. Let's go to the kicking game. Our punting game doesn't look bad. We're covering the kick. After that first bad kick we came alive. We received to start, so we will kick off this half, and the kick-off team will go down there and cause a fumble. Any questions, comments? Bradford?"

Bradford McClure was seated on the floor, his purple headband stained with sweat. "I think that a lot of quick passes, um, like to the, um, flank-erback, I think they'll go. Very quick. I don't know about the long passes."

"I'll buy that," Coach Fowles said. "They're one-on-one in the flats. We scared them to death with the one long pass, and we probably won't be able to do that again. Good point. Jonny?"

"We can eat 'em up outside in the flats, but the backs have to look up really quick, because if we send them out for passes I've got nobody to block for me."

"Good point. Boys, we won't have all day to pass back there. A couple of times Jonny was set up, but receivers did not look up quickly enough. Look up quicker."

"Another thing," Jonny said, "their defensive left end, number 83. The referee warned him three times about punching and stuff. Like, uh, he told him the first time he was going to kick him out."

"All right," Coach Fowles said. "We're not the officials, and we don't want to complain. Who's the end on that side, Dan Miranda? Dan, tell your captain."

"I told the referee," Dan said. "He's warned him three times."

"All right, then we want to know about it. One of you captains tell us, after you give them one more chance. Karl Walsh?"

The slender cornerback cleared his throat. "They have yet to send the left end out for a pass," he said.

"Well, there's always a first time. You still play it safe now, Karl. Uh, what were we in that time when they went for about 30 yards on the ground. Was that a five-four half-barrel in?"

"That was a double-barrel," said Bruce Stacey, who called the defensive alignments.

"Stay away from it, Bruce."

"I know. The gaps were opening, and it looked, you know . . ."

"Okay, that's all right. No more."

"Coach, it seems they're closing in on the middle."

"Right, they are. That's why we're going to run the inside belly wide."

One of the officials poked his head in the locker room door.

"Coach?"

"Yes sir."

"Three minutes."

"Thank you. All right boys, anybody notice any of their players tipping?"

Bradford McClure leaned toward Stan Beronski. "Hey Stan, do you feel when they're running to our side they close the gaps?"

"Yeah, I definitely do," Stan said, "and they also keep their end in on that side."

"Hey, Coach?" Bradford said. "When they're running to our side, they're closing their gaps."

"Okay, good. But you know what? There's no place for them to go because we've got our linebacker and our laura man as fillers, and we've got our cornermen coming up on the outside."

Coach Fowles waved off other questions. "Boys, we've got t-w-e-n-t-y-f-o-u-r minutes. This is just like our break during practice. Our best part of practice is always the second half. Put your hats on."

"They're HURTIN right now!" Jonny yelled, pushing his long hair back and pulling his helmet down over it.

"Twenty-four more minutes," Coach Fowles said. "Who's got more pride?"

"LAKETOWN!"

"Who works harder?"

"LAKETOWN!"

"WHO WE GONNA BEAT?"

"LOURDES, LOURDES, LOURDES!"

Lourdes came out strong. They drove into Laketown territory, then passed down to the 20, the end eluding safetyman Ted O'Neill for a step. Then the quarterback passed into the end zone. Ted O'Neill was step-for-step with his man, and leaped to make a brilliant over-the-shoulder interception.

The ball was brought out to the 20. Laketown was held, and punted it away. Lourdes came right back, running and passing into Laketown territory again. They began concentrating on their left side, pushing Steve Barker out and sending their halfback between Steve and tackle Jim Marshall. Again and again they worked that spot, getting a first down on the 10. They went up the middle to the seven, then the five, then to the three. On fourth down they passed over the middle deep in the end zone, but once again Ted O'Neill leaped to tip it away. Yorktown had held on the three.

Three running plays gained three yards, and Laketown was forced to punt. Steve Barker was standing nearly under the crossbar of the goalpost. Rich Merrill's snap looped high, and Steve had to jump to reach it. Under pressure, he kicked out only to the 15.

Lourdes promptly passed up the right side for the score, and suddenly it was 8–6, despite the goal-line stand moments before.

"ALL RIGHT, BRUCE!" Coach Fowles yelled to Bruce Stacey who had lined up the defensive huddle. "SIX-THREE GOAL LINE. Tell em to go UNDERNEATH, Bruce."

As the Harvesters submarined, the Lourdes quarterback fumbled the snap, and they were stopped. The score remained 8–6 as the third quarter ended.

"Wow!" I said, caught up in the frenzy with the crowd and the Laketown bench.

"It's going to be a rough fourth quarter," Coach Fowles said over his shoulder as he walked quickly over to talk to Jonny. "They are pushing us around now."

And they were. The Harvesters' offense was dying, and it seemed to be only a question of whether the defense could stand the strain.

With third down on his own 30, Jonny threw deep to Don Heidner, the same fly pattern on which they had scored earlier. Don again was a step open, and the pass came in well, but the Lourdes defender made a sensational diving interception on the 50.

Lourdes passed down and out. Safetyman Ken Furst slipped, and Karl Walsh was barely able to catch the receiver on the Laketown 24.

Rich Schenkle hobbled off, and the bench groaned. He flopped down on his back behind the bench, and the team doctor felt along his leg around the knee. "Can you move it?" he asked. Rich moved it. "Nothing's broken. Try to walk on it."

Rich got up and limped along the sideline, holding an ice bag against his knee.

Meanwhile, Lourdes gained five, to the 19, over Jim Marshall, who was tired from playing both ways, and who was being sorely tested now. Jack Forrest had been sent in at linebacker for Rich Schenkle, and after that one play he came back to the sidelines.

"Rich's back in, Coach," he said. Rich had immediately put himself back in at linebacker.

The doctor shrugged. "All I can do is check to see if anything's broken, then it's pretty much up to the boy."

Jim Marshall and Bruce Stacey threw the quarterback for a small loss. It was third and nine on the 23. A pass was overthrown at the 10. On fourth down, the quarterback rolled left and looped one high into the end zone. The receiver was five yards behind Ken Furst and Karl Walsh, but the pass went just beyond his reach.

The bench cheered wildly and Coach Branahan grimaced.

"How did that man get behind you?" Coach Fowles barked angrily to his defenders as they came off. "How could that happen in that situation?"

There were about four minutes left. The electric scoreboard was not yet connected. The public-address announcer called out ball-carriers and tacklers, but he could not know the time left. Laketown needed a first down or two to run out the clock.

Jonny inadvisably called a pass, firing a bullet out to the right. A defensive lineman got a hand on it and tipped the ball high into the air. Players on both teams dove for it, but Lourdes came up with the interception, the fourth of the day on Jonny.

Jonny came off the field dejected. Coach Fowles did not take time to talk to him. "All right, DEFENSE!" he cried, sending his tired defenders back onto the field.

First down Lourdes on the Laketown 27.

On the first play the quarterback rolled to his left. As Bruce Stacey barreled into him he ducked and tossed the ball blindly behind him. Somehow his running back caught it and got to the line of scrimmage. A screen pass up the middle gained just three. On third and seven, Laketown was called offside, making it third and two on the 19.

Lourdes sent a man in motion to the right, and the quarterback took the snap and rolled in the same direction. Tackle Bradford McClure sliced into the backfield and almost caught him as he threw, incomplete on the five.

Fourth and two. Fearing that Lourdes might try to pass for a touchdown, Laketown could not risk its 6–3 submarine defense which would ordinarily have been called on a fourth-down play. Lourdes ran with power inside, over Steve Barker and Jim Marshall down to the 13 for a first down.

A power play on the right gained three, to the 10. Then they tried the left side again, but Bruce Stacey smashed the ball-carrier at the line of scrimmage.

On third down the quarterback dropped back to throw. End Stan Beronski was in on him, chasing him back to the 20. But the quarterback swung to his right, eluded Stan, and dashed through the now spread-out defense down to the three-yard line.

Lourdes had a first down on the three, with less than two minutes to play. Laketown dug in with a six-man front.

A straight-ahead power play over the right guard gained one. Then they ran at weary Jim Marshall again. Bruce Stacey caught the fullback by the shoulders and pulled him back to the four, but Marshall had been offside. The ball was put on the one, with second down.

The quarterback kept it and tried to duck in at the same spot, but Jim and Bruce dropped him inside the one.

Third down, and less than a minute to play. The Harvesters' defensive line groggily pulled itself up. The fullback hit the left side again, and Jim and Bruce and others stacked the play up three inches from the goal line.

"LAKETOWN NEVER QUITS!" Coach Fowles yelled. And then he was silent. Jim Marshall came slowly to the sidelines, limping.

"Too tired, Coach," he gasped.

Vince Carradino, with his bad back, loped in to take right defensive tackle for the climactic play.

The Laketown line had its hands down actually in the end zone for the fourth-down play. The head linesman sighting down the line of scrimmage was straddling the goal line.

Lourdes came out in the wishbone. The quarterback handed to the fullback, who plowed into the line to his left, at Carradino. Jim Petrowski, diving from his middle guard spot, got an ankle. For an agonizing split second, the fullback leaned forward for those three inches. Like a white streak, Bruce Stacey hurtled over the line and hit the fullback full in the chest and dropped him like a stone.

Stan Beronski, looking along the goal line, assessed it instantly and raised his fists skyward. Then Rich Schenkle leaped in the air and swung a fist happily. Then the whole defensive team began to dance and hug each other. Lourdes was stopped with the tip of the ball two inches from the goal line.

The official picked up the ball and waved the game over. Coaches Fowles and Branahan shook hands, and then were engulfed by leaping, yelling, battered, exhausted Harvesters. And not one of them knew that it was Coach Fowles's thirty-ninth birthday.

5

Coach Fowles stood on a bench in the locker room and told his grimy, happy team: "Boys, you were lined up in the end zone, and you didn't quit. There's *no way* we're going to quit, *ever*. That was a beautiful victory. I have never been more proud of anybody than I am of you boys today."

I thought there were tears on Bradford McClure's usually scowling face, but it could have been sweat.

After the team showered and dressed, several of them piled into Bradford's VW van and drove out to a local hamburger shop where they were treated to free sodas. Harvesters sauntered wearily in, along with green-sweatered cheerleaders, strangely subdued and spent.

Later, Jonny and I just drove around in the twilight, starting to relax. We had statistics: Lourdes out-gained Laketown on the ground, 135 to 22, and overall 231 to 130. Lourdes had ten first downs to Laketown's four, and Laketown didn't get a first down after the first quarter. Jonny threw three completions in fourteen attempts, and had four interceptions. The statistics made it seem impossible again.

Jonny chuckled. "I'd hate to run against our defensive team," he said. "They are some mean dudes. I wouldn't like to have Stan or Rich or Bruce coming at me all afternoon, you know."

I mentioned that the statistics on his passing didn't look too good. "Were you choked up?" I asked.

"Naw. We'll get that smoothed out, get our timing down. Donnie Heidner's going to be getting open all season, you know, and like we connected on that. I always play better in a game. You know why?" He chuckled again. "I can't play without anybody watching me, you know?"

It was dark, and we stopped by Coach Fowles's house. There was a birthday party for him, so we wanted to just go in and out. Coach Fowles greeted us joyfully at the door, and then grabbed Jonny in a hug and lifted him off the floor.

"Jonathan Penchak," he said, "I have waited seven years to see you play this game, ever since fifth grade."

"We were a team today, Coach," Jonny said, shrugging off the compliments which trickled from the guests filling the living room.

SUNDAY, *September 19*

The New York Times headlined the Harvesters' upset victory on its high-school sports page. In the evening twenty-five players crowded into the Fowleses' basement rec room to see the game film. They sprawled in various postures of repose on the floor, dressed modishly in old clothes, military surplus greens, dungarees, work shoes. Coach Fowles sat beside the projector and clanked it forward and backward, sometimes taking it frame by frame, then running it back again, with a steady commentary.

". . . Now what happened here?" (Clank, clank).

"This is where we had the double-barrel stunt with me and Rich," Bruce Stacey said.

"Yeah, well, boy, we really got annihilated here. This is the last time we called this one." (Clank, clank) "Wooooow!"

"Look at Rich and Bruce!" Jonny said, "Watch 'em fall over each other."

Players laughed.

"Is Steve Barker here?" Coach Fowles asked without pausing. "Steve's gotta be tougher than this or he's not gonnna play end. That kid drove him five yards down field—right *there*. Look, he's *still* got him. . . . All right, good angle of pursuit here, and here. . . . All right, this is a nice cut-back. . . . Karl Walsh, see here? Where you are here? I couldn't believe this, but it didn't happen any more. I'll tell you what happened here."

The film showed the Lourdes halfback faking Karl in and running outside him. "He came in and you followed him in, rather than holding your area. Now it's all over, the kid is off to the races. Ted O'Neill is just barely going to catch him. That would have been the ballgame, gentlemen, right there. One mistake by a cornerback and we all suffer.

"All right, it's their ball on their 20-yard line. Now watch," (clank, clank) "and see if we're watching the ball," (clank, clank) "and not the man. . . . Now we start to play defense here."

"Way to go, Stan," Jonny said as the film showed Stan Beronski spinning the ball-carrier down with one hand.

"Nice job, Bruce," Coach Fowles said when the film showed Bruce Stacey's tackle jarring the ball out of the quarterback's arm.

"Now, see right here," (clank, clank) "Bruce, is that guard trying to pick you off? See, he misses Bruce, he throws an elbow out and misses him." (Clank, clank) "I don't know if that kid ever saw Bruce coming.

"Now here we are dug in on the goal line. Jim Marshall you're too *high!* Look there," (clank, clank) "the kid's got you standing *up!* You know what? I think they made a mistake down there giving it to the first man through every time."

Coach Fowles rewound the film and the players traded barbs about each other's performances.

"Boys, that was a great victory," Coach Fowles said. "But now we have a choice to make. We can replay that Lourdes game every day this week . . ."

"Right on!" Jonny said, raising a fist.

"Heh, heh, heh," Coach Fowles went on, "but we're not going to do that. We're going to get ready to play Mamaroneck. We have never played a school that big before. They are a Double-A school. Coach Branahan and I have looked at some films from last year, and we've checked around, so we know a little bit about them. Last year they weren't very good. But they have one very impressive running back. They run a pro set with a split-backfield. Defensively they like a Notre Dame four-four, with the tackles turned slightly in."

"Do they stack their linebackers behind them?"

"They almost stack them, Jonny, but usually they put them just outside. The only stunts we saw were the two inside linebackers coming inside, and the two tackles going straight ahead—like our double-barrel half-in.

"Now I was really impressed with the way we hit Saturday. But we *have* to play better offensive football. We have to move the football on the ground consistently, to beat Mamaroneck. Our defense played too much Saturday, men. I mean, the pressure—our defense was in the game the whole last quarter. Our offense was not carrying their share of the load. So, a couple of things we can do to correct that.

"Number one: We can block better, linemen *and* backs. And backs can fake better. And on our passing game, everybody's got to run the right patterns, not one way one time and another way another time. And we have to work on our pass defense, to eliminate the easy touchdown. That's why Lourdes lost that football game—they gave us an easy touchdown and never recovered. Plus our goal line defense. We've told you, how many times? You can't run on that defense, not if we do it right. There's no place to go. We proved that yesterday.

"We also proved something else. Laketown never quits. That was beautiful, just two inches to go.

"And I'll tell you something else: In all fairness, I've got to give the coach and players of Lourdes a lot of credit. They had class. Their coach came clear over to our side of the field after the game. It was a heartbreaking loss for them, but he had no excuses, no alibis, just said congratulations on a good ballgame."

The players left as informally and comfortably as they had come, talking and laughing. Coach Branahan and I stayed, and the three of us had glasses of cream sherry.

"How many plays did you call from the sideline?" I asked Sandy, who was wearing sandals, a faded Wrangler shirt with the sleeves cut off, and a wide woven leather watchband.

"Oh, I guess seven or eight."

"Hey, Coach," Buddy said, "we called more than that, really. I'll bet we called a third or a half of the plays."

Sandy had been fidgeting with index cards on which were diagramed plays, and he kept tapping his foot nervously. "What would you think of putting Ted O'Neill at tight end?" he asked.

"Hmmm," Buddy said, "I think it's risky. He wants to play quarterback. He might quit."

"He might *not*," Sandy said, "and he's got awfully good hands."

"Know who else might quit?" Buddy said. "Keith Allen. After the game he asked why he didn't play more. Another one who's discouraged is Stu Rosenman—even though he started, he didn't get much action. Stu is like a diamond in the rough. We better let those boys know *we* know they're there."

"What about Freddie Delaney at defensive end instead of Steve Barker?" Sandy said, draining his sherry.

"Hmmm," Buddy said. "You know, we really didn't play that good of a football game. Lourdes wasn't all that good. We were very fortunate and had a lot of heart, but technically we made too many mistakes, had too many interceptions, got up too high on blocking, stuff like that. We've got a lot of work to do, lot of guys banged up."

"I was surprised that Jim Marshall took himself out for the last play of the game," I said.

"No, that was the right thing to do," Buddy said. "Jim was afraid he was going to hurt the team because he was really dragging. Remember, he hadn't hit for a week because of that chipped bone in his wrist and the bruise on his thigh. He was really exhausted. I'd rather have a fresh second-stringer in there than a really tired first-stringer."

"You sure pointed out a lot of mistakes in the film," I said.

"Yeah, well they made a lot. But also I don't like them to think that they can't lose just because they have a lot of heart. And I want them to be able to lose too when the time comes. They're probably going to lose this season, or next year, or at least sometime in life. The point is, I thought they could play better, whether they won or lost."

MONDAY, *September 20*

The rain was back again, beating against the classroom windows. So far it had been one of the rainiest Septembers in memory.

Players were passing around the clipping from *The New York Times* and laughing, when Coach Fowles came into the room. He went to the blackboard and erased it as he spoke to them over his shoulder.

"Hey, all that publicity was *great*. We all love it. But that was last week. Now it's today. A new week." He turned to them and dusted off his hands.

"Hey, listen. One game is over, already just a memory. Seniors, most of you have just seven games of organized football left in your entire lives. This season's going to go so fast from now on you won't believe it. So pay attention."

The room quieted.

"All right, Mamaroneck. This will be their first game of the season, so we haven't had a chance to see what they have. On films from last year they looked big, but a little flat-footed. They impressed us as a big, lumbering team. But that was last year, and we don't know for sure what they have back. But we *do* know they had *four coaches* up here scouting *us* on Saturday. And their four coaches would probably say: Number one, Laketown can be passed on; number two, the screen pass will go; number three, stop the long pass and Laketown has no offense.

"But we will have some surprises for them. For one thing, we will reincarnate our split-backfield, which we did not run on Saturday. We ran only out of the I against Lourdes. Mamaroneck's four-three defense is weak against dives, so we will run the dive from the split-backfield, and they haven't seen us do that.

"Now, we know they like to pass. They like the screen pass, and they like the option. If they come out in a wishbone, we will go into a laura center. Otherwise we will feature a regular five-four laura with stunts. They like to use a reverse-pivot dive from the split-backfield. So linebackers, don't watch the quarterback, watch the ball. They come out upright, in a two-point stance, and sometimes they go on that. Usually they shift down into a three-point stance. In the films, they took a long time before they shifted, so they may be calling automatics."

"Backs," said Coach Branahan, "really explode when you hit. We should be able to dive against them. Backs should be able to hit the hole in 0.9 seconds from the split-backfield."

"Yeah," Coach Fowles said. "If we really fire out we can bother them. The record for hitting the hole since I've been here is 0.8 seconds. On the quick dive, the lineman just has to block for about one second, move the man any way he will go, and the back hits in 0.9 and cuts for daylight either way off the block."

"So all backs," Coach Branahan said, "run the dive this week with a stopwatch, all the time."

At the end of the meeting the coaches handed out stars—little decals for the helmets—to the defense. The coaches felt that the offense gets more press publicity, so to balance that they usually gave the stars to the defense. Ted O'Neill got one for his interception in the end zone. Karl Walsh, Ken Furst, and Vince Carradino got them for recovering fumbles. Bruce Stacey got one for most tackles.

The rain had stopped when the team went out, but all was mud. Running through the swampy area to the manbuilder, Bruce Stacey slipped on a rock and twisted his ankle. He went limping into the locker room while the coaches fretted.

Defensive backs went off by themselves to practice reaction drills, but instead found an old soccer ball and practiced kicking.

Ted O'Neill was told to try right end, and he didn't complain. Jonny threw to him in the mud. On a down-and-in pattern, Ted seemed to pull up as the pass was thrown.

"Don't hesitate, Ted!" Jonny hollered. Ted responded by running out his patterns at high speed. His hands were like glue. The question of whether Ted would take direction from Jonny, who had the job Ted really wanted, was settled immediately. Ted smiled at the quarterback. "Throw to me a *lot*," he said.

Coach Fowles called for the offense to line up, and Rich Schenkle tried to join the huddle in the tight-end spot. "Stay out of the offense, Rich," Coach Fowles said, trying to guard against further injury to the linebacker.

Rich put his head down and drifted away. He kept drifting and went into the locker room. Later when Coach Fowles called for the defense, Rich wasn't around. Coach Branahan went into the locker room. Rich was sitting on a bench with his head down. Bruce Stacey, who had twisted his ankle, was combing his hair in front of the mirror.

"Why can't I play offense?" Rich asked, glancing up at Coach Branahan. "I mean, I just, uh, I don't understand it. I was playing tight end a couple weeks ago. Why don't, I mean, if, why can't I play?"

"Cause your knee hurt," Bruce said, combing. "You just told me, you were practically *crying* in the game."

"No I wasn't, no I wasn't," Rich said, smiling sheepishly. "I wasn't, Coach, really. It just, I mean, I feel, uh, it's okay, Coach. Why can't I play?"

"This is only Monday," Coach Branahan said.

"Yeah, but I didn't play all last week, and now I'm not playing."

"Okay," Coach Branahan said, tapping Rich's shoulder, "I can tell you, you *will* play this week on offense."

Rich kept looking at the floor.

After practice, Coach Fowles took Bradford McClure aside. "One of the players came into the guidance office this afternoon," he said, "and he told me that you, Bradford, were the one that really fired up the defense on Saturday."

Bradford went into the shower. As we soaped up I said, "Does it please you to hear that?"

"It's all bullshit," he said, "that stuff is always bullshit."

On each Monday night following a football game, Coach Fowles showed the game film for parents. They met in a classroom. Ten parents and four players and three girl friends showed up for the Lourdes film.

"It might interest you to know," Coach Fowles said to them as he threaded the projector, "that the entire Lourdes team went to football camp for a week during the summer."

There were a couple of soft gasps. He showed the film, stopping frames here and there to single out John Curtis's blocking, Jonny Penchak's perfect long pass to Don Heidner, Jim Petrowski's indefatigability at defensive middle guard.

"How much do you weigh right now, Jim?" he asked.

"One forty-five," said Jim, who was leaning against the wall watching the film with his glasses on.

"See, we're just peanuts, this football team," Coach Fowles said. Several times he went over Bruce Stacey's fierce tackles, and the goal line stand. He finished the film and then went to the front of the room and hoisted himself up to sit on the teacher's desk. He explained the theory of the Laketown goal line defense, and praised the team for its courage. Parents nodded at his points.

"Why didn't Lourdes throw on the goal line?" Jonny's mother asked.

"Well," Coach Fowles said carefully, "you generally go with your best play." He held up his index finger and thumb in a U. "Remember, they had just *that far* to go. I wouldn't want to have to do that over." He smiled, and there were pleasant chuckles in response. "You all know that when I came here I taught fifth grade. And this is the first of my fifth-grade classes to come up and play varsity football. These boys are very special to me."

Mrs. Forrest, Jack's mother, got up to announce that the sale of the oven mitts had netted $510, which would go toward the cost of new green vinyl capes for the team. Last year the team had no coats at all, and suffered through two games when the temperature was below freezing. Mrs. Forrest said that there still wasn't enough money to pay for installation of the new scoreboard. "So we're raffling a car on December 22," she said. "We need door-to-door work to sell tickets. There will be 1,500 books of five tickets each, and tickets cost a dollar. Saturday's paper will have a feature story on our endeavors." She smiled warmly and started to sit down. Then she stood up again. "We hope there will be a football banquet this year—catered, because we've been washing too many uniforms."

"Wow," said Coach Fowles softly, swinging his feet.

WEDNESDAY, *September 22*

For the third day the team drilled against the "Mamaroneck" offense and defense. Coach Branahan had the stopwatch on the backs constantly as they ran dives against the Mamaroneck four-three and four-four defenses. They were not yet hitting the hole in 0.9 seconds, but they were getting quicker. Keith Allen had been putting himself in more at tailback. Ben Schenkle, Rich's younger brother with the wired-in tooth, had also been running. Jonny liked to work with Ben.

Jonny had been running both the Laketown and opponent's offenses and occasionally had confused the "HUT-ONE, HUT-TWO" Mamaroneck count with the "GO, GO" of Laketown.

In separate drills, the line, working with Coach Fowles, seemed as usual to be working harder than the backs. Up on the rise behind the school they sweated and groaned through high-speed belly-flops, bunny-hops, forward rolls, cariocas, and blocking.

"QUICKER, QUICKER!" Coach Fowles hollered. "Hit the knee, work up to the waist, move him laterally."

Stan Beronski had been gimpy from a groin pull suffered in Saturday's game. He said nothing, but dragged his leg. Coach Fowles spotted the limp. "Get Stan outta there!" he shouted.

"It's okay. I loosened it up on the track, Coach."

"Yeah, I know you did," Coach Fowles said, pushing Stan away from the drill. "You always tell the truth."

Stan smiled and stood aside. "It's a plot," he said to me. "Schenkle must have said something."

Sugarbear was having problems of his own, limping from time to time on his damaged knee. But he refused to leave the drills, and Coach Fowles did not insist.

In the pit drill, Cary Grimes, the lanky black end who hadn't received a regular varsity jersey, challenged Mike Schultz, a tall, husky end who had. They collided in dust, and Cary snarled and grunted bitterly and held his own. Then he stalked out of the circle.

Coach Fowles threw passes to Don Heidner. From 10 yards away he snapped bullets into Don's hands in various around-the-clock positions.

Don's hands grew red. Coach Fowles kept at it, delivering his hard passes in a fluid motion, with pinpoint accuracy. Don began to shake his hands between catches.

"I love to throw," Coach Fowles said, smiling, continuing to bombard Don's palms. "I'm a frustrated quarterback. In high school I could throw better than anybody else, but we ran a single-wing and they wouldn't let me throw."

Don blew on his red hands.

"How does that feel, Don?" Coach Fowles asked, throwing again.

Don shook his hands.

"Think how strong your hands are going to be."

"Yeah," Don said, looking at them.

THURSDAY, *September 23*

It appeared there might be a teachers' strike. They had been negotiating and threatening for several weeks, but now it was getting serious. Both Coach Fowles and Coach Branahan said that while they sympathized, they would still coach during any strike. All the athletic coaches were meeting today to talk about what their policy would be in the event of a strike.

Stan Beronski was supposed to be in charge of the team meeting in the coaches' absence. "We should do everything just the same way without the coaches," he said. But he didn't have his heart in it, couldn't think of anything to do, so rather than sit in the classroom and laugh, the team went out and began practice on its own.

It had been decided by the coaches not to approach the manbuilder through the swamp anymore, because players had been slipping on the rocks—that was how Bruce Stacey had twisted his ankle. Instead, the team was to run an extra few hundred yards up a hill, around the end of the swampy grove, and back down to the manbuilder. As the team headed up the long way, John Finch split off and headed through the swamp.

"Don't go the short way, John," Bruce Stacey called.

"Long ways suck," John called back cheerfully.

On the hill, Jonny and Bruce took over to push the team. "I'm not gonna lose on Saturday!" Bruce yelled, chugging up the hill.

"Remember, Laketown," Jonny shouted, "Losers SUCK!"

"Hey, Schenkle, get off the hill," Bruce said to Rich. Rich continued to limp up and down on his bad knee. "Come on Rich, do it for the FAMILY." Rich ignored the pleas.

Bruce, Rich, and Jim Marshall were in shorts today, still kept from contact because of a twisted ankle, bruised knee, and bruised thigh, respectively. With helmets on, the three jogged together on the running track while the team began the scrimmage.

The coaches came out. "The teachers will picket tomorrow," Coach Fowles told me, "but not during school hours."

All the running backs got shots at hitting the line on dives. Ben Schenkle was the last. "I would start Ben at fullback," Jonny told me, "and Al Stacey at tailback. Ben will be starting before long. Wait and see."

The three injured joggers completed their run and came to stand and watch the rest of practice. Jonny and Rich started wrestling, and Jonny threw Rich down.

"All right, Rich," Coach Fowles said casually, "take a couple more laps."

Rich took a deep breath and hauled himself up and returned to the running track alone.

Stan Beronski and Steve Barker had switched defensive ends, putting both back at the sides they played last year. Little Rich Merrill, who centered for punts, was playing safety. The coaches watched him. "What are we gonna do about Rich?" Coach Fowles asked. "He keeps putting himself in back there. He's down in the dumps. He's got a lot of guts, but he's not good enough to play back there."

They didn't take him out.

FRIDAY, *September 24*

Rich Schenkle collected ballots for honorary captain in Stan's motorcycle helmet. Jonny was elected. Then the green jerseys for the away game at Mamaroneck were passed out. Some were missing. That caused Coach Fowles to fume.

"I'm a little hot about the green Laketown jerseys that are walking around town," he said. "*He* deserves a jersey," he pointed to a player, "so does *he*, and *he*. The only reason they don't have jerseys is because they've been stolen. Number 40, where is it? Number 41? Four jerseys have been stolen. We got four kids in this classroom who worked their guts out since

August 25. They deserve jerseys. If some guys want to look like Joe Namath, they should go down to Korvette's and get some cheap thing. Otherwise they can come out and earn them just like *you* did. They belong to the *family*. I'd love to see somebody find them.

"All right, let's review Mamaroneck." He went over the offenses and defenses, sketching them quickly on the board. "One reminder: If Jim Petrowski makes a mistake at middle guard, it's maybe six yards. If Ken Furst makes a mistake at safety, it's six points, and everybody on the field is looking at him. So you secondary men, play your keys and don't give up the easy touchdown. Let's force them to make mistakes."

He opened a folder on the desk and took out a small letter.

"This is something I received in the mail that I'd like to share with you."

He read: "Coach, I realize now why everyone writes letters. It's because we'd all like to be on that field every Saturday playing for Laketown High. I'd give my right arm to break a sweat for Laketown again. . . . I regret those days I took it easy and they'll always be burned into my memory. . . . Never again will I hit one-on-one, run the hill, it's all memories. Coach, I believe this year's team is stronger than ever, they want a winning season with an 8–0 record more than any team before. I only wish I was part of such a team at this moment. Have a great season, never quit. Let them have no regrets, Coach."

Coach Fowles read the signature of one of last year's players. The room was quiet.

"Wow," Jonny said softly from his seat on the floor at the front of the room. "It's hard to believe it was him. He was a hardnosed kid."

"It's up to *you*, gentlemen," Coach Fowles said, putting the letter back in the file. "All right, game time tomorrow is 1:30. We will leave here at 11:30 and get there at 12:30. If you're *really* gonna play from 1:30 to 3:30, you need food. So get up early enough for breakfast. Phone calls tonight at ten minutes to ten."

Bradford McClure had skipped practice yesterday to go to New York to see the rock opera, "Tommy."

"When I skipped practice," said a friend named Sam, a reserve defensive back, "I didn't get to play."

Bradford shrugged. "So I probably won't play," he said.

"This team pisses me off," Jonny said angrily as he slammed the ball into the dirt. Backs were running lazily out for passes. "Look at those guys fucking around. I only get to throw a few passes anyway before they start working on defense. Also I feel lousy today, ache all over. I don't know if I'm getting sick or it's just bruises."

Stan Beronski had a huge boil on the front of his right thigh. He said he was going to try to bring it to a head tonight and open it up. He wore sweat pants at practice to cover it. Coach Fowles looked at it and sighed. "Whew," he said as Stan trotted away. "That kid has a tremendously high pain threshhold. He's been hitting with that all week."

Coach Fowles called the starters out for a two-minute, stop-the-clock drill. He called them by name. Keith Allen expected to be called for halfback. But Ben Schenkle was named. Keith walked away sadly. Ben was surprised.

"See?" Jonny said. "I knew he would start."

Jim Marshall went over to talk to Coach Fowles. He was not named to start at defensive right tackle. Because of the bruise on his leg, he hadn't hit all week. Freddie Delaney would start in his place. "Coach," Jim said mournfully, "I just don't understand why I'm not starting on defense."

"Well, we just have to see how it looks tomorrow," Coach Fowles said. "We might make a spur-of-the-moment decision, but right now this is the way we want to try it."

At the end of practice, Coach Fowles called the team together. "Tomorrow you've got to be mentally ready," he said. "You're not mentally ready now."

Still, physically it had been a good week, with crisp, hard hitting and smooth play execution. Coach Fowles was pleased with that aspect.

SATURDAY, *September 25*

Game day was sunny and cool, still shirt-sleeve weather. Players came early in the morning to watch the JV team roll up its second straight victory, then began drifting into the locker room to dress at about eleven. John Finch roared into the parking lot on his motorcycle and sat aboard it to discuss with Jonny whether he could stand it up on its rear wheel.

Then he demonstrated, revving it up and abruptly letting out the clutch. The bike reared, suddenly went higher, and then was almost up straight on the rear fender, sliding forward leaving a trail of sparks. "Hmmm," John said, bouncing down again, shutting it off, and looking at the rear fender. "Bent."

"Crazy," Jonny said.

A reserve end named Joe Knowland stood disconsolately outside the locker room. He was not allowed to dress because he had not been home last night when Coach Fowles called. Coach had tried to get him twice.

The team clattered aboard the yellow bus at 11:30, jamming into seats, leaving a few reserves standing. The coaches took their customary seats next to the front door. The bus was neither silent nor noisy; players talked but didn't laugh.

"How do you feel, Buddy?" I asked the coach, who had been silent after giving the bus-driver directions.

"Nervous," he said, pursing his lips and looking straight ahead out the front window. "I'm really nervous. I don't know why exactly. I thought it was the best week of practice we've had."

The Mamaroneck Tigers were on the field when we arrived, running through drills in white jerseys and silver pants. Bleachers lined both sides of the field.

The Harvesters filed into the locker room to put on their shoulder pads. "Ready to play in forty minutes," Coach Fowles said. "Right now we'd like to have the passers and receivers, and specialists, right here behind the school—not on the playing field—as soon as you're dressed."

The team went through drills on the grass behind the school, then went in to talk to itself in the locker room, without the coaches.

The casualness of the drills disappeared the instant the locker room door closed. Jim Marshall spoke first, his voice shaking.

"You know what their coach is saying in there right now? He's saying 'STOP THEIR DEFENSE AND WE'VE WON THE GAME,' because our offense DOESN'T GO NOWHERE!"

"It's true," Rich Schenkle said, as Jim stomped this way and that, huffing. "They think we're not that strong on offense, but today we're going to prove them wrong. Today we're going to come across a Double-A school. And it's great that we're playing these big schools, because everybody thought we were going to be so bad. I'd rather have it this way than play these little cake schools and win 30–0. Cause I KNOW we can do it. WE'RE GOING TO WIPE THEM OUT!"

Jonny sat on a bench and swung his helmet against his leg. He spoke calmly. "I don't know how many of you guys are seniors, but we never had an eight and 0 year, and I want it to be this year. If we lose today we're not eight and 0. Every game is as important as every other game. Let's go out there and whip their asses. And uh, don't worry about, you know, who's getting all the stars on their helmets, because if we win, you know, everybody looks good. We're a *family*."

Rich Schenkle held his arms out, as if to grab onto Jonny's last words. "Yeah, if somebody recovers a fumble, the *team* recovers it!"

Bruce Stacey shouted from a corner of the room, jabbing at the team with his index finger, his eyes focused somewhere on the floor in front of him. "Last night when we were home POLISHING OUR SHOES AND WATCHING TV, you know what these guys were doing? They had their PEP RALLY AND FIRE last night. This is their FIRST GAME, and these guys are UP! THEY'RE

UP! They're saying Laketown beat Lourdes because WE were UP. AND WE'RE NOT UP TODAY! We're just LOAFING AROUND!"

Now he strode over legs to the center of the team, yelling louder. "YOU GUYS THINK WE'RE GONNA WIN THIS WAY? You're CRAZY! We gotta GET UP! WE GOTTA BEAT HEADS!"

Rich's voice filled in softly. "This is no picnic, Laketown."

Coach Fowles walked in, followed by Coach Branahan chewing gum. Both were wearing green shirts and ties, their usual sideline attire.

"All right," Coach Fowles said gently. "Let's listen. Coach Branahan, anything you want to say?"

"Just two words: Pass defense."

"Okay. Couple things I want to say. We won last Saturday in the last few seconds with our guts hanging out, right down on the two-inch line. And the reason that we won there is because we don't know *how* to quit. We had a better state of mind than that other football team last week, gentlemen. Coach Branahan and I agree that in many respects we've just completed the best week of practice we've had. Now we are at the critical point. We've worked too hard, come too far, to lie down now. And you can do it today because it's right up here," he tapped his head, "MENTALLY! Mentally you can do it. First time we've ever played this high school, first time we've ever played a school this big, and you're lucky enough to be here."

He paused and looked over his players, and the room was soundless except for their breathing.

"Think about those last few seconds," he said, even more softly, "on the goal line. We did it together. Who's in better shape?"

"LAKETOWN!"

"Who hits harder?"

"LAKETOWN!"

"WHO WE GONNA BEAT?"

"MAMARONECK, MAMARONECK, MAMARONECK . . ."

As the team trotted out on the field, past the Mamaroneck bleachers, there were taunts. "Look at the Laketown GIRLS!" somebody yelled down as Jonny and Stan trotted by together, their blond hair flapping below their helmets.

Mamaroneck won the toss, received, and ran the kickoff back to their 35. The Laketown defense had a few changes from the week before. Steve Barker and Stan Beronski had switched ends, putting Stan on the right side; Freddie Delaney had replaced Jim Marshall at right tackle; Karl Walsh had moved from right corner to left safety, replacing Ted O'Neill; and Ray Meister was at right corner.

Mamaroneck gained three yards in three running plays, and punted to Ken Furst, in single safety, who took it on his 22 and got to the 27.

The offense had Ben Schenkle at fullback and Al Stacey at tailback. They began diving through holes punched out by the middle of the line, guards Clifford Albert and Jack Forrest, and center Jim Marshall. The line was quick. Mamaroneck pulled in tighter, and Jonny hit his new right end, Ted O'Neill, down and out for 20 yards into Mamaroneck territory. Then Jonny fired down the middle to Don Heidner who took it to the 18.

Husky Brian Purcell, a tight end last week, this week alternating with Al Stacey at tailback, brought in a play. He took Jonny's hand-off behind right tackle Tom Kase for six yards, to the 12. A Mamaroneck offside brought it to the seven for a first down. Fullback Ben Schenkle sliced through the middle to the three. The line was hitting so quickly that the linemen bounced up after each play and seemed impatient to get to the huddle. Brian Purcell took it to the one.

On third down, Jonny called a quarterback sneak against the tightly packed goal-line defense, and got half a yard. The Laketown bench was up, and pressed together at the 35-yard line, which is as close to the end zone as rules permit.

On fourth down, Jonny kept it again, this time behind a barely successful wedge of blocks by Jim Marshall and Jack Forrest, and drove in by inches.

The crowd and bench reacted wildly to the first real offensive display of the season, and Jonny came off the field with his head characteristically down, silently grasping all the hands offered him.

Coach Fowles grabbed him in a hug, smiling, then said into his ear above the noise of the crowd: "Jonny, what is it we want other teams to run on us down there?"

"Hunh?" Jonny said, looking at him.

Coach Fowles repeated the question, and Jonny frowned and nodded.

"Quarterback sneak," Jonny said.

"Right, because that's the easiest thing to stop. But don't worry about it. Good work, Jonathan Penchak."

"Do a job, defense," Jonny said as he went past the defensive team lining up to go in.

Ben Schenkle stayed in to kick. Because he kicked soccer style, he stood back at an angle to his left from holder Don Heidner. The snap from

Rich Merrill was high, forcing Don up off his knee, but Don got it down and Ben kicked it perfectly. It was 7–0.

Then the bigger Mamaroneck Tigers began to move. Behind a heavy line, the quick backs cut through the tackles, past Bradford McClure and Freddie Delaney. They pushed quickly downfield to the Harvester 19. A fourth-down pass fell out of bounds.

Laketown took over but was held in its own territory. Ted O'Neill punted to the Tiger 38 as the first quarter ended.

To start the second quarter, Mamaroneck again went at the tackles. Bradford McClure on the Harvesters' left side was being trapped, and behind him linebacker Rich Schenkle was being pushed first inside, then outside. In nine plays Mamaroneck was back at the Laketown 15.

The Tigers' quarterback rolled left on an option play, but end Stan Beronski ripped through and hit him just as he tried to pitch to his trailing back. The ball rolled free. Jim Petrowski tackled the back, who was struggling to reach the loose ball, and Stan recovered on the 20.

Two Laketown running plays got eight yards. With a third and two on the 28, the coaches sent in Bruce Stacey for a power dive. Jim Marshall and Jack Forrest opened a gaping hole on the right side, and Bruce shot straight up the field, shedding tacklers, and dragging the final two with him, for a 21-yard gain.

Jonny continued to work the right side of the line, behind Jack Forrest and Tom Kase. Brian Purcell and Al Stacey alternated at tailback, sometimes bringing in plays. Little Ben Schenkle, leaning forward and twisting like an eel, cut sharply on either side of Jack Forrest's blocks.

With fourth and two on the Mamaroneck 49, Bruce Stacey was again sent in. From the fullback spot right behind Jonny in the I, Bruce went straight up the middle, butting into the back of center Jim Marshall, for eight yards.

The half was drawing to a close. Jonny dropped back and threw for Don Heidner on the goal line, but two defenders were there; the ball was underthrown, and they batted it away.

The team banged into the dressing room ahead of the coaches.

"That defense sucked. . . . Where's the Gatorade? . . . Let's GO defense. . . . They're running ALL OVER US! . . . Coach is gonna come in here and say our defense SUCKED! . . . Roger, where's the Gatorade?"

The tiny blond manager looked around bemusedly for the drinking bottles.

"They took it down to the field, Jack. . . . Now who the hell. . . ."

"All right boys, listen up," Coach Fowles said, walking over bodies to the rear of the locker room, where there was a blackboard.

"What in the world is going on in *here?*" he asked loudly, sketching the defensive alignment and tapping the chalk over the left tackle spot. "How is that possible, to run up there when we've got all those *people* there? What's going on?" The team was crowded into the end of the locker room, with not enough room for all to sit on the floor. "Hey, the people that have been playing, sit down, give 'em room. What's going on, Bradford?"

"What they're doin, uh, their back is *really* quick and he can cut *really* well. He's running for the hole, and if it's blocked up he'll cut in or out. . . ."

"Rich Schenkle! Where's Rich? Rich, are we showing your stunt too soon over there?"

Bradford answered instead: "If I line right up head-on, the tackle doesn't know which way I'm going, but if I move into the gap. . . ."

"But you're not supposed to be in the gap. Rich, are you telling Bradford to line up in the gap?"

"I didn't say line up in the gap," Rich said.

"Well something is—okay, listen! That's a *mental* mistake. We want you head-up on that boy, so he is *confused* and doesn't know which way we're coming. Now if Bradford goes outside and that boy steps inside and picks up Rich, our stunter, then we're in trouble. Because Bradford's actually taking himself out of the play. You line right up on his *nostrils*, Brad."

"Okay, Coach, but on that stunt, three guys are coming out to get Rich."

"Okay, now when that happens you got problems. But there's one thing you can do. Believe it or not you are going to force those blockers to tackle their own man. You know how you're gonna do that? You're gonna go right down underneath everybody and grab legs and cause a pile-up."

Rich raised his hand. "Uh, coach, I think we are really working good in the six-three, because then somebody's always getting through to them."

"Instead of the five-four laura? Well, okay, then let's stay with our six-three awhile and see how it goes. The only thing about the six-three, our pass-rush better be really good, because the secondary is weaker. Yes, Jim?"

"On that, I hit the guy and I go inside," Jim Petrowski said, his padded hands waving descriptively in the air, "every time I get hit and go this way, I look for the ball and then I have to go back and by the time I go back . . ."

"Okay, okay, but you've done your job. You've eliminated one man. The people that ought to be making the tackle are right behind you, Jim."

"Gimme some Gatorade."

Bottles clanked and were passed on.

"Okay boys, I'll tell you what: Defensively we've got to cause some mistakes. That quarterback had some people open early in the game, and I'm sure the coach over there is telling him that. Our pass-rush looks pretty good. We took control of the ballgame because we had both a running *and* a passing attack. We had the ball more than they did. Offensively we're moving the ball. Jonny, you're mixing up your plays well. Dive looked good, the four or six hole. Any comments?"

"Counter at the four and six holes."

"Uh, the only thing about a counter—they're running a six-man line, and that's tough for a counter. This is what they're doing, boys." Coach Fowles sketched a six-man line on the blackboard. "Maybe they got out of this from time to time, but this is what they were doing before. It's a six-two-three, that's all it is. They're taking their monster man—this linebacker here—they're just taking him and setting him to the wide side of the field. Now this man does not have any pass responsibility, and that's why we've got people open a lot. Questions?"

"They're calling automatics on us," Rich Schenkle said.

"Well then, we've got all day on the stunts. Stay back and let them look it over and do whatever they want. Don't show the stunt right away. Ted O'Neill?"

"We had about 12 yards to go and ran a 71 pass. And I did a 10 yards-and-in like I'm supposed to, and their whole secondary moved over that way. And like the other receiver was open on the other side. So if Jonny was able to look over—I don't know if he had enough time—it was wide open."

"You mean look over to the tight end?"

"Yeah."

"All right, that's something to keep in mind. Now gentlemen, I can't believe they cracked our six-one frankenstein *twice*. It's gotta be somebody's not protecting their inside gap when that happens."

"Coach, it's a case of that back changing directions so quick," Bruce Stacey said.

"Yeah, well he's gotta start out someplace, and when he starts out there should be a man in that hole."

Coach Fowles erased the blackboard and turned to face the team. "Gentlemen, I'll tell you what: We're not playing as well as I think we can. Now what do you think of that? Seven to nothing? I'm not satisfied with that performance and I'm not going to lie to you. We're not good enough yet. I'll tell you another thing: You people better improve. I know you can play rougher than that. We pay thirty-five dollars per shoulder pad. And let's use em. We're not as aggressive as we should be, not yet. It may be good enough for somebody else, but not for Laketown, not for this *family*. Coach Branahan, anything you want to say?"

"Just again, concentrating on pass defense. We can keep rotating toward their strong side. And Stan, if you see them coming for a pass, just fire in hard. The cornerman can come up too."

"Okay, boys, twenty-four more minutes. We're not good enough yet. We are in better shape than they are, but we're not proving it right now. Go out the second half and knock these people down on the field. Twenty-four more minutes. Who's gonna hit harder?"

"LAKETOWN!"

"Who we gonna beat?"

"MAMARONECK ..."

Laketown took the kickoff and began driving right away, with Jonny working the right side of the line just as before. Ben Schenkle at fullback and Al Stacey at tailback hit behind Jack Forrest and Tom Kase again and again.

Players began to heat up. End Dan Miranda, returning from a deep-pass pattern downfield, paused to trade words with the safetyman. Coach Fowles yanked him immediately. "You're in there to play football," he shouted at Dan. "The officials are there to keep law and order. Sit down until you're ready to play football."

After one play Dan came up to Coach Fowles. "I'm ready to play football now, Coach," he said.

"Go on in," Coach Fowles said.

With a third down on the Mamaroneck 47, Jonny hit Don Heidner on the right sideline at the 35 for a first down. As Don tumbled out of bounds, a tackler pounced on him late. I yelled the message to the official that he was blind for not calling a penalty. Coach Fowles grabbed my arm and quickly pulled me away.

"Much as I like you," he said, "you cause us a 15-yard penalty and you'll be up in the stands."

Jonny passed deep for Don, who was tripped on the 15. The official called interference and marked off 15 yards from the original line of scrimmage, putting the ball on the 20.

"MR. REFEREE, SIR," Coach Fowles called. The official glanced over and then looked away again. "MR. REFEREE SIR, MAY I HAVE A RULE INTERPRETATION, SIR?" The official reluctantly blew his whistle to halt the action and came trotting over.

"Excuse me, sir," Coach Fowles said, "but may I have a rule interpretation on why the ball was not moved to the point of the interference?"

"The penalty is marked off from the line of scrimmage," the official said.

"Okay, thank you, sir."

Since Coach Fowles was a certified official himself, I asked him how it could be that he didn't know that rule.

"I know it," he said, "but that's *my* way of letting them know I'm paying attention. It's better than yelling at them."

On first down on the 20, Jonny bootlegged to the left, then reversed and threw quickly to O'Neill in the other corner of the end zone, but the ball was thrown too far, incomplete. Jonny rolled right and hit Brian Purcell, the tailback, at the 17. On third down, Ben Schenkle dove again behind the quick block of right guard Jack Forrest down to the seven, for a first down. Jonny called the same play again, and Ben went to the three behind Jack and Jim Marshall. But an offensive holding penalty pushed the ball back to the 22.

Running now from a split-backfield instead of the I, Jonny pitched out to the right to Ben, who cut inside a crushing double block on the cornerback by Ted O'Neill and Tom Kase, and went to the 15.

Now Jonny came back to the other side, throwing a long, looping screen pass—just clearing the arms of a defender who would have had an open field—to Brian Purcell on the left. Brian spun one tackler off over his head, Clifford Albert chopped down another, and Brian went to the seven.

On third down Bruce Stacey came in with a play, which was simply himself straight up the middle. Jim Marshall drove straight ahead, left guard Clifford Albert dove low and knocked the feet from under his man, and right guard Jack Forrest turned his man out. Behind them came Bruce, straight-arming the only man left, the umpire, to go in for the touchdown.

This time the pass from center was perfect, as was Ben Schenkle's kick, and Laketown led 14-0.

Mamaroneck took the kickoff to their 33, then went back to work at their right side, at tackle Bradford McClure and linebacker Rich Schenkle. Their first try gained nothing. Then a well-executed draw play caught linebacker Bruce Stacey shooting in on a stunt. Bradford was pushed to the outside, the ball-carrier faked Jim Petrowski aside, Rich dove at him and missed, so did Ken Furst. Finally Ted O'Neill grabbed the ball-carrier around the neck and brought him down on the Laketown 43.

On first down they tried to suck Bradford McClure in with a counter, but Bradford submarined and tripped up the halfback at the line of scrimmage. On second down the quarterback rolled out to his right, and Bradford slipped in and hit him just as he threw. The ball floated along the sideline and was intercepted by cornerback Al Stacey.

Laketown drove for two first downs before being stopped on the Mamaroneck 33.

With the third quarter nearly over, the Mamaroneck quarterback abandoned his right side, which had been so fruitful in the first half, and began working the left. Two sweeps got a first down. Then a pass to the deep left was complete behind Ken Furst and Ray Meister to the Laketown 18. Finally the Harvesters held, and a fourth-down pass missed in the end zone.

To start the fourth quarter, Laketown drove out to the 40, then was forced to punt it away. Mamaroneck moved again. Running successful options right and left, the Tigers brought the ball to a first down on the Laketown three.

They came out in the wishbone, and Bruce Stacey instantly called the team into a laura-center defense. A huge hole opened between Bradford McClure and Steve Barker, but Bruce smashed into the ball-carrier for no gain. Then they ran a delayed counter at the same hole, but the Stacey brothers, shoulder to shoulder, straightened the fullback up and sat him down on the two.

On third down they ran a dive at the other side, at tackle Jim Marshall, but again Bruce Stacey shot over to cover the hole, stopping the runner inches short of the goal line. Finally, on fourth down, they ran at Jim again. Jim grabbed the runner, but couldn't hold him back. He scored, and that made it 14–6.

Mamaroneck elected to run for two points rather than kick for one. The quarterback rolled left on an option, but end Stan Beronski cut him off, forced him to dump the ball back wildly, and the try failed.

In the waning minutes, Mamaroneck got the ball again in its own territory. But now the Laketown pass-rush was smothering. Bradford Mc-

Clure threw the quarterback for a big loss, and finally Karl Walsh picked off a desperation pass at midfield to end the game.

"You did some terrific running at fullback," I said to Bruce Stacey as we boarded the bus.

"They were just giving me great blocking," he said.

"Hey, Ben Schenkle," I called, "You were really slicing up that line."

"It was Jack Forrest's blocking," he said.

"I guess it's the best game I ever played," Jack said, smiling shyly.

The bus ride began with raucous spirit. Freddie Delaney was leaning out the window. We passed a chubby girl hitchhiker. "You'll never get a ride, YOU FAT HORSE!" Freddie called. A body was passed back over the heads of the players. It was Brian Purcell, who didn't seem to mind. Freddie Delaney was hoisted aloft and passed forward in exchange. A small, but game, reserve named Jerry Spitz was joyously depantsed. The bus bearing Laketown spectators and cheerleaders pulled abreast of the team bus at a stoplight, and the cheerleaders were still chanting, dutifully.

Gradually our bus became quiet, and players put their heads down on the seatbacks in front of them and rested.

When we arrived at the school, the locker room was locked. Coach Fowles went around the building and found a way in. He punched the locker room doors open from the inside, and then went into the coaches' room and telephoned a custodian. "If any of my kids get sick because they had to stand around in that cold," he growled, "it's going to fall on somebody's head."

Jim Marshall's parents hosted a hero-sandwich supper for the team. Players milled around outside, moving carefully as muscles tightened and bruises began to sing pain.

"I guess that's the worst game I ever played," Rich Schenkle said, smiling and looking at the ground, dangling a root beer in his hand.

Bruce Stacey was holding an arm across his chest. "I hope I didn't break my ribs," he said a few times.

There was to be a party later at the Schenkles'. Meanwhile Jonny and I went to his house. Parked in front was his faded red Saab for which he as yet had no driver's license. He showed me some photographs he had taken and processed himself at school, arty black-and-whites of weeds, girders, a wheelbarrow. He took out his guitar and picked out rock melodies. His parents came home and congratulated him. I suggested he and I go out for a drink.

"Okay," he said.

"When are you coming home?" his mother asked. "Eleven? Half-past eleven? I'll pick you up."

"Aw, ma, I can get home from Schenkles'. Don't pick me up."

"I'd like to pick you up."

"Please, don't pick me up."

"Half-past eleven?"

"I'll get home okay."

We went to a pub outside of Laketown. I ordered a double Scotch. Jonny ordered a Coke.

"Surprised?" he asked.

"Not really, I guess," I said. "But I thought you were going to have a drink."

"Naw. I mess around and joke a lot, but underneath all this I guess I'm really a jock. If I compromise here, I'll compromise on the field." He rubbed his neck.

"Hurt?" I asked.

"Not really. Remember when I got hit on that bootleg, on the far side of the field? I really got knocked dizzy. I couldn't think what play to call next. I was sure I was going to screw up and fumble. But . . ." he sipped his Coke, "I didn't."

On the way to Schenkles' we drove down a narrow blacktop road where he had been in an accident the year before. Stu Rosenman, the fullback, had been driving with Jonny and two other boys. Jonny said they were going nearly 100 miles per hour, when Stu swerved to avoid an oncoming car.

"I had been looking at the speedometer," Jonny said. "I kept telling Stu to slow down. We flipped over three times."

He pointed out the slash, still visible, angling from the road over a gully and into the woods. "You ever know what it feels like when you're going to die?" he asked. "I was sure we were all dead. While we were flipping up in the air, you know, I was absolutely sure. I heard a voice. I couldn't tell what the words were. I didn't see any images, just the voice. It was the voice of Coach Fowles. Isn't that weird?"

He sat quietly for a few seconds. "I think once you've gone through that you're never quite the same person. I had trouble sleeping for a long time, dreams and shit, you know? It's funny. Like, for a long time after that the thought would come back that maybe I *was* dead, you know, and that whatever I was doing at the time was just, like, still just thoughts compressed into those seconds before I died. Like, it's hard to explain, but sometimes I would have the feeling—wherever I was, at school, or any-place—that suddenly there was going to be this crash and pain, and then I would be dead. Like the crash wasn't finished, you know? Anyway, there are some people I just won't ride with anymore, no matter what."

The Schenkles had a fire going in the backyard, and players had sand-wiches and sodas. Many had brought girls with them. I saw Ted O'Neill. "How'd you like playing end, Ted?" I asked.

"You know what?" he said, smiling broadly, "I really loved catching Jonny's passes—no shit!"

"Hey, Bradford," I said, "how come you stand by yourself on the side-lines all the time?"

"Hi, Richard," he said, adding confidentially, "Did you smell all that grass in the stands?"

Rich Schenkle brought out two beers, for me and a friend with me. "Mom thought you might prefer this," he said.

Jim Petrowski came over. "Look at this," he said to me, nodding at the whole scene of players talking and joking in the flashing light of the fire. "Isn't this incredible how everybody's together? Like, Bradford and Bruce Stacey, they say each other sucks, Bruce is a hardhat and Brad is a freak. Look at 'em sitting together. All these different types on this team, and we're all one team now. Isn't that unbelievable?"

Some players and their girls began to melt into the shadows and into the house. I went out to my van. The back door was ajar. Inside on the floor were a girl and a Harvester.

"Hi, Richard," said the player.

"I . . . well, uh. . . ."

"Don't worry," said the player brightly, "we won't tell anybody."

7

MONDAY, *September 27*

The stage was set for the game the Laketown Harvesters wanted more than any other: Horace Greeley. Greeley, the high school of a wealthy, small, exclusive neighboring town had been the class of the county for the past two seasons, rolling up an undefeated streak of twenty straight. The last two years, they had beaten Laketown 38–0 and 24–0. In fact, Laketown had not beaten Greeley since these seniors were in Buddy Fowles's fifth-grade class, seven years ago.

Last year, to try to psyche up his players, Coach Fowles had secretly ordered a cake delivered to the Laketown locker room before the game. On the icing was the greeting: "To the Laketown Cake-eaters." It was assumed, of course, that this prime insult had been supplied by Greeley players. The Harvesters splattered the cake all over the walls of the locker room. Then they went out and lost anyway, and Coach Fowles wrote a letter of apology to the Horace Greeley custodians. There are still Laketown players today who don't know the cake came from Coach Fowles.

This year there would be no tricks. "You don't win football games with gimmicks," Coach Fowles said. "Even I had to learn that."

Coach Fowles respected the Greeley coach more than any other opposing coach. Greeley had dropped its opener this year, but to a tough urban team in a squeaker, and the loss was largely due to the fact that

Greeley fumbled away three punts. This would be the first of five league games for both teams. Laketown, with two upset victories behind them, would nonetheless be the underdog for the third week in a row. But there was a growing confidence on the team. Players from earlier years began passing on grudging praise to these players that Coach Fowles called "peanuts." Local area radio stations planned to broadcast coming Laketown games.

All season so far, past Greeley games had been recounted. Now rumors of what the Greeley team was doing to get ready flitted through the halls of Laketown High School.

"You know what Greeley has in the locker room?" Bruce Stacey said to the group that hung out at the school cafeteria. "They got a dummy hung up there, with number 12 on it, and they kick it and punch it."

Twelve was Jonny Penchak's number. It was not only that Jonny's passing attracted notice around the area, but also that he had played against many opposing football players in lacrosse, and they remembered.

Jonny did not hang around the cafeteria. Neither did Stan Beronski or Bradford McClure or Rich Schenkle. But other players did, and often I would stop by before practice. Usually I would find myself admiring the luscious nubility that strolled the halls and would recall my high school fantasies of the broad powers I supposed emanated from being a football star.

I tried to assess the differences between my high school time in the early 1950s and this, my situations then and now. A lover of sports but not a jock, I had been in the band, which meant that I traveled to away games and enjoyed that marginal participation in the sporting event.

Were the students more sophisticated now, were they wiser, older than we were? When I was in school, there might have been a minor scandal about drinking, but now there were debates in the local press about whether drug use was widespread at the high school. We had a student council, but it was not concerned with so serious a matter as getting a representative on the school board, as was the student senate at Laketown. Our war was Korea, but I recall no student protests. Last year some students at Laketown held special antiwar seminars instead of attending a day's classes.

Two aspects of high school life seemed to me distinctly unchanged. One was the steel lockers lining the cinder-block hallways. The other was girls.

Perched among football players on the low book counter that separated the cafeteria from the hallway, dressed in dungarees as they were, dangling my feet as uncomfortably as they, I watched the girls as avidly and distantly as ever. As irony would have it, I was separated from them now just as surely as before by both age and station—then too little, now too much.

Perhaps in my day I had only imagined the lure of the football star. In any case, the stars seemed as unawed by the girls as the girls by them. "We see them every day, don't forget," Jonny Penchak once said to me.

So the players gathered there not to ogle, but mainly to relax among themselves. Ben Schenkle was often there, begging rides to the shopping center where he could get snacks before practice. The Stacey brothers were often there, and the group never seemed to tire of teasing Al about his light curly hair, which they called "the white Afro." Jack Forrest was there, talking with a Bronx accent, walking bowlegged, tussling with passers-by. Stu Rosenman was there, fretting about failing schoolwork or forgetting plays or not carrying the ball enough. Big Bob Mills was there, identifiable by his food-stained shirt and rusted black shoes. Bob was always merry. His straight brown hair sat on his head like a bowl, covering his ears, and he had a paunch and spindly legs. He played football with a jolly toughness, and was being used more and more where Jim Marshall used to play at defensive right tackle.

What was different about all of them, compared to the players of my high school years, was the hair. Almost all our jocks had crewcuts. On the Laketown football team the hair was almost universally long, at least to below the ears. But even on that point I couldn't draw a firm generalization. No football team the Harvesters would see all year would have hair so long.

What was different about me was that the adult monitors, posted in the halls to guard against intruders or class-cutters, would let me, now the writer, roam freely.

I stopped by to see the principal, John Leary. Mr. Leary was a direct, outspoken man with short hair and narrow conservative neckties. He sprinkled his conversation with casual hells and damns, visited classrooms often, and was generally spoken of with respect around the school by students and faculty alike.

This was his second year at Laketown, after twenty years at a Long Island school where they didn't have football.

"I love football," he said. "I think it knits the school together. And it's festive as hell—the bands, flags, the leaves . . ."

"Why wouldn't you let Coach Fowles schedule a ninth game this year, like he wanted?" I asked.

"Make the season too long," Mr. Leary said.

"But isn't basketball even longer?"

"Sure. Basketball is too long. Wrestling is too long. I think there should be a break between sports. Hey, I *love* sports, but I think the kids need a rest between seasons."

"I was surprised when I came here," I said, "at how the kids dressed, dungarees and so on, and at all the long hair on the boys. Don't schools around here have rules about that?"

"I don't know if other schools do. I don't even want to be concerned. We don't have any dress code, or hair rule, or any of that. Sure, I might think girls look better in dresses, for example. But that's not the way it is, so I just put it out of my mind. It's only a question of taste anyway. And besides, I trust the basic good sense of kids. If we have a banquet, the kids dress well for it. And hair—I think hair is a safe, convenient way to show your individuality. I think it's fine. What do you think of the team?"

"They seem to be doing well," I said. "Does it bother you there's going to be a book about it?"

"Naw. Why?"

"Well, I just thought there could be some things that might embarrass a school or principal."

"I'm not worried about it," he said, smiling. "I depend on Bud Fowles. He's a good coach, a damn good man."

Coach Fowles was not so much worried about being able to score on Greeley as he was about stopping their straight-ahead, hard-running offense. Greeley ran from an unusual box formation:

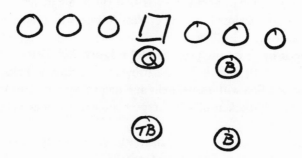

For the past two seasons, Laketown had tried unsuccessfully to stop them with the five-four laura. This week the coaches instituted a special four-four. Jim Petrowski would drop back out of the line to play inside linebacker with Bruce Stacey, and Barry Brill would be brought in to join Rich Schenkle as the other outside linebacker.

"Inside linebackers," Coach Fowles said, sketching the alignments on the blackboard, "watch for the counters." A counter had the quarterback turning toward the box and faking to the man going to that side, and handing off instead the other way, to a back crisscrossing to the weak side. "Your job is, don't watch the quarterback, watch the football. There's an imaginary line through the center. If the quarterback starts in the direction away from you, don't cross that imaginary line until you're sure where the ball is. Because they will counter right back at you. Any questions?"

"Have they ever run a wingback reverse?"

"No. I've looked at movies all the way back six or seven years ago, and I've never seen that."

"Well, we can't go by that," Bradford McClure said, "because Laketown has never run a four-four defense against them either."

"Okay, good point. Let's assume that they do try to run some kind of reverse to that wide man coming back to the other side. We still have the linebackers watching the ball, and, on paper at least, we've got people accountable for every area. The outside linebackers will hold their areas.

"Now, they've been scouting us, and they can read the papers too. They know we won the first game on a long pass. They know we threw the ball well in the second game too. So it's obvious they will be working this week on pass defense. There are two ways to play pass defense. One is what we call almost an eight-three principle, eight people trying to get the quarterback. The other is to have a lot of people playing back. I can't stand here and tell you exactly what they're going to do, but I would guess they'll try to play us a four-four-three. They might try to play us a five-three-three which is what they did last year when they shut off our running game. But it makes no difference. If they try to play us a five-three-three, they're giving us one of the flats, on one side or the other. They *have* to. That's *their* problem. I'm not going to tell them they're making a mistake. But even if they use a four-four, which is stronger against the pass, we *run* better than they realize. It turns out that we run *very* well.

"Their coach traditionally does not believe in a lot of stunts, but they might change that. They might have their linebackers coming some of the time. But that isn't any problem either, because our linemen are taught to protect the inside gap first."

He sketched what he assumed the Greeley four-four would look like, the four linebackers close behind the four linemen, but spread a bit wider. He drew in the Laketown I formation, with a flanker on the right. "Now don't quote me on this, but I feel almost sure they'll have to give man-and-a-half coverage over here, on our flanker, on Don Heidner. Their outside linebacker will have to be involved helping the defensive halfback on Don—almost *have* to do it. Then we *should* be able to run in through there, with Don drawing that linebacker out. And I'll tell you what: We should be able to *throw* on it too, on whatever defense they put up. I don't think it matters, I really don't. We've got a passer who really throws accurately, and we've got several kids who catch." Rich Schenkle frowned slightly as he looked at the floor. I didn't then understand why.

Coach Fowles put the chalk down. "Boys, people have been calling me. A coach called me today and he said, 'Wow, what a victory!' He couldn't believe what we did last week, and the week before. I know we've been surprising a lot of people. But it's not surprising to me, because this team has improved day by day. You can see it. I think we hit our all-time low about four weeks ago down in Port Chester, but that was good for us. That was a learning experience. I'm glad it happened. Because now we are improving so fast people can't believe it."

The team drilled especially hard. Juniors pushed so quickly through the tires that a few seniors, like old unionists whose work pace is threatened by ambitious apprentices, hissed at them to ease up. Linemen sweated in the still-warm temperatures as they banged into the blocking sled. The backs, with both a running game and a passing game now confirmed, seemed to take themselves more seriously.

Jonny ran the Greeley box attack at the defense. During the scrimmage period, when Laketown worked against a mock opponents' lineup, the reserves scrambled into the huddle for a chance to work with the regulars. The coaches, of course, watched the Laketown lineup more closely than the opponents'. Therefore, the opponents' lineup was often devoid of regulars, who didn't particularly want to bang themselves up when the coaches' eyes were on the other side. (Laketown used no dummies in its scrimmages, the players preferring to practice against live bodies.)

Jonny ran both offenses, partly because he could so deftly pick up and organize the opponents' attack, and partly because he liked to play all the time. Occasionally, when Ted O'Neill took over the helm, Jonny would try to sneak into a defensive linebacker spot on the opponents' team, but he was always chased by the coaches.

This week, the "Greeley" offense seemed confused and erratic. I asked guard Jack Forrest, another who worked with both offenses, if it wasn't too much each week to try to master the other team's offense to test the Laketown defense, while at the same time trying to improve the Lakeown offense.

"Naw," he said, "we gotta do it."

"Wouldn't it be better," I asked, "if the team just concentrated on doing what *it* does best, rather than worrying about what the opponent is going to do?"

"No way," he said. "We wouldn't know what to do on Saturday if we didn't work this way."

To save the center of the game field, the team scrimmaged along the sidelines at the ends, moving across the field rather than up and down it.

On offense, so many backs were trying to get first-string action that none of them got to play much. Stu Rosenman, who had lost his fullback's job to Ben Schenkle, and Keith Allen, who so badly wanted to play tailback, pushed into the huddle often. Then there were Ken Furst, who wanted to play tailback besides defensive safety; Brian Purcell, who also wanted to take the tailback's job from Al Stacey; and Bruce Stacey who wanted to play fullback full time. Competing players set their own rules about frequency of alternating. Ben Schenkle didn't like to argue, so he got to run with the ball least of all.

On defense, Coach Fowles was trying to solve his end problem. On one side, Stan Beronski was unchallenged. But Coach Fowles was not fully satisfied with Steve Barker at the other end. "Steve is tough," he said to me, "but we never know what he's gonna do. We don't know where he's going to line up, we don't know whether he's going to get penetration in the backfield or drift along the line. He makes too many mistakes."

So he tried Stu Rosenman there, and was disappointed again by the same characteristic which had lost Stu the fullback spot: He didn't seem aggressive enough. Then he tried Freddie Delaney. As long as somebody told Freddie where to line up on each play, he was all right.

And Freddie was trying hard. He was concentrating so fully on lining up correctly against the various offensive sets that he didn't know he was dragging an eight-foot tail.

John Finch had come up to him and patted him on the back, telling him he was doing fine. Freddie had grinned shyly. Meanwhile John had tied a long cloth strip onto the back of Freddie's headband. The coaches said nothing. Freddie didn't discover it until he tripped over it four plays later.

Not only was I sharing more and more the emotion of the season with the players, but also I was becoming more vicariously involved with the game itself. The simple donning of football shoes on the opening day of practice was my first intrusion into a game I had never been big enough to play. Later I enjoyed retrieving the ball between plays. And now, with Ben Schenkle sitting it out so much while other backs ran, I got the chance to center for him for extra-point practice. I was proud of my snaps back to his holder, Don Heidner. But then Ben connected too far up on the ball and drove it into the back of my head. I went over to stand beside Freddie Delaney.

"Hit in the head, huh?" he said.

"You finally got rid of your tail," I said brusquely.

THURSDAY, September 30

I sensed a letdown. The defense had been tenacious all week, the offensive line quick as waterbugs. "Never has Laketown been quicker off the ball than this year," Coach Fowles said.

But now they seemed bored defending against the Greeley plays, and driving easily through the Greeley defense.

"Coach is really psyched up for Greeley," Jim Petrowski told me.

"How about you?" I asked.

"Aw, you know, I'm always ready. Since I'm not big, mental attitude is like 100 percent of the game for me. But Coach is, wow! He's really freaked out."

Jim Marshall said to Bradford McClure, "You're going to be eaten alive on Saturday. That guy on you is six-two, two hundred and five."

Bradford shrugged.

Bruce Stacey missed practice again this week, due to a groin pull and to another huge mysterious boil—apparently of the same type that Stan Beronski had last week—on his rump. The appearance of the boil led of course to comments about its sexual derivations. Bruce had been out with the team, but not making contact. This was his third week without full practice, and Bradford grumbled about it.

"Other guys have been hurt, but they still practice," he said. "Like Stan, or Rich—they're always working and hitting."

"I'm surprised to hear you say that," I said. "Before Bruce got hurt, it seemed to me he worked awfully hard."

"He's not a bad guy," Bradford said. "But he worked hard at the beginning because he thought he had a shot at being captain. He's got a thing about showing how bad he's hurt."

There was almost a curricular disaster during school today. In phys.-ed. class, Jonny was supposed to be pitching horseshoes. He deserted the pits, however, and wandered into the cafeteria, dressed in his white gym shorts. According to the Laketown High School Athletic Department's rules and regulations, discovery of a football player cutting class would mean suspension from the next game. Jonny was alert to that, and would have slipped cleanly away if somebody hadn't sneaked up behind him and ripped his shorts off. The athletic director let him off with a warning.

FRIDAY, October 1

On the blackboard today for the prepractice meeting was a diagram of the Greeley offense with the first name of each player written over his position.

"We're not going to purposely antagonize people," Coach Fowles said. "But I do want you to go out there and purposely try to disturb their concentration. In golf, if you're putting, people aren't allowed to make noise. At a gymnastics meet it's like a morgue, it's so quiet. In football you're allowed to make noise. Not when the quarterback is calling their signals, but other times. Disturb their concentration. Because concentration is all a state of mind. One reason we're going to beat Greeley is because our state of mind is going to be better than theirs. Also we're going to hit harder than they will. We're going to be quicker. And I'll tell you something else: We are going to be better football players. We're prepared physically and mentally. We've had a good week.

"Now. A couple things we have to talk about, and then we'll get out of here and have another good practice. *Does everybody hear this?*"

The players were stone quiet as if breathing were a violation of the Laketown High School Athletic Department's rules and regulations.

"We got a break today like you wouldn't believe. I was down in the cafeteria today, so I know what the situation was completely. I spoke to my boy, Ted O'Neill." He looked down at Ted O'Neill, and the tall quarterback-end was smiling nervously. "Hi, Ted, how you doin?"

Ted twitched in his seat. He had been the second athlete, the second football player, the second *quarterback* to cut a phys.-ed. class this week. Instead of shooting arrows, he'd shown up in the cafeteria.

"Boys, the athletic director did not *have* to give Ted a break. And if that happens again, I don't care if the boy is all-universe, he is not going to play in the next game. I don't want you to wander off into Lower Slobovia if you're supposed to be pitching horseshoes or something else. And if you do it, that's *it*. Nothing I can do about it. *Do we all understand that?* But I want to compliment you on not cutting classes generally. You've been pretty good about it. All right, let's talk about the football game we're going to play tomorrow."

He turned to the blackboard and drew the offensive and defensive Laketown alignments. "I want everybody who's going to play football tomorrow to come up here and tell this team what his job is at his position."

While they were filing up one at a time, a big reserve lineman named Bill McCord drew a caricature of Ben Schenkle on the desktop. Stan Beronski leaned over his desk to remove his contact lenses for practice. He, like Jim Petrowski, shunned visual aids for games, and played with dim eyesight.

"Will we start right off with the four-four defense?" Bradford Mc-Clure asked.

"Sure," Coach Fowles said. "Keep in mind they will probably try to get a quick score on us. But we know that defense. We *know* it. I can't believe how well we've learned it in one week. All right, phone calls."

He put his foot upon a chair and leaned forward, his eyes narrowed in a wry smile. "Tonight if I make a phone call and I don't hear somebody's voice. . . . " He put his foot down and walked slowly up the aisle, sweeping his gaze across the room as bits of laughter broke out. ". . . If I don't hear somebody's voice tonight, that's *it*. Understand me, Joe?"

Joe Knowland, the reserve end who had not been allowed to dress last Saturday because he hadn't been home for the phone call Friday night, grinned and blushed and nodded.

"That's *it*. I mean, I think you're a great guy, but that has nothing to do with it. The team comes first. I don't care if your name begins with an S, when that clock strikes ten, who do you think I'm calling first?"

"Me," Joe said, with laughter around him.

"Heh, heh, that's right, Joe. Hey, Joe, your mother sounds like a great woman." He walked back to the front of the room, still smiling. "You listen to her and you'll be all right. When I called Joe Friday night, his mother answered and she said, 'Oh, he doesn't have to be home yet.' I said, '*Doesn't* he?' And she said, 'Naw, he doesn't have to be home because the coach never calls until 10:30.' "

The room erupted in laughter, cheers, and applause.

"Jim Marshall, you had a question?"

"You said you make the phone calls at ten o'clock. What happens if somebody's not home at 9:30 and you call then?"

"Hey, Jim, that's the first thing somebody would ask that knows nothing about you people. All anybody with that question would have to do is go out there on August 25, the first day of practice, and watch you guys hanging on the bars, running up the hill, doing the sprints—and they'll see the price you people pay to play football. And after doing all that hard work, who wants to throw it away? I been making the phone calls for six years, and that's the first time somebody stayed out, and I know that's going to be the last time."

He looked out the window, then spoke softly to his team. "Okay, gentlemen, this time tomorrow we are going to be defeating Horace Greeley in a football game. We are going to be fine tomorrow. I can't wait." He shook his head as if in wonder. "I *can't wait* for tomorrow to come. Because this is a different year, a different team, and we are going to win."

Coach Branahan stepped up to the blackboard. "Uh, guys, I don't know whether I ought to be doing this, but here it is." On the left he wrote "116," and on the right, "12." He pointed to the figure on the left. "This is the total score in recent years for Greeley, and this," he pointed to the other figure, "is Laketown's. We have not scored on Greeley in three years. Maybe you want to think about that."

In the locker room Keith Allen and Bob Mills got into a friendly wrestling match, and Keith dumped Bob heavily against a locker. Jonny threw down his shoulder pads. "Come on!" he yelled at them, "We have a serious game tomorrow, guys. Cut it out before somebody hurts somebody."

After he made the phone calls, Buddy Fowles and I sat with glasses of cream sherry at the kitchen table. Squeegy was putting dishes in the dishwasher. Buddy had broiled a steak outside, and served it with rosé wine in chilled glasses.

"I don't know how to evaluate practice this week," he said thoughtfully. "You never can tell. I think it probably makes less difference who scores first this year than in any of the last three years. Because the team's attitude is different. These guys will never quit, they'll come from behind if they have to. Last year we went into the Greeley game undefeated, and then they scored quickly on us and I had the feeling the heart just went out of our boys. I don't think that will happen this year."

He turned the wine glass in his hand and stared at it. "I never told the kids we'd win before, never told them flat-out we'd win. Maybe it was a mistake. I'm not sure we will. But in a way we can't lose. The kids will do their best. They've really got class. Jonathan Penchak is the best quarterback Laketown has ever had." He took his wife's hand and squeezed it. "Maybe we'll come out with the laura center against the pass. . . ."

8

The morning was cloudy and mild. A dozen Laketown players drove to the nearby town to see the JVs against the Greeley JVs. They stood along the sidelines and up in the visitors' stands and saw Greeley win 20–14, handing the Laketown junior varsity its first loss. Members of the Greeley varsity sat on the other side of the field. They were wearing their blue game jerseys.

The Laketown players sneered at that. "Will you *look*," somebody said, "they got to wear their game jerseys to be psyched for us."

In Laketown, players came to the locker room early, around twelve, to get taped and dressed. Coach Branahan taped Stan Beronski's thumb, which had been jammed in practice.

"Does your thumb hurt a lot?" I asked the lean, muscular defensive end.

"Just when it gets bumped," he said, "then it feels like it's broken."

Bruce Stacey delicately pulled on his game pants. "How's your rump?" I asked.

"Hurtin," he said.

"Where's the screwdriver?" Bradford McClure called. Somebody passed it to him and he tightened the screws which held his faceguard onto his helmet. Ted O'Neill did the same.

Several of the players were ready at one o'clock, a half hour before they were supposed to start warming up for the two o'clock game. They milled around quietly. At 1:30 the team started loosening up outside.

"I am going to be *so* loose today," Jonny said, firing a bullet into Al Stacey's gut. "I'm gonna pick 'em apart."

Bruce Stacey paced tensely back and forth alone, staring at the ground, clenching and unclenching his fists.

"How about his injuries?" I asked Coach Fowles.

"He'll be ready," he said.

Just before the team went in for its time without the coaches, a shower whirred across the woods and swept over the game field, sending cheerleaders and baton twirlers scurrying toward the school. Then it passed.

The team shoved into the locker room.

"Let's go Laketown," Jonny said quietly. "Let's think about it."

After a moment, Jim Marshall said, "There's over 200 kids who played here and never beat Greeley. And they'd give their RIGHT ARMS to be in your place RIGHT NOW! Because they know WE can beat them!"

"Just think, Laketown," Rich Schenkle said, barely controlling his voice, "Seven fuckin years. SEVEN FUCKIN YEARS WE HAVEN'T BEAT THIS SHIT TEAM!" He turned and slugged a locker with his padded fist.

"They're no pros, Laketown," Bruce Stacey said.

"Think about it, Laketown," Jonny said, "think about it. Last time we beat them the seniors were in FIFTH GRADE."

Rich Schenkle's fists were still clenched. "We got a chance today to be the first team in eight years to beat a Horace Greeley team," he said. "They proved they could lose last Saturday. But don't think, I mean, they might have had a twenty-game winning streak busted, but they don't plan to start no fuckin LOSING STREAK."

"They're good, Laketown," Jonny said, his voice low, "but we're better."

From the back of the room came a voice: "Just remember that fuckin CAKE they sent us in the locker room. It just shows you how much fuckin RESPECT they have for us. They think we're SHIT!"

"We're still nobody to them."

"We got a lot to prove to them, seniors," Jack Forrest said.

"Hey, we've won by 8–6 and 14–6," Jonny said. "Those aren't big scores. We have to WORK."

"Laketown," Bruce Stacey said, "we were undefeated last year too when we met this team."

"We ain't never scored on 'em, seniors," Jack Forrest said. "We ain't never done SHIT!"

"They don't give two shits WHAT our record is," Rich Schenkle said.

Bradford McClure slapped a dingy brown arm pad against his leg, and pulled it on. "For seven years we been talkin about how bad we wanna beat em and shit," he said. "Let's not talk about it anymore. It didn't do any good last year, it didn't do any good the years before. Talk doesn't do anything. Let's go out and show 'em."

"Let's just DO it," Jonny said.

"Just pop somebody as hard as you can," Bruce Stacey said, "and we'll win the game."

"Know yourself," Jonny said, "and then we know we can do what we want to. This is the team that can do it, Laketown, because we can move the ball, and we can take it down their throats. This is a FAMILY this year, not like last year. Last year they were great guys, but they couldn't pull together when it counted."

The room was quiet as he went on.

"Think about the way we've won, Laketown, like champions, playing our guts out. That's all we got to do today. Don't get all emotional and start crying like last year. Just go out there and beat the shit out of Horace Greeley."

"Can't get much simpler than that, Laketown," Rich Schenkle said. "You do your job and we'll win, don't do your job we'll lose. Just think about it."

"I hope everyone in here is really, really scared shitless," Bruce Stacey said.

"I know I am," Rich said.

"You BETTER be," Bruce went on, "because. . . we were at their school today. You know what they had? You should have seen their locker room. Get Penchak, get 12, get 42, get 51—get these guys and you win. They think if they can get two or three of us out, they got it. They don't realize that we're a FAMILY, and we ALL HIT. Everyone STINGS on this team."

"That's all it takes," Jonny said. "This year I want to be 8 and 0. I don't wanna be any cake 6 and 2, 7 and 1. That's when you compromise, when you lose. You go out there and say, well, maybe we won't win. Maybe I'll slow down on this play. That's when we lose. If

:145:

you're hurt, get out of the game. But if you're not, you better hit like you mean it."

Coach Fowles walked in quickly, speaking in a calm voice as he came. "Boys, this is it. Coach Branahan, you have anything you want to say?"

"Yeah. Hey, let's remember, first play of the game last week they went for the bomb. Their JV team has done it two weeks in a row. Outside linebacker—Rich or Bruce or whoever it happens to be—hit that end as hard as you can if they're in that box. Ray Meister, make sure you're keying on that slot man or that blocking back. Ken Furst and Karl Walsh, let's really play football out there in the secondary, on every play, but *really* be ready on that first play for the long one."

"Boys," Coach Fowles said, "the last time we beat this football team was on *this* field, here at home. You people were in the fifth and fourth grades. Of all the teams we've had, I have more confidence in you than in any other football team. And I'll tell you why. Rule number one: You do your best. You believe in yourselves, and *we* believe in *you*. Forty-eight minutes out there. Do your best. This is it. You've got the ability to win this football game, gentlemen, and you *will* win this football game. Who we gonna beat?"

"GREELEY!"

"WHO WE GONNA BEAT?"

"GREELEY, GREELEY, GREELEY!"

By game time it was sunny and warm. A large crowd overflowed the bleachers and surrounded the field behind the snow fence.

Rich Schenkle, wearing bright new white hand pads, and Jim Marshall went to the center of the field for the toss. The other two captains, Stan Beronski and this week's honorary captain Al Stacey, waited at the hashmarks. Laketown lost the toss, and would kick off.

The band slogged onto the field, wearing green blazers. A breeze ruffled the American flag, carried by a girl at the front, and the green miniskirts of the baton twirlers. Bruce Stacey stood apart from the team and watched. Jim Petrowski paced along the bench behind the team, seething with tension, gritting his teeth. Across the field, Greeley stood attentively for the National Anthem, their white helmets glistening, their blue short-sleeved jerseys neatly tucked into their white pants.

Greeley returned Jim Marshall's kick to its 41, then opened up passing as expected. The first was incomplete over the middle. Next, the quarterback rolled to his left on an option, but Stan Beronski got his arm, and then Jim Petrowski piled into him for a loss of two. On third down, the quarterback dropped straight back to throw, and was hit by Stan and Jim before he even got a foot planted, for a loss of nine. Greeley punted to the Laketown 28. Jonny led the offense onto the field, and Bradford McClure shook his hand as they passed.

Al Stacey tried the right side twice for four yards. Jonny's pass aimed for Ted O'Neill slanting out was batted dead at the line of scrimmage. O'Neill's low punt barely cleared the arms of the rushing linemen, and rolled only to the Greeley 43.

Mixing straight-ahead power plays and tricky counters, Greeley marched quickly to the Laketown 20. Then the quarterback faked a running play to the left and rolled back to his right. Linebacker Barry Brill came up the middle on a stunt, lunged, and got the passer's waist just as he cocked his arm. But still he threw as Barry tried to drag him down. Safetyman Karl Walsh had let the end get behind him in the end zone, and the pass floated perfectly into the end's arms for the touchdown.

They tried running to the left for the extra points, but Stan came through untouched and dropped the runner in the backfield. Six to nothing.

"Barry, grab his ARMS when you get in there!" Coach Fowles shouted at the linebacker who had almost stopped the touchdown play. Then he spun on Karl Walsh. "Karl, what happened back there? HUH? Tell me Karl? Don't walk away, just tell me what happened."

"He just beat me, Coach," Karl said, his head down.

"Wow, just like that we're behind," Jack Forrest said, shaking his head.

"Okay, okay!" Coach Fowles yelled, clapping and walking briskly among his stunned defense. "It's all right. We'll get it right back. The offense will get it right back, and the defense will do it's job. Let's go!"

Ken Furst brought the kickoff back from the 10 to the 25. Jonny overthrew Don Heidner in the left flat. Second down was supposed to be a wide sweep, but Jonny's pitch to Ben Schenkle swinging to his left bounced off the little fullback's leg. Jonny dove to recover, but for a loss of seven.

"We should be running *dives*," Coach Fowles muttered to Coach Branahan.

Ted O'Neill juggled and lost a down-and-out pass as he went out of bounds. On fourth down Ted punted miserably again, to the Laketown 37.

Stan Beronski continued to blast into the backfield. As the quarterback cocked his arm to throw, Stan barreled into him and knocked the ball loose. It looked to us like a fumble, but the official ruled it an incomplete pass. Greeley was held, and punted to the Laketown seven.

A Greeley offside penalty moved the ball to the 12. But then Jonny, rolling right and looking for Don Heidner, was trapped and thrown just a yard from his own goal line. Al Stacey on a dive went up the middle to the 12. Then on third-down tackle Tom Kase jumped offside, and the Harvesters were back on the seven. Jonny rolled right and this time hit Don Heidner in the flat. Don spun away from a tackler and bulled ahead to the 17, where he was tumbled out of bounds in front of the band. That made it fourth and inches for a first down.

Jonny called time-out and came over to the bench. "Can we go for it, Coach? Quarterback sneak?"

Coach Fowles looked out at the ball, contemplating the dangerous field position. He sighed. "Wow," he said softly.

"We can do it, Coach," Jonny said. "They'll push 'em right out. We only got a couple inches to go."

"Okay, Jonny, go ahead. Go on a high number. DO A JOB, OFFENSE!"

They lined up, with Jim Marshall hunched over the ball. Jonny started the long count, meant to draw the defense offside. He would go on three. "GO, GO, HUT-ONE. . . . " But Jim, tense and anxious, moved the ball early. The official whistled the penalty before the play got off, and Jim, his head down, trotted off the field to be replaced by Rich Merrill who would center for the punt.

"What the hell is this?" Bradford McClure muttered, standing as usual behind and away from the rest of the team. He kept his arms folded. "This sucks."

Ted O'Neill punted out to the 40, but the Greeley blockers chopped down the onrushing tacklers like tenpins, and the ball-carrier cruised to the sideline and down it to the Laketown 12. The first quarter ended.

On first down, the quarterback handed off to the first man through on the right, and end Steve Barker brought him down hard on the 10.

"HOLD 'EM, DEFENSE!" Jonny yelled from the sidelines. "WE'LL GET IT BACK!"

The Harvesters lined up in a goal-line stance, heads low, rear-ends high, with Rich Schenkle in the middle of the six-man line. A play came in from the Greeley bench, and the lineman whispered it to the quarterback. Greeley lined up in an I. The quarterback faked to the first man through and went back, spun, and threw a jump-pass intended for the back to whom he had faked. Somehow Rich Schenkle had got back, and he leaped, tipped the ball with his hands, then grabbed it and brought it down, curled around it like a baby, with Bruce Stacey standing over him protectively on the five-yard line.

The crowd and bench erupted in cheers, and Jonny brought his offense back on with his fist waving in the air.

Ben Schenkle wove beautifully to the 15. Then Al Stacey followed Ben's blocks for three straight plays to the 26, and Laketown had its initial first down of the day. Greeley stopped two running plays. Stu Rosenman brought in a pass play from the bench, and on third down Jonny threw for Stu on the 50, but the Greeley defender made a leaping interception, turned, faked the tacklers around him, and headed for the sideline, trying to outrace the last man he had to beat, Jonny Penchak. Jonny played the angle perfectly, and threw a body-block that dropped the runner on the 25. A clipping penalty against Greeley moved the ball back to the 45, but the Laketown offense came off the field sagging.

Jonny kicked the turf on the sideline. A man who'd been invited to sit with the team waved a pedantic fist at Jonny. "Threw off balance, boy, off balance. Got to set up better, boy. . . "

"For CHRISTSAKE," I found myself yelling at him. "Not NOW. LEAVE HIM ALONE!"

Laketown continued stunting its linebackers, forcing Greeley linemen to block them, and leaving Stan Beronski free to rush. Stan hurried the quarterback on second down, then hit him and forced him to throw wildly on third. With fourth and five, Greeley ran a straight power dive from the box and got the first down on the Laketown 30.

The quarterback was again rushed on first down, and threw into the ground. The Greeley coach sent in a screen pass from the bench, but Al Stacey read it perfectly, slipped through the blocking wall, and popped the receiver for a 10-yard loss. On third down the quarterback was again rushed and threw incomplete.

The Greeley punt bounced on the seven, but rather than let it roll into the end zone, Brian Purcell fielded it and turned upfield. He slipped and went down at the 11.

"Know where you are on the *field!*" Coach Fowles barked at Brian.

Ben Schenkle dove twice behind Jack Forrest's blocks, bringing the ball out to the 15. Then Jonny threw long to Stu Rosenman, playing tight end, but he and Ted O'Neill ended up at the same spot. They bumped, the ball bounced off Stu's hands, and then Ted's, and fell incomplete. Laketown punted to the Greeley 47.

On first down Bradford McClure ripped through and got the quarterback by the ankles for an eight-yard loss. The line was in on the passer twice more. Greeley punted into the end zone.

The half ended. The team started dragging toward the locker room. Coach Fowles ran in among them. "Come on, RUN IT OFF! Laketown NEVER walks!" And they ran in.

The team angrily pushed into the locker room.

"Crummy pass, ONE CRUMMY PASS!"

Gatorade bottles clinked around.

"Let's get it together. We can do it. Keep our energy."

"Cause their defense is WORRIED about us," Jack Forrest said. "They don't know what the hell we're doin, and all we're doin is runnin at 'em. Hey backs, just cut right off us and you GO, guaranteed."

"Hey look," Jonny said, waving a Gatorade bottle in his big hand, "nobody wants to lose to Greeley. Don't compromise. NO COMPROMISE!" He was answered by several assenting shouts. "Hey, listen. They're not that tough. They got SIX points, right? They're not hittin us. NO MORE! They got that because we weren't ready. WE'RE READY THIS HALF!"

Jim Petrowski's high-pitched shout came from a corner of the room. "Hey, guys, they got ONE touchdown on us, and we could get it all back if everybody would THINK, and get on the punting team and the kickoff team and do everything RIGHT! WE CAN BEAT 'EM! Hey offense, hold that ball longer."

"That offense is big," Rich Schenkle said, "but they don't HIT. For their size they just don't hit, not half as good as they could. Defense, a little secret: Just give em one shot in their stomach with your flipper and they won't want to block again. Because I know. I did it to THREE GUYS."

"Get it together, guys."

"Their defense is pussies."

"All right," Coach Fowles said, striding into the room. "Heads up. Let's start with defense. First of all we made a mental mistake on that touchdown. Karl Walsh is not superman. Our end was not lined up properly on defense, so he didn't slow up their end, and therefore their quarterback had time to throw the football. And Steve Barker, that's one reason why you're on the bench right now. And Stu Rosenman, you're going to *play*. You line up outside the end and you fire across the line. The best pass defense in the world, gentlemen—you've seen it—a good, hard rush. They don't know *who* to block on that rush. That quarterback is *shaking*. Right now we've made every mistake in the book, believe it or not. I can't believe what I've seen this team do wrong the first half. And we're *still* in the game. And you know what that's a sign of? We're going to *win* it."

He smiled and held out his arms. "We are going to win. Our kicking game stinks—one time we even lined up a man short because Barry Brill's picking his nose instead of being on the field. I saw somebody stop to see if one of their men was hurt, trying to be a nice guy instead of a football player. And Jim Marshall—I don't know what *you're* doin, centering the ball when we're not ready.

"Everything in the world went wrong, and think about it: We're still in the football game. We are going to win it. We are in better shape than they are. They are *dragging* right now. They're tired.

"Now, they are going to kick off to us. Jonny, when we get the football, their defense can't possibly stop a dive from the split-backfield, it's impossible. Is there any reason why you want to continually run that I and dive Ben Schenkle? Tell me now, if there is. . . "

"I only ran the dive with Ben once," Jonny said.

"Okay, all right, uh, but from the split-backfield Ben got nine yards first time we ran it."

"Coach?" Jack Forrest said. "When we run from the split-backfield they shoot their ends inside, and our ends are taking them in, and our backs are still going inside. They're not cuttin wide."

"All right, then we got to get the ball to the dive man a little sooner, and make that cut if you can. I don't know about the play-action pass against this team. Forget that, it's too slow.

"I'll tell you what, gentlemen: Our defense, we look like Laketown." He chuckled. "We really do. They don't know what to do. They don't know where we're coming from. They don't know what to do with their bootleg. Their quarterback is over there yelling at his linemen, 'Are you guys going to block or what?' We've *always* been a second-half football team. You know that. Twenty-four more minutes, and we're going to take it right down their throats.

"Stu Rosenman, you dropped a pass you should have caught with your teeth. Where's Stu? Come on, Stu, that should never happen.

"We want more gang-tackling. Jim Marshall, you're still asleep the first half. You're not going to play defense until you're ready to play—I'm TELLING ya. You might be the greatest guy in the world, it doesn't matter to me. The team comes first.

"Eddie McArthur," he looked over at the reserve end, "you're off the punting team. Jim Petrowski, you're *on* it. Jim, I expect you to go downfield and *belt* somebody. And don't stop to see if one of their players is hurt, like Eddie McArthur did. Brian Purcell, know where the ball is on those punts. If it's going to bounce into the end zone, let it do that. Ken Furst, when you field those kicks, turn upfield and get positive yardage. All right, any questions, comments? Ted?"

"The option will go because the end is coming inside."

"*Yes!* Jonny? Where's Jonny? Jonny, I thought you were going to call a bootleg off the inside belly a couple of times. It's there if you want it. Good comment. The stomp, pack it up! Our lineman didn't block them, Ben. Jonny Penchak recovered that fumble and saved a touchdown. Our line is not getting off on the count for the stomp, boys. It should go, I agree with you. It was a good call. . . . "

"Their ends are so quick," Jonny said.

"Well, we've got to be quicker. Rich?"

"Number 75, that tackle, is way downfield illegally on passes. One time right in front of the referee. I told him."

"Well, tell *me* too."

"He sees him come walking right back to the huddle too."

"Well, we are not going to complain about the officials. We're going to beat Greeley playing football. Gentlemen, I'll tell you the truth. In the second half we're going to beat them. It's as simple as that. But you've got to give it everything you have in your stomach. You're wearing them down. And you're in better shape than *anybody* we play."

An official leaned in. "Coach," he said, holding up one hand, "five minutes, two to get down there and three to warm up."

"All right, thank you. Now boys, think about what we've just said. We are making more mistakes than we've made since the Port Chester scrimmage, and we're still in the football game. And we've got the kind of a team that's going to win this football game. Who's in better shape?"

"LAKETOWN!"

"Who hits harder?"

"LAKETOWN!"

Coach Fowles paused and looked slowly around at the faces leaning toward him in anticipation. Then he said very softly, "Who we gonna beat?"

"GREELEY! GREELEY. . . . "

The cheerleaders were still dancing joyfully when Al Stacey took the kick-off and broke free for a second to the near sideline. Then, he was hit head-on, the ball popped out, and Greeley had it on the Laketown 35.

"MY GOD!" I yelled at Coach Fowles, but he was already urging on his defense.

"You got that quarterback rattled," he yelled as they trotted onto the field.

Two line plunges got Greeley nothing. On third down the halfback took a pitchout wide to his right and appeared to be setting up to throw, when end Stu Rosenman tore into him right above the knees and drove him over backward into Stan Beronski who had come all the way from the opposite side. The halfback was helped off the field.

Greeley punted short, and Ken Furst took it near the 15 and returned it to the Laketown 22. Ben Schenkle, slipping like a trout, got a first down on the 34. Then Al Stacey butted tacklers aside and went straight up the middle for a first down on the Greeley 49, putting Laketown in Greeley territory for the first time in the game.

Jonny started using the bootleg. He faked beautifully to Ben, and hid the ball on his hip and went around right end to the 44. He repeated the play, running by the defensive right end who was still watching Ben, getting down to the 30.

Jonny hit Ted O'Neill on a slant-out to the sidelines at the 18. Cowbells and horns and the band's drums joined the crowd's cheering. Ted O'Neill couldn't get up.

"What is it, Ted?" Coach Fowles said, crouching beside his end who was lying across the sideline on his back.

"Cramp, coach, this leg."

"All right, pull him off, get him off the field."

We carefully pulled Ted across the sideline so that Laketown would not be charged with a time-out. Ted massaged his calf and stood up.

Ben Schenkle sliced to the 13. Jim Marshall leaned over to speak to Jonny before they huddled. Jonny nodded. On the next play, he faked to Ben, sucking the defense toward the fullback, and hid the ball behind his hip and swung all alone around the left end for the touchdown. He raised the ball triumphantly over his head as he crossed the goal line.

Ben's kick was wide to the right. With the score 6–6, it was a new ballgame, for a few minutes.

Greeley took the kickoff to the 31. Then seven straight times they ran power plays over right tackle. Catching Bruce Stacey stunting, and moving tackle Bradford McClure both in and out, they went to the 46; then countered to the Laketown 48; then drove to the 32; then to the 14. It was like a nightmare; the coaches strained to see what was happening in the line. Then to the 12. Then to the 2. And finally through the same hole for the score.

On the try for the extra points, Bruce Stacey finally slammed that hole shut, ramming the fullback behind the line and driving him over backward. Greeley led, 12–6.

Jim Petrowski, playing linebacker today, had been removed during the Greeley drive, and had paced the sideline fuming. Now his words blistered the air as he stomped back and forth in front of the bench. Coach Fowles said something to him, and he yelled back, "I'LL SHOW YOU ON THE FIELD!"

Coach Fowles wheeled to face him. "Just keep your mouth shut and help the *team* right now!"

He called Bradford McClure over. "They're not just blowing through," Bradford explained. "Lot of times Bruce is calling me outside, right? I'm going out and the linebacker in back of me is getting blocked in. I don't know what in the hell he's doing. And they're just running right off tackle."

"We'll get it right back," Jonny said, adjusting his helmet. The offense, not disheartened, was poised on the sideline, anxious to get back to work.

Don Heidner ran the kickoff back to the 30. Inside power plays moved it to a first down on the Laketown 44. Jonny pitched right on a stomp to Ben, and the fullback swept to the Greeley 48.

The fourth quarter began, with a fourth and two for Laketown on the Greeley 48. Coach Fowles signaled for a time-out. Jonny came over to the bench.

"Want the bootleg again?" he asked the coaches.

"What do you think?" Coach Fowles asked Coach Branahan. They both looked out at the ball and thought for a few seconds as Jonny watched them.

"Fake the inside belly," Coach Branahan said, "and Jonny on a bootleg."

"That's a slow developer though," Coach Fowles said, "really gotta hustle."

"I like to fake it off the dive better, Coach," Jonny said.

"Okay," the coaches said together.

Jonny faked to Ben Schenkle straight ahead and bootlegged to his left, diving over a tackler to make the first down by inches.

Then Jonny rolled right and threw deep for Don Heidner, who stole it away from two defenders, falling on the six.

Coach Fowles sent in Bruce Stacey with a pass play. "It's dangerous," he said, "but let's try it."

Ted O'Neill slanted to the right side and Jonny drilled it to him in the end zone.

With the score 12–12, Jonny came to the bench to discuss the extra-point play which might decide the game.

"I think we can get two," Jonny said, hoping to run the ball.

"We don't *need* two," Coach Fowles said. "All we need is one. What do you think, Sandy? Want to kick it? We got a good kicker."

Coach Branahan chewed his gum and stared off into the distance.

"I think we can kick it, Coach," he said.

"Let's kick it, Jonny," Coach Fowles said.

Jonny stepped off the field, the kicking team went on, and the two coaches turned to face each other and silently shook hands.

Don Heidner called the signals, took the snap from Rich Merrill and Ben kicked it through perfectly. The team ran off proudly, grasping thumbs in power handshakes. Laketown led for the first time, 13–12.

Coach Fowles gathered his defense together at the end of the bench and told them to get down on one knee. "All right, defense," he said, "this is it. Now the offense got us two touchdowns, so it's up to you people."

"We'll do it."

"We can do it."

"I *know* you're going to do it. Play back, watch for the long passes. We're going to do it. Where's Bruce Stacey? Bruce, we're not calling any stunts right now. Play square, heads-up, hardnosed football."

Then he walked away and called Jim Petrowski over alone. Laketown would now abandon the four-four defense and return to the familiar five-four laura. He planned to put Jim back in at middle guard.

"First time you don't cover your area you're comin back," he told Jim.

"I can explain. . . ."

"There's nothing *to* explain, what are you talkin about! I want to see *action* out there!"

Greeley took the kickoff to its 37, and the regular Laketown defensive team went in. Jim Petrowski dashed to his middle-guard post and got down on his knees to await the play, bouncing up and down like a coiled spring.

They came right at Jim on the first play, and he hit the fullback directly in the midsection and put him down for no gain. Then they swung wide to the right for a first down on the 49. Laketown's defense angrily charged back into its huddle.

Greeley came back at the same right-tackle spot through which they had run seven straight times for their last touchdown. Rich Schenkle lunged at the big fullback and caught his arm, spilling the ball. Tackle Bob Mills dove on it, and the Harvester defense came jubilantly off, its job done to near perfection.

Laketown was held, and punted to the Greeley 15. With five minutes left in the game, the Harvester defense was called upon again.

The strong Greeley fullback ripped through the right side for eight. Bradford McClure was rolling on the ground in pain. Coach Fowles and the team doctor sprinted in.

"It's just a cramp," Bradford said.

The doctor kneaded the calf, and Bradford got up and came slowly off.

The fullback went again at the right side, but this time four Harvesters hit him behind the line. Again they ran that side, opening it up this time for a first down on the 40. Bradford went back in. The Greeley quarterback glanced over at him, then called the same play. Bradford and Rich Schenkle hit the fullback for no gain, and the Greeley star went off holding his arm.

Greeley then went the other way, running wide to the left. But Stan Beronski threw his blocker aside, caught the runner around the waist, and spun him down for a loss back to the 35. On fourth down, they threw deep to the left, but safetyman Ken Furst was with the receiver, and the pass was overthrown.

The Laketown offense could now eat up the clock if they could get a first down or two. There were about three minutes left.

Inside running plays gained only five yards. With fourth and five, Jonny called time-out and came over to the bench.

Coach Branahan wanted to go for it, to try to hold onto the ball. Jonny said they could do it. Coach Fowles drew in a long breath through his clenched teeth and shook his head.

"I think we should punt, Ben, try to get it out of bounds down deep."

"We can do it, Coach," Jonny pleaded.

"Let Al Stacey run it around left end," Coach Branahan suggested.

"I don't like it, Sandy," Coach Fowles said, "but you call it."

Jonny pitched left to his tailback, but the Greeley end and cornerback were in the backfield immediately, and dragged Al down for a five-yard loss.

Greeley had the football with less than two minutes to play.

"Okay, defense, just hold on for TWO MORE MINUTES!"

"Jack Forrest was hurt on that last play," the public-address announcer boomed.

Jack was lying on the grass by the bench, holding his ribs.

:156:

"Where does it hurt, Jack," the doctor asked, gently probing the guard's rib cage, "right in here?"

"Ooooh, yeah."

"Jack," Jonny said, standing over him, "I'll send you to the best hospital in the world."

Jack smiled and groaned.

"All right, Jack, get up and walk around," the doctor said. "I think it'll be okay. Just a bruise."

The crowd cheered and applauded when Jack got up.

Greeley was now throwing, and the Laketown secondary dropped deeper to protect against the bomb. Two passes were overthrown at the Laketown 30. Coach Fowles pulled defensive end Stu Rosenman out of the game and yelled at him.

"We been working on our ends staying *outside*, why did you line up *inside?*"

"Rich Schenkle said. . . ."

"I DON'T CARE WHAT RICH SAID! When you go in you stay OUTSIDE!"

There were forty seconds left.

Greeley passed deep over the middle. The receiver, looking back for the ball, ran over safetyman Karl Walsh. Offensive interference was called. But Greeley came back to get the first down with a sideline completion on the Laketown 44. Another pass over the middle hit Rich Schenkle in the chest, but he fell over backward and dropped it. On the next play, Ken Furst stepped in front of the receiver on the 20-yard line and picked it off, to end the game.

The team raced around the field in a frenzy. Coach Fowles hugged Jonny and yelled again and again, "We DID it!"

Rich Schenkle could not speak, only groan with satisfaction as tears rolled down his cheeks.

The Greeley coach raced across the field and lifted Coach Fowles off his feet in a bear hug, congratulating him.

The team danced and jigged off the field and up to, but not into, the locker room. The players stayed outside, catching their breath, savoring their victory. Fans, parents, girl friends, came up to shake hands, hug, take pictures, watch. Then the team wanted to go into a huddle to yell out its next victim. But so heavily had Greeley weighed on their minds, that they stood looking dumbly at each other.

"Hey, Coach," Bradford McClure called to Coach Fowles, who was headed toward the Greeley locker room, "could you tell us before you go, please, who we gonna beat next week?"

He smiled and joined the team in the huddle. "Hey boys, who's got more pride?"

"LAKETOWN!"

"Next Saturday, who we gonna beat?"

"FOX LANE! FOX LANE! FOX LANE!"

The Greeley team sat on the asphalt outside their locker room, waiting to board their bus. Antiglare grease paint ran like mascara with the tears on some faces. Other faces were just somber. None spoke. The Greeley coach introduced Coach Fowles to them.

"Boys," Coach Fowles said, "you played a real fine football game today, nothing to be ashamed of. You did your best. I admire you and your coach, you played your hearts out down to the last play, and you never quit. You can be proud of yourselves. And I'll tell you something: I hope you win every other game on your schedule. You've got a fine football team."

A few of the beaten players looked silently up at Coach Fowles.

Then the two coaches went into the Laketown locker room, which was alive with happy shrieks, bustling with the joys of victory.

"You all know Coach Perelle," Coach Fowles said. "He'd like to say a few words to you."

Coach Perelle climbed up on a bench, smiling. "You might say that we two coaches have a Fowles-Perelle mutual admiration society," he said. "You've got a tremendous coach, and your game shows it. A really fine football team. Now, I know this is nonprofessional, and I hope it doesn't ever go beyond this locker room, but I hope you guys go all the way."

Cheers cascaded over the Greeley coach as he stepped down.

Outside, the two coaches stood for a few moments together.

"Nick," Coach Fowles said, "that was a real fine high school football game."

"Yes it was," said Coach Perelle, and they shook hands and parted.

"What a difference," Coach Fowles said to me as he watched the Greeley players straggle sadly toward their bus. "If we had lost, we would have looked and felt like that. But we won, and you saw our locker room. One point in a football game can make that difference in the way you feel. That really is like life. I think maybe winning and losing are too important. And it's a shame that these two football teams—one on top of the world, the other down in the dumps—can't communicate with each other right now, can't sit down like human beings and talk about how they feel. Someday we'll do that. Maybe not this year. But some day we'll sit down with our opponents after the game and get to know each other. This is not war, you know. It's just a football game. And who has more in common than two football teams?"

Running back Keith Allen, who had not played, came up to Coach Branahan in the coaches' locker room. "I finally realized today," he said, "that it was the team that counted, not individuals. That's been my trouble all along."

The team went to the Penchaks' to be served hero sandwiches, sausages, meatballs, and sodas on the backyard patio. Players served themselves from large pots, and took metal soda cans from washtubs filled with ice. The cheerleaders were there. The players were relaxed and content and tired.

"Were you very worried about making that kick?" I asked Ben Schenkle about his game-winning extra point, "or were you sure you would make it?"

"I was sure I *wouldn't* make it," he said. "I knew for sure when I took my first step that I wasn't going to hit it right."

"But you kicked it perfectly."

"Yeah."

"Hey, what a *family* this is, guys," Jonny said.

Some of the players were trying to collect money to buy goods for a party tonight at the Petrowskis'. Was I coming? I was asked.

No. My own marriage of thirteen years had just broken up, and I was in no mood to join the celebrants of Harvester togetherness. But it was a hell of a party, and echoes of it would reverberate through the season and even to the school year beyond. There would be some who would feel that the team never fully recovered from that party.

9

Perhaps it was inevitable that this team, presumably one of the weakest in years, yet now having won three straight games it was supposed to lose, all by narrow margins, capped by beating the awesome Greeley for the first time in eight years—perhaps it was inevitable that they would bust loose in a party.

Apparently it was a simple drinking party, involving maybe fifty to seventy kids at one time or another, a lot of beer, some Southern Comfort, a little grass, and a few pieces of broken china. It didn't last long. "Guys were hanging from trees by 7:30," a player said, "and it was virtually over by nine."

It did not involve the entire team, and those who did not attend, or did not stay to drink, were rankled by those who blatantly broke the training rules. "I knew if I stayed I would get into that," said one player who had looked around for ten minutes and then left, "and I just don't want to do it during the season."

Ever so tiny a wedge was thus driven into the core of the family.

Players laughed about the party, and tossed playful barbs at each other in the Fowles rec room before the coaches came down with the projector.

Coach Fowles ran the film, which for the third straight week was a technical disaster. The players had collected twenty-five cents apiece to pay the extra cost of filming this big game in color. But a hundred feet in the middle were woefully overexposed, so that the players looked like snow figures skating on ice, and only occasionally could the viewers distinguish the numbers or yard lines.

In the Lourdes film, huge hunks had been blank or overexposed; the whole first quarter of the Mamaroneck film was missing. The films, like the sod on the playing field and the zippers on the game pants, seemed to deteriorate week by week.

Typically, coach Fowles ignored that and kept his critical eye on those aspects of the game he could discern. While players joked and teased about themselves and Greeley, their coach was serious.

"It's the little things that count," he said, clanking the film back and forth over frames. "We are taking longer in the huddle on passes—that gives them away."

Receivers were shown to have been running pass patterns too close together; Ted O'Neill changed patterns en route, and Stu Rosenman didn't know the patterns to start with. Blockers were getting too high, especially Jim Marshall. Jack Forrest was wasting a step as he pulled to lead the sweeps. Kick-returners, mainly Ken Furst, were dancing too much laterally and not turning upfield quickly enough. On punts, the three men in the blocking wave five yards behind the center were leaving areas unprotected, a fault that would haunt the team a couple of weeks hence.

The turning point in the game was clearly Rich Schenkle's interception on the five-yard line. Coach Fowles ran the film back and forth several times over those frames. "That might have killed us," he said, "if they had scored right there. But what I can't figure out, Rich, is how did you get back there when you were supposed to be up in the line on the frankenstein?"

Rich smiled and looked at the floor. "I don't know," he said. A few people laughed.

"I yelled at him where the hell was he going," Bruce Stacey said.

"What were you doing, Rich?" Coach Fowles asked.

"I don't know, Coach," Rich said, squirming, smiling nervously. "I just had a feeling they were going to throw."

"Had a *feeling*, huh?" Coach Fowles said, chuckling. "Well, if they'd have run through your spot, you would have had *another* kind of feeling."

Players laughed, and Rich kept smiling and looking at the floor.

The film revealed that often Greeley players were standing around with hands on hips as plays developed away from them. Some of their blockers seemed bored.

"I think," Coach Fowles said aside to me, "he's got some kind of problem over there, some dissension or something, because it's clear some of his players didn't want to play football."

The Laketown Harvesters, too, were ripe for a letdown. Coach Fowles had that on his mind. It was time for what later became known as the "So Long, Oolong," speech.

MONDAY, October 4

The players sat in sober apprehension as Coach Fowles entered the classroom at 3:00 P.M. sharp. Around the cafeteria today the talk had not been about Fox Lane—despite the fact that the Foxes were also undefeated—but about the party at Petrowskis', whether the coach knew about it, and what he would do if he did. One rumor was that a fink player from last year had spilled it to Coach Fowles. "We're going to start off today by running a mile," Keith Allen said. "I got it from the coach himself."

Coach Fowles went right to the blackboard.

"Yesterday or Saturday or last week or the last three weeks doesn't mean a thing," he said, erasing the words left over from the English class. "All that matters is today, and getting ready for the Fox Lane game. That's the only game on our schedule. So let's start with the most important part of the football game, our defense, how to stop their offense.

"I expect everybody in this classroom to know the starting count for Fox Lane. It's 'READY, SET, HUT, HUT, HUT.' Sometimes they go on 'READY,' so be alert for that. On 'SET' they'll shift down to a three-point stance. Know their starting count. Most quarterbacks, especially in high school, will inadvertently go to the same number pretty much of the time. They run an I, they split their ends, and they like a slot left. They like to run their tailback on first and second downs, and pass on third down."

The tension in the room seemed to relax as Coach Fowles talked only football, only Fox Lane. Coach Branahan leaned against the wall, unsmiling, chewing gum, and wearing dark glasses. He had been hit in the eye with a tiny stone during the Greeley game.

Coach Fowles sketched the Fox Lane defense:

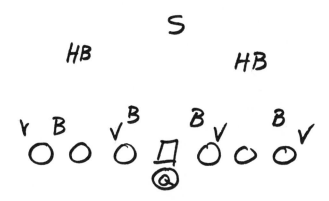

"This is a split-six," he said, "or it looks like a gap-eight. The flats are open. But one of their defensive halfbacks is six-feet-four."

He paused, and the players filled the air with questions, as if to keep this line of talk alive: "Do their linebackers stunt? . . . Are they always outside shoulder? . . . Is that guy really six-four? . . . Are their linebackers really close? . . . Are they really quick, Coach? . . ."

Coach Fowles put down the chalk. "We have a couple other things to to talk about," he said.

"The first thing I'd like to say is, we've got *five* football games left, twenty-five practices—five of them are on Friday, so you can't really even count those—and five games. And then it's all over. I get letters from kids who are disillusioned about college football, and they say, 'boy, it's not the same.' I don't care where you go to college, Notre Dame, Oklahoma, Penn State, it's not the same as high school football. We were totally dedicated at the college where I played, it was great, and yet there was something missing from high school football.

"Now, we have an opportunity, I mean *we*, everybody, the dedicated kids and the kids who right now aren't as dedicated as they should be, yo-yos and non-yo-yos alike have an opportunity to have maybe the best football team that this high school has *ever* had. So if some of you want to go out and get your head screwed on backward, you're not going to stay on this football team. It's that simple.

"If you are not committed to having a good football team, GET OUT OF

OUR LIVES! I'm not even going to *argue* about what drinking does to you physically. That's not the point. The point is, we've won three football games. At the first game every single kid on our defense was lined up in our end zone. And you know why we won the game? Because mentally we didn't have any flake-outs, or quitters, or gutless wonders on the field. That's why we won the game.

"Next, we had no business beating Mamaroneck. We have 135-pounders playing—that's a *joke*. But it's not how big you are. It's what you have in your head. It starts with your mind.

"How about wars? I think wars are sick. But wars don't start overnight, gentlemen, or not in one week. You start with a little decay here and there, and a little more and a little more—and pretty soon human beings are shooting other human beings.

"Now get the analogy. With a good football team you start with a good mental attitude, and build on it. Did it ever occur to you when we stick you up on the bars, what that does for you, hanging up there? It forces you to have a better mental attitude. I can tell you right now who the flake-outs are. You want names? I can tell you who drops off the bars when my back is turned. The flake-outs are not going to win. The winners are going to hang up there and *force* themselves to get stronger. Because it starts with your mind."

He looked around the room, which was absolutely silent.

"The third football game. You realize what you did Saturday? We did something *twice* Saturday that last year's team never did *once*. We came from behind twice. Because gentlemen, you're not quitters, you're not gutless wonders. You've come too far. You've got class.

"But we also did something Saturday that last year's team *never* did during the season. Some of you pulled a stunt I couldn't believe. There are no squealers in this room. I'm not a detective, but I hear a lot of things. People tell me things, a lot of people in town. I go down to buy a gallon of milk and people come up and tell me about things you wouldn't believe. All I have to do is listen, and I'm a good listener.

"You've only got thirty days left. If you want to get your head screwed up, you've got the rest of your life to do it. But don't do it and stay on this football team. You want to drink, get out of my life. We've got too many dedicated people on this football team. And if you don't feel that way, SO LONG, OOLONG! Have a nice life. Have enough guts to quit like a man. Quit messin up this football team. Turn in your equipment and we'll give it to some freshman. And then *we'll* get on with it. This has to come from within. If you have to be leaned on to help this football team, GET OUTTA HERE! AND GET OUTTA HERE NOW!"

Coach Fowles hitched a thumb toward the door. "Let's see if you have guts enough to walk outta here." He looked around the room from player to player, waiting.

"So we beat Greeley. *Big deal!* Are you satisfied with that performance? I'm not. I thought we *stunk* the first half. We've got work to do. If you want to blow your mind, *take off* and do it. Because, gentlemen, I'll tell you what: I'm not trying to win a popularity contest. I'll start bouncing bodies off this team. My job is to put the *team* first. You like to win? Then you gotta work harder. You want to be a loser, then just be one of the boys, part of the herd."

Coach Fowles affected a cocky air and walked back and forth, snapping his fingers. "Sure, hey, I'm one of the *boys.* Hey, man, I'm one of the boys!" He snapped up straight and smacked his hands together. "That takes *no guts.* You want to think for yourself? *Then do it!* GET SOME BELLY IN YA! Some of you people had guts enough to turn around and get outta there Saturday night. Some people didn't.

"Boys, don't disgrace this football team, don't disgrace yourselves. When you get your mind screwed up, that is a mental compromise. If you want to have a good football team, we can do that. People tell me this team has guts. And I agree, you *do* have guts. Flake-outs, get up in the grandstand and wave a big green-and-white banner or something. Leave us alone.

"Okay boys, you have a decision to make. I *can't* be one of the boys. This is *your* football team. If you want to have a good team you better get together, and you better do it from within. I'll tell you what, gentlemen: If you're not going to make that decision yourself, I'm going to make it for ya. Heh, heh, heh—no sweat. I'm not going to hesitate next time. I'm just going to bounce you right off the football team. I'll bounce bodies out of here like you wouldn't believe. And I don't care if you're all-universe. You do that again and, SO LONG, OOLONG!"

He looked around the room, and his voice softened. "Boys, you're going to have a lot of automobiles in your lifetime, color TVs, lots of things. But you're only going to play high school football once. *Just one time.* And for the seniors, thirty days from now it's all over. All over but the memories.

"We are a football family. We were, and we are. I know we've got guts and we've got class and we don't have quitters. And you might say I was a little disappointed when I heard what I heard. That is the *last* time that's going to happen."

He stopped and looked around the room again, his gaze steely, icy. For a full fifteen seconds he looked from face to face.

"Does anybody have any questions?"

Again he looked at each face in the room, at the downcast eyes. Then, after another fifteen seconds, he said in a voice almost inaudible:

"Okay, let's go outside and play football."

"That was fucked up for those kids to tell the coach about the party," Bradford McClure said. "It wasn't necessary."

Bradford, after having been told he would be "eaten alive" last Saturday, won the star for most tackles. Rich Schenkle and Ken Furst got them for interceptions; Tom Kase got a rare one for an offensive player, for making two blocks on one play; Bob Mills got one for a fumble recovery; Stan Beronski got one because it seemed that he made the quarterback fumble even though the officials didn't call it.

Jack Forrest's ribs were okay. Bradford and Ted O'Neill still suffered from leg cramps. "It's a question of diet," Coach Fowles said, "the kids need more salt." He was prohibited by state law from dispensing salt pills, but he urged the boys to take them. "It won't help to take them just before a game," he told them, "but start a day or so ahead of time."

What really bothered the coaches were boils. Al Stacey had some which were now gone; Stan Beronski's had healed; Bruce Stacey had a bad one which burst and drained after the game Saturday; Keith Allen had some starting; Ben Schenkle had a huge one develop on the back of his thigh over the weekend. He had had it lanced. Where were they coming from?

There was a suspicion that the bad septic conditions at the manbuilder—which smelled always of sewage—were the source, or that there was something lurking in the muck of the baseball outfield where they sometimes practiced. Coach Fowles didn't think so. "I think it's just a question of not keeping clean," he said. Still, the coaches were worried that the boils might sweep the team, like a staph infection. To prevent further outbreaks, they changed manbuilder hills. Today they ran a very steep but shorter incline of tall grass and weeds and rocks just behind the school.

The coaches watched the team run the manbuilder. Ben Schenkle limped over to Coach Fowles with a note from the doctor stating that he could not play until the doctor later notified the coach that Ben's leg, where the boil had been lanced, was okay.

"What should I do?" Ben asked. "I feel like I could play tomorrow."

"This note says no, Ben," Coach Fowles said. "And that's it." Then he looked off, as if musing, and said without expression. "Doctors are as different as coaches, they feel different ways about things. All I know is I have to get a note from *a* doctor saying you can play."

Ben limped away. "What are you going to do?" I asked him.

"Go to another doctor," he said, smiling.

Bruce Stacey challenged Stan Beronski in the pit drill. When Bruce was on defense, he bulled Stan back a step. But when Stan took his normal defensive charge, he slammed his forearms up under Bruce's chin and nearly snapped his helmet off.

"Wow," Coach Fowles said to me, "and Stan's arm is so sore he can hardly lift it. When he was running the tires he tucked his hand into his pants to keep his arm from bouncing."

Vince Carradino and Bob Mills, then Jim Marshall and Stu Rosenman, went at each other. Altogether it was the roughest pit drill of the season.

As we were walking away from the players during the break, Coach Fowles stopped and looked down at a small red leaf that held tiny sparkling beads of rainwater. "There are so many beautiful things around if you look for them," he said.

Ben Schenkle stood by himself watching the team scrimmage. "The doctor didn't even give me any anesthetic," he said, lightly touching the back of his leg.

"What was it that really happened," I asked, "at the beginning of the season when you got your tooth knocked out?"

"Uh, well, Rich came home and something was bothering him, I don't know what. Like, when he's like that I just try to stay out of his way, you know. But, I don't know, he just got mad at something and we just wrestled around. And I ducked and got punched. The tooth came out on the floor. But I can't really get mad at him, because things just bother him."

Practice ended. As I walked into the locker room, Coach Fowles was telling Rich, "I didn't think you played too well on Saturday." Rich stood looking at the floor, his dark hair coiled and wet down over his ears, his hand pads caked with new mud. "You can do better, Rich."

The coaches got dressed and left. I chatted with some of the players and then dressed slowly in the coaches' room. Suddenly there was screaming in the locker room. I ran out to see Bruce Stacey and Rich Schenkle, naked, face-to-face, with tears streaming from their eyes and their fists clenched down at their sides.

"I DIDN'T tell HIM! I DIDN'T!" Bruce yelled at Rich, wiping grit and tears from his cheeks.

"Who the fuck TOLD him if it wasn't YOU!" Rich yelled back, his bare feet moving up and down. He groaned and yelled and tried to form words, while his body shivered with tension. "SOMEBODY TOLD HIM. It was YOU! I can't . . . you have to . . . WHY'D YOU HAVE TO DO THAT?"

"I DIDN'T tell him! ASK him!"

Jonny gently pushed them apart with his arms, and Rich turned away, trying to make his sobbing understood.

"I DIDN'T tell him," Bruce yelled again, pleadingly.

Jonny and Stan and Bradford quietly steered Rich away and urged him to take a shower. Rich snatched up a towel and turned away from the varsity shower, where Bruce was headed, and stomped down to the JV shower stalls. Bruce showered quickly and left. Rich stayed in the shower for a long time with his three friends.

I sat on a bench with Ben.

"I hope I still have *all* my teeth left after tonight," Ben said.

"What do you mean?"

"Cause Rich is, you know, he might be angry. Sometimes, the day before a game, like when he's asleep, Rich is so tense that he hollers things, like 'HIT 'EM! KILL 'EM!,' you know, 'GO, GO! TACKLE 'EM!' Like he's playin the game, you know, havin a nightmare. He doesn't usually wake up or nothin."

Rich emerged from the shower somewhat calmed, but sad. I asked Jonny what it was all about.

"Rich thinks Bruce told the coach he'd been drinking, and that that's why he hadn't played well against Greeley."

"Yeah," Rich said, his voice still choked. "You know what it was? You know what it *was*? Remember those two beers I brought out for you and your friend at the party at my house last week? Bruce saw that and so he told Coach Fowles I'd been drinking. My *mother* gave me those beers because she said she thought you looked uncomfortable around all us kids, and maybe you'd like a beer. And Bruce told the *Coach* I'd been *drinking!*"

Faintly disturbed at my contribution to the problem, I asked Rich, "What makes you think Coach Fowles believed Bruce?"

"Cause I heard he did. I heard he said that explained why I didn't play so good."

"That doesn't sound like something Coach Fowles would say," I said.

"Yeah, well what am I supposed to think, in my position? I got no way of fighting back. What about my reputation? I care about that."

Rich sat down on a bench and with two fingers pulled back the lock of wet hair that came down over his forehead.

"Like, Coach Fowles is a good guy," Jonny said, "he really is. But Rich saved that Greeley game with that interception. You call that a bad game?"

"What was I supposed to do?" Rich said. "I'm a linebacker, right? And I'm up on the line in the frankenstein, and I just felt they were going to pass—like we knew they had that jump pass. I'm a linebacker, so what do I do? It's just instinct, I guess. I drop back and get it. And Bruce says, 'What the hell are you doing back there?'"

"You don't think Bruce is trying to hurt the team," I said.

"No, it's not that. But I think he's bitter because he's not captain. I know Coach Fowles was disturbed about who they elected captains. I mean, I'm not dumb. I know that he never came to me and congratulated me for being captain. Last year he congratulated the captains . . ."

"Like the thing is," Jonny said, "Bruce's okay. But like he's been out for all these days with injuries. Other guys have had injuries, and they're still out practicing every day. Like Rich had pulled ligaments at the start of the season. When we hung on the bars, somebody had to help him lift his arm so he could reach the bar. And some of the guys are bitter about today, you know. Bruce comes back after missing all those practices, and he goes right back into his old position, calling defensive signals."

"And what about *Ben*?" Rich said, more angrily. "Ben's been fullback, and so today he's out by doctor's orders, and Bruce is all of a sudden the fullback. So what happens now to Ben?"

"What makes you think your brother won't get his job back as soon as he can run?" I asked.

"Well how do we *know*? I mean, like Bruce is *really* good, and we need him on the team. But why does Coach Fowles have to listen to just *him* all the time? I think I been working hard. What about me? Look what happened to me when I got hurt. My knee still hurts from the Port Chester scrimmage, but I been working right along. So why don't I get *my* job back, why don't I get to play offensive end like I did before I was hurt?"

"It's like with Bradford," Jonny said. "Bruce has been down on Brad ever since freshman year, when he thought Brad stole his sweat pants. Remember that big team meeting a few weeks ago, when Bruce talked about training rules? That was actually all about Brad; Bruce wanted him off the team because he had seen him over at somebody's house drinking a couple of beers on a Sunday afternoon. So he called that big meeting that never got off the ground—all to get Brad off the team. Now look where Brad is, starting, making most tackles. This really *is* a family."

"You going to tell Coach Fowles about this?" Bradford asked me.

"No," I said. "The deal is I don't tell him what I hear from you guys. But I *do* know him pretty well. And this sounds like a misunderstanding. Why don't *you* go and talk to him, Rich?"

"Aw, what could I say? I don't want to go and complain." He started pulling on his clothes. "I'm not going to hurt the team anyway. I'll go to Bruce tomorrow and talk to him. I'll tell him that I think he is a great guy and player and everything, and just ask him to quit talking about me, explain how I feel. I just want to play football . . ."

I walked down the hall to where Coach Fowles had just finished showing movies of the Greeley game to the parents. "It may be a staph infection," he explained to the parents as they put on their coats. "What you do is use strong soap. If boils appear, soak them."

"Sometimes the boys think they're helping us," Mrs. Forrest said, "by not bringing practice pants home to wash every day."

Coach Fowles wound up the cord to the projector.

"Buddy," I said, wondering if I were violating a confidence, "tomorrow, on the field, why don't you just be especially alert to any unusual vibrations."

He looked at me for a couple of seconds. "Okay," he said.

"I mean, maybe if you. . . ."

"You don't have to say any more," he said.

TUESDAY, *October 5*

It was still sunny and warm, though some of the trees were red with fall. The cheerleaders were out on the sidelines practicing in white gym bloomers. While the team hung on the bars, the coaches stood aside and debated whether to use man-to-man or zone-pass coverage. Coach Fowles felt the zone was more effective. Coach Branahan felt that they didn't have fast enough secondary men to risk a zone. They had been debating it off and on all day.

Jonny finished hanging on the bars and threw some passes nearby. The coaches moved away. "I don't want him to hear us argue this," Coach Fowles said. "This is something we work out ourselves, a coaching matter."

Coach Fowles was in a bright mood. Before the scrimmage session he challenged Jonny to a distance-throwing duel. Coach Fowles heaved the football from the 50-yard line, five yards deep into the end zone. From that spot, Jonny took a hop-step and threw it back to the 50—a tie at 55 yards. "I told you I was a frustrated quarterback," Coach Fowles said.

For the scrimmage, he put Bruce Stacey in at fullback and moved Ben Schenkle to tailback. Then he put Rich Schenkle in at offensive end.

The offense seemed transformed. Bruce Stacey broke up the middle all the way. Rich caught two bullet passes over the middle, and blocked savagely with his overactive forearms. Ben skittered and spun through quick holes in the line. The offense was high-spirited, blazing.

"This is amazing," I said to Coach Fowles, "what you've done today."

"I just listened to the vibes," he said, laughing, "and I put certain things together and it hit me like a brick. Communication, that's all it is. I was not being sensitive enough to certain people. I was not praising Rich enough."

The team went on exuberantly. I asked Ben how he liked tailback.

"Holes are bigger," he said, breathing heavily after a run. "I get to run more wide stuff. Just have to get my timing. Instead of hitting the holes as quick as I do at fullback, I have to hesitate a split second for Bruce to get out of the way. Am I okay?"

Offensive guard Clifford Albert hooked an arm around Jim Petrowski's ankle to keep him from making a tackle. "Shit!" Jim said, yanking himself free. "He's always doin that."

Jack Forrest was repeatedly crab-blocking Bob Mills, slipping in low on him on all fours and buckling his legs. "You feel like termites crawling all over my legs," Bob said, grinning and slapping Jack's helmet.

Bradford McClure tried linebacker. Before practice Coach Fowles had asked him to try that spot, in the four-four since Jim Petrowski couldn't see well enough. Coach Fowles had told Bradford, "I hate to move you out of that tackle, because you're playing it so well."

"I'll give it a try," Bradford had said.

Bradford did not like it. Most of the plays were running to the other side. He went over to Coach Fowles. "I feel so useless," he said. "I'm not helping the team. Should I still drop back and cover my flat when I see the play's going the other way?"

"Yup, you still do your job."

Bradford raced along the line after a ball-carrier. Rich Schenkle chased him and threw himself across the backs of Bradford's legs.

"You *clipped* me!" Bradford yelled.

"You should *run* faster," Rich said.

When Ted O'Neill went in at quarterback, Jonny wandered away and started punting along the sidelines. He kicked one that dribbled 15 yards and wrenched his knee. Jonny fell over backward, groaning. A crowd gathered.

"Who's down?" Coach Fowles called.

"Just Jonny."

"Can I be a punter?" Jonny called, still flat on his back.

I said to Jonny, "The team looks like it came back together today."

"Coach Fowles is a smart dude," he said.

Coach Fowles broke the scrimmage to have his players run over and cheer the soccer team, which was having a tough game. The team gathered at the soccer sideline and cheered, in their way.

"GO, LAKETOWN, SCORE!"

"MAKE 'EM FUMBLE!"

"How do you play this game?"

"*Why* do you play this game?" Stan Beronski mumbled.

"TACKLE THE MOTHER!"

The supportive appearance of the football team seemed to have all of the boosting effect of a thunderstorm on a croquet match.

What preceded the day's splendid practice was this: Word came to Coach Fowles in the morning that Rich Schenkle had missed the first two periods of school. Coach Fowles called him at home, and he said he had overslept and was coming in, but his tone caused Coach Fowles to be suspicious.

He called Jonny into his office. "How's the team?" he asked the quarterback.

"Okay," Jonny said.

"What does that mean?" Coach Fowles asked.

Jonny said simply that Rich was very upset because he felt he earned a chance to try offensive end, and that some guys on the team were leaning on him and saying he could have played a better game if he hadn't been drinking. "And there are guys on the team who know he *wasn't* drinking," he told Coach Fowles. Jonny never mentioned Bruce, or the dispute.

"I don't know why Bruce does this to people," Coach Fowles said.

Then he got Bruce into his office and told him he knew there had been some trouble between him and Rich. Bruce asked him how he knew. Coach Fowles explained the difference between deductive and inductive reasoning, and said that he had used the latter process.

:*172*:

"You see," he said to Bruce. "Rich is a fine football player, so I expect more of him than the average player. When I criticize him, it is not to say that he played a bad game. But the point is that now we must pull together even more as a team."

Bruce sought out Rich. Rich told him, "Why don't we just forget it. It never happened. Everything is fine."

"Whether it happened or not," Bruce said to Rich, "I'm here to apologize right now."

WEDNESDAY, October 6

On the Guidance Center bulletin board, outside Coach Fowles's office, was a cartoon drawn on white paper by reserve guard Bill McCord. It showed a smiling ghoul of a man in a top hat standing over a tombstone marked "FOX LANE—R.I.P." in the background were three similar stones for Our Lady of Lourdes, Mamaroneck, and Horace Greeley. Looking over the scene was a vulture perched on a sign that said "Laketown Hill."

Outside Coach Fowles's windows, girls in shorts and miniskirts, and boys with equally long hair, and dungarees, swarmed toward the yellow school buses. Huge thunderheads rose in the blue sky over the woods, and leaves swirled around the legs of the departing students.

Coach Fowles was on the telephone with the coach of a team that had scrimmaged Fox Lane. As he talked, he doodled on a tiny white pad.

"Does the tailback have good speed? . . . We *thought* it was a split six. . . . They like to stunt those linebackers? . . . Are those guys lined up on the outside shoulder of the tackles, in the gap, or inside shoulder of the ends? . . . Are they down in a three-point stance, or up? . . ." He drew the alignment on the pad. "Wonder what he will do with the flats with the three-deep. . . ." He wrote "FLATS" and underlined it three times.

He finished his talk and invited Mrs. Forrest and Mrs. Allen in. "We came to meet the boys in the cafeteria to hand in the oven-mitt money," Mrs. Forrest said, "but the boys didn't show."

Mrs. Allen had a tube of black ointment with her. "The doctor says that the infections the boys are having are not boils that come from within," she said, "but infections that spread from without, like impetigo." The doctor had prescribed the black ointment for Keith, and Mrs. Allen recommended it for the others.

When they had gone, Coach Fowles said, "The team looks good. But we're not out of the woods yet. I think the reason for no letdown is, in fact, Saturday night, the party."

He doodled on his pad. "Know what? We might try a fake punt if we're somewhere around midfield on fourth down on Saturday. Part of the reason I'd like to try that is that Peekskill—we play them next week —has a reputation for blocking punts. If they see us pull a fake against Fox Lane, they'll *have* to watch out for it. Did you know Fox Lane has scouted us all three games? I can't believe it."

"The team really seems tight together right now," I said.

"One of the unique things that I really love about football," he said, "is that the team gathers together for a meeting after every single play. They come together as a unit. Remember how I sometimes call out to Bruce Stacey, if he's calling defensive signals, 'Bring em together.' What I'm really telling him is to have a meeting, get the family together. And that's what they do."

A cold front came through as the team gathered in the classroom. Sudden bursts of wind sent leaves in through the open windows, and then the rain pelted down.

Coach Fowles recounted the tips he had received on Fox Lane. He told the team he had received an interesting letter from one of last year's tough linebackers, and that he would read it to them Friday or Saturday. He said that the infections spreading around the team probably had to do with cleanliness. "Get your practice pants home and washed more often. The worst possible thing to spread infection is to borrow towels. Bring your own."

He informed them that radio stations were planning to broadcast at least the next four Laketown games. "You don't have to be Dr. Albert Einstein to figure out why we're getting a little attention," he said, "because you have all been willing to pay the extra price, like on the tires and the hill. If we go into this game thinking Fox Lane won't be tough, we're in trouble. But if we keep improving as we have been, we will have the time of our life Saturday afternoon. Right now you shouldn't be ready to play Fox Lane. But Saturday afternoon you should be ready."

Fox Lane had won its first two games of the season, but with difficulty, against weak teams. The Laketown scouts had not been impressed with the Harvesters' next opponent.

Ted O'Neill got a haircut today, to the neighborhood of his ears. "My parents hassled me," he said. The Schenkle brothers had been finessing.

The other day they were directed to get haircuts, but they came back unshorn, reporting that the barbershop was too crowded.

At the start of the scrimmage, Ted O'Neill said to Jonny, "You're going to throw more to me today, right? Right?" Catching passes seemed to give him adequate fulfillment. The more he caught, the harder he blocked.

Keith Allen had been fumbling all season. He was perhaps the fastest back, but his hands had been betraying him more and more. His hands were one reason he got teased about wanting to become a pediatrician—that and the fact that he got queasy at the sight of blood. He went out for a flare pass. The ball slid off his palms, and immediately he slapped his hands over his face mask in a gesture of humility and regret. The next two times he ran, though, he broke for the distance.

Keith was to carry the ball on the fake punt. He lined up in the blocking position just ahead of the punter, then darted back to take the hand-off. On such a play in practice, the defense was supposed to cooperate by pretending not to know what was going on. But on the first try, Brian Purcell, playing defensive end, went straight in at Keith and caught him for a 15-yard loss.

"Way to cheat up, Brian," Jonny called.

On the second try, Brian let Keith get back only to the line of scrimmage.

"Hey, Purcell is fantastic," somebody hollered to Coach Fowles. "Put him in if they try a fake punt against us."

Brian turned his palms up innocently.

Freddie Delaney, the tough and vacantly friendly defensive lineman, was put in at defensive left end, where neither Steve Barker nor Stu Rosenman had been satisfactory so far. On the first play, Ben Schenkle swept to his right with a pitchout from Jonny, and Delaney drove him down for a loss. On the next play he dropped Jonny before he could throw. Then he slanted in and pinned Bruce Stacey who was headed for the four hole.

Coach Fowles walked by Coach Branahan and said under his breath, "Coach, we found a left end."

I stood on the sideline with three players waiting to alternate in, and asked them about drugs. Driving through town today I had noticed a new sign, perhaps six feet by ten, yellow, with a revelation in tall red and black letters from the local drug guidance council: "There is NO HERO in HEROIN"

"There's a lot of acid around school these days," said one of the players. "Not many guys on the team drop it—not guys that want to play. There's a little coke around. Not much heroin at all."

"Hey, I gotta get my plants inside for the winter," another of them said. "Would you take them and let them grow in your house?"

"Come on," I said, though secretly appreciative of his confidence in my knowledge and discretion.

There was wild yelling and responsive laughter in the locker room as some of the players got dressed. Only some got dressed because somebody had taken all the open combination locks and locked them all over the place on the wrong lockers, on urinal pipes, on chair backs. All locks looked the same, and trial and error was the only way to find yours.

One group of six locks was fastened together like barnacles around the handle to the bathroom door. Most of the yelling was coming from there, from Freddie Delaney. He was kicking and screaming maniacally at the door handle. Even his obscenities were frazzled. "Pricking fark puck goddamned shicking bastard!"

Bob Mills was laughing hysterically behind him.

"You do this?" I asked Bob.

"Me?" he said, doubling up ecstatically as Freddie tried to control himself enough to have another go at the combinations.

In the coaches' room, I told Coach Fowles that the pass protection looked weak against the "Fox Lane" defense.

He seemed unconcerned. "I don't think they'll be able to stunt those linebackers like that on us. We'll do a quick pitch to the outside, and our guards will pick them up. Besides, I don't care if we look bad Monday through Friday. Saturday we'll look good."

"Jim Marshall can't block at all," I said. "He's hurting you. He seems so sure of his position, almost cocky."

"Jim, cocky? Hey, he's not cocky, not at all. Jim needs more confidence. You know what he needs? He needs a lot of T.L.C. He needs to be patted on the back more. He'll be fine."

THURSDAY, *October 7*

At the meeting, Coach Fowles reviewed the Fox Lane offense, then he said, "One more thing, and I'm very serious about this. Let's all understand what I'm about to say about this next subject. It has to do with stealing.

"Now gentlemen, there are a lot of ways to make sure we stop stealing, especially from within the family. The last people I would think anybody'd want to fool with is probably the football team, because you've got a lot of people going to be down on your neck."

Several players laughed quietly. ". . . I'll tell you what, if I hear of anybody taking *anything* that does not belong to him in this school—I'm not just talking about uniforms now, I'm talking about other things, like money—that's going to be the end of the road. When we go into a football game we've got to trust each other, know that we are going to do our best for each other. Everybody has to know he can rely on every single person. That is like *critical* on every football team.

"If you don't feel that way, please don't play football, because there are too many kids that *do* feel that way. Now, are there any questions about stealing?"

Coach Branahan suggested that they try the bull-in-the-ring drill instead of the pit. The former has a man in the middle, surrounded by six players numbered one to six. The man in the middle doesn't know which man on the ring has which number. Numbers are called out in rapid succession, and the man with that number charges the man in the middle and tries to drive him out. Thus, players are coming from all directions. The idea is to make the man in the middle quick and alert. Coach Fowles didn't like the drill.

"In the first place, Sandy," he said, "I've seen too many guys hurt that way. Secondly, the idea of the pit drill is to build confidence, because if you just go in there and do your job, you'll do okay. But the bull-in-the-ring destroys confidence, Sandy, it really does. There's no way you can hold your own. Eventually you get racked. Let's stick with the pit."

In the pit drill, Freddie Delaney went against the second-string offensive center, quiet Mitch Gordon. Delaney launched himself like a shot. He caught Mitch under the face mask with his forearms and ripped his helmet off.

It became cold during the scrimmage period for the first time this season. The mosquitoes disappeared. Players awaiting turns shivered. Most of the players were still wearing tee shirts.

Running the Laketown offense against the "Fox Lane" defense, Jonny hid the ball on his hip and ran the bootleg to his left, completely fooling defensive end Stan Beronski, who ran right by Jonny with his eyes on the faking back.

"Stan," Coach Fowles said to him, smiling slightly. "On *our* defense, who would you key."

"The quarterback."

"Mmm-hmm," Coach Fowles said, walking away.

On the next play Jonny barely handed off to a back when he was caught in a severe bear hug by Stan. Stan easily spun him around and threw him down. The two friends rolled over and over in the grass, laughing. "S-t-a-n B-e-r-o-n-s-k-i," Jonny announced, in the manner of a broadcaster calling a tackle.

"You know how beautiful that is?" Coach Fowles said to me, looking warmly at the two boys. "How many people would recognize how beautiful it is to see so much love between two football players?"

Ben Schenkle was back at full strength, having recovered from the old boil and ignoring the new. He never changed his wide-eyed expression, and sucked on his mouthpiece like a pacifier. When he ran, he leaned well forward, slipped off pile-ups, cut smoothly either way, never taking a direct hit from a tackler. It seemed sad that he, like others who were only five-seven and 160, with but moderate speed, would not play football beyond high school.

In the locker room, Jack Forrest painfully pulled his shirt off. He was wearing a double pad over his bruised ribs.

Bruce Stacey complained to Coach Fowles that his knee was bruised. When Bruce had gone I said to Coach Fowles, "I'm waiting for the day Stan Beronski comes in and says he bumped his knee."

"Well," Coach Fowles said, "some guys need more reinforcement than others."

Ken Furst, the safetyman, had bitten his tongue in making a tackle; it was sliced open underneath. Coach Fowles said that the doctor had recommended against stitching such a cut, "so put ice on it, and we'll see if you can play."

No new boils were reported.

Mrs. Schenkle put candles on the table for a spaghetti supper with me and Ben and Rich. Ben sat by the table, carefully slitting the tiny hem on the legs of his new bell-bottomed dungarees to give them a fashionable ragged look. Rich quietly held his two-year-old sister on his lap, and looked at her and at the table.

Mr. Schenkle was working late at the telephone company, "because of the strike," Mrs. Schenkle said, as we ate. "One thing I always tell the kids they can be proud of is that their father, without a college degree, worked his way up. He started out working over a manhole. Now he's a supervisor. I think it's sad how so many times people like him get pushed aside in companies by people who have degrees, regardless of ability or experience. That's one reason we want Rich to go to college, so that he can get a decent job and not be pushed aside."

"Do you want to go to college?" I asked Rich.

"Not all that much," he said.

"We don't want to pressure the kids," Mrs. Schenkle said, "but just want them to get good jobs. . . . "

"But that's pressure right there," Rich said. "You have to go to college to get a decent job, whether you want to go or not. It's the thing you *do*."

"Do you feel a lot of pressure playing football?" I asked.

"Well, I'd like to get a football scholarship to help me go to college," Rich said, "but you mean like getting psyched up? Not really. I don't really have to get psyched up. The idea is to think about what you're doing, what your job is, about the team staying together. Sometimes when I get there Saturday mornings I may seem psyched up, but it's just that I'm concentrating so hard on what my *job* is that day."

He retrieved his sister's pacifier. "Like, we're not really psyched up out there. In the Greeley game, when Greeley scored the first touchdown, we didn't have to get all psyched up and worry about how we had to get it back right away. We just took the ball and got back in the huddle and said, okay, now we're just going to play football and stay together. Like out on the field when we yell at each other, it's just to say move faster, cover a hole quicker, do this or that better—it's just communication, not squabbling or getting all psyched."

He bounced his sister on his knee. "Like, I feel that way down deep everybody cares about *some*body. I really feel strongly about the team as a *family*. That's very important. Like we all work together. There aren't any *stars* on this team."

"I guess you're proud," I said to Mrs. Schenkle, "about Ben being vice-president of the junior class."

"*Are* you, Ben?" she asked, widening her eyes.

"Yeah," he said, continuing his work on the hem.

"He never told me," she said.

"Me neither," Rich said, smiling.

"When did that happen?"

"Oh, couple weeks ago," Ben said.

Ben left to telephone his girl friend. Rich went upstairs to study for a driver's education test the next day.

"Your sons sure don't brag much," I said. "I can't imagine not telling anybody if I were elected a class officer."

"No, they never did brag. But they are like night and day, so different. See, Rich has to work hard for everything he gets, and Ben doesn't. Ben's very easygoing. Rich worries more, I think."

Mr. Schenkle, a trim, tall, quiet man with neatly combed black hair, arrived and sat down for his late supper. We chatted about the success of the Greeley game, the prospects for Fox Lane.

"Rich's hand is still badly swollen, isn't it?" I said.

"Yeah," Mrs. Schenkle said. She turned to her husband. "Is that the same hand he fractured in the doorjamb?"

He smiled. "I don't know. I don't remember which hand that was. He's had so many injuries."

"Like with the motorcycle," Mrs. Schenkle said. "A year or so ago Ben bought on old motorcycle for fifteen dollars, and Rich wanted to try it, you know, just around the yard. But Rich. . . ." Rich came back and sat down, his hands in his lap, looking at the table. ". . . *You* tell it, Rich, about the motorcycle."

He shook his head.

"Come on Rich, tell him that story. All right, I'll tell it. Rich kept asking to try it. He just wanted to take it around the lawn once—but Rich, *you* tell it." Rich was silent. "Okay. He took it and was just going to go around the lawn once. . . . "

"The story is I went around the lawn once and went through the playroom window in the basement."

I chuckled. His mother continued, "Yeah, and he cut two fingers pretty badly. But you know how Rich is. A neighbor was helping him, and I came running up, and Rich kept calling to me, 'I'm all right, I'm all right'—so I wouldn't worry, you know?" She smiled at Rich.

"At the beginning of the season your arm or shoulder was hurt," I said.

"I had torn tendons," he said, "from when I hurt myself playing football on the beach."

"Does it still bother you?"

"Only when I lift my arm," he said, carefully raising his left arm. "I couldn't lift my arm for a while. It still hurts when I do."

"Did you get your car inspected yet?" His father asked. Rich shook his head, looking down at the table. "What? I told you about it last week. You *have* to get it inspected."

Rich squirmed, but didn't lift his eyes. "I *can't* get it inspected. The lights don't work, the horn doesn't work."

"Get them fixed."

Rich sniffed. "I just don't have the money right now."

Ben came back, wearing his new bell-bottoms.

"Coach seemed upset about stealing today," I said to him.

He grinned. "Yeah. That was about Jim Petrowski's watch and ring. Some tall skinny kid stole them. Jim was going to beat him up, but he really didn't want to." He named a reserve on the team.

"Was *he* involved?" I asked.

"I think he *knew* about it," Ben said. "Like a couple of times I caught him in the locker room just sneaking around. Once he was looking into the equipment room, and he was saying, 'Wow, look at all that stuff up there. I could go *crazy* looking at all that stuff!' " He laughed.

"Is there a lot of stealing?" I asked.

"Naw. Well, except maybe in the lunchroom." Ben laughed gleefully, and Rich smiled. "Like one time last year we were hiking stuff past the lady. Like somebody was standing outside, you know, calling plays—like 'Cookies at two'—and we'd just bend over and hike 'em right out of the room. And another time a guy was out in the hall with a lacrosse stick. When the lady wasn't looking guys would just pick up a sandwich and throw it out. The guy would reach around the door and catch them with a lacrosse stick."

I was to stay the night. Mr. Schenkle had converted an upstairs dormer-room into a bedroom for Rich and Ben. It was stocked with trophies, baseball mitts, road signs, and lacrosse sticks. Ben didn't like to sleep in there with Rich because Rich kept the radio on all night. He took his sleeping bag and headed for the living room. Rich and I went up.

"Do you mind having the radio on?" he asked.

I said I didn't, and he tuned in a New York all-night rock station. He went to sleep, but I lay awake all night, listening to the music and thinking about families.

FRIDAY, October 8

It was sunny and warm when the team went out in shorts. The girls' field hockey team had a contest on the football field, so the football team took their field.

The team began its drills. A man from the Midget Football League —coach of the team on which Coach Fowles's son Jeff played—came over to talk to the coaches. The team began horsing around. Linemen ran in backs' positions, players fell down laughing, two footballs were used at once.

Coach Branahan watched for a moment, and then went over, yelling. "DON'T YOU GUYS KNOW YOU GOT A GAME TOMORROW? YOU THINK THEY'RE JAGGING AROUND RIGHT NOW OVER AT FOX LANE?"

He was red-faced. Coach Fowles came over. Coach Branahan snatched up the football and turned his back to the team and moved his lips angrily. Coach Fowles stood eyeing his team. The players stood cowed before his silent gaze. "All right," he said softly, "bars and tires."

They ran off. Coach Fowles watched them go. "It was right on the tip of my tongue, Sandy," he said. "I almost sent them in. I almost said, 'You don't want to practice, get off the field!' I've done it other years. I don't know if they're ready, Sandy."

"Boy, that made me mad!" Coach Branahan said.

Stu Rosenman got a tear in his shorts while running a play. Other players quickly completed the job, darting at him from behind like dogs at a bear. Finally, stripped, he went in to recover himself.

Ken Furst, still not sure he could play tomorrow because of his cut tongue, worked out with the team. Bradford McClure, having tried line-backer, was back at defensive tackle. In the four-four, Coach Fowles now had as linebackers Rich Schenkle, Bruce and Al Stacey, and either Barry Brill or John Finch at right inside linebacker. John was new to the position, but seemed quick.

The specialty teams worked briefly at the end of practice—a couple of punts, a couple of kickoffs. They were clumsy units, employing a few starters and virtually all of the reserves. From time to time I mentioned to Coach Fowles my fears that these ragtag teams might be costly.

"Yeah, I know, but I do it to allow more kids to play. I hate to tamper with them by putting regulars in."

The team filed into the classroom for its last pre-Fox Lane meeting.

"Last year Fox Lane used a three-triple-stack, five-three defense," Coach Fowles said in review, "with three linebackers lined up right behind three linemen. They haven't used that five-three this year. If they *do*, that's *their* problem. We feel there are too many weaknesses—the counters go, the flats are open. So far we've seen a split-six, practically an eight-man line. They can't possibly play us with an eight-man line because we *pass* too well. But that's their problem too."

He announced the starting line-up. There was one change in the line. "Freddie Delaney will start at defensive left end," he said.

Freddie's head popped up from his desk. He looked around the room, then clapped his hand over his eyes.

"I'm not sure about right inside linebacker," he went on. "Both Barry Brill and John Finch be ready."

That evening, over the phone, he would tell John he was going to start.

In the secondary, Mark Ferenzi, a competitive little back with black curly hair and a prominent nose, would replace Karl Walsh, whom the coaches felt was getting beaten too often on passes.

The new scoreboard was tested today, its hundred of little lights blinking on and off with quarter, score, field position, and time remaining. It was to be operative tomorrow. Coach Fowles reminded the team that the scoreboard was not official. "The only clock that makes a difference is on the field judge's wrist."

Coach Fowles announced that Bradford McClure had been elected honorary captain. Then he said, "Boys, there are right now two undefeated teams left on our schedule—Fox Lane, and Sleepy Hollow who we play in our last game. Don't let the opportunity to defeat an undefeated team slip through your hands. There are still a couple of people who believe we have been lucky so far. Tomorrow will be the day we're going to prove that we weren't lucky. Phone calls at 10 o'clock."

"This *could* have been a crucial day," Coach Fowles said, tinkling the ice in his glass of Scotch, "like after Port Chester. We'll see. I'm worried about them letting down. I'm worried about them not being up for Fox Lane."

"You were angry today, when they were messing around," I said, "but you didn't send them in."

"Well, it's all a question of timing. Earlier in the week, I could have been wrong bringing up that whole thing about the party. I thought about that. I could have ignored it. And today, I could have sent them in. Sometimes the kids are really trying to tell you something. Sometimes they *want* you to get tough, crack the whip, make them work harder, show them you are the boss. But it has to be done at exactly the right time. We'll see."

10

SATURDAY, *October 9*

A strange lethargy blanketed the team as it loosened up behind the school a half hour before kickoff time. They went through normal drills, but more quietly than before, without a certain nervous spark. When they lined up for calisthenics, the four captains facing them didn't yell the familiar dramatic words, but merely called out the exercises.

Perhaps, I thought, the team was a bit spent, having come through three close ones with upset victories. This was the first week they had been favored.

Coach Fowles had chills, and suspected a fever was coming. He stood watching with his hands in his pockets. "I almost shouldn't say this," he said to me, "but we were three and 0 the last three years too."

The team filed into the locker room for its four minutes without the coaches. Words seemed more forced, less spontaneous, than in previous weeks.

"Everybody's been saying that we've just been lucky the last three games," Keith Allen said calmly.

"Maybe we *have*, but today we got to show 'em different."

"They think they're going to beat the CAKE-EATERS from LAKETOWN!"

"All right, Laketown," Rich Schenkle said, "let's just shut up. There's nothing that should be said. Just go out there and play the game we really should play. We got pride, we're going to win. They're looking for an upset, it's as simple as that. That's all that has to be said. We just go out and play."

"Don't think they plan to lose, cause they're just as big as WE are."

"They ain't lost yet—take that into account."

"Don't underestimate 'em."

"Don't underestimate the man in front of you," Rich said, "that's all."

There was a silence.

"Just hit 'em hard the first few plays, Laketown."

"Hit 'em *every* play."

Another silence.

"Nobody likes losers," Jonny said.

Silence.

"If we lose today," Jonny said, "then everything we've done so far is just a fluke, a mistake."

"Boy, that's for sure," Bradford McClure said.

"If we're four and 0 after today," Jonny said, "we're halfway to eight and 0, you know."

"Three and one SUCKS."

"Three and one," Jonny said, "that's great for some people, but it's shit for us."

"We don't settle for second best."

"Seven and one, or eight and 0, Laketown."

"Just remember," Rich said, "they're psyched out of their minds down there. Cause they've got a chance to beat LAKETOWN."

"Hey, uh, if somebody throws a punch at you," Jonny said, "or kicks you in a pile-up, you know, just get up and walk away from 'em—just walk away."

"Got that, Delaney?" Bruce Stacey said.

"Everybody got it," Jonny said.

"Let's GO," Bradford said. "Kickoff team, get that ball right away."

"Go down there and put your head right in the guy's chest," Jonny said, "and pop the ball loose. That's all football is. We beat teams because nobody can *hit* harder than us. Look at Greeley, their backs were hurtin. They carried one kid out. They were hurtin, they didn't *want* to play football. We just out-hit em."

"If we're not up, they're going to beat us. And I don't think we're up."

The coaches came in. "All right boys, listen up," Coach Fowles said. "First of all, Coach Branahan, you have anything you want to say?"

"Just a reminder: Any team that throws the ball *eighteen times* in a game, they are potentially a dangerous team. Linemen, you've got to get a good pass-rush on. Freddie Delaney, Stan Beronski, you should eat that quarterback alive when you get a shot at him. Don't let him roll out around you, cause if he rolls out around you he's got too much time."

"Put your head into his," Jonny said. "Stan, hit him right in the head."

"And that secondary," Coach Branahan went on, "let's just key out there."

"Boys, I'll tell you," Coach Fowles said, "the family comes first, the *family* comes first. If somebody's not doing their job in there they're going to sit down and somebody else will do it. But everybody will do their job today."

He had in his hand a folded piece of paper, and now he opened it up slowly.

"I received a letter from a college man. The letter is written to *you*. I'd like to share what he has to say with this family."

He read:

Dear Coach Fowles:

I've been told by my sister that Laketown is now three and 0. Boy, was I happy to hear that Laketown had beaten Horace Greeley. Congratulations to you and to YOUR family (MY family). I am very proud of what the Harvesters have done so far this year. And I don't have to tell you what I HOPE happens the rest of the season. I would like very much to see the team in action this year because they must have an unbelievable amount of pride and determination. I realize with big victories like the ones Laketown has had this year, that there could be a letdown. Or an overconfidence, or whatever, that has happened before, when the teams I was on were three and 0. And then got one's head handed to us. Now is the time to work even harder. I think because of the lack of size that I've been told we have on the team this year, that mentally the guys have to make up for it, and so far they have.

Remember—if you are willing to give all of yourself whenever you are on that field, then not only will you be proud of yourself and your team but EVERYONE who has been on the

Laketown football team will be proud of you too, and will be prouder to say that they are a member of the Laketown family! I am very proud of the Laketown family. Do me a favor—make me even prouder!

Coach Fowles read the signature of last year's linebacker and folded up the handwritten letter quietly and tucked it back in the envelope.

"Who we gonna beat?"

"FOX LANE! FOX LANE! FOX LANE!"

Laketown lost the toss and kicked off. The defensive line asserted itself immediately, stopping the Foxes cold. They punted to Ken Furst in single safety on the Laketown 35. Ken started to his right, then cut back and was tripped. The ball slipped out behind his arm and was recovered by Fox Lane. The Foxes had the ball on the Laketown 36.

The quarterback rolled out to his right, with Bradford McClure and Freddie Delaney after him. They pulled him down for a six-yard loss. But Laketown was offside. Instead of second and 16, it was first and five on the 31.

They wedged a big hole in their left side, over Jim Marshall, and the halfback swung wide down the near sideline to the 15, where Al Stacey and Ray Meister rolled him out of bounds.

The halfback took a pitchout to the right, but Bradford, Freddie Delaney, and Rich Schenkle sifted through and pinned him for a five-yard loss. Laketown was offside again.

"WHAT NUMBER?" Coach Fowles called out to the officials, pointing to his chest.

"Number 51," the official said, indicating Jim Marshall.

Instead of second and 15 on the 20, it was first and five on the 10. The center of the Harvester line held for one play, but then the fullback spun up the middle, cut sharply to his left, and went in for the score. The kick was perfect, and with less than five minutes elapsed on the new scoreboard, Fox Lane led 7–0. Laketown was behind for the third time in two weeks.

Ben Schenkle ran the kickoff back to the 25, and the Laketown offense took the field confidently. But they couldn't move, and Ted O'Neill kicked a low, line-drive punt which rolled dead at the Fox Lane 27.

Fox Lane couldn't move either, and punted back to the Laketown 43.

On first down, Al Stacey knifed up the middle to the Fox Lane 44. But the Harvesters were stopped there. Ted O'Neill's punt rolled into the end zone.

There was no hint of alarm on the bench; the team seemed almost to be biding its time.

With first and ten on the 20, the Fox Lane quarterback again rolled to his right, and again Bradford McClure, Freddie Delaney, and Rich Schenkle chased him, catching him on the 18. The right side of the line stopped a running play. On third down, Stan Beronski chased the quarterback all the way back to the five-yard line before he threw a wildly incomplete pass.

Laketown took the punt at the 50, and, as the second quarter began, the offense finally began to roll. Jonny hit Rich Schenkle, cutting across the middle from the left end, to the 32. Ben Schenkle followed John Curtis's block over left tackle to the 29. Bruce Stacey brought in the full-back-counter play from the bench. Jonny faked right, handed back to Bruce over the left side, behind Clifford Albert and John Curtis, and Bruce ran over three tacklers down to the 12.

Fox Lane stiffened. Al Stacey got to the 11, Ben Schenkle to the 10. Coach Fowles signaled for a time-out.

Jonny trotted over. "All right," Coach Fowles said, putting his arm on Jonny's shoulder. "We got to get eight yards."

"Ben," Coach Branahan said, "Ben behind Bruce Stacey, double-dive."

"Try somethin wide?" Jonny suggested.

"That end's way outside already, Jon," Coach Branahan said. "We got to go inside of him."

"The double-dive with Ben sounds good," Coach Fowles said. "Strong I left, tailback double-dive on this side, at the seven hole. Do we have our big boys in there? Hey, Al Stacey, get in there."

Al joined Jonny to trot back to the huddle. The hand-off went to Ben right behind Bruce Stacey. But there was no hole. Ben swung wide to the left. The six-foot-four-inch Fox Lane cornerback chased him, grabbed him around the shoulders, and threw him down like a grain sack on the seven-yard line.

On fourth and five, Coach Branahan sent in the 70-quick pass, calling for Ted O'Neill to slant out sharply to the right. He was bumped and slowed as he went out, and Jonny threw incomplete. Laketown gave up the ball seven yards from a touchdown.

Fox Lane could not advance, and punted. Ray Meister took it on the

Laketown 47, and, cutting behind a sharp block by Ken Furst, brought it back to the Fox Lane 46.

"All right, Jonny," Coach Fowles said as his quarterback started in, "run inside, the three, four, six, and seven holes, okay?"

Jonny alternated hand-offs to Bruce Stacey and Ben Schenkle inside the ends, and they advanced steadily to the Fox Lane 21. Then Jonny faked a hand-off, rolled to his right, and threw a strike to Don Heidner, who had faked left and slanted out right. Don took it all alone on the five and scampered in.

Ben kicked wide to the right, leaving Laketown still behind 7–6. But the offense had come alive.

Ted O'Neill stopped by the coaches. "I'm getting double coverage," he announced proudly, "so Don just had one man to beat."

Jim Marshall kicked off to the Fox Lane 20, but the Foxes set up a blocking wall that erased the Harvesters on the left side, and the runner brought it all the way to the Laketown 42.

"What's going on?" Coach Fowles mumbled. "Sandy, we gotta change that kickoff team."

On third down, they passed over the middle. Ray Meister was behind his man in good coverage. But he tried to reach over the receiver's shoulder to get the ball, and was called for interference.

From the 27, the quarterback repeated the play, but this time Ray cut in front of his man and made the clean interception in full stride on the eight, cutting to the far sidelines and bringing it back to the 25. Laketown was held, and punted to the Fox Lane 38.

On first down the quarterback delayed slightly, then kept it himself and sneaked to the right of his center for five yards. On second down he dropped back to throw, and got it away just before Stan Beronski rammed him. The pass was incomplete, but Stan was called for roughing the passer, and the penalty moved the ball to the Laketown 44.

Again the quarterback threw, deep over the middle. Ray Meister leaped to tap the ball with one hand, then gathered it in and fell over backwards on the 12 with his second interception.

Ben Schenkle and Brian Purcell ran the ball to the 21, where it was fourth and one, with only eight seconds left in the half.

Coach Branahan wanted to go for it. Coach Fowles tried to get the attention of an official. "How many time-outs does Fox Lane have?" he called, but he wasn't heard.

He turned to his assistant. "Geez, if we don't make it and they call a time-out—hey, Sandy, we *got* to punt the ball, are you kiddin? Hey, they're right down on our 20-yard line if we don't make it."

"Just eight seconds?" Coach Branahan said.

"They can get one play off down there. I'd rather make them try and run back a punt. PUNTING TEAM!"

"Awright," Coach Branahan said, as the punting team went on.

"We can't consume eight seconds on a running play," Coach Fowles said. "The clock doesn't start until the ball's snapped, don't forget."

"I know," Coach Branahan said, resignedly.

"Hey, they get four seconds and they're on our 20-yard line. It's not worth it."

Ted O'Neill punted, and it was well covered by Jim Petrowski who watched it roll dead at midfield as the half ended.

The team clacked impatiently into the locker room.

"Keep MOVING!"

"Shit, unbelievable!"

"Did you rough that passer, Stan?"

"I didn't think I was *that* late."

"Sit down, come on."

"Fucking. . . . "

"Sit DOWN!"

"Somebody got an opener for the sodas?"

"We made every mistake possible—a pile of SHIT!"

"If we're going to play like this the second half," Jack Forrest said, "let's go over and concede or somethin."

"All right, gentlemen," Coach Fowles said as players moved aside to let him among them, "let's start pulling together this half. The first half we did everything we could to help Fox Lane. Penalties all over the place. I–I–I can't remember the last time we were penalized for so many stupid things.

"Where's Ted O'Neill? Ted, the head linesman says you're coming out of the huddle and swinging your arm into the neutral zone. That's an automatic five yards, Ted. Don't do it the second half. The roughing-the-passer penalty I didn't see, so I couldn't comment on that. Now the interference call, Ray Meister, that was a judgment call, and we don't complain about judgment calls. Let's play football.

"We think we know one of the things they're doing. When we split a flanker, they are keying the fullback man-to-man on the flanker side.

Which is beautiful. So our fullback counter should go. And it did. Bruce Stacey, I thought sure you were going all the way on that.

"Okay, defense. Our defense hasn't really hurt us that much. On pass defense a couple times we looked a little shakey, but not bad. Our kicking game *destroyed* us! That first touchdown we handed to them with a fumble. And gentlemen, we told everybody in here that they will return kickoffs up the short side of the field—and they still did it, broke somebody almost all the way.

"Well, the first half is over. We can't cry over spilt milk. It's done. But this half we have complete control over. And we're going to take the kickoff and start to play football the way *Laketown* is able to play football.

"Any questions, comments, suggestions?"

"Rich Schenkle," Coach Branahan said, "if they split a man in the slot, you just forget him. We're just going to play him man-to-man."

"Play right off Delaney's tail?"

"That's right. Put pressure on the quarterback. Don't let a man come out of that backfield."

Jonny banged his helmet on the floor. "Let's talk about *offense*," he said.

"All right, offense," Coach Fowles said. "Suggestions?"

"We gotta get that number 55," right guard Jack Forrest said, "that linebacker over me, cause we run like at the three hole, he's makin all the tackles."

"All right, do we have a reach call on?" Coach Fowles asked. The center yells, "reach" at the line of scrimmage if he thinks a linebacker is stunting, indicating that he will take the linebacker in the direction the play is going.

"We're callin it," Jack said, "but he's like just about straddling the tackle's leg, and it's real hard to get him. I can get him when we go away, to the other side, but Jim can't get to him when . . . "

"The linebacker is on me," left tackle John Curtis said, "and the defensive end is outside me. So when we run at three, I have to take him."

"The bootleg is freezing the end," Jonny said. "The end just stands there waitin for me."

"So the end shouldn't be the problem," Coach Fowles said. "Don't worry about the end. Go for that linebacker. Anything else?"

"*Pass*-rush!" Bradford hissed. "We can't get *in* there."

"What's the problem?" Coach Fowles said. "He's got all day back there. What's the story?"

"I have no *idea.*"

"Looks like they're going real low and cutting our legs out."

"Gentlemen, I can't believe the amount of time their passer has. Last week the pass-rush was tremendous, it won the game for us."

"Lucky that kid can't throw," Jonny said.

"Bob Mills," Bradford said to the right tackle, "why aren't *you* getting in there"

"I got two men on me on the pass-rush," Bob said.

"Same with *me,*" Bradford said.

"Let's stunt a little bit," Coach Fowles said. "*One* of you two linebackers, Bruce or John, is gonna get in there. Bob, who's double-teaming you, the center and the guard?"

"Yeah."

"All right, that means that John Finch, you're gonna be all by yourself on the other side of the center and you're gonna be going down the quarterback's throat."

"But they're double-teaming me also," Bradford said.

"Now *wait* a minute! What's Freddie Delaney doing?"

"Freddie's going to the outside," Bradford said, "and they're pushing *me* to the outside, double-teaming me to the outside, and getting Freddie caught in the wash."

"Well, another thing we could be doing: the laura, in passing situations."

"That's what we worked on during the week," Bradford said.

"Yeah, the laura is a much better pass-rush, because we can stunt up the middle real quick."

"We're a second-half team," Jonny said, "Let's GO!"

Coach Fowles held up a hand. "It was a rough half, but I got to be honest with you. I was not worried. Because we've got too much class, too much guts in our stomachs—and you know we're *never* gonna quit. That's a fact. Now, we've got twenty-four minutes . . . "

The Harvesters took the field to loosen up. Coach Fowles watched them, somberly.

"They are mentally flat," he said to me. "They are thinking about their next game, and they are not ready for this game. I can tell you right now, we are in *serious* trouble."

In the huddle, he said to them, "This is the half when you do everything you can to help the family. The family comes first. Right now. We got twenty-four minutes boys, and *you* can *do* it. I told you one time before, I'm going to say it again: I've got more confidence in this football team than any team I've had at Laketown, *ever!* And that is a fact. Too much class to let one mistake bother us. Twenty-four more minutes . . . "

"WE CAN DO IT!" Jonny shouted into the huddle.

Al Stacey took the kickoff back to the 38. Jonny kept and sprinted to his right for five yards. Then he handed off on a quick-opener to Ben Schenkle for another five and the first down.

Jonny threw a screen out to the left intended for Brian Purcell. It bounced off Brian's hands and rolled free. On the chance that it was a lateral, a free ball, the Fox Lane cornerback scooped it up as Brian stood still nearby, and ran it all the way to the end zone.

The pass was ruled incomplete, but Coach Fowles yanked Brian immediately. "Brian, are you *sick* or what?"

Brian shrugged, embarrassed, and headed for the bench.

"Got a *temperature?*"

"No."

"Then you better play football. You ran harder last week. You're not doing anything today."

Ben swept to the left for a couple, but the tackler grabbed his face mask, and the penalty moved the ball to the Fox Lane 37.

Ben shot up the middle, diving, twisting, to the 26. Bruce Stacey replaced him and ran the same play, to the 18. Ben came back in and hit behind Jim Marshall for the third straight time, but this time the ball dribbled out of his hands. Jim Marshall and Tom Kase were still driving their men forward as Ben lunged behind them, trying vainly to reach the ball which rolled lazily just beyond his fingertips. Fox Lane recovered on the 13.

Jonny came angrily off the field, with Ben trailing, speaking to him, trying to be understood with his mouthpiece still in his mouth: "I dithn't ether rearry gethe bawr, Jonny. . . . "

"He stunted and nobody picked it UP!" Jonny shouted.

"Take it easy, take it easy."

He spun on Jim Marshall. "Let's go, Jim! It was a simple reach call! They're STUNTING!"

"No one stunted!" Jim shouted back. "I got *my* man . . . "

"We'll get it back . . ."

"Everybody SIT DOWN!"

Fox Lane ran inside left tackle for a first down on the 27.

"LAURA!" Coach Fowles yelled, "get into the LAURA!"

Jim Petrowski went in at middle guard as the Harvesters switched from the four-four to the five-four laura.

"How about your secondary, want to change it?" Coach Fowles asked Coach Branahan.

"Naw, we got time."

The quarterback rolled left to pass, but Bruce Stacey had stunted and was on him, grabbed his jersey at the neck and flung him down on the 20, for a loss of seven.

The quarterback sneak again. Linebacker John Finch was stunting so fast that the quarterback simply ducked under him and went up the middle for a first down on the 39, where Al Stacey and Ray Meister caught him from behind. A holding penalty against Laketown moved the ball to the Laketown 46.

Barry Brill went in for Rich Schenkle. "Just gonna give you a rest, Rich," Coach Fowles said. "Take your hat off and get down on one knee. Just a rest, Rich."

The fullback hit hard on the right side, dragging Barry Brill, Bradford McClure, and Bob Mills with him to the 38. There, Laketown held. Jim Petrowski submarined to stop the fullback for a three-yard loss; Ken Furst leaped high to knock away a pass. Fox Lane punted dead on the seven.

Jonny got out with a pass in the right flat to Don Heidner, who butted over one tackler and brought the ball to the 20.

Then disaster. Jonny threw deep and off to the left sideline for Don again, but the huge Fox Lane cornerback reached high to intercept at mid-field. Unmolested, he sped down the sideline for the Foxes' second score.

The extra-point kick was good, and Fox Lane led 14–6 with four minutes left in the third quarter. There was an increase of tension noticeable along the Laketown sideline.

Ben Schenkle ran the kickoff back to the 40. Jonny rolled to his right and threw for Ted O'Neill near the sideline, but it was underthrown and intercepted, and brought back to the Laketown 32.

The offense came off sadly. Coach Fowles clapped encouragement. "Come ON! Get that ball BACK, DEFENSE!"

Fox Lane inched forward to a fourth and four on the 25, then blasted over its left side for a first down on the 20. The quarterback went back to pass, stumbled, and fell, and then Stan Beronski piled into him. Stan looked quickly up at the official, but no penalty was called.

The fourth quarter began.

On fourth down, the quarterback went back to throw, but the line had slipped through. Jim Petrowski, Stan, Freddie Delaney were after him like hounds. He went further back, then looped to his right, all the way across the field on the 45. He ducked under Stan, slipped by Bruce Stacey. Bradford was blocked. Finally, the quarterback stopped and threw complete, but for a loss on the 33. Laketown took over.

Coach Branahan put an arm on Jonny Penchak. "Jonny, what will work? Fake dive and bootleg?"

"It won't work because no one blocks the end," Jonny said, "I'll get destroyed."

"Even though you make a good fake?" Ted O'Neill asked, adjusting his helmet to go in.

"It doesn't matter, because the outside end always sees the ball anyway, and he's not blocked."

They trotted away from the sidelines, Ted persisting. "Well then, fake one way and. . . ."

Al Stacey went up the middle for a first down on the 47. Ben Schenkle struggled to the Fox Lane 49. Ben then took a pitch around right end to the 35, but Don Heidner was called for clipping, and the ball went back into Laketown territory.

Jonny hit Rich Schenkle down-and-in to the Fox Lane 41. Rich was dropped hard, and got up groggily. Stu Rosenman replaced him at left end. There were eight minutes and fifty-four seconds left.

Bruce Stacey used brute power up the middle to the 33, then again to the 28. Rich Schenkle went back in. Bruce and Ben got the first down on the 15. Then Bruce again, slashing through tacklers, took it to the one-foot line, and finally in for the touchdown. It was 14–12.

Jonny called time-out and came to the bench to discuss the crucial extra-point play which could tie the game with less than six minutes to play.

"Beautiful, Jonny, beautiful," Coach Fowles said, tapping his quarterback on the shoulder pads. "All right now, we got three yards we gotta get. Three yards. Coach, what do you think?"

Coach Branahan looked out at the ball.

"They're jamming the middle," Jonny said, breathing hard.

"Fake the bootleg and send Heidner in the corner?" Coach Branahan said. "Let Jonny try the bootleg? And if he can run it, make it an option?"

"Yeah," Coach Fowles said, "I like that, with you running the ball, Jonny."

"Okay?" Jonny asked, edging away.

"From a split-backfield?" Coach Branahan asked.

"How you want your backfield set up, Jonny?"

"In an I."

"All right," Coach Fowles said.

"Fake the double-dive at three," Jonny said, confirming the play, "bootleg it, hit Donnie down-and-out, and if he's not open I'll just run it."

"All right, listen," Coach Fowles said calmly. "Tell your people this is it. We're gonna do a good job. Jonny, get the family together in there, one family. We can do it."

Jonny headed back in.

"WE CAN DO IT!" Coach Fowles called after him.

"LET'S GO, LET'S GO," Coach Branahan yelled, clapping, "for the FAMILY!"

Jonny took the snap and rolled to his right. But there was the defensive end, unblocked, just as Jonny had warned about earlier. The end hit Jonny just as he threw, and the ball floated weakly short and into the ground.

Jonny got slowly to his feet. He ripped up a handful of sod and slammed it back to the ground. The score was 14–12 with 5:48 showing on the new scoreboard.

Fox Lane brought the kickoff back to the 43. Laketown lined up in the laura. Rich Schenkle became an unstoppable terror on defense. On first down he shot through the left side on a stunt and caught the runner for no gain. On second down he fired in the same gap, between Fox Lane's right guard and tackle, and hit the quarterback just as he handed off, and the play gained nothing. A little pass to the flat gained four, leaving fourth and six on the 47.

Fox Lane lined up to punt. Rich was in a rage, and crashed into the line before the ball was snapped. The offside penalty made it fourth and one foot. Fox Lane punted anyway, to the Laketown 23.

On first down, Al Stacey darted through a huge hole opened in the right side by Jack Forrest and Tom Kase, and only the last defender caught him on the 44.

With three minutes and forty-three seconds left, Jonny called another time-out.

"I think we should try running on 'em, Jonny," Coach Branahan said.

"Yeah," Coach Fowles said, wheeling to look down his bench. "Where's Bruce Stacey? Want Bruce in, Jonny?"

Bruce came over. "Yeah, Bruce, you and Ben."

"All right, go ahead in," Coach Fowles said. Then he grabbed Jonny's jersey. "Hold it, wait a minute. A draw might possibly work. Right now you're doing a good job. Bruce, you all right?"

"Yeah," said the weary fullback.

"All right, take your hat off, Bruce, get down on one knee. Go in next play."

Jonny gave first to Al Stacey, who was stopped cold, then to Bruce on a fullback counter to the 47. With three minutes and ten seconds left, Jonny called Laketown's last time-out.

He stood silently by his coaches.

"We got two downs to get about seven yards," Coach Fowles said.

"Eight-man look-in?" Coach Branahan suggested, indicating a quick slant-in pass to Rich Schenkle.

"We haven't tried that yet," Coach Branahan said, "Jonny, pro right, eight-man look-in."

"Okay."

Rich slanted in and Jonny fired the ball into his chest. Rich was hit immediately by the six-four cornerback, but wrestled free, banged off another tackler on the 45, and finally went down on the 40, with the first down.

Jonny dropped back again, looking over the middle, but no one was free, and he heaved the ball far over the right sideline.

On the second down Jonny threw deep for Don Heidner on the goal line. Don went up with two defenders and the ball fell incomplete through six flailing arms.

Then Jonny looked again to his left, deep for Rich Schenkle. The pass seemed headed for his arms, when the giant Fox Lane cornerback reached up and snared it with one hand. He turned up field along the sideline all the way to the Laketown 25, where Bruce Stacey dragged him down.

A clipping penalty took the ball back to the Fox Lane 36, but hope was now truly fading. Jonny came off and stood by himself, his arms folded, looking at the ground.

Rich Schenkle was not finished. On first down he stunted through the line and stopped the fullback for a yard loss. On second he hit the same man for no gain. On third down he caught the halfback by the ankles for another yard loss.

Fox Lane punted, Ken Furst signaled for a fair catch on the Fox Lane 47, and the Laketown offense had the ball with 40 seconds left.

The crowd was on its feet cheering; the team had shown magic before in this season.

Fox Lane went into a deep prevent-type defense, dropping its secondary men far off the line.

Jonny went back, watching Don Heidner slant deep over the middle, and whipped the ball to him on the 30. A lone defender timed his tackle precisely, and hit Don with a shot just when the ball arrived. The ball bounced off Don's chest incomplete, and both Don and the tackler lay motionless on the ground.

Coach Fowles and the doctor raced out, but both players had started to move by the time they got there. They had had the wind knocked out of them.

With twenty-seven seconds left, Jonny went back again to pass, found nobody open, and scrambled to his right out of bounds. Eighteen seconds left.

Rich Schenkle faked a move inside, then took off, angling for the left end-zone flag. Jonny scurried back and watched him, and as Rich broke free, several steps behind the defender, Jonny arched a beautiful spiral. Rich strained forward and dove for it on the 10, but the ball went a few inches too far.

As Rich got slowly to his feet he, or the play, or the team, got a standing ovation from the crowd.

The Laketown bench was hushed. Coach Fowles stalked down the line in front of his players, yelling and clapping. "Laketown NEVER quits! Come on, GIVE EM SOME SUPPORT!" The team responded, lining the sideline to cheer the last nine seconds.

Jonny dropped back to pass, but the Foxes were all over him. He tucked the ball in and went down under a swarm of red jerseys as the final whistle blew.

Coach Fowles dashed immediately for the far side of the field to congratulate the Fox Lane coach. The Harvesters loped drearily off.

"That's what we GET you guys!"

"All that FUCKIN AROUND!"

The players straggled toward the locker room, heads down. Some went in. Some sat down on the grass. Jonny and Rich lay on their backs. Ted O'Neill flopped face down on the knoll. Coach Fowles came running up.

"Come on, everybody in! Everybody in! Nobody stays out here feeling sorry for himself."

They pulled themselves up and followed him in.

He jumped up on a bench. "All right, let's get together," he shouted through the locker room, "bring it in, bring it in." Players pressed toward him. "All right, let's pay attention. First of all, we have no alibis, no excuses. When we win, we win like men. And if we *have* to lose, we're gonna lose like men, with no alibis, no excuses. We made too many mistakes today, gentlemen, too many mistakes. Fox Lane scored more points than we did, we gave away two touchdowns. But I'll tell you one thing: Get your heads up! We never quit. Laketown never quit. First of all, I'm going to be very honest about it, we were not ready to play today, mentally. We were not ready to play—you know that as well as I do. Now we can't go back and undo what just happened, it's impossible. So from this . . . second . . . on, we're gonna start thinking about next Saturday, about Peekskill High School. We can't go back.

"Hey, boys, listen: Nobody wins all the time in life. And when you *do* lose, I'll be able to tell more about you than any other time. When you lose you have to take a look at yourself. And you're tempted to make excuses, tempted to be a flake-out, a quitter. But we didn't quit today because Laketown *never* quits. On the very last play of the football game we played our guts out, and believe me I'm proud of you for that. So get your heads *up!* And from this second on start to think about Peekskill. Who we gonna beat?"

And from the team it surprisingly burst, "PEEKSKILL!"

"We are gonna beat them, gentlemen. Do you know why? We will be *ready*. Peekskill has no idea what they're in for next week. Who we gonna beat?"

"PEEKSKILL!"

11

In the little coaches' room Sandy Branahan slammed his locker shut. "Yeah, I'll look at the films tonight, and again and again. I'll play the whole fucking game over and over all night long."

Out in the parking lot, Mrs. Forrest, Jack's mother, greeted and congratulated several of the players as they came out lugging their gym bags. She gave Ray Meister, her neighbor, a warm hug. "Great game, Ray," she said, "wonderful interceptions."

The team was given postgame pizzas and sodas at the Staceys'. They lived in a simple, comfortable, two-story brick house with trees, picnic tables, and a small asphalt basketball court in back. The players sat at the tables, mixing with cheerleaders and a few other girls, and munched the endless supply of pizzas brought out by Mrs. Stacey from a hot oven. Some of the players shot baskets. The team seemed tired, but not badly down.

"Am I a prophet, Richard?" Bruce Stacey said to me. "Didn't I tell you we'd lose?" I couldn't remember that he did.

"I agree with Coach," Ted O'Neill said, hassling a drooping piece of mozzarella. "Peekskill has no idea what's in store for them next week." He chewed his pizza. "You know what? I think this loss goes right back to Saturday night, that party."

"That's bullshit," said John Curtis, sitting next to him. Other players at the table agreed with the tackle that the party was not the reason.

Rich Schenkle was leaning against a tree. "What are you going to do tonight?" I asked him. "Have a party?"

"Naw," he said, chuckling. "There's a double-feature, *Mash* and *Patton*. I think me and Ben, and maybe Jonny, and a couple others will go to see that. I just want to relax."

Jonny and I went over to Jack Forrest's. Jack got out his 250 Suzuki motorcycle, which he had not been able to get going, and he and Jonny tinkered with it. Ray Meister roared over from his house nearby aboard his 350 Yamaha, which was not yet registered. Ray joined the tinkerers examining spark plugs, fuel-line connections, wires. They could not solve Jack's problem.

Jonny got aboard Ray's bike and fired it up.

"Take it easy, Jon," Ray said. "The clutch is sensitive."

Jonny slowly let out the clutch, and the bike lurched forward. The rear wheel spun on the damp early evening grass, and Jonny slid sideways. Then the bike leaped forward across the lawn and burrowed into a hedge. Jonny crawled out unhurt, and extracted the bike. After Ray had checked it over for damage, Jonny got on again and chugged slowly around the lawn.

Then he and I got back in the car and took a ride.

"Tough game, Jonny," I said. "You almost had Rich open there at the ... "

"I'd rather not talk about the game, okay? Let's talk about my guitar. This beautiful black Aria I saw at the shop. I'm buying it. Waiting for the money to come from my bank. When I get that guitar I'm going to play and play ... "

He sat back in the seat strumming an imaginary guitar and moaning a soft rock melody to himself.

Coach Fowles greeted me at the door holding a glass of cream sherry.

"Boy, I'm exhausted tonight," he said. "I had a couple Scotches earlier and started to fall asleep on the couch. So I switched."

A handful of his friends, who traditionally spend postgame Saturdays with the Fowleses, sat around quietly with drinks. Buddy and I went into the kitchen where Squeegy was putting together a goulash.

"Maybe we didn't lose anything at all today," he said. "Anyway, no team in this county lost today with more poise and class than Laketown."

"I saw you run across the field to congratulate their coach," I said. "How come you ran over there so fast?"

He chuckled. "Hey, when we lose, that opposing coach is not going to get beyond the *hashmark*. That's just the way it is. Did you know I got on the Fox Lane bus and talked to their team? I just told them they played a fine game, and I hoped they went all the way. They were really quiet, listened. Remember that big black tackle, with the tape across his nose? He said to me, 'Coach, you got some guys really *hit* out there.' I thought that was a nice thing for him to say. When I finished they cheered."

"How come you chased your players into the locker room right after the game?"

"Because they were just going to lie in the grass and feel sorry for themselves and wait for people to come up and lick their wounds. I wasn't having any of that. If they want to come out later and lie in the grass— after they have made certain decisions for themselves in the locker room— then fine."

"I was surprised I saw no tears in the locker room," I said.

"Yeah, well I think that just reflects again the fact that we weren't emotionally up for the game and didn't have far to come down."

He shook his head. "You know, this is the first time Fox Lane has beaten Laketown in the six years I've been head coach. We shut them out the last two years with the laura defense. And when we switched back to the laura today we stopped their running game cold. They aren't really very good. Sandy and I agree that they'll probably lose three games out of their next four."

He sighed. "I just didn't do a good teaching job this week. Stan Beronski disagreed with me after the game, about mental attitude. He said that regardless of mental attitude, we still should have won. Which is probably true. Four turnovers in the second half, all three interceptions and Ben's fumble on the 15. Other than that, Fox Lane didn't get inside the Laketown 30 in the whole second half."

We went back to the living room. Coach Fowles put the projector on a little table, and took a mirror down from the wall, so he could show the game film for his guests.

SUNDAY, *October 10*

The players were jovial, sprawled on the floor of the Fowleses' rec room to watch the Fox Lane film. Coach Fowles went over it quickly. He pointed out when running backs seemed hesitant, when linemen didn't stay with their blocks. He agreed with several players that they had underestimated the Fox Lane linebackers, who had moved very quickly along the line of scrimmage to shut off running plays.

"That one kid," John Curtis said, "that tackle, he kept saying, 'I'm Dick Butkus, you can't run at me.'" The room cracked up with that recollection.

"He *hit* though."

"*Yeah!*"

"All right, boys, lights," Coach Fowles said. "First of all, I don't think our attitude *was* good. Let's face it, we were not as ready to play football as we were against Greeley. But I was talking to one of our kids after the game, and I think maybe he was right. Even with the attitude the way it was, we still could have won the ballgame. We came *very* close.

"We allowed that team one touchdown. The other touchdown they scored on a turnover. You know how many turnovers we had the second half? Four. You just can't have four turnovers in one half and win, you just can't do it. On the other hand, we were down inside their 10-yard line early in the game, and we should have scored down there. Another time we fumbled inside the 20.

"One great thing about this football team though is that we really never *do* quit, never. And even on the very last play of the game, in fact, some of the people who were there will tell you they couldn't believe we were going to lose that game. And I think that's a compliment to the whole team.

"Now. Next week we play a very tough football team. We play Peekskill. They are always a very rough, physical team. And this may be the best team they've had in years. They have one halfback, Crayton, who is probably the quickest, the toughest back to put down, that you will face all year. They have a sophomore fullback that weighs 240."

"Crayton is old, too," Coach Branahan said, "late 18."

"Good," Jonny said. "Maybe we can catch him in a bar."

"They are really rough," Coach Branahan went on, "they always are. Peekskill is completely emotional kids, always keyed up. Hotheads. If they get you in a pile-up, they'll go for your eyes."

"I keep mine closed," somebody said.

It was Columbus Day, a school holiday, so practice was at 9:00 A.M. It was hot and muggy, with pools of water in the grass from yesterday's downpour. Tiny players from the Midget League were there in uniform for a clinic.

Coach Fowles's son was a star runner for one of the teams, but Buddy was ambivalent about Midget football, both because he feared it gave them organized football and emphasis on winning too early in their lives, and also because of the danger of injury. He called my attention to their cheap equipment, especially helmets, whose protective value he doubted.

"But when the kids want to play," he said, "it's difficult not to support them. Parental responsibility is an interesting thing. I get a lot of credit from many people for spending so much time with the boys on our team, helping them in different ways. And yet what about my own son? Jeff had a football game last Saturday, and where was I, his father? I was down here with *my* team. I'm not sure I'm spending all the time I should with my own son."

But this morning he was walking among the tykes, watching with deep pleasure. Harvester players were paired off with small groups of Midgets to drill them briefly in fundamentals. We could hear Coach Fowles's words echoed: "Hit him at the knee, slide up to the waist, and turn him laterally. . . . Get off on the COUNT, off on the count. . . . QUICKER. . . . Use your hands and get rid of the blocker. . . . "

After serving the clinic, the team had a spirited practice, with hard hitting. Don Heidner was there but not dressed. His ribs had been severely bruised near the end of the Fox Lane game when he had the wind knocked out of him. Rich Schenkle's right hand was badly swollen, and swathed in tape.

"What's that from?" I asked.

"From *that*," Rich said, snapping his forearms up under an imaginary chin, and smiling.

The coaches introduced a new offensive set, a *strong*. The tailback lined up behind the quarterback, with the fullback outside the guard on the flanker side. That put blocking power a little quicker on that side. Coach Fowles said he was installing the new set because "I don't feel Peekskill adjusts well."

The defense concentrated on the laura.

"If there's a weakness," Coach Fowles said to his defensive linemen, "it's right *here*." He pointed to the gap in the laura lineup on the weak side of center, where only two of the five men were positioned. "But we'll have Bruce Stacey cover that."

The humidity got to a few of the players. Some got dizzy and took themselves out for a few plays. Keith Allen went inside and threw up.

Bees got to others. Stan Beronski and Freddie Delaney were allergic to bee stings. When bees came around, those two stopped whatever they were doing and devoted full time to dodging and swatting.

Bob Mills smacked his head into Ben Schenkle's belly on a hard tackle. Ben got up, expressionless, and slunk back behind the row of on-looking players. Then, privately, he doubled up and held his stomach. Finally other players made him lie down. Protecting his pride, they shielded him from the coaches' view.

TUESDAY, October 12

It was a rough day for the team even before practice. The athletic director suspended Stan, Steve Barker, and Keith Allen from the day's workout because they had goofed off in gym class. Stu Rosenman was even more discouraged because he had played so little against Fox Lane. In the cafeteria he said, "I'm just looking for a place to start. I used to be a fullback, but now I'll play anywhere."

Ben Schenkle came to the meeting carrying his pads and eating a roast beef sandwich. Coach Branahan wrote the numbers and names of the Peekskill players on the blackboard.

Coach Fowles said Peekskill ran from the split-backfield, from which they liked to throw, and from the I. "In the I, Crayton, their best runner, is the up man. He carried eighteen times last week. We will use the laura center against that, with the laura man—probably you, Bruce Stacey—keying Crayton. Like I told you, this is perhaps the best Peekskill team in years. You better make up your mind right now that you're going to sting some people on Saturday. You'll probably get stung some, too."

Last year, Laketown had won 14–0. The most memorable event of that game was that Jonny went in at quarterback for the last play of the game, called a quarterback sneak, and went 63 yards for what seemed to be a touchdown. The official ruled the game had ended before the play got off, and Jonny's run was nullified.

"What the hell's the matter with the team?" the athletic director, Rick Bronson, said to Coach Fowles. He was referring not only to their earlier goofing-off in gym, but also to what was going on at that moment.

The team was supposed to be doing calisthenics, but instead they were laughing, dancing, falling down.

Coach Fowles watched them. "I am really tempted to send them to the showers," he said angrily, "I really am."

He walked over to the team. He spoke brusquely. "All right, get down on one knee, take your hats off. My philosophy is simple: If you want to have a good time, *have* a good time. If you're happy, *stay* happy. If you're *not* happy, *get* happy. It's simple. If you *want* to have a football team, *have* a football team."

He looked icily down at the faces of the players. "Now if you don't want to have a football team, you should leave. Right now."

Nobody moved. He looked slowly around at them. "Any questions?" Nobody spoke. He went on in a softened voice. "If there are no questions, then this is a contract with me, because everybody understands. Any questions?" Still no one moved or spoke. "All right, bars and tires."

The team scampered off, and he walked dejectedly behind them. "I may have just made the biggest mistake of the season," he said to me, "by not sending them in. It's a question of timing. Psychologically, it's really harsh treatment to send them in. Well, I didn't send them in *now*, anyway. We'll see."

He folded his arms and watched the players hop briskly through the tires. "It has to come from *them*," he said. "Captains are important right now. In some ways Bruce Stacey could have been the type to bring the team together now."

The backs went to the playing field, and Coach Fowles took the linemen up to the practice field behind the school. And then he whipped them.

"All right, on the SLED! Hurry up, let's GO! On TWO—GO, GO, HUT-ONE, HUT–TWO. . . . All right, second line, GO, GO. . . . Come on, QUICKER, QUICKER! . . . On the COUNT. . . . Hey, John, you want to take a SHOWER? NO? Then you work as hard as everybody else! . . . Come on, Jim, you're too SLOW. . . . Next line, quicker, GO, GO. . . . All right, on the whistle, forward rolls. . . . Move with the ball, on your bellies, MOVE!"

The linemen struggled to keep up, puffing and sweating under the sun and the lash—up, running in place, down on their bellies, forward rolls. He drove them without relief. Finally he stopped them. They stood sucking for breath, streaked with sweat, their feet still moving from the intensity of their pace.

Coach Fowles smiled. "On Saturday, we're going to beat Peekskill," he announced. "You know why? Because we're going to *outwork* them. Not outlaugh them. *Outwork* them." He paused, still smiling. "Get the message? All of you get the message? *All right!* One-minute break."

"Wow!" I said to him.

He chuckled. "They *love* it," he said.

They went back to work, the pace undiminished. I suffered with Don Heidner as he flopped out time after time on those bruised ribs; I gasped with Jim Marshall who was beginning to lag; I watched Bradford McClure with awe as he drove himself uncompromisingly.

"Boys, I'll tell you what," Coach Fowles said, between drills. "If everybody out here worked as hard as Bradford, there would have been no worries the last four games. All right, on the whistle, leap out on your bellies. . . . "

Rich Schenkle was trying to conceal a limp. Every time they belly-flopped, Rich came down on his damaged knee. Players privately urged him to stop, but he ignored them. I whispered the fact to Coach Fowles. He watched Rich, then walked over to him and handed him the tattered football he had been using.

"Hey Rich," he said, "go down to Coach Branahan and get me a better ball. I don't want this lousy ball."

Rich hesitated, looking at the ball.

"Go on, I mean it."

Rich took the ball and walked off. He disappeared around the corner of the school, then came quickly back, with the same ball.

"Hey, go *on!*" Coach Fowles hollered at him. "I don't want that ball, Rich, I'm not kidding!"

Rich went.

Coach Fowles shook his head. "You have to watch out for their pride," he said.

"Why didn't you send the team in today?" I asked. "The second time in a week you bawled them out."

"This just wasn't the time to send them in. You have to understand, for some of the guys it's a catastrophe to miss practice—in their minds."

"But Friday, before Fox Lane?" I said.

"Mmm," Coach Fowles said. "On that day they were still an undefeated team. Maybe they should have gone in then."

In the pit drill, Stu Rosenman out-muscled John Finch. Jack Forrest smoothly blocked Ray Meister out of the circle. Ben Schenkle wanted in against Tom Kase, but Bradford McClure shoved Ben aside. Tom drove

Bradford into the ground. Then Bruce Stacey and Rich Schenkle stepped in. They went at each other savagely with their forearms, hammering, lifting, grinding into each other. At the whistle Bruce tapped Rich on the rear, and Coach Fowles smiled.

"Maybe the kids have just been trying to tell us they wanted to work harder," he said.

Freddie Delaney drove a beaten-up old Dodge station wagon with a clanking transmission. He usually parked it outside the locker room on the asphalt sidewalk atop the grassy rise that led down to the field. Some players rolled it down the hill. Freddie discovered it there and angrily drove it back up. When he went inside, the culprits rolled the car down again. Freddie came out and drove it back up.

"Why don't you lock it?" I asked.

"Cause I leave the keys in it."

"Why?"

"Cause once I took the keys out and I dropped them into the gas tank, by mistake."

WEDNESDAY, October 13

Cheerleaders occupied the hanging-bars, sitting atop them to have their pictures taken. Coach Fowles took backs together with linemen to the linemen's area for a consolidated drill. There had been some grumbling about the backs having it easy. So today they got a taste of what linemen did. The backs started out cheerily, but soon were disenchanted. They struggled to keep up with the well-conditioned linemen in forward rolls, belly-flops, cariocas, and so on. Jonny was disgusted. "*This* is getting ready for Saturday?" he said. The linemen gloated.

Then they all went down to run the blaster. The backs formed a gauntlet for the linemen to run through as they emerged from the rubber-pronged blaster. They jabbed and laughed at the slower linemen who cursed the unfamiliar machine. Then the linemen formed a gauntlet for the backs to run through. They pummeled the backs. Only cornerback Ray Meister made it through.

Rather than give up his arm pads as the coaches wished, Keith Allen showed up today with new bright green ones. In the pit drill, he and Ray

Meister traded victories. Tom Kase stayed low to drive Clifford Albert out. Jim Marshall used his great strength to out-bull Vince Carradino. Don Heidner and Mark Ferenzi hit weakly.

"Some guys don't belong in there," Coach Fowles said later. "Like Don Heidner. He's a good football player, tough, but he just doesn't belong in that drill. The pit's not his thing."

After practice, Rich Schenkle sat outside and pulled off his soccer-style shoes. He stared at them sadly. The soles were ripped nearly off. "I paid ten dollars for these three weeks before the season," he said. Coach Branahan looked at the dilapidated shoes and shook his head. "I haven't got money to buy new ones," Rich said.

Don Heidner brought him a pair of low-cut football shoes with long spikes. They were too small. Coach Branahan went inside and brought out a pair of his own soccer-style shoes for Rich to try. They were just right. They would be Rich's for the rest of the season.

Last year, as a junior, guard Jack Forrest hardly ever played. He became more and more depressed about his small size. Not fast enough to be a back, not big enough to be a lineman, his feeling of unsuitability grew even as he did not, and finally he believed there was no spot for him at all in high school football.

"I was really down," he said, toying with a chicken leg at a family supper at his house. "Then I went to football camp last summer. There were guys from all over the country, big guys. I was sure I couldn't play with these guys. But you *had* to play against them. We had three sessions a day, just football, football, football for a week. I found myself playing against a 220-pound tackle. There was nothing to do but try. I found I could move him. I could actually block that monster. I found out I could do the job. It changed everything around for me."

The family had moved to Laketown from a mean neighborhood in the Bronx when Jack was a freshman. His father, a round, jovial, hospitable man with dark, curly hair, still commuted to his job as a splicer with an electric company.

Jack and his younger brothers drank from quart bottles of soda. Mr. Forrest handed me a beer and scowled playfully at the two main dishes on the table, fried chicken and stew. "Two things I really don't like," he said, smiling, "and she makes them both."

"Go cop a walk," said Mrs. Forrest with feigned belligerence. She was a small, high-strung, delightfully open woman with short, dark hair and thick glasses.

"This team seems unusual in so many ways," I said, "such small players, such good spirit, such long hair . . ." Jack's dark hair curled neatly over his ears and down the back of his neck, enhancing the benignity of his dark, sloping eyes and gentle, innocent smile.

"Some parents are still uptight about the hair," Mrs. Forrest said. She mentioned another starter on the team. "*His* father would belt him if he tried to grow his hair long." She mentioned another player. "*His* father made him shave off his goatee yesterday. We don't think long hair matters at all."

"I'm still not sure about him playing guard," Mr. Forrest said, looking at Jack. "The point is, Jack loves football so much, maybe he should switch to another position where he would have a better chance to play further, in college. I mean, there's no use kidding ourselves about Jack playing guard at college at—what do you weigh, Jack?"

"One fifty-six now."

"Yeah. So I keep thinking maybe he ought to try the backfield."

"I don't *like* the backfield. I've tried it. I just don't like it."

"But if it's the only chance he's got to *play*. . . . See, I loved football, really wanted to keep playing when I was younger. I wanted to play semi-pro, but I couldn't see well enough. I'm *blind*." He chuckled. "But it's just that I hate to see Jack not get to play after this year, when he wants to so bad. And then there's the matter of scholarships. . . ."

"I ain't gettin no football scholarship," Jack said. "And so I *won't* play at college. I'm enjoying *this* year."

"I think it's wonderful kids as small as Jack get to play at all," Mrs. Forrest said, "and the *coach* they got. . . ."

"Jack's workin hard in that line," Mr. Forrest said, "that's for sure."

THURSDAY, October 14

I ran into the principal, Mr. Leary, in the hall. "Of course I was disappointed Saturday," he said, "because Laketown clearly was the better team. We won the game in all respects except the damn *score*." He chuckled and looked out of the window and watched the leaves blow under a cold, dark sky.

Coach Fowles was absent from his guidance office. I found him in an empty classroom with Coach Branahan, going over changes for Saturday. They changed the frankenstein short-yardage defense from a 6–1 to a 6–2, to give the line more help against Peekskill's off-tackle threat. They made personnel changes on the kickoff team. They worked out a new play, the tailback going in motion, and then hooking in for a short, quick pass over the line.

And they decided that they would open up on Saturday with the long bomb to Don Heidner. For that first play, they would put in the strong set, with Bruce and Al Stacey in the backfield to pass-block for Jonny.

"I talked to Stu Rosenman's parents yesterday," Buddy told me after Sandy had left. "They were in the guidance center to see somebody else, with Stu, and I ran into them. Mr. Rosenman asked me how much I weighed, and I said about 180. And he said it was a good thing I didn't weigh 150, or I would have had my block knocked off last Saturday. It was because I didn't play Stu more. You know what? I took that as another positive sign from the game. I have always felt that Mr. Rosenman could perhaps support his son a little more, not always attack him. And now he was defending him. I thought that was beautiful. Stu needs lots of support."

In the pit drill, the two reserve ends, Mike Schultz and Cary Grimes, battled again. Mike drove Cary out of the circle. Bradford McClure urged Cary on. "Use your HANDS, Cary," he yelled, "what do you think you HAVE 'em for?" Cary fought back, and was driven out again by his larger foe. Stu Rosenman beat Freddie Delaney twice.

"Good *job*, Stu," Coach Fowles said.

Bruce Stacey complained about his knee, which was puffed up. Coach Fowles moved it, felt around it with his fingers. "You've got a little fluid on it. When'd you hurt it?"

"Couple days ago."

"They don't drain fluid anymore. For the first forty-eight hours you should have put ice on it. Now it needs wet heat. Tonight put an Ace bandage on it, not too tight, and it will press the fluid out."

The scrimmage was lethargic. My mind wandered. Over on the soccer field, three small boys were shooting up a toy rocket which soared into the sky and then returned to earth beneath a little parachute. Huge cumulous clouds edged with bright gold moved in front of the sun.

The "Peekskill" offense was running against the Laketown defense. The defense was jamming up. "Hey, hold it!" Coach Fowles yelled, coming over to the left side of the defensive line. "We got three guys trying to go through the same gap. Come *on*, we can't have anybody stunting like that unless it's called in the huddle. Good way to get killed."

For a while the team looked sharper. They moved into the 40-yard sprints. Back and forth on the playing field they ran, from the goal line to the 40, and back, in three waves. But only a handful of boys seemed to be running hard. The coaches talked about that as they watched. Coach Fowles grew angry. After the fifteenth sprint, he stalked out to the center of the field, facing the team.

"Anybody with guts enough to say he put out at least 100 percent on these sprints, step forward five yards."

Nobody stepped. He looked at them, up and down the line. "I'll tell you what, with this attitude we'll never beat Peekskill. Take a shower. I don't even want to see you run the last sprint."

The coaches walked together toward the locker room, looking at the ground. "We're not ready for Peekskill, that's for sure," Coach Fowles said. "Maybe they should have a meeting."

Coach Branahan agreed. "It's all right to say the kids should do things on their own," he said, "motivate themselves, but sometimes they need to be prodded."

"Hmmm," Coach Fowles said. "That's the trouble with having captains who don't *lead*."

"There's one guy who could be doing it right now," Coach Branahan said. "Bruce Stacey."

They both nodded. Outside the locker room, Coach Fowles called the three captains together.

"Boys, we are headed for a *bad* loss. We've had a good week of practice, looked good, but mentally we're not ready."

Rich Schenkle, Stan Beronski, and Jim Marshall stood uncertainly and looked at the ground.

"It's not that I want us *up* today," Coach Fowles went on, "or even tomorrow—that's not the point. But we're not putting out. We better do something. Any suggestions?"

Rich shifted his feet and pulled back a lock of hair with two fingers. "I guess just talk it out," he said.

"You mean have a meeting?" Coach Fowles asked.

"Yeah."

"Okay, that's a *good* idea."

They decided to have it tomorrow, Friday, after practice, without the coaches.

They went in. "Buddy," I said, "maybe I shouldn't be telling you this, but I think one problem with your captains is that they feel they've never really been accepted by the coaches."

He looked at me, his eyes slightly narrowed inquisitively. "Really? Is that a fact, or an assumption?"

"I think it's a fact."

"Then we've made a mistake," he said.

FRIDAY, October 15

The team ran through brisk no-contact drills in good spirits. Play execution was sharp, the players were attentive to the coaches.

"They look better today," Coach Fowles said to Coach Branahan as they went in. "They don't need a special meeting."

"Last year on the JVs," Coach Branahan said, "to psyche up the guys on game day we had each boy run by and shake the coach's hand and say, 'I want to *win* today.' There are a lot of ways to psyche them up. Maybe something like that. . . ."

"I don't know if we can do that kind of thing, Sandy. There's an age difference between JV and varsity, you know, the boys on the varsity are a little different. It still has to come from within the boy himself."

"Hmmm," Sandy said.

In the classroom, guard Clifford Albert, the only starter whose hair did not protrude from the back of his helmet, was elected honorary game captain in a close vote over tackle John Curtis.

"Boys, we think we know three automatics that Peekskill calls," Coach Fowles said, referring to coded play changes the quarterback can call at the line of scrimmage. "If they're lined up and the quarterback yells 'Red,' that's a pass over to the right. 'Green,' pass over the center. 'Blue' is a pass to the left."

"How'd we get those, coach?"

"Never mind. But we did it the right way—no hanky-panky. But let's not get hung up on that. Let's out-hit them first, then worry about colors. Let's review Peekskill a little bit."

He reminded them of the straight-ahead power of the 240-pound fullback, and the open-field prowess of halfback Crayton. He taunted them with the information he had heard that the Peekskill quarterback was not allowed to be tackled in practice, so was not used to being hit. He quickly ran the Peekskill film from last year for the final time, showing the team's power on wide sweeps.

"But don't worry about that," Coach Fowles said as he rewound the film. "Just go out and play football. They'll go down just like anybody else when you hit 'em right. Bradford?"

"I don't understand why we don't always go for a two-point conversion, since we're not consistent with our kicks."

"Well, Ben's been pretty good. If we get one point in the bag, we can go for two points next time. In the Horace Greeley game, we went for one point and made it and won the ballgame. Hey, it's *hard* to get three yards down there on the goal line.

"Okay boys, last Saturday is gone. We could play Fox Lane nine times and beat them nine times. But that's *gone*. And you just have one crack at Peekskill. For the seniors, this is the last time you're *ever* going to play Peekskill. This is it. Forty-eight minutes. And we shouldn't have to come in and hit you over the head with a board to get you fired up. The rest of your life I want you to remember tomorrow. It can be the kind of day you *want* it to be. Okay, any questions?"

Nobody spoke. He looked around the room carefully. "Captains want to say anything?"

The captains were silent. "Okay. I can hardly wait for tomorrow to happen. Because we're gonna be an entirely different football team."

12

SATURDAY, *October 16*

Ben Schenkle and Ted O'Neill got dressed early, and went onto the home field to practice kicking extra points before leaving for Peekskill. Ben wanted Ted as his holder, rather than Don Heidner who didn't really want the job and whose holds had been unsteady. Ted had big, sure hands, and Ben kicked confidently with him holding.

Stan Beronski sat outside the locker room daubing his shoes with black polish. Another starter came walking slowly up, a little bent over. "Where's that cold spray?" he asked, looking for the aerosol can of Nitrotan spray used for minor cuts and bruises. "My parents were away this morning, so my girl came over, and I overdid it. I really got sore balls." He went inside, opened his pants, and shot some of the numbing spray down in his crotch.

"This weather sucks," Stan said, still polishing his shoes outside. "It's too hot to play football."

The bus pulled away for the half-hour ride to Peekskill. The players were nearly silent. So were the coaches.

"How do you feel about today?" I asked Coach Fowles.

"No special feeling, I don't know," he said quietly.

"I have a feeling," Coach Branahan said. "I have never coached a losing team against Peekskill."

We drove through Peekskill, a dingy town gnawed at by urban renewal, and got out at the public park where the game would be played. The game field stretched over two baseball diamonds. The players went into the locker room to put on their shoulder pads, and then trooped out to sit in the shade until time to warm up.

A group of small black boys watched as Jim Marshall walked by. "*That* motherfucker don't *need* no shoulder pads," one of them said.

The players climbed over some rocks on the bank across the running track from the field, and lounged under the trees. The player who had had the busy morning went behind a bush and applied some more Nitrotan spray. Finally it was time.

Ben Schenkle and Ted O'Neill got permission from Coach Fowles for Ted to hold for kicks, and they went out to practice. Rich Merrill, after packing cotton into an infected ear, centered for them. Jonny threw to backs and ends. Linemen sprinted and banged shoulders. Coach Fowles wandered among them.

"They look really ready to play today," I said to him, "not like last week."

Coach Fowles was pensive. "Yeah, but you know, this is a funny game. You start out with a funny shaped ball. And it takes weird bounces . . ."

Rich Schenkle called "heads" and won the toss. They elected to receive the kickoff, choosing to risk facing into the bright sun. Roger, the little manager, jogged among the players, stopping to apply antiglare greasepaint under their eyes. A few players refused at first.

"You *will* use it," Coach Fowles directed. "We're not listening to any excuses about the sun."

A large contingent of Laketown fans was there, filling the stands behind their team's bench, and already the cheerleaders were whipping them up as the Harvesters retired to the locker room to psyche themselves.

Jim Marshall slammed his helmet repeatedly into the lockers. "They think we're CAKE, Laketown! They think we SUCK! CAKE!" (bang). "CAKE!" (bang). "CAKE!" (bang).

"EVERYBODY together now, we got a FAMILY!"

"Let's fuckin GO!" Jonny yelled. "Let's kick some ASS today, huh?"

"Whole damn WEEK. . . ."

"It's the ATTITUDE that's going to win today," Rich Schenkle said.

"We gotta pull it all together today, offense AND defense."

"We owe Coach Fowles. . . ."

"We don't just owe Coach Fowles," Bradford McClure said. "We owe

OURSELVES something because we practiced like a BITCH all week. The linemen worked their BALLS off this week."

"EVERY PLAY, Laketown, put 'em on the GROUND!"

"Let's get TOGETHER, LAKETOWN!" Jim Marshall hollered, banging the locker again.

"GET THAT QUARTERBACK!" Jim Petrowski cried. "He's CAKE, he's a HOTHEAD! He can't get HIT in practice!"

"BREAK HIS KNEES, Laketown, BREAK HIS KNEES!"

"Do it Laketown, for ALL of us, the whole FAMILY!"

"Don't TALK, Laketown" Rich Schenkle said, "We gotta DO it."

"THEY'RE not nice guys," Jonny said, "SO WE'RE not nice guys."

Through the thin walls, Peekskill could be heard whooping it up in the adjacent locker room.

"LISTEN TO 'EM!" Jim Petrowski screamed, "LISTEN TO 'EM!"

"Everybody make NOISE, Laketown. . . ."

The room was filled with screams and taunts.

"YOUR TEAM SUCKS! . . . WE'LL KICK YOUR ASS!"

"You know why they're YELLING," Jonny shouted, "BECAUSE THEY'RE SCARED!"

"Right now they think they're better than us," Rich Schenkle said, "AND I DON'T GIVE A FUCK!"

"We paid too fucking high a price. . . ."

"Hey, whenever you get a shot at anybody, KILL 'EM! PUT 'EM OUT OF THE GAME!"

"They're SCARED!"

"NO MISTAKES, Laketown."

"Just think about last week," Jonny said, softer, "how SHITTY it was. Think about how you felt after the game. THINK about it!"

"All right, boys," Coach Fowles said as he pushed his way in through the raging players, "that's enough. You know, there are a lot of words, and there are a lot of actions. And as far as I'm concerned, actions *always* speak louder than words."

As he spoke, there was persistent muffled banging on the lockers around the room, and from the Peekskill side.

"All you've got to do now is go out on that football field and do what we believe—what we *know*—you can do. Cause action speaks louder than words. The key word is hit, hit, *hit!* That's what we're gonna do today, gentlemen. Coach Branahan, anything you want to say?"

"Hey, fellas, come on now. You know, we've waited for this—I don't know just what it is that makes me feel—I've *never lost* to Peekskill. Never.

In *anything*. I played em in *high school* and never lost to them."

"It better not start today, Laketown," Jonny said, "it BETTER NOT!"

Bradford tried to speak. "It's not, it's not. . . ."

The Peekskill team was pounding on lockers.

"Hey, boys . . ."

"THEY'RE POUNDING AWAY," Jim Petrowski yelled, "IT DON'T MEAN NOTHIN . . ."

Coach Fowles spoke calmly. "On the receiving team we're going to take it up the left. And if we don't break it all the way we're going to get one on the first play, the bomb . . ."

Bradford tried again: "The sign of a fabulous team, the sign of a fabulous team. . . ."

"Boys, who works harder?"

"LAKETOWN!"

". . . is a team that can come back from a LOSS!"

"Who we gonna beat?"

"PEEKSKILL! . . ."

The stands were nearly full. The flashy Peekskill band retreated. The defensive teams were introduced over the public-address system. And then Peekskill kicked off to start the Harvesters' best game so far.

Al Stacey brought the kick back to the 30. Along the bench, the players were tense in anticipation of the bomb to Don Heidner. Jonny dropped back behind good protection, and Don streaked downfield past two defenders. Jonny whipped his arm forward and delivered—too far. Don dove on the Peekskill 25 but the ball was just beyond his reach.

Keith Allen went in to launch the running game, and sliced for six yards behind John Curtis and Clifford Albert. Then he limped off with an injured knee.

Peekskill held, and Ted O'Neill dropped back to punt. The second blocking wave of three men lined up five yards behind the center. Two Peekskill linemen shot through on the left side and blocked the ball right off Ted's foot. Ted whirled and dove back to recover. But it was Peekskill's ball on the Laketown 17.

"Son of a BITCH!" somebody shouted on the bench.

"Where'd they come in?"

"He stunted. DAMN!"

"He came right up the middle, Coach."

They pitched out to their swift back, Crayton, around the left side. Everybody was blocked in, and safetyman Mark Ferenzi on that side had taken a step toward the middle. Only Bruce Stacey was in close pursuit as Crayton swept in for the score.

The Peekskill kicker missed off to the left. The score was 6–0, and the Harvesters were quickly behind for the third straight game.

Coach Fowles turned sharply to his assistant. "Coach, we can't stay in that six-two. We gotta have corners."

"Coach, we gotta keep Al *in*," Bruce Stacey protested, indicating that his brother should not cover the flat.

"No, Bruce, we gotta have corners. Forget the six-two double-stack. Stay in the six-one frankenstein, Bruce."

"Okay."

Brian Purcell fumbled the kickoff, but scooped it up and wrestled his way to the 15. Ben Schenkle on a counter ripped through the left side for a first down on the 27. Two more first downs put the ball on the 50.

Running plays brought it to a third and one, on the Peekskill 41. There was a mix-up in the backfield, and Jonny was thrown for a loss to the 45. With fourth and five, he called time-out.

"Jonny, what happened there?" Coach Fowles asked him at the sideline.

"I called a double-dive at the three hole, but Bruce lined up on the other side and blocked at seven."

"Okay, right now, what do the linemen say? What looks good in there? Think we can make it?"

"Might be able to stomp with Bruce," Jonny said.

"Yeah, uh, which way?"

"Stomp right."

"What do *you* think, Sandy?"

Coach Branahan hesitated, then said, "Tailback-motion pass."

"I don't know," Coach Fowles said, rubbing his chin. "What do *you* think, Jonny, tailback motion, or the stomp?"

"I think stomp, giving Bruce the ball."

"Let's go," Coach Fowles said.

"All right," Coach Branahan said.

"Tell your people we gotta *do* it now," Coach Fowles said as Jonny moved away. "Tell em we have faith in everybody in that family!"

"That's a good call, Sandy," he said to Coach Branahan. "Either call would have been good."

Tom Kase pulled sharply to lead the blockers around to the right, and Bruce swept behind him for the first down on the 39.

Jonny threw a flare pass to tailback Brian Purcell on the right, and

Brian jumped over a tackler and got another first down on the 26. Ben Schenkle, on dives, went to the 20, then to the 18. Bruce Stacey bulled over center for Laketown's sixth first down on the 15. Jonny threw to Don Heidner on the sideline at the two. Then Jonny kept around the left end and dove just inside the corner flag for the touchdown.

With Ted O'Neill holding for the first time, Ben kicked the extra point smoothly, and Laketown led, 7–6.

Peekskill ran the kickoff to its 33 as the second quarter began. The quarterback went back to throw, looking to his right. Stan Beronski hit him from behind for a loss to the 24. The quarterback sprinted to his left to throw, but Bruce Stacey and Stan threw him out of bounds, back on the 18. Peekskill punted to its 45.

Rich Schenkle slanted in to take Jonny's pass on the 31. Ted O'Neill came across the middle from the other side and caught another on the 20, for the ninth first down.

Then Jonny faked into the line and bootlegged to the right, behind crisp downfield blocks by John Curtis, Al Stacey, and Don Heidner, and was thrown out of bounds on the five. He called time-out.

"Motion pass?" Coach Branahan said.

"I don't like the motion pass down there," Jonny said. "I'll hit Rich comin across."

"Well, we've got four downs to get five yards," Coach Fowles said.

"I'll call the 71 pass," Jonny said, "and if Rich's not open I'll just throw it away."

"Sandy?"

"Yeah, fine."

"Tell the linemen, do a job, baby," Coach Fowles yelled after his quarterback, clapping. "Tell em we got *complete faith* in 'em out there."

Rich slanted in from left end and was tripped; the ball dribbled through his fingers as a flag went down for interference. Rich pounded his fist in the dirt.

The ball was moved half the distance to the goal, the 2½-yard line.

Ben Schenkle took it in on a counter the next play.

His kick was perfect, and Laketown led, 14–6.

"All right, all RIGHT!"

"Let's keep ON 'em now, keep on 'em!"

Jim Marshall kicked out of bounds, so the ball was automatically placed on the Peekskill 40, as specified by state rules.

On third down, Stan Beronski again blind-sided the quarterback and left him lying there.

"I think he's hurt, Coach!" someone yelled cheerily.

"I don't *want* him hurt," Coach Fowles snapped back. "I don't want *anybody* hurt." The Peekskill quarterback got up and walked slowly to his bench. The Laketown defense trotted off. "Not bad, defense, not bad."

Peekskill punted out of bounds on the Laketown 35. Bradford Mc-Clure came over to Coach Fowles. "They're going on 'Set' on almost every play," he said, "that's why we're getting stung when we shift."

"Okay, *defense*. From now on we move on their *first sound*, we move on 'Ready.' "

"The quarterback looks right at the hole they're runnin, and he looks at the slot man when he's going to pass."

"All right, *defense*, the quarterback is looking . . ."

A clipping penalty moved the ball back. With a third and 23 on the 22-yard line, Jonny drifted by the sideline. "How about a draw?" he called, cupping his hands over his mouth.

An official immediately waved him away. "There's no time-out," he said to the quarterback.

"YES, Jonny, YES!" Coach Fowles answered.

The Peekskill safetyman had seen the exchange. "SOMETHING'S COMING," he yelled to his line. "WATCH IT, THEY GOT SOMETHING ON. . . ."

Keith Allen, put in to run the draw, found no hole at all.

Ted O'Neill dropped back to punt from the nine, and again the wave of blockers set up in front of him. But Peekskill's left end fired through, brushed Keith Allen aside, and slapped the kick down. Ted recovered again, but it was Peekskill's ball on the five on their second blocked punt of the day.

Crayton ran it in. A pass over the middle gave them two extra points to tie the game, 14–14, with three minutes left in the half.

Keith Allen slunk miserably off behind the team to sit on the bench, his head down.

"Who came through there?" Coach Fowles asked his team angrily. "Who let him through? What are you doin out there, Keith, throwin FLIPPERS? You're off the punting team, Keith. We can't be nice guys now. You may have cost us the whole ballgame."

"YOU CAN'T WANNA WIN A GAME AND LET THAT HAPPEN!" Coach Branahan yelled hoarsely at Keith.

Jonny was also raging. "You wanna walk across the field RIGHT NOW and GIVE 'EM THE GAME?" he yelled at no one in particular. "WE GAVE 'EM TWO TOUCHDOWNS!"

:221:

"I want Keith Allen off the punting team, Sandy. Let's get somebody in there who wants to block."

Through it all Keith Allen sat alone rocking, his face buried in his hands.

Al Stacey brought the kickoff back to the 27. Ted O'Neill made a diving catch of Jonny's pass on the 45, for Laketown's twelfth first down. Ted struggled up and limped off.

"Cramp again, Coach."

"You gotta take more SALT."

Jonny continued the passing show. He hit Rich Schenkle on the sideline at the 28, then again at the eight where Rich made a leaping catch and was driven over backward hard. For a few seconds he lay on the ground, then slowly got up and waved off a substitute.

With first down on the eight, Jonny called for Ted O'Neill to slant out to the right. Jonny rolled to his right, but Ted was not there; he had come back across the center. Jonny finally spotted him and, now under pressure, threw off balance. The ball floated short, and was intercepted in the end zone.

Coach Fowles took his end's arm as he came off. "Why'd you turn in, Ted?"

"It was full outside and . . ."

"Yeah, Ted, but we been working on that play all season long, and then we confuse it right here on the goal line. You're supposed to know what you're doing. Jonny's depending on you to carry out your assignment!"

"Let's GO, TED!" Jonny said angrily, kicking the dirt.

The Peekskill quarterback tried to pass, but was dumped by Rich Schenkle, as the half ended.

The Harvesters swept into the locker room on a torrent of wrath and frustration. Jonny was screaming, his voice raspy from abuse. ". . . WHOLE FUCKING TEAM, the OFFENSE plays its GUTS OUT, run the hill, hang on the bars, WORK ALL THE FUCKING TIME AND WE GET OUT THERE AND PEOPLE FUCK UP!" He slammed his helmet against the wall, then against a bench, then a locker.

Jim Petrowski howled unintelligibly. Jim Marshall stomped and cursed and banged his helmet into lockers. Rich Schenkle beat the wall with his padded fists.

"WHAT THE HELL'S THE MATTER?" Jonny cried. "DOESN'T ANYBODY WANNA WIN THIS FUCKING GAME?"

Coach Fowles came in, his jaw set in vexation, but he held up his hand to calm the locker room. "Boys, I just can't believe this. We are pushing this team *all over the field*. And we are tied at halftime. A couple mistakes, couple boys don't do their job, and the whole team suffers. We are not going to make any more *stupid mistakes!*

"Now, we all know that the punting team—a couple of guys—just killed us. But that will be fixed. Don Heidner, you've been just jogging your pass patterns when the ball's not coming to you. So the guy *knows* it's not coming to you. Hey, Don, if you're that tired, get over on the bench and rest the second half. Jim Marshall, when you kick off this half get your mind down out of the clouds and *hit it right. Don't kick it out of bounds.* There's no excuse for that. Coach Branahan, anything?"

"Jonny, you're moving the ball *beautifully*. The offense looks great."

"Hey, Coach," Bruce Stacey said. "They're starting to push and shove now."

"All right, listen to me. When *anybody* gets tired, they start to take shortcuts. And a shortcut in football is holding, pushing, personal fouls. That's what I meant when I said it's going to boil down to conditioning. And *pride*. And right now I'll *put my house up* on you people. That's how much I trust you. Pride and conditioning—right now we've got more of these things than any other football team in this county. That's a fact. But if you go out there and don't think properly, you're not going to win. Bradford?"

"Coach, I think they're catching on to how we shift on defense. I'm getting stung all the time."

"Which way are they blocking you, Bradford?"

"Mostly to the inside."

"All right. Bruce, what are you running, the laura center?"

"Yeah, when they run the I."

"All right. But when they have a man out in the slot, don't go laura center. Use the regular laura and shift *to* that slot man. And once in a while throw that Penn State quaker at 'em, the four-four. Any comments?"

"On punts," Clifford Albert said, "can we go toe-to-toe on the line now?"

"Well, we can tighten up the splits on the line a *little* more. The trouble with toe-to-toe . . ."

"See, we're getting . . ."

"WAIT A MINUTE, CLIFFORD! WAIT A MINUTE! I can't be nice now. LISTEN! If we go toe-to-toe how we gonna block people comin outside? We're *dead*. We *can't* go toe-to-toe. They've got too much outside pressure on us. That's my point. However, *you* have a point too. We *are* going to tighten up, but we have to find a happy medium. We can't go berserk because they blocked two punts. They're not gonna block any more. Let's cut the splits in half, one yard between linemen. And hold your blocks a little longer on the line, two seconds instead of one, because that second wall is not picking everybody up."

He looked around the room. Faces were still set in anger.

"All right, we'll be all right the second half. I told you that you had conditioning and pride. There's another thing. You know what you guys are really outta sight on? I been in Laketown eight years, and this team is head and shoulders above any team I've ever coached in that *you never panic*. I've never seen anything like it. You get behind, you go out there and get it back. We blow two touchdowns, you still come right back. You know why? You got the faith, the faith in the family. I've never seen a high school football team quite like this, ever. And maybe I never will again. Whatever happens this half, I know I can be proud of you.

"And now we want twenty-four minutes of the finest football you can possibly produce."

Crayton brought the Peekskill kickoff back to midfield. Karl Walsh came off complaining, "I got punched so many times it was unbelievable."

Three plays later, Crayton ran wide to the left, then cut back inside Al Stacey, and broke up the middle of the field for a touchdown run of 50 yards.

They faked the extra-point kick, but the quarterback, trying to throw, was smothered. Laketown was now behind for the fifth time in three weeks, 20–14.

Rich Schenkle, whose chinstrap was covered with blood from a cut under his mouth, said, "We'll get it right back."

Following the kickoff and an exchange of punts, Laketown started from its 20. Jonny threw to Ted O'Neill for a first down on the 30. Jonny, hit just after he threw, hollered to the bench that he had been punched in the face. Jonny sent Don Heidner deep again for the bomb, but it was underthrown and intercepted on the Peekskill 35. Jonny came off quietly, already thinking of what that play had revealed to him. Don Heidner was getting triple coverage deep. Ted O'Neill, lined up on the same side at end, had drifted out in the flat and was wide open.

But now Crayton broke through the left side, again cut back inside Al Stacey, crossed back over the middle, and headed for the far sideline. Al, though, had immediately launched a perfect angle of pursuit and went all the way across the field to catch the fast halfback on the Laketown 32, just when it looked like he would go all the way.

"You gotta *watch* that guy," Vince Carradino muttered.

"HEY, GET THAT COACH OUTTA THE END ZONE!" Coach Fowles was waving his arms at the official. "HEY, THERE'S A COACH BEHIND THE END ZONE! GET HIM OUTTA THERE! HEY, GET THAT GUY OUTTA THERE!"

A tall man with a clipboard had been standing just outside the end zone, sighting upfield and jotting notes as the Laketown defense lined up. Finally, an official waved him away.

"He wasn't on the playing field, Buddy," I said.

"I know, but if he's one of the Peekskill coaches, then he's gotta stay between the 35-yard lines, and if he's *not* a Peekskill coach, then he's not allowed to stand where spectators are not allowed."

The huge Peekskill fullback bulled three times over the middle to a fourth and one on the 23. Coach Fowles sent Jim Marshall in for Jim Petrowski, to add beef to the middle of the line. "Submarine on them," he told Jim. But the fullback plowed ahead for a first down on the 18.

"LET'S GO, DEFENSE, COME ON!"

But Crayton picked his favorite spot again on the left side, and burst the rest of the way for his fourth touchdown of the day. A pass over the middle got the extra two points, and Peekskill led, 28–14.

"Okay, Jonny, you can handle this, you know what to do . . ."

Following the kickoff to the 20, Jonny sent Don Heidner deep, intending to fake the bomb to him and hit Ted O'Neill on a delay in the flat. But Ted had not delayed at the line. He had struck out immediately for the flat, and so the defender had not been fooled, and was on him. Jonny then threw desperately for Don, 45 yards in the air, but not far enough. A defender stepped in front of Don and intercepted it on the Peekskill 38.

The Harvester defense took the field to start the fourth twelve-minute quarter. They were fired up, and charged the bigger Peekskill line viciously. Peekskill was forced to punt. Jim Petrowski slithered through and almost blocked it. Laketown started from its 30, and Jonny went back to work in the air.

He hit Rich Schenkle slanting out for five yards. Then Rich's little brother Ben pushed through behind blocking by Rich and John Curtis for the first down on the 42. On the way back to the huddle, tailback Brian Purcell stopped to console an injured Peekskill player, lying on the ground.

"GET BACK AND PLAY FOOTBALL," Coach Fowles yelled. "YOU'RE NOT A DOCTOR!"

Jonny hit Ted O'Neill in the right flat, and Ted broke two tackles before being dropped on the Peekskill 45. Rich went deeper now on a down-and-in, and Jonny laid it in his arms just inside the 30. Rich then ran a shallower pattern and took Jonny's pass on the 18.

The Peekskill secondary was now yelling back and forth, trying to adjust to Jonny's pinpoint passes. Again behind solid protection from his blockers, Jonny hit Ted O'Neill on the eight. Brian Purcell took it to the six. Ben Schenkle came out.

"Coach, the counter might work."

"I'll buy that," Coach Fowles said, sending Bruce Stacey in at fullback.

Jonny faked the hand-off to the right, spun and handed off to Bruce on the left side, and Bruce banged through to the end zone.

For the extra points, Jonny looked for Rich slanting in from the left. But he was covered. Jonny threw quickly for Ted O'Neill coming from the other side, but a linebacker jumped in front to intercept. The score was 28–20 with five minutes left.

The bench was alive and yelling confidently as the kickoff team went in.

Peekskill started from their 20. On the first play, Stan Beronski caught the heavy fullback around the neck and wrenched him down. But then Crayton swung to his left, cleverly cut away from Rich Schenkle's lunge, and dodged his way to midfield.

The Laketown line dug in. Coach Fowles stalked back and forth in front of his offensive team, poised on the sideline. "They'll get the ball for you," he told them, "and you will take it right in."

A running play gained five. Then a fumble. In the middle of the line the Harvesters piled on top of Bradford McClure, who had the football. Jonny led his team jubilantly onto the field.

The Laketown partisans screeched encouragement from the stands. Cowbells rang and aerosol horns tooted and cheerleaders bounced as if on Pogosticks. There were four minutes remaining.

Jonny drilled one over the middle for Rich Schenkle, but a solid tackle by two men caused the ball to bounce off his stomach incomplete. A running play was stopped, then Jonny overthrew Ted O'Neill. Fourth and ten with three and a half minutes to go.

"GO FOR IT, JONNY!" Coach Branahan hollered. Jonny dropped back and looked for Rich. Three defenders surrounded the end as he zigged out, then back in. Jonny fired it into the crowd, and Rich elbowed free for a split second to take it on the 28 for the first down.

Ben Schenkle went up the middle to the 23. Jonny threw wide, missing

Don Heidner. Then he handed off to Brian Purcell who wedged his way for five yards. The chains were brought out. The ball was just over the 20, a foot short on fourth down.

Bruce Stacey went in with the play from the bench, a double-dive over the right side, behind Jack Forrest and Tom Kase. Bruce got two yards for the first down.

"ATTA BOY, JONNY, YOU SHOW 'EM!"

Again Rich Schenkle slanted in from the left, crowded by defenders. Jonny rifled it to him on the seven. Rich went down under tacklers. Then immediately he struggled free and sprang up and down like a jumping jack, pointing to his face mask and to one of the tacklers. An official had seen it, and tossed a red flag down for the face-mask penalty. The ball was moved to the three.

Bruce Stacey went straight ahead from there to score. It was 28–26 with less than two minutes to play.

The coaches and Jonny discussed the extra-point play.

"Every time we slant Rich in," Coach Branahan said, "they're adjusting, putting two men on him. Flanker look-in? How about pro-I right, tailback in motion to the left—that will pull them to that side—then hit Don back on the right side?"

"Against the motion?" Jonny asked.

"Yeah, they're double-covering Rich. So motion that way, and come back to Don."

"Mr. Headlinesman, *sir*? How much time is left?"

"One minute and twenty seconds."

"All right Jonny. Now listen. Tell your linemen to stay low. We got it made. You can do it, baby, you can do it."

The team came out of the huddle in the I, with Don Heidner flanked to the right. Jonny flicked his heel to start the man in motion. But Ben went to the right instead of the left. Jonny took the snap, quickly dropped two steps back, and fired for Don just over the goal line. Don was covered, then tripped, and the ball bounced off his fingertips as he fell.

Harvesters yelled for an interference penalty, but the official turned his back and walked away.

Ted O'Neill yelled at Ben as they trotted off, "He said motion LEFT! Motion LEFT, he said!"

Rich Schenkle, battered and tired, was downhearted on the sidelines. Coach Fowles put a hand around behind Rich's helmet and looked into his eyes. "Hey, Rich Schenkle, get the ball back and we're going to take it all the way in the *last second*."

Peekskill recovered the short onside kick and then began to plug away at the middle to use up the clock. Laketown called time-out to stop the clock.

Coach Branahan stood with his hands clasped behind his head, his eyes closed, as if basking.

". . . Laketown has twenty-three first downs so far," announced the voice over the public-address system, "to Peekskill's six."

Coach Branahan slammed his fist into his head.

Bruce Stacey stumbled off the field, groggy from his day's work.

"Nice job, Bruce," Coach Fowles said. "COME ON, LAKETOWN! LAKETOWN NEVER QUITS!"

The big Peekskill fullback banged into the line again, and was stopped. Laketown had no more time-outs, and the clock kept running. The official stepped in, snatched up the ball and waved it over his head. The game was over.

The team climbed slowly and quietly aboard the bus. Beside the bus their cheerleaders chanted faithfully. Peekskill kids ran by taunting, but several of them also said, "Nice game, Laketown."

"All right, sit down, boys," Coach Fowles said, standing in the front of the bus and looking back over his exhausted players. "Now we're going to get ready for Brushland. Boys, you can't score four touchdowns, give your opponents two as gifts, and then expect to win the ballgame. But you guys still have class and you *never gave up*. Laketown never quits."

He slumped to his seat. "Let's get outta here," he said to the driver.

As the bus approached Laketown High, it stopped for a light. Two small boys walked by, wheeling a bicycle. "Hey, did you *win?*" one boy called. Players looked silently down at them. The other boy chuckled. "They lost," he said.

The bus stopped in the parking lot, and Coach Fowles stood up and faced his players. "Boys, the first game we played, one touchdown was good enough to win. This time we got four. We completely dominated the game, and you will see that on the statistics. But we made two bonehead plays, we had two punts blocked. Now, we can cry about this all weekend, all next week. But the way I look at it, we've got *eighteen days* left. That's all. Eighteen days left, and we'll never be together again like we are now as a family. *Never*. Eighteen more days. Three football games. And we're gonna win all three of them. Three more victories. Eighteen more days."

He stood looking at them. Bradford McClure said softly from the rear of the bus, "Let's make the best of those eighteen more days, guys."

Coach Fowles got off the bus first and walked alone toward the locker room, spinning a football lazily on his finger. The only sound came from the clatter of the players' cleats on the asphalt, behind him.

Coach Branahan slumped in disbelief on a chair in the coaches' room. "Twenty-three first downs to seven. We controlled the ball something like eighty plays to their fifty." He shook his head. "I think we're not going to win another game, the way things are going. These two losses cost Buddy coach-of-the-year. Even with seven and one he could have been coach-of-the-year."

Coach Fowles came in, and smiled. Coach Branahan looked up at him. "Buddy, we should be five and 0 right now, five and 0."

Coach Fowles chuckled.

"Buddy, I would have given up earlier. I'm too emotional. These kids have *incredible* class."

Coach Fowles smiled broadly. "Well, we're giving the fans their money's worth. That's what makes football an exciting game—a *game*, Sandy."

13

The team showered and dressed quickly, anxious to be free of the depressing confinement of the locker room. Then they went to the home of Tom Kase, where they were treated outdoors to sausages, pizzas, and sodas. They were tired, but as usual the postgame depression was dissipated quickly by the assembly of the family for a feast on paper plates.

Don Heidner's right hand was badly swollen. He couldn't move it.

"Why'd you come?" I asked.

"I'm hungry," he said.

I asked Ben Schenkle why he'd gone in motion the wrong way for the last extra-point try.

"All I heard in the huddle was the set," he said, shrugging. "I didn't hear the direction given for the motion. So I just went the way I been going in practice." He took a long drink from the can of soda. "I gotta tell Coach I gotta run more in practice. There are so many backs alternating in, I only got to run about three times all week."

Jonny lay back on a car hood while his date massaged his knee. "Ben's funny," he said, laughing lightly. "You know, he can't remember nothin. Like, he'll bring a play in from the bench, you know? And by the time he gets to the huddle he can't remember it. He'll say, 'Uh, let's see, pro-right—no, that's not it, uh. . . .'"

The players ate, and sat with their girl friends, and laughed, and threw crab apples at a hornets' nest.

As the team gathered in the basement to see the Peekskill film, Buddy and Squeegy Fowles arrived back from New York City, where they had seen the Jets beat Buffalo 28–17. "It was the first time we ever went to a game by ourselves," Buddy said, "without the kids or friends. And I loved going with Squeegy and loved the food she packed and the thermos full of wine. But the game bothered me a little. For example, there was an ordinary screen pass to a man who gets paid a lot to catch them, and here were all these people around us screaming and yelling as if it was the most fantastic thing on earth. I just couldn't get excited about it. I guess I just reached saturation on football."

There was a refrigerator downstairs in the rec room. John Curtis opened it up. He started in surprise, then reached in and hauled out a gallon jug of cream sherry and held it up for the other players to see.

"Hey," he said, "Coach Fowles is going to get his head screwed on backward." He shoved it back into the refrigerator and wobbled to the center of the room. "And then it's SO LONG, OOLONG!"

The coaches came down. "I still feel *terrible* about that game," Coach Branahan said.

Coach Fowles ran the film. Keith Allen was there, despite his humiliation at allowing the second punt to be blocked. Coach Fowles pointed out the mistakes made by the blocking wave in abandoning its positions, but did not dwell upon them.

The statistics reaffirmed how Laketown had dominated the game—or at least the airways—on Saturday. Laketown's total yardage was 345 to Peekskill's 237. Jonny had set a Laketown record of eighteen completions in thirty-two attempts for 205 yards, while Peekskill—apart from extra points—went zero for one in the air. Rich Schenkle caught eight passes, another Laketown game record.

Jim Petrowski was still angry. "They hit the least of any team we've played this year," the little middle guard said.

A few of the players were annoyed at the extra-point strategy, and they confronted their coach.

"Why did we try to pass three times for extra points," Bruce Stacey asked, "rather than run?"

"All right, good question," Coach Fowles said. "You can second-guess every call, of course. But to get three yards against a six-five goal-line defense is really *tough*, Bruce. Nobody has been able to do it against *us* this year. We felt we had the percentages. The most difficult thing to stop on the goal line in high school football is a kind of roll-out pass."

"But with a run," Stan Beronski said, "at least he has a chance to keep his feet moving and plow ahead."

"Three yards is a long way to plow down there," Coach Fowles said.

"We passed last week too and missed," Bradford McClure said.

"But how about Lourdes?" Coach Fowles said. "We passed and won the game."

The argument died there.

Coach Fowles called upon Ian Bush, the JV coach, who had scouted Brushland, for a report.

Brushland was Laketown's crosstown rival, a much larger school, Double-A. It would be the Homecoming Game. In last year's JV game, won by Laketown, there had been a brawl between teams at the end. Many of the same players would face each other on the varsities Saturday. This year, Brushland was 0–4. Ian accentuated the negative in his report.

"They haven't scored since their opening game," he said. "They're big, but not quick. They were off last week, so they haven't played for a couple of weeks. . . ."

"So they've had two weeks to think about us," Coach Fowles interjected, quickly changing the course of the report. "This is their big game, against Laketown. As far as I'm concerned, they're a good football team. Let's get something straight right now: I don't want the team psyched up Monday, Tuesday, Wednesday, Thursday, or Friday. But I *do* want you to work hard all those days. Then put it all together on Saturday—110 percent effort *and* psyched up.

"And boys," he said as they stood up to leave, "our kicking game will improve 100 percent, *mark my words!*"

After the players had gone, Coach Branahan produced Jonny's statistics so far this year. He had a total of forty completions in ninety-six passes for 531 yards, a completion average of 41.7 percent. He had thrown twelve interceptions.

"When you throw that much in high school football," Coach Fowles said, "Jonny's passing percentage is really outstanding."

The coaches sat together to sift through the dittoed scouting sheets on Brushland and to break down every play to assess strengths and tendencies.

"I'll tell you," Coach Fowles said, "we can't let these kids think they're playing a bad team."

"Did I make Brushland sound bad?" Ian asked.

"Yes, you did. I think it's better to accentuate the positive aspects of opponents. Not con the kids, not lie. But every team has positive sides. Like you can say they are big boys, you don't have to say they're slow. Take Jonny's statistics. When they're looking at him for awards, I'm not going to mention the twelve interceptions, unless they ask."

They poured over more play sheets.

"They're not a bad team," Coach Fowles continued. "They lost to Sleepy Hollow 16–0," referring to Laketown's final opponent of the season, still undefeated, "but actually they just gave up two long passes. Sleepy got only six first downs. And you know how Brushland is gonna be against us. They haven't won yet. This is our Homecoming, so they're gonna be up. And they *are* big."

MONDAY, *October 18*

Bradford McClure, who had urged the team on Saturday to make the best of the days left, in shop period cut the tip of his thumb nearly off with a hacksaw.

"The doctor says I'll be out at least two weeks," Bradford told Coach Fowles in the guidance office, holding out his thumb with a fat bandage on it.

"Well, if he says that," Coach Fowles said, "that's probably *it*."

"I'll go to another doctor," Bradford said, as he left.

Coach Fowles shook his head. "What a shame for a guy like that, worked *so* hard all season."

Bradford won two stars for the Peekskill game, for a fumble recovery and again for the most tackles.

As he walked down the hall toward the classroom for the prepractice meeting, Coach Fowles reflected on the tightness of the games so far. "Wow, five games this close, every week the kids holding on by their teeth. They're getting tired, beat up. I think today maybe I'll have 'em practice without pads, no contact. The games have been so close that we haven't even been able to get reserves in. This is the first year I can remember when we haven't had a chance to play *everybody* even once in five games."

Stu Rosenman, who had tried fullback and end but had been playing little, stood next to the wall. "Coach, can I talk to you?" Stu's eyes were moist.

Coach Fowles looked at him closely. "You aren't thinking about quitting, are you Stu?"

Stu nodded. He said he was disheartened at not playing, and was bothered by digs he was getting from Coach Branahan which he didn't think were funny. "I didn't think I did that badly when I played," he said, a tear on his cheek. "I don't think my attitude is good anymore."

"First, Stu," Coach Fowles said, "I want to compliment you for telling me this. Secondly, let me say this: We have to make judgments based on practices. Freddie Delaney looked terrific at defensive end during the week before Fox Lane. Steve Barker looked good before Peekskill. So they played. But I'm not all that pleased with their performances in those games. If you were graded for the Greeley game, I would give you a B. The position is wide open, Stu, and you can play it if you work hard."

Stu drew a hand across his cheek.

"Listen, Stu. Why don't you skip practice today and think about it. I'll tell you what: If you work hard Tuesday through Friday, there's a *good* chance you'll be able to play a lot on defense against Brushland, get in early. This is not a special chance because you talked to me, but because you *may* work harder. Okay?"

Stu nodded and walked away. He walked quickly and sadly past the team which was filing into the classroom.

Players scrambled in, most of them late, carrying parts of their equipment they had not yet donned. They sat in seats and on the floor pulling on pads, pants, socks.

"Gentlemen, everybody who has ever participated in football has at one time or another had the experience of sitting on the *bench*. I think that is one of the most courageous things that anybody could possibly do—and stay with it instead of quitting—to come out and practice football day in and day out, go through what you people do, and do your best *in spite of the fact* that you sit on the bench during games.

"For the kids who haven't gotten into any of the five games, I'll tell you, you have *not* been forgotten. We have certain decisions to make as coaches, and one of them is that the team's gotta come first. But the first chance we have to get you into a football game, we will *do* that. Nobody has more respect for you people on the bench than I do, because

I sat on the bench in high school and college, and I know what it's like. Don't get discouraged. I know that's easy for me to stand here and say that, but it's still the best advice. I know it's especially hard for *seniors* in that situation.

"For the juniors, I'd like to point out a couple of things. I don't want to embarrass anybody, but is Rich Schenkle here?"

"He had to go home first, Coach."

"Well, I have very deep respect for Rich Schenkle. I have never seen a kid hit any harder than Rich. In the fourteen years I've been coaching, I have never seen a boy give more of *himself* for the good of the team than he has. Last year, we played eight games. How many did Rich start? One. Now he didn't suddenly become this really tough person. He was tough last year too. And he has worked hard every single day.

"Stan Beronski didn't just suddenly become what he is. Last year Stan started the first game . . ."

"And never again," Stan said.

"He said a *nasty* thing, Coach," Jonny said.

". . . John Curtis didn't start any of the games, neither did Tom Kase, or Jack Forrest. Nobody was more discouraged last year than Bradford McClure—*nobody*. Yet he had courage enough to stay with the team for most of the season. And it was no bed of roses for him at the beginning of *this* season either. Think about it. You never know when you're going to get that chance, that break. And when you do, do your best.

"And you people who *are* playing, I think you have an obligation too. One of your responsibilities is to encourage some of these other kids who aren't playing much, don't let them get down in the dumps. Really and truly let them know that you understand. Nobody's a big star all the time— *nobody*.

"All right. Now we've got to prepare for Brushland, and we've got to do it in a hurry. Brushland is big—brontosauruses. They are very rough. Probably be quite a few penalties. And we've got to be ready. They will be ready for us. The teams we play are really getting ready for us.

"Hey, you know that coach who was in the end zone over at Peekskill? He was from *Gorton,* and we don't play them until a week from Saturday. You know what he was doing? He wanted to know *exactly* where we were lined up on the laura."

He looked down and watched Jonny hurriedly pull on the last of his pads. "All right. Now I don't want any complaints about this. Go in and put on shorts. No contact today. Any complaints?" He smiled as nobody took the dare. "The reason is, we've had five heart-stoppers in a row, and we've had contact every day but Fridays since August 25. Okay? Let's get outside."

"You know what?" Coach Fowles said as we went out. "The Peekskill coach kicked his team off the practice field last Friday for clowning around."

Bradford McClure watched practice, his thumb embedded in the white bandage that made him look like Little Jack Horner with a gauze plum. "I went to another doctor," he said. "He told me three and a half weeks. So I guess it will be at least two weeks, like the first doctor said." He sneered at the drills. "This sucks, practicing without pads."

Rich Merrill still had an ear infection. Ken Furst playfully clapped his hands over the earholes in Rich's helmet, sending him reeling in pain. Rich decided to go to a doctor.

In the evening, Coach Fowles ran the Peekskill film for the parents. Then he sat on a desk in front. "Your kids have class," he said. "They won't quit. You've got to keep in mind that these people are only sixteen, seventeen, eighteen years old. They made mistakes, but they didn't quit."

He looked around the room, with a small smile. "I thought sure somebody would ask me right away about the two-point conversions, about why we passed instead of running. It is very, very hard to run against a goal-line defense. Actually, we hate to see somebody throw on *us* down there, cause we can't stop everything. If I had it to do over again, I would still throw."

Mr. Schenkle asked, "How about passing when you had first and eight for a touchdown?"

"Just one of those things," Coach Fowles said. "Ted was open when it was thrown, but the man got in front of him and took it away."

"What was the pattern?" Mr. Schenkle persisted.

Coach Fowles avoided focusing criticism by name, on the play when Ted O'Neill ran the wrong pattern in the end zone. "Well," he said, hesitating, "one of our boys made a mistake. We didn't run the right pattern."

Mrs. Forrest asked how the punts got blocked.

"Nobody wants to win more than these boys," Coach Fowles said carefully. "A boy made a mistake, but that's all. They never quit. Right after the game, the kids didn't jump on the one or two kids who made mistakes. They went over and congratulated Peekskill on a fine football game. I think this is the most exciting football team Laketown has ever had.

"You know, we're peanuts, little fellows. Bruce Stacey is one of our big boys, and he weighs about 175. Don Heidner, how much?"

"One fifty-seven," his father said.

"Jack Forrest is what, about 150? Clifford Albert about 165. We just have big shoulder pads. But nobody has more *heart*, more *guts*, more *class*."

Ray Meister's mother said, "I think a lot of that can be attributed to the coach."

"Well," Coach Fowles said softly, "to *everybody*. We're one big family."

"I think that's true," Jonny's mother said. "That's what's different about this team."

"Brushland is *huge*," Coach Fowles said. "They are *brontosauruses*. And they like to hit. We will be ready for them."

He swung his feet and looked around at the parents. "Well, the season is rapidly coming to a close. Fourteen more days of practice. . . ."

Outside on the dark sidewalk, Bradford's father stood with Coach Fowles. Mr. McClure was the manager of a food-processing plant in Brooklyn, and in his spare time restored classic old cars in their garage. "It's very strange," he said. "There were Bradford's older brothers, you know. Next year will be the first year in twelve years I won't have a son to watch playing football on the Laketown varsity." Mr. McClure would be dead anyway, before Christmas.

TUESDAY, *October 19*

Parked outside on the asphalt was a car with high shocks and a tachometer. "That's Allen's greaser car," somebody said. A few of the players raised the hood and stacked a bicycle and some chairs atop the engine. Keith came out as they stood nearby.

"You guys are so fuckin *mature*," he said, angrily yanking out the bicycle and chairs and hurling them away. He also had a big bag of apples on the backseat. Later he told the players they were welcome to them, that he had brought them for the team.

Coach Fowles lined up the punting team. He made some changes, putting Ben Schenkle and Brian Purcelle in the second blocking wave, and moving Barry Brill up to the line. Then he had everybody else on the squad line up to rush and try to block the punts. Ted O'Neill got the ball cleanly away every time.

"You'll never get another kick blocked, *ever*, Ted," Coach Fowles said.

Jonny had been trying to grow a beard. What he got was a few wispy strands of barely noticeable blond fuzz. "It's coming," he said. "Hey, I've already cut it off three times this season."

Coach Fowles called a break to have the team cheer the soccer team, which was losing 1–0. The Harvesters lined up inside the snow fence and yelled encouragement across the running track to the soccer field. Jonny took a loose piece of lath and ran down behind the row of players, rattling the stick across the backs of the helmets like a boy at a picket fence.

WEDNESDAY, *October 20*

At precisely three o'clock, Coach Fowles said, "All right, let's get started." There were twelve players present in the classroom. He began describing defenses as Bruce Stacey and Jack Forrest walked in. "Gentlemen, you're late. If you're late tomorrow, take five laps. I'm serious about winning this football game." Ted O'Neill and Jim Marshall walked in. "Take a lot of salt tonight so you can run laps if you're late tomorrow. When I say three o'clock, that doesn't mean two minutes after." Ben Schenkle, Steve Barker, and Tom Kase arrived. "Don't be late tomorrow, boys. On the four-four quaker, we'll make a slight change. We'll put the tackle *in* the gap, to make as much penetration as possible." John Curtis, Brian Purcelle, and Ken Furst came in. "You'll take laps tomorrow if you're late. We're getting too much pressure on the right inside linebacker. If the ball goes in that direction, Stan, you're on inside shoulder, and I want the linebacker to scrape *hard* right off Stan's butt on the inside. Same with the linebacker on the other side. John Finch, if you're late tomorrow you take laps. Now yesterday we had twenty people and more trying to block a punt, and they couldn't do it. The punting team *blocked* them out. It's not how long you spend on the practice field, it's *quality* we want.

"Uh, by the way boys, the Peekskill film is on the way to West Point. They want to look at a couple of our players."

"Who?" John Curtis asked.

Coach Fowles stared at him, and players laughed.

"In other words," John said, "it's none of my business."

"Yes, it is your business, John, but I don't want to tell you right now. Don't be late tomorrow, Jonathan Penchak."

"Brushland is such a greaser school you slide off the doors," Jack Forrest said as the team went outside.

Ben Schenkle told me proudly he got twenty-one right out of twenty-five on a math test. "With help from Clifford Albert. He gave me most of the answers."

Ben had two new boils on his left leg. "Hunh-unh, no doctor," he said. "I'm going to hit harder than ever. I been doing bad lately."

As the team went into calisthenics, there was conjecture about who West Point was interested in. Coach Fowles said it was Jonny and Al Stacey.

"I hope there are no close-ups," Jonny said, swishing his hair.

Coach Fowles got the idea of scraping his linebackers to the inside of the ends by talking with coaches at Penn State and West Point. "Hey, Sandy," he said, "you know what my phone bill was last month? two hundred twenty dollars. Hey, those Penn State defenses are *expensive*."

"You just pick up the phone and call these big-time coaches?" I asked.

"I always ask advice," he said, "and the coaches are generally happy to give it." He reeled off the names of secretaries to the coaches, listing details of the lives of each: age, children, interests, attitudes, mannerisms. "I tell people I talked to the coach at Navy and they say, 'You're full of shit,'" he said, uncharacteristically using the profanity, "but I get through to them because I can talk to the secretaries."

"You're a con," I said.

"I'm interested in people," he said, smiling.

Barry Brill fought Tom Kase to a standoff in the pit drill. "Surprising!" Coach Branahan said.

"Barry did better against Tom than anybody else has all year," Coach Fowles said.

Jonny jumped in against reserve end Eddie McArthur, and drove him back by slamming up under him ferociously with his forearms. "Wow," Coach Branahan said softly, sighing with relief when it was over.

"I'd like to try this sometime with arm pads on," Jonny said, rubbing his bare forearms.

Brushland practiced under the lights beginning at 6:00 P.M. Yesterday

Rich Schenkle hid in the bushes and watched them. "They ran everything to the right," he told some of the players today. Coach Fowles asked him, "Is it true, Rich, what I heard about you being a superspy?"

"I was told we were going for pizza," Rich said.

I went to the Petrowskis' for supper. Jim and his parents and I had meatballs at a small table in their compact kitchen.

"You heard about the fight with the Brushland JVs last year?" Jim asked. "There were little fights all game. And then at the end we tackled the quarterback, and guys just jumped on me and somebody kicked me in the head. I guess I just passed out for a couple of seconds. I figure there will be a fight on Saturday. But, you know, a lot of guys, including me, would not like to fight because we figure we would be letting Coach Fowles down."

Mr. Petrowski, a lean, pale, light-haired man who was an electrician for the railroad, told me that Jim almost died from whooping cough as a child. "That's why he has bad eyes," he said, "from being in an oxygen tank so long." He took out some old yearbooks to show me pictures of Jim and his older brother when they were in grammar school. He was very interested in Jim's wrestling—which had cost Jim a tooth last year—and followed the matches closely. He was looking forward to watching Jim wrestle this year, especially since it was expected he would do well in the championships.

Each school class was making a float for the Homecoming parade on Saturday. Jim and I went to one of the juniors' homes where his float committee was constructing a turtle going under goal posts—meant to be outracing a hare. Junior classmates in dungarees worked in the garage shaping crepe-paper flowers and sticking them on the wire mesh which was the turtle's back. Without the head, the turtle looked like a colorful bump in the road. The juniors figured they would lose the competition.

We decided to invade the lair of the probable winners, the senior class, and so we drove to Nick Calbano's to watch them finishing their crepe-paper airplane which would have a propeller that really turned.

Nick Calbano, a pleasant, open, slim senior, stood watching progress in his garage and told me why he had quit the team. "I started both ways on the JVs, wingback on offense and halfback on defense. This year I couldn't come out at the beginning for medical reasons. So I asked Coach Branahan if it was worth my while to come out late, and he said sure.

"I knew Don Heidner was a better flanker, but I thought I could play defensive halfback. But I never really got a chance to get in on defense. I got the idea of quitting when Coach Fowles yelled at us for messing around. Remember? He said the most important thing in life is to be happy, and if you're not happy, *get* happy.

"I just got to thinking about that. It was a beautiful thing to say. I thought about whether I was happy, and decided I wasn't, that I could not be happy sitting on the bench and not getting to play. I could go crazy on the bench.

"So I went in to Coach Fowles the next day and said I thought I should quit for that reason. He didn't want me to quit, of course, but he didn't seem terribly concerned. He just said, 'In the final analysis it has to be up to you.'

"Many of the things Coach Fowles does are tremendous, he's a tremendous psychologist. I don't blame anybody, really. With just two coaches they have too much to do to watch each individual in all situations."

THURSDAY, *October 21*

Players gathered early in the classroom. They looked at Ben Schenkle's boils. "He got those because last night he slept in Rich's bed," Jonny said. "You ought to see where *Rich's* got 'em."

Coach Fowles stood just outside the door as the team counted down the last ten seconds to 3:00 p.m. As they said, "zero!" he came in. Coach Branahan went to work taping Ken Furst's ankles as Coach Fowles talked.

"Two days of practice left before Brushland, and one of those is really a loosening-up day. Then four hard days and a loosening-up day for Gorton, and the same for Sleepy Hollow. So boys, it's down to nine real practice days. It will *never* be the same again. And no matter how much you want to turn that clock back, you'll never play high school football again. That's a part of your life, and it's gone.

"And so I'd just like to leave you with one big thought—and the funny thing is, no matter how many times you hear it and think about it, the full impact is *not* going to hit you until it's too late. The thought is this: *Have—no—regrets.*

"A lot of kids who played football here come down to watch practice, and they wish they could be part of the family again. But it's never the same. And it *shouldn't* be the same because you've got a lot of *other* things to do in your life. Don't have any regrets.

"To have no regrets, you must follow rule number one: Do your best. Nobody in here knows what his best is. Maybe your best today will not be as good as your best next Tuesday.

"I'm not trying to embarrass anybody, but I've got to be honest with you. A year ago if somebody would have told me that this little shrimp right here in the front seat would have the kind of year he's having, I wouldn't have believed it. And now I don't think we've ever had a better blocking guard at Laketown High School than Jack Forrest. And you know why he's done such a good job? *Watch* him out there sometime. Or better yet, try to keep up with him.

"Last year at this time if somebody had told me Bradford McClure was going to be a real fine tackle, I wouldn't have believed it. And here we are. You don't have to be 340 pounds to play tackle. You've got to have a lot of guts. And the ability to come back, pick yourself up, and do your best.

"Hey, boys, we've got a lot of people like that on this football team. And in just a very, very short time it's all going to be gone. *Except* the memories. Have no regrets.

"You know, on the last day of practice I always have the seniors take a last lap around the track. And the seniors will start around, and they'll be yacking it up for a while, and the juniors will be halfway paying attention. And juniors, in one—very—short—year, it's going to be *you* jogging around that track for the very last time. There are some juniors in here right now who are thinking, 'What's he talking about?' And you know what?"

He chuckled. "You're going to find out, just like the seniors are finding out now. Nine more practices in uniform. Three short games. And the rest is memories."

He looked over his team and said softly. "Don't have any regrets. Let's play football."

The coaches watched the team run up the manbuilder. "I heard a cheerleader was in the locker room today," I said.

Coach Fowles was silent.

"Yeah," Coach Branahan said. "I met Ben in the hall, and he asked me if I was going into the locker room. I said yes, and he looked kind of funny and scooted away. When I went in I just caught a glimpse of her long blond hair flying out of the door at the other end. They were giving her a tour or something, as a joke."

"Her *mother* won't think it's a joke if she hears about it," Coach Fowles said.

Right tackle Tom Kase, usually unbeatable, lost his second straight pit-drill match today, this time to a reserve lineman. Coach Fowles was disturbed. "He's losing weight to wrestle," Coach Fowles told me. "He started the season at 184, and now he's down under 170. I told him during the *wrestling* season he could be a wrestler."

I asked Tom about it. "I'm not trying to lose weight," he said. "I'm just losing it. I'm down to 167."

I found myself becoming bored with practices. They were now a repetitive drudgery from which the magic had been removed by two straight defeats. I wondered whether the players, too, weren't bored.

They practiced goal-line defense today, where the field had turned to dust. Rich Schenkle went down under a pile-up, but the players didn't get off him right away. They jumped cheerfully up and down on his back and pushed his face in the dirt. Clifford Albert danced across his back with his cleats.

"HEY, be CAREFUL of him!" Coach Fowles shouted. Rich got up shaking dirt off his face mask and smiling.

Freddie Delaney missed practice yesterday because he had to attend a bricklayers' union meeting. "That's why I couldn't come out at the beginning of the season," he said. "I had to work."

Freddie didn't go into the locker room directly after practice. He took a bow and arrows from his car and began shooting at an archery target, still in full football gear.

Coach Fowles called Tom Kase into the coaches' room. Tom couldn't explain his weight loss. He said he got tired in practice, and had cramps. Coach Fowles called his mother. He suggested she get some wheat germ, and asked her how she cooked meat for Tom. "Rare? That's good." She told him Tom had been taking vitamin C, but Coach Fowles said that was just for colds.

He hung up and turned to Tom. "You been weight lifting?"

"Every day," Tom said.

"Every *day*? Hey, Tom, that's too much. What do you bench-press?"

"About 220. Curl about 110."

"That's good, Tom, but every day is too much."

"I been doing it every day since summer."

"Wow. Listen, you should do it only every other day at *most*. Leave the weights alone for a few days. Go to bed early."

Al and Bruce Stacey were both seniors, though Al was sixteen and Bruce seventeen. The quirk occurred when they transferred into Laketown from another school system years ago. "Think what kind of an athlete Al could be if he could be here another year," Bruce told me once outside the cafeteria.

"Bruce is the one who exaggerates everything," his father said. We were sitting in their comfortable Americana home, a well-applianced, small-roomed house. Mr. Stacey was a pleasant, tall, bull-necked man with wavy blond hair. He was a national sales manager for a hardware concern. "He will exaggerate how many guys were in on a tackle, how many tackles he made, how many road signs they stole after the last game. Al is more brainy, quieter."

"Al's the one that always has to take you down on whatever you do," Bruce said. "Hey, who made all the tackles in the Peekskill game?" he jibed at his brother.

"Who made all the blocks?" Al jibed back quietly.

"See?" Bruce said, and they both smiled.

"I know our kids are known as 'straight,' " Mr. Stacey said. "I don't think that bothers them. As far as drinking and stuff like that is concerned—even smoking marijuana—my main feeling is that certain things are against the law, and you shouldn't do them for that reason. But we try not to be stuffy about it. Like after the last football game last year I said, okay, you kids are old enough now. If you want to have a few brews after the game then go ahead. Just if you get smashed someplace, call me, don't try to get home."

I had been thinking about Bruce's disappointment about not being a team captain. I asked whether he felt that Jonny was a real leader on the field.

"Yeah, he is," Bruce said. "Like in the huddle if somebody is mouthing off—you know, try this, try that, try this hole here—Jonny will just tell 'em to shut up, and they respect him. I respect him."

Al nodded. Al lost out today in the balloting for king of Homecoming dance.

"Stan Beronski got it," Bruce said, with a smile I took as signaling delicately mixed emotions.

The Harvesters, in shorts, without pads, went through some drills, ran some plays. Coach Fowles, dressed in slacks, a short-sleeved shirt, and a tie, directed them. Though the weather had been unusually warm so far, the leaves in the hills around the school were deep red, at their color peak for Homecoming tomorrow.

The team went in for its final meeting before Brushland. Jim Marshall handed them scraps of paper on which to write their votes for honorary captain. Jack Forrest was elected. Coach Fowles started to review Brushland's defense. Players were mumbling, turning around. Suddenly he exploded.

"HEY! SHUT UP!" The noise stopped immediately. "If anybody's got anything to say, raise your hand, and I'll shut my big mouth. We've got a football game tomorrow, whether you know it or not!"

He looked sternly at his players. "In order to win, we are going to have to *concentrate*. You people want to do other things right now, just go home, have a nice life. We have to have *concentration* if we want to win tomorrow. A good golfer, good student, doctor, lawyer—in any walk of life, that is a key word: *concentration*. You can eliminate mental mistakes if you concentrate. You can get off on the *count*, you can watch the *ball*.

"Now, they are predicting rain. Whatever the weather—if we have a *snowstorm* it doesn't bother me. You know what we are going to do? If we kick off, we will *onside kick*. Got it? They are definitely going to be caught flat-footed. We'll get the football before they even know what happened.

"Remember, once that ball goes 10 yards, you can run with it. Everybody understand that? It's *anybody's* football. Go down there wild-eyed and just dive straight out and *get* it. All right. Jim Marshall will start for the ball, like he's going to kick off. Ben Schenkle, you will be lined up beside him and come at an angle, and cut in front of Jim at the last second, *quick*.

"Now Ben, I don't want you to kick that thing to the *end*. Kick it just over the head of the tackle, just over his head. Even if the tackle gets the ball, he's a *lineman*, and he's not used to handling it. He's probably saying to himself, just like any lineman up there, 'Geez, I hope they don't kick it to me.' And we'll have our fastest kids lined up on that side of the field. We want that ten yards covered in maybe 1.1 seconds. And *throw* yourself at the football."

"Is that if it *doesn't* rain?" Jonny asked.

Players laughed. Coach Fowles looked up.

"*Hey*, we're gonna see how many jokes we have after the game tomorrow." He chuckled sardonically. "Nobody likes to laugh more than I do, brother. But I've got total recall about some things. I got a memory like an elephant. I love jokes. Let's have a party! But I want you to know one thing gentlemen, as of tomorrow afternoon, if we don't play football the way I think we should play football, you better get plenty of sleep Sunday night, because when you come to practice Monday—heh, heh, heh . . ."

Monday was Veterans Day, a school holiday. "Are we gonna have practice Monday, win or lose?" Jonny asked.

"Are we gonna have *practice?* Oooh, you better *believe* it. I love to joke, but boy when we play that football game tomorrow, you people—and that includes you, Jonathan—are signing a contract with me. If we don't have a good football team on that field tomorrow, Monday's going to be a very interesting day."

Coach Branahan spoke, "I don't imagine Clifford Albert and Jack Forrest are thinking it's a joke right now because that guy that weighs 244, he's a defensive tackle, and he's going to be on one of those guys. He's got almost a hundred pounds on Jack, ninety pounds on Clifford."

14

SATURDAY, *October 23*

It turned out to be a warm, sunny day for Homecoming. Several of the players went to Brushland High to watch the JVs beat Brushland, 21–0. Then they returned to Laketown High to dress for their last home game.

At about one o'clock, the parade of floats, pulled by cars, arrived, accompanied by the band playing from the back of a flatbed truck, and cheerleaders chanting and swinging their arms. One float was a Laketown covered wagon; another was a Laketown dummy football player leaning among cornstalks; then came the turtle and the airplane. Spectators crowded around the parking lot to welcome the festive parade and add to the decibel level.

Inside the locker room, Barry Brill applied tape to what was left of his shoes. As they ripped week by week, he had applied more and more tape, so that now the entire toe sections were taped, making them look like clown shoes. "They gotta last three more games," he said.

Coach Branahan taped Jonny's ankle, which had been injured in Peekskill. Jonny said the tape hurt when he did it himself. Sandy said he would try to put it on more carefully.

The team went out, in home-game white, to loosen up. The backs ran the tires. Some of the linemen joined them. Jim Petrowski and Ray Meister banged shoulders. Jonny threw long passes to his ends, testing his ankle. Jack Forrest, who had sore ribs and an aching back, stretched and bent to relax the muscles.

Coach Fowles had gone back into the locker room, and now he appeared and called me over. "Remember that coach who was in the end zone at Peekskill? The guy from Gorton? I just caught him in our locker room. He said he had gone in there to 'tinkle.' So I said to him, 'You got a lot of guts. This your first year as coach?' He said it was. I said, 'Well, someday you'll be a good coach.' Then he got all excited and started telling me all about himself, where he went to school, where his brother coaches. I just stood there watching him, and he said I made him so nervous he couldn't tinkle."

He looked around. "And now he isn't even doing the thing he *should* do, which is to be out here watching us warm up, if he really wants to learn something."

The coin toss was to be held on the field at 1:35, and Coach Fowles sent his captains down. They trotted to the middle of the field and waited. Brushland, in dark green jerseys, was warming up on the sideline, but neither their captains nor the officials joined the four Laketown captains. Rich Schenkle looked around at the big crowd, which filled the bleachers and surrounded the field.

"It's too hot to play football," Stan Beronski said.

After several minutes, the Laketown manager ran down from the school where the team was warming up. "Coach says to come back up. He doesn't want you to wait for them."

Just then the officials and the Brushland captains came over. Rich called heads and won the toss, electing to receive. Then the Laketown captains headed back up the hill to rejoin their teammates.

"They're not brontosauruses," Stan said.

"What's a brontosaurus?" Rich asked.

Coach Fowles was steaming. "All right boys," he called to the team, "take four minutes in the locker room, then let's play football."

". . . If they can win ONE game," Jim Marshall shouted, "they want to beat Laketown. That's all they want."

Rich Schenkle was trembling. "Last night we went over to watch 'em," he said. "When we were still on the road and couldn't even SEE the team we could hear it . . . ."

"We didn't even get off ROUTE SIX," Jim Petrowski yelled, "and we could hear them guys YELLIN! They're so ready to kill us it's UNBELIEVABLE! They remember that fight so well it's UNBELIEVABLE!"

"We just about got out of the car . . ."

". . . And they're gonna be out there to KILL us!"

"And this morning, this morning," Rich said, dancing nervously on his toes, "I was talking to one of their captains, and you know what he said? He said, today they're starting a NEW SEASON, Laketown! All week long their coach has drilled into their minds, the Laketown game is the beginning of the 1971 SEASON!"

Jim was almost crying as he shouted, "You think we can walk out there and throw our helmets on the field and beat 'em you're CRAZY! YOU WANNA BE THREE AND THREE? THAT SUCKS! WE BETTER NOT LOSE AGAIN TODAY! BE-CAUSE I'M TIRED LOSING TWO GAMES IN A ROW!"

"They're 0 and 4," Rich said. "But we're 0 and 2 for two weeks, almost as BAD as THEY are. And we've got THREE TIMES the team they do. Not as big, but as SMART AND QUICK as any team in the COUNTY!"

There was a silence.

"And who knows, maybe Gorton will come up and beat us too."

"Just think about it, cause I know THEY are."

"Right from the captain's mouth—today is a new SEASON for them."

Coach Fowles came in. "Anybody else have anything to say in here?"

"Get ready," Jim Marshall said, "RIGHT NOW!"

"Do you know what it said in the paper yesterday?" Coach Branahan said. "That somebody is going to stop a *losing streak* in this game. It didn't say anything about anybody winning. Secondary, let's play heads up and watch for that option pass. Cornerbacks, you got to come up and take the pitch man. *No* mistakes today on the field."

Coach Fowles started off softly, gently. "Hey, boys, I really in all honesty thought we had respect from the other teams. Now I'm not so sure we have respect from this team."

His voice rose a notch. "We tell them we're gonna be out there at twenty-five minutes to one, and what do they do? THEY THINK SO MUCH OF LAKETOWN THAT IT GOES IN ONE EAR AND OUT THE OTHER!"

The sudden crash of his voice seemed to stun the room.

"THEY LEAVE US STANDING THERE LIKE FOUR DUMMIES. IS THAT RESPECT? I say, no, it's not respect."

He was striding back and forth, emphasizing his words with his arms. "We catch a coach RIGHT IN THE LOCKER ROOM. He had guts enough to walk into OUR LOCKER ROOM! I wouldn't do that on a BET! IS THAT THE KIND OF RESPECT YOU PEOPLE WANT TODAY? CAKE-EATERS! TODAY THEY LEAVE YOU STANDING OUT ON THE FIELD LIKE FOUR MONUMENTS! THAT'S HOW THEY RESPECT YOU!"

His voice cracked and the cords stood out in his reddened neck. The players stood awed by the angry tone.

"YOU THINK YOU HAVE RESPECT YOU'RE CRAZY! YOU GOT FORTY-EIGHT MINUTES OF FOOTBALL TO EARN RESPECT! WHO WE GONNA BEAT?"

Three times he bellowed the question, and three times the team bellowed back, "BRUSHLAND!"

"All right, boys, bring it in, bring it in," Coach Fowles said as the huddle formed around him. "Right now, everybody in the family. Hey, gentlemen, this is our *last* home game, our last football game on this field together. We're going to make it one we'll *never* forget, *never!*"

Ken Furst brought the kickoff back up the middle to the Laketown 33. The first play was to fake the jet-pass deep to Don Heidner, and hit instead Ted O'Neill who would delay and drift out to the right flat—the play that misfired at Peekskill.

"Let's see what they're in right away," Coach Fowles said, peering at the Brushland defensive lineup as Laketown came to the line of scrimmage. "... They're in a five-two monster...."

Jonny rolled out to his right, seemed to hesitate, then threw on the run toward the sideline. But the linebacker had dropped back. He cut in front of Ted and intercepted on the Brushland 45, in front of the scaffolding from which the game was being broadcast.

"He underthrew me by EIGHT YARDS," Ted O'Neill shouted as he came to the bench.

"I know he threw a bad pass," Coach Branahan said calmly, "but you should delay a little bit longer, all right?"

"Jonny, come here," Coach Fowles beckoned to his quarterback. "Listen," he said softly, holding Jonny's arms and looking into his eyes. "Why did you throw the football?"

"Cause Ted was open."

"Yeah, but you weren't on balance when you threw it, and it didn't have any gusto on it. Did you think of running?"

"Ted was *open.*"

"Okay, let's forget that."

Jonny walked away, kicking the dirt.

Stu Rosenman started at left defensive end. Bob Mills filled in at Bradford McClure's left tackle spot, and Tom Kase was to play both ways, offensive and defensive right tackle.

A flag was thrown on Brushland's first play, and the usually tranquil

Bob Mills was hopping up and down angrily. The official signaled a face-mask penalty.

"Hey, Vince Carradino," Coach Fowles yelled along the bench. "In for Bob Mills, hurry up."

"He had his hand right around his helmet," Coach Branahan said.

"I don't know what it was," Coach Fowles said, "but I'm gonna find out. Hey, Bob, what was it, Bob?"

Bob spit on the grass. "Face mask." He walked away.

"Now wait a minute, come here. Did you have your hand on his face mask?"

"NO! I had it like this. . . ."

"All right, go back in on the next play."

Aided by the 15-yard penalty, and using straight-ahead power plays, Brushland drove to the 13, where the Laketown line held for three running plays. On fourth down, the quarterback dropped back to pass. Stu Rosenman, coming from left end, was on him when he turned around. He hooked his hand in the passer's shirt and dropped him on the 20. Laketown took over.

Al Stacey ripped up the middle for a first down on the 34. Ben Schenkle and Al brought it to the 41. Brian Purcell took a third-down play in from the bench.

Jonny bootlegged to his left and was dropped for a yard loss.

"Hey, Jonny," Coach Fowles said to him as he came off. "That wasn't the play Brian brought in."

"I didn't know *what* you sent in. He came to the huddle and mumbled —'Bmbmbmbmbm.' "

Ted O'Neill punted, but suddenly there was turmoil along the bench. A Brushland player was standing there, and players were yelling to Coach Fowles and to the officials. Somebody shoved the player. "Don't PUSH me, man!" the Brushland player said.

Coach Fowles came running up, yelling. "All right! KEEP QUIET! SHUT UP! EVERYBODY SHUT UP!"

"What the hell's he doing pulling a trick like that. . . ."

"Don't say ANYTHING," Coach Fowles said, "DON'T OPEN YOUR MOUTH!"

An official had seen the violation. The Brushland player had simply been caught by a late substitution and had tried to get off the field the closest place possible before the play started. Brushland was penalized for illegal procedure, and Laketown got the ball back.

Al Stacey and Ben Schenkle ran inside plays for two first downs to the

Brushland 31. Then Jonny faked to Ben up the middle, dropped back, and threw to Don Heidner slanting to his left and all alone on the five-yard line. Don took the pass in full stride and went in for the first score of the day. Ben Schenkle missed the kick, hooking it to the left. The score was 6–0.

As Brushland lined up to receive, Coach Fowles thought he caught a signal. "They're coming over HERE!" he yelled out to his kickoff team, "going to run it THIS WAY!"

But they ran it the other way, back to the 40. They were held, and punted. Brian Purcell watched it come down, right through his hands. It rolled out of bounds on the Laketown 25.

"Let's get him outta there, Sandy," Coach Fowles said. "Last week it was the sun."

Bruce Stacey limped off. "Got a cleat in the knee," he said. The doctor surveyed the knee and pronounced it okay.

Ben Schenkle stuck a finger in his mouth. "My tooth is loose again," he said, out of earshot of the coaches. "It hurts."

Jonny called a 72-flood pass, sending both Ted O'Neill and Don Heidner down-and-out into the same area, and hit Don who knocked one defender over on his back and went for 20 yards.

Two running plays gained nothing. Then Jonny dropped back, looking for O'Neill, and was hit by two rushing linemen. Ted O'Neill punted. Brushland was held and was set to punt back. Stan Beronski charged, just missed blocking the ball, and fell across the punter's legs. The roughing-the-kicker penalty gave Brushland a first down on the 50.

The quarterback went back to throw, was rushed, and threw wildly. He looked at the nearest official, and his head snapped up and down with apparently angry words. The official threw a flag and marked off 15 yards against Brushland for a personal foul. The Brushland coach yanked his quarterback and yelled at him on the sidelines.

Brushland punted, and Don Heidner ran it back to the Laketown 35. On the first play, Jonny hit Ted O'Neill on a quick slant-in for a first down on the 45. On the way back to the huddle, Ted said something to the defender who was covering him.

"IGNORE NUMBER 11!" Coach Fowles yelled to Ted. "HE DOESN'T EXIST!"

Laketown couldn't move, and punted back.

With the ball on the Brushland 30, the quarterback went back to pass. Stan Beronski chased him. He tried to spin away, but Stan locked his arms and knocked the ball loose. It rolled backward from the 15 toward the goal line and Jim Petrowski dove on it on the six.

But the ball was brought back to the 15, and the official signaled it Brushland's ball. The Harvesters protested, and looked toward their bench. The referee was already heading over to Coach Fowles.

"I'm sorry," he said, "but the umpire blew it dead in possession of Brushland. Nothing I can do about it, Bud. He made a mistake."

"Okay."

Brushland punted, and time ran out in the half.

". . . Hey, you know what that was? That was CAKE! . . . Is there any more of that, what is it, orangeade?"

"Would have been first and goal on the SIX," Jim Petrowski said.

"They said that was a mistake, Jim."

"MISTAKE? Would have been a TOUCHDOWN!"

"Okay, Jim, okay. . . ."

"Hey, Laketown," Jack Forrest said, "they're not the hardest hitting team we've played, they're nowhere near it. We're not hitting hard enough, that's all it is."

"Should be 24 zip now," Rich Schenkle said.

"Let's face it," Jonny said, "those guys aren't any fuckin good."

"Aw, shut up, man!" John Curtis said, with a hurt expression. "What are you TALKIN about! Don't get overconfident."

"I'm REALLY overconfident," Jonny said.

"Jonny, I was OPEN . . ."

"Ted, I KNOW . . ."

"Hey, Jon," Rich said, "I was open on that . . ."

"Well I REALLY HAD A LOT OF TIME, Rich."

"I know, I know, I was just saying . . ."

"If you could just look over at ME first, I'm open . . ."

"Don't TELL me, Ted, OKAY? I know I know I know. I know who's out there. CHRIST!"

"Jonny's been getting the CRAP kicked out of him," Jim Petrowski said.

The room quieted down as bottles of orangeade and Gatorade clinked around.

"Way to go, defense," Jonny said. "They can't MOVE the ball."

"Hey, DEFENSE!" Jim Marshall said, "we haven't had a SHUTOUT yet this year."

"All right," Coach Fowles said, "let's go over some things. Defensively we're not playing a bad football game. We've made some mistakes. Roughing the punter was *inexcusable*. Once the boy kicks the football you can't touch him, Stan, unless you touch the football first. It's that simple. Our

:*253*:

tackling isn't bad, our punt coverage is excellent. We're making a lot of mental mistakes on our SETS, gentlemen, on lining up in the backfield. We seem to be a little more excited out there than we *should* be.

"Again, we're a second-half football team. Lot of people on the Brush-land football team looked awful tired. That doesn't mean they *will* be however. Because it's a state of mind. We gotta go out there and *prove* to them that they are tired.

"Offense. For the first time this year I've seen our quarterback dumped two or three times in the first half. Anybody have any reasons for that? We've got to throw quicker on these patterns. Coach Branahan?"

"Use quick slant-ins, all right? To Ted especially."

"Yeah, that linebacker is lookin for Don," Jonny said.

"They got *two* men on Don," Coach Fowles said.

"But you can throw to Don also," Coach Branahan said, "if you can get him on a quick slant-in, cause they're givin him all the short patterns in the world. But they want to stop the bomb."

"But they got a monster on Don's side, you gotta remember," Coach Fowles said. "Ted O'Neill should be open all day long. But not the long in-and-out, that's too slow. Just the quick-in or quick-out."

"Also, Jonny," Coach Branahan said, "let's try a pro-right, strong left," indicating the flanker split to the right, but the backfield weighted to the left. "Let's see what they do with their monster. If they just keep the monster on Don. . . ."

"We can run it back the other way, at the seven hole," Jonny said.

"Actually I'm amazed they've stayed in a six-man line," Coach Fowles said. "Wherever Don Heidner goes, that's where the monster goes. It's that simple.

"You know what bothers me? We haven't caused that team to fumble. By the way, that fumble down on the five- or six-yard line, the referee came over and said the umpire just made a mistake. . . ."

Jim Petrowski slammed his helmet on the floor.

". . . They made a mistake," Coach Fowles went on, looking at Jim, "and that's *it*, there's absolutely nothing we can do about it."

"Okay. John Curtis and Clifford Albert." He looked at his left tackle and guard. "When Don goes over to the other side, the right, how do those people line up on you, outside shoulder?"

"Yes," John said.

"All right, then I think we've gotta stop splitting Rich Schenkle. We need him in tight to help. When we split Rich we lose him as a blocker.

Let's not waste a split on the other side with Rich just to look fancy. If we're gonna throw to him, then split him."

"Coach," Coach Branahan said softly, "it's pretty warm in here."

"Yeah, it is. Let's go outside, out alongside the building. Don't go down to the field yet."

They walked out of the locker room. I asked the players what the Brushland quarterback had said to cause a 15-yard penalty and get himself temporarily pulled out of the game.

"He said, 'I wish that motherfucking referee would open his goddamned eyes.'"

The players leaned back against the wall outside. The sky had darkened. Down on the field, the float parade was finishing, and cheers and music, muffled and blended by the distance, wafted up to the team.

Coach Fowles stood apart from the team and looked down at the pageantry. "I love all that," he said, "the whole scene, the game, the floats. Of course, too much of anything is bad. But I don't think this is too much. So much time and love have gone into this. And people say today that kids won't work. The dedication of kids is tremendous."

He walked over to the team. Players got quickly to their feet even before he spoke, and pulled their helmets on. He clapped his hands. "Okay, let's go down, Laketown."

The Harvesters assembled and began their last, somber, single-file walk down to their own playing field, a line of pubescent gladiators in grass-stained white; boys who had girl friends, motorcycles, social studies, boils, but on whose minds at this instant was only the second half of their last home high school football game.

Brushland took the kickoff to their 20. They came out in a new shotgun formation, with the quarterback five yards behind the center. He took the ball and threw quickly to his right. It was tipped up at the line and fell incomplete. A draw gained one. The quarterback slipped to one knee trying to pass. They had to punt.

Don Heidner took the kick on the Brushland 45 and drove straight ahead, over one tackler, to the 35.

On a quick dive behind Tom Kase, Ben Schenkle went for seven.

"That's going to work," Coach Fowles said to Coach Branahan. "Let's try it again. LOOKING GOOD, JONNY, LOOKING GOOD!"

Jonny heard his coach, and twice more Ben hit the seven hole, for the first down on the 23. Then Jonny faked to Ben and spun around to hand to

Brian Purcell on a tailback counter to the other side, to the 18. Brian took another counter to the 11.

Then, lining up at tailback, Ben took a delayed hand-off, swung to his right around the end, dove over the last tackler at the three, and landed in the end zone.

Jonny trotted to the sideline, to the accompaniment of wild cheers and a cowbell and drums of the band.

"Try for two?" Coach Branahan asked. "Outside-belly action pass, with Rich coming across the middle and Ted O'Neill and Don Heidner running a 72 flood to the right?"

"Sounds good to me," Jonny said.

"All right," Coach Fowles said, "and you'll need a blocker. Who's the best tailback to block?"

"Bruce and Al Stacey are in," Coach Branahan said.

"All right, let's go."

Ben Schenkle came off. He angrily snapped his chinstrap off and went away by himself.

"What's wrong?" I asked.

"I can block!" he said with uncharacteristic heat. "Every time they want a blocker they take me out."

Jonny faked to Al Stacey, hid the ball on his hip as he rolled to the right, then fired a bullet to Don Heidner in the corner of the end zone for two points.

It was 14–0 with six minutes and forty-seven seconds left in the third quarter.

"We're just gonna grind 'em into bits now," Jack Forrest said happily as he came off. "We got 'em all psyched out."

Indeed, everything seemed to be coming together. Jim Marshall's kick-off bounced into the end zone.

Brushland again came out in the shotgun.

"TELL RICH TO DROP OFF IN THAT ZONE," Coach Fowles instructed from the sideline. "HEY, AL STACEY, PLAY THE SHORT PASS."

Karl Walsh intercepted the pass over the middle on the 32 and squirmed back to the 25.

Ben Schenkle plunged for four yards on the right side. Then Jonny faked to him at the same hole, spun and gave to tailback Al Stacey on the other side. John Curtis had opened the hole, and Don Heidner had tangled up the cornerback. Al swung wide and ran it in untouched for the score.

Jonny stayed in, so they would go for two points. I asked Coach Fowles why, with the score 20–0, they didn't kick instead.

"I don't know," he said, "this is Jonny's call."

Jonny fired a quick slant-in to Ted O'Neill for the two. Ted said something to the defender he had just beaten, and then came off.

"I played basketball against that guy," Ted explained. "He's been hollering, 'Get O'Neill.' So after the touchdown I said, 'Please, Jonny, call the slant-in.' And he did."

Brushland started from its 28. Coach Fowles began substituting on defense. Big Harry Wallace went in for the first time this year, working his tiny feet like pistons under his round, 270-pound body. Don Heidner went in for deep pass coverage. Vince Carradino and Freddie Delaney went in. Opposing players began to exchange words.

"HEY, FREDDIE DELANEY!" Coach Fowles yelled. "IF YOU WANT TO PLAY FOOTBALL, DON'T TALK TO HIM!" He turned toward Jim Petrowski on the sideline. "Jim, you're not going to play football either unless you stop talking to them."

On two passes, Brushland moved to its 40, then was forced to punt.

Laketown took the kick on its 30. Coach Fowles sent in his entire second-string offense for the first time in the season. The band played a bugle charge. Ted O'Neill took over at quarterback, Stu Rosenman at fullback, Ken Furst at tailback, and Karl Walsh at flanker. The result was an immediate collapse that turned the game around.

Even before the first play was run, Laketown was penalized for illegal procedure when a lineman moved. Ken Furst gained three up the middle. Ted O'Neill called a flanker reverse. Karl Walsh swung deep with the hand-off, was trapped near the goal line, and whirled down. It was third down and 28 to go on the two-yard line. Next, the hand-off was fumbled, and Ted fell on it one foot from the goal line. They had lost 30 yards in three plays.

Coach Fowles sent in his regular punting team. Ted O'Neill had to stand near the rear boundary of the end zone, only 10 yards from the center instead of 13. He hurried his kick. It dribbled out only to the 19.

The first-string defensive unit went in. But on the first play, Brushland's quick halfback ducked through the line, cut back to his left, and went for the touchdown. They faked a kick and threw for the extra two points. With the third quarter nearly over, the score was 22–8.

The defense was disturbed only that it had lost the shutout, but they said little, for it was the fault of the offense. Or even the coach. "It was almost too early to substitute," Coach Fowles said musing on the sidelines. "I took the momentum away from my football team."

The coaches yelled to watch for an onside kick, but Brushland kicked off normally. Jonny worked his team into Brushland territory with running plays before Ted O'Neill finally had to punt.

The third quarter ended, the band began playing a loud march, and Coach Fowles called an official over.

"Sir, I am *not* a complainer. But I think number 22 is awfully free with his forearms. Okay?"

The official waved acknowledgment.

The band continued playing as the fourth quarter began, with the ball on the Brushland 15. Brushland fumbled on the first play, Laketown recovered in the pile-up, and it seemed the Harvesters' momentum might be restored.

"Let's power it right in, from a split-backfield," Coach Fowles told Jonny. "Ram it in."

Jonny sent Keith Allen into the line for two, then yelled something to the sidelines.

Coach Branahan ran down to where the band was still blasting. "Hey, knock it off. They can't hear Jonny's signals."

The band leader shrugged and smiled, waving his arms in front of him to still the musicians. "You gotta admit," he said, "there was not much time between quarters."

Then Jonny threw three times incomplete. Brushland took over.

"Fuck," Jonny said.

"Watch your language, son," the official said.

Using the shotgun formation off and on, Brushland drove to midfield. Then a receiver slipped by Karl Walsh to take a pass over the middle. He sailed down the far sideline until Ken Furst caught him and dragged him out of bounds on the three.

On the next play they scored, running over right tackle. They repeated the play for the two extra points. With three minutes left in the game, the score was 22–16. The Harvesters were shaken. Only Bradford McClure, standing on the sidelines in a sport jacket, his bandaged thumb sticking up from his folded arms, was slyly pleased.

"They ran over my spot," he said, smiling. "That'll help me get my job back."

"BRADFORD!" I said.

"Long as we win," he said.

Now an onside kick was almost a certainty. Coach Fowles sent out his surest receivers: running backs, ends, and Jonny Penchak. Magically the short kick bounced toward Jonny, and magically it dribbled through his big hands. He scrambled after it, but was beaten by the onrushing Brushland wave. It was Brushland's ball on the Laketown 46 with two minutes and fifty seconds left and only six points separating the teams.

What had earlier been a joyful rout was now impending calamity. Brushland opened up with running plays, using its time-outs to stop the clock. They got a first down on the 35. Then they came out in the shotgun, with receivers spread wide to either side. The quarterback threw over the middle. Ray Meister was on his man closely. But he gambled for the interception, reaching over his man's shoulder. He missed; the receiver took it and spun away. Mark Ferenzi pulled him down on the 11.

First down, with fifty-three seconds left. The crowd poured out of the bleachers and packed around the snow fence near the end zone.

From the shotgun, the quarterback threw over the middle for the end zone, but Bruce Stacey knocked it away at the line of scrimmage. Again the quarterback threw over the middle, and again Bruce leaped and tipped it up. His brother Al, sweeping across the end zone with the intended receiver, snared it and ran it out to the 14.

As Jonny prepared to call a final quarterback sneak to run out the clock, Coach Fowles turned and faced his bench. He commanded all their eyes.

"No matter what happens after the game," he said sternly to them, "everybody stays right here. First guy crosses over this white line onto that field, he's finished. If anything happens, Coach Branahan and I will take care of it."

Before Jonny took the snap, a linebacker hurdled the line and smashed into him. Brushland was assessed five yards for offside. Jonny took the team back into the huddle, with the clock running, and they waited there until the final whistle blew.

For a brief few seconds the teams were apart. Then the players advanced and began to shake hands with their opponents. After some hesitation, the Laketown bench swarmed onto the field to join. There was no hint of trouble. The Harvesters ran off the field side by side with Brushland.

15

Coach Fowles climbed onto a bench in the locker room and shook his head. "Gentlemen, we had the football game under control until—well, I don't know what this is. For the sixth week in a row, a cliff-hanger. We're gonna put this whole thing to rest next week, and the following week. All right, Coach Bush saw the Gorton game today. Give us a quick summary, Ian."

And so, even before they had a chance to shower after the Brushland game, the inexorable season proceeded—the team was pushed into preparation for Gorton.

Ian reported: big line, fast tough backs, sometimes run the wishbone, won today by seventeen points. "And boys I'll tell you something else: We better not look past Gorton," Coach Fowles added. "We *all* know Sleepy Hollow's undefeated. But we don't play them for two weeks. We're gonna play *one game at a time*. Gorton, that's who we want now."

Some of the Laketown players stood outside waiting for rides home. They watched silently as an ambulance came, its red light flashing, to remove a Brushland player who had collapsed after the game.

Ben Schenkle, Ken Furst, Ray Meister climbed into a car. "Should we wait for Rich?"

"Naw," Ben said, "my parents are waiting for him. He thinks he broke his thumb."

"I gave up eight points," Ken Furst, the safetyman, said. "On their first touchdown run, I had the guy, then I lost him. And on the extra points, I went in instead of covering my zone where they threw."

"This one was the coach's fault," Ray Meister said, "for sending in the second-string so early in the third quarter."

It was a very warm night. A breeze swirled the leaves on the ground and brought new ones down. Coach Fowles and I stood on his lawn in the dark and listened to the leaves. He seemed very tired. "Yeah, it was my fault. The team was ready to run away with one, and they almost did. The kids on the bench wanted to play too. But it almost cost us."

The first raindrops pattered down on the dry leaves. "Jonny came up to me after the game and said he wanted to call his own plays. He was right. Sandy and I have taken the game away from him little by little. The game today was not Jonny's game. See how important communications are?" He was silent for a few seconds. "I can hardly wait for next year. These kids this year are fantastic kids, beautiful kids. Each year is a new challenge. I'm already thinking about some of the kids who aren't playing this year, who will be playing next year. It never ends. I really love it."

SUNDAY, *October 24*

Coach Fowles prepared to run the film. Rich Schenkle's thumb was in a splint.

"Did you have it x-rayed?" Coach Fowles asked.

"Yeah. It's not broken."

"Does it hurt?"

"Throbs a little."

Rich had hurt his thumb on the second play against Brushland but won the star for most tackles in the game.

Jonny flopped down on the floor. "Hey, Coach, does it show that on-side kick that I fumbled?"

"Yup."

"Wake me up," he said, rolling over on his belly. What had caused him to fumble, Jonny revealed later, was that his long hair had got into his eyes.

It was a rainy, dark day, matching my mood. I had become tired. I was tired of the practices, the players, the lingo; of the smells of sod, bodies, Nitrotan Spray, Firm Grip, adhesive tape; of the tires, the manbuilder, the films, the psyching up. Winning and losing were tedious. I wanted the season to end.

In the locker room, Rich Schenkle built a fortress around his damaged thumb. He applied a sponge-rubber pad, then a metal splint shaped like a V, then another pad, then wrapped it with several layers of tape. He did this painstakingly alone, with his teeth and good hand, not daring to show it to the coaches.

Coach Branahan was absent, suffering from the flu. Coach Fowles put the backs and linemen together for a series of demanding agility drills. After them, the players stood panting. Coach Fowles put his hand on Jim Petrowski's shoulder.

"I'm not knocking Jim," he said, "but he's not naturally that good of an athlete. But I *defy anybody out here* to keep up with him in agility drills. This is why he's a good football player."

He announced that they would play King of the Mountain on the manbuilder, which was a wall of mud.

Guards and tackles assumed their positions at the top, to be charged by the backs and ends. While they tangled, grunting and roaring, spilling down the mudwash together, Jonny slipped over to the side and climbed unnoticed, arriving behind them all and proclaiming the hill to be his. Ray Meister had been sat upon facedown in the mud, and arose looking like a melting gray monster. Bruce Stacey staggered off the hill, groped his way across the ground, and stumbled into the seven-man sled, all the while moaning about mud in his eyes. Coach Fowles sent him in to wash his face.

In the pit drill, husky Stu Rosenman opposed lanky reserve end Joe Knowland.

"Hey, Stu," Coach Fowles yelled, "now's the time to help the family. You're going to help Joe become a football player by hitting him as hard as you can."

Stu did, and Joe held his ground for a few seconds before being driven out.

"How does that help Joe?" I asked.

"Cause he found out he can take it. I didn't want Stu going easy on him. He gave Joe some success. Joe is going to be a football player next year, you'll see. He'll help the family."

They went into the scrimmage session. Rich jumped into the huddle.

"Get outta there, Rich!"

"Aw."

"Not today."

Rich stomped off. He angrily ripped the bandage from his thumb. "What did I put this *on* for anyway?" he said. Both his hands were swollen.

"Where are your new hand pads?" I asked.

"I threw them away for a play on the goal line at Peekskill, or someplace."

Coach Fowles said that Laketown would destroy Gorton's punting game in the following manner: A tough Harvester would line up head-on the Gorton center. His job would be to smash into the center as hard as possible. "That boy will center the ball the first time to the punter. The next time he will be so worried about getting hit that he will center it into the end zone."

"Coach?" Stan Beronski said, "Can I be the man assigned to belt the center?"

"Yes."

"Why do you want to do it?" I asked.

"Cause he's in such a helpless position," Stan said, smiling.

To relieve Jonny of the confusion of running both offenses, Coach Fowles was the "Gorton" quarterback. He faked to backs excellently, and threw beautiful long bombs that drew "oooohs" from the team. He was serious, and scolded rushing linemen when they disturbed his throws. "The point of this is to give the secondary work on pass defense," he said.

Once Barry Brill shot through and bumped him as he set up to throw. "I *told* you not to do that," Coach Fowles said. "It doesn't help the family."

I picked up broken glass from the practice field, swatted the ubiquitous little black bugs, watched the girls play field hockey, and wondered if the weather would ever turn cool.

Defensive end Steve Barker had hurt his knee. Coach Fowles felt around the knee carefully, and sent Steve to the locker room.

"I'm afraid it might be cartilage or ligaments," he said.

On the Laketown offense, Keith Allen took several pitchouts from

Jonny and followed Tom Kase, who pulled from right tackle to lead around end on stomps. "GO, GO, GO," Keith yelled at Tom, pushing him with his hand.

"He's really fast," Tom said. "He's the only one who runs up my back."

After practice, Stu Rosenman stayed out to get some pointers on defensive end from one of the last year's strong linebackers. "Get rid of those guys coming at you," Stu was told, "give 'em an arm, get rid of 'em. Hate those guys. Then you're free to make tackles."

Later, in the car, Stu Rosenman talked to Jonny. "Coach has so much bullshit," Stu said. "You believe it for a while, about how good you are and how well you're doing and all that, but after a while it's just bullshit."

"Coach Fowles is a lot smarter than some of you guys think," Jonny said.

"He sure can play quarterback," Stu said. "When he hid the ball on his hip, and watched the back go into the line, I was standing three feet away. I couldn't believe that back didn't have the ball."

Stu and I went to his house. It was a spacious home on a hill, with a swimming pool in back. We ate roast beef.

The Rosenmans owned a women's clothing store in the shopping center. Mr. Rosenman was a compact man with bushy gray eyebrows, a gruff voice, and a direct manner. Mrs. Rosenman seemed milder, spoke more softly.

I asked Rosenman about his chastisement of Coach Fowles for not playing Stu more.

"I don't believe in second-guessing people," he said. "I just felt I should speak my mind to him. He's a great gentleman and a fine psychologist. One of the first things he said when we were there outside his office —he turned to Stu and said: 'You deserve a tremendous amount of credit this season for sticking it out while you're on the bench.' I think he's got a message and he really believes in it."

Mrs. Rosenman, busy at the store, didn't get to see the games. "I listen on the radio," she said, "and I just keep hoping for the time when they say number 25, Rosenman, did something. But it never happens. He never gets in."

"I watch Stu all the time," Mr. Rosenman said. "I sit up in the stands and watch him every minute, whether he's on the bench or not. Sometimes I wish he'd at least pick up the water bucket or something, just do *something*."

"One of the reasons I think Stu should play," Mrs. Rosenman said, "is that Stu has been playing since he was ten, in fifth grade. He did everything. He won the run, kick, pass, punt competition—or whatever that is. He started as a sophomore on the JV. Last year he went away to a private school. I wonder if that might have been resented by Coach Branahan."

She thought for a moment, and then said carefully, "I wonder if something is going on with Coach Fowles. He's had four assistants in four years. Since he's delegating so much responsibility to Sandy Branahan, I wonder if either he is planning to move up somewhere and let Sandy take over, or if he's just trying to keep an assistant coach for once."

"I started the Lourdes game, remember?" Stu said. "And did you know that I never got to carry the ball *once*? Coach Branahan is supposed to be responsible for the offense, and I don't know if he is down on me or what. Like he makes little remarks in class that are supposed to be jokes, about the store, and about my car accident last year. I don't appreciate that. But I *did* go to him—before the Peekskill game, I think it was. I didn't talk about the jokes, but I did ask him about not playing. And he told me on that day, Tuesday, 'You *will* get the ball, in the first half, and if you keep doing well you will stay in there.' But I didn't get the ball until the fourth quarter, and then for just one play."

"How'd you feel when your father talked to Coach Fowles, with you there?"

"I was embarrassed. But I was getting more and more down every day. So that day when I saw him in the hall, and he asked me if I was thinking of quitting, like I couldn't really talk and come right out with it, how I wanted to quit. So I started to cry—really. So he talked me out of quitting."

"Do you think you're playing as well as other years?"

"I don't know. It's funny. Like tonight after practice when I was talking to that guy from last year, and he was telling me certain things to do? I began to get the feeling that the problem this year is that I'm not aggressive enough. I started thinking back. I hurt my knee as a sophomore, and just possibly that's in the back of my mind—like I don't run quite as hard because I don't want to hurt my knee again."

"You like playing defensive end?" I asked.

"Even more than running back. Because at least you get to hit somebody every play."

"Where do *you* think Stu should play?" I asked his father.

He shrugged. "I don't know all that much about football," he said.

"Why don't you come to some practices?" Stu asked.

:265:

His father smiled. "I'm afraid to come to practice," he said. "I'm afraid I would start telling the coach how to run his football team."

WEDNESDAY, October 27

"Well, seven more practices," Coach Fowles announced at the start of practice. "Don't have any regrets."

The coaches put in a wishbone formation today, designed to give Ben Schenkle a quick shot at either the four or the six hole, behind the guards. He lined up close enough behind Jonny to be able to touch his rump, with the other two backs a step behind him to the right and left.

In the scrimmage session, Coach Fowles again was quarterback for the "Gorton" offense. "He has a good arm," Coach Fowles said, referring to the Gorton quarterback, "but in my judgment they will not come out passing. They will try to run it down our throats."

Ted O'Neill took over the "Gorton" offense. Before anybody could stop him, Jonny lined up at tailback and took a hand-off, smashed over center, and was piled up.

"GET OUTTA THERE, JONNY!" Coach Branahan yelled.

Jonny got up to his knees, his hair down over his face, his helmet pushed forward over his eyes. "It's FUN!" he said.

"Whew!" Coach Branahan said, looking at Coach Fowles, who shook his head.

Bradford McClure came back to practice, his thumb still protected by a huge bandage. He tired quickly, and said he felt lousy. His thumb hurt. "I probably came back a little early," he said.

Jim Petrowski was one of the few who ran all out for each of the sixteen 40-yard sprints at the end of practice. The coaches usually called out the names of the winners for the last two or three sprints. Today that was making Jim especially angry.

"I win the sprints up to the last ones," he said, "and then I'm tired. Then the guys who haven't been working, they run hard and get their names called. Like it makes the guys who are loafin look good."

There was a letter to the editor of one of the area dailies. The writer complained about the "shabby treatment" of spectators at Laketown games, pointing out that some who paid a dollar to get in got no seats, and got their clothes torn on the broken-down snow fence around the field. The fence was broken because the football team ran over it like a stampede every day, leaving an occasional player or piece of equipment hung up in the wire.

THURSDAY, *October 28*

Another hot, sunny day. Bradford McClure was out sick, so was Keith Allen. A flu bug was going around. Steve Barker was on crutches. He tore cartilage in his knee, and would be operated on next week. Rich Schenkle rejoined the practice. He put a splint on his thumb and taped it to his first two fingers for more support.

Rich got into the pit drill against Jack Forrest, and drove the little guard out of the circle. "Your thumb is sharp," Jack said.

Stan Beronski went in against Harry Wallace. Their first go was a standoff, Stan unable to budge the mountain of a boy. Jonny tapped Stan on the rump. "Show him where you live, Stan," Jonny said, laughing. Stan then hit Harry so hard he tore his helmet off and sent him reeling. "S–t–a–n B–e–r–o–n–s–k–i!" Jonny announced. Coach Fowles quickly went up to Harry, put his hands on his shoulders and looked into his eyes. "You sure you're okay?" he asked.

During the break, Jonny came out of the locker room tipping a Carling Black Label can up to his lips, spilling down his chin. Coach Fowles looked at him. "It's water, Coach. Want some?"

Jonny had been having trouble in throwing his usual smooth spiral the last couple of weeks. Coach Fowles watched him carefully, then suggested he move his index finger a bit farther back on the ball.

In the scrimmage, Stan got through and rocked Jonny with a tackle. "S–t–a–n B–e–r–o–n–s–k–i," Jonny said, hurling down a wad of grass. Jonny ran three straight plays around left end, sending blockers ahead to knock Stan out of the way.

"Jonny got mad," Stan said.

Twice Jonny faked over the middle and sent runners through the tackle holes, beating linebacker Bruce Stacey. He teased Bruce about it. Bruce clenched his fists. On the next play Bruce shot through the line aimed at the running back. But Jonny faked, kept the ball himself, and ran right up the middle through Bruce's vacated spot on a quarterback draw.

"Good hustle anyway, Bruce," Jonny said, chuckling.

Jerry Spitz was playing defensive safety in the "Gorton" lineup. Jerry was five-seven, and weighed about 140. He was delicate and clean and quiet and slow. He never missed a practice, but was always among the last to get into a scrimmage, and seldom made contact. Time after time he drifted blankly toward the line of scrimmage, and let Don Heidner lope behind him to take the passes easily from Jonny.

"He's killing us," Coach Branahan muttered to Coach Fowles. "Can't we put somebody back there that will give us a little defense?"

"I hate to take anybody out who's trying to help," Coach Fowles said, looking dolefully out at the little defender. "Hey Jerry, you sure you know how to play that? Okay. . . ."

In punting practice, Stan Beronski got his chance to try belting the center. He lined up opposite Rich Merrill. Rich looked between his legs and centered to Ted O'Neill. Stan whacked him over backward with his forearms and ran over him. Rich gritted his teeth, silently. Next time he glanced up at Stan as he made the snap, and the ball rolled back to Ted. On the third try, Rich looked between his legs again as he made the snap, and Stan destroyed him.

The team lined up for sprints. "One more week of practice," Coach Fowles said. "Uh, how many don't have green jerseys?" Thirteen Harvesters held up their hands. "Hey varsity," Coach Fowles said with annoyance, "we're short thirteen jerseys. That means we have to pull jerseys off the JVs. You all played JV, so you know how that feels. Now maybe some of you can, uh, *find* some jerseys home or someplace . . ."

It was Parents' Orientation Night at the high school. Several football players demonstrated gymnastics and exercises for the parents. I went to Sandy Branahan's social studies classroom. Parents sat in their children's seats. Sandy introduced me as the fellow writing the book on the football team. Three mothers whirled around.

"You're the guy who thinks the cheerleaders are ugly," said one.

". . . Who doesn't like the cheerleaders," said another.

I remembered telling Ben Schenkle I thought the cheerleaders had fat legs. I made a mental note to tell Ben I was in love with them.

FRIDAY, *October 29*

Football players were wrestling in the gym before practice. They had pushed some tumbling mats together. Some of them, like Rich Merrill, Tom Kase, and Bob Mills, were on the wrestling team. Bruce Stacey was not. Bruce lost to Tom Kase, then to Bob Mills. He yelled maniacally and insisted on rematches. Coach Branahan chased them into the locker room.

The weather maintained its vernal fraud, hot and sunny, and the team seemed infected by a fever. Practice, in white shorts, was sloppy and unserious. Players not directly involved in plays joked on the sidelines and punted balls back and forth.

Bruce Stacey stood near the offensive backfield, arms folded, not alternating with other running backs.

Coach Fowles approached him formally. "Bruce, could I respectfully invite you to participate at fullback next play? Would you accept?"

Bruce returned Coach Fowles's smile. "Okay," he said with his head down.

"He's upset because he's not playing more on offense," Coach Fowles told me. "And I'm not sure he *shouldn't* be playing more. That's what's difficult about coaching."

When Coach Fowles called for the punting team, some of the players, punting and joking and wrestling on the sidelines, didn't hear him. Other players ran into each other lining up. "HEY, WHAT IS THIS!" Coach Fowles stormed, stomping down the line of scrimmage. "You think we're going to play Little Sisters of the Poor tomorrow? I'll tell you what: If we don't do the job we *should* do on Saturday, Monday's going to be a great day! A *great* day. This is not a threat. That is a *promise.* Let's wake *up!* You guys in the end zone, get *outta* there! On the sidelines, get *outta* there! Move back! Pay attention!"

He ran a few more plays, then called a halt. "All right boys, bring it in." The team crowded around him. "This time tomorrow the game is over. Can't bring it back. Meeting in twenty minutes, and we'll go over the scouting report again and answer questions. Run it in . . ."

The coaches watched the team run toward the locker room. "I'll bet a thousand dollars right now there'll be ten people late to the meeting," Coach Fowles said.

Players were yelling in the showers, and spraying water out and throwing soap. Coach Fowles opened the door of the coaches' room and leaned out. "Hey, John Curtis, who's messing around in there?"

"You want *names?*"

Coach Fowles leaned back in and slammed the door. "Tell you what," he said to me, "we're going to get our ass wiped tomorrow. They're not ready to play football. Or, well, they just might pull it all together and be great. You never know."

Nobody was late for the meeting.

"Traditionally for the last game, Sleepy Hollow," Coach Fowles told the team, "we have all the seniors go out to the hashmarks as honorary captains. So if there's anybody you think deserves to be the honorary captain tomorrow, at Gorton, this is the last chance to elect one."

They elected John Curtis, the left tackle.

"If you think we're playing a girls' team tomorrow," Coach Fowles said, "you better get it out of your head. Ask some of the kids who have played Gorton in the past. This is the fifth year we've played them, they've won two and we've won two. They put a lot of our kids out of action over the years. I'm not trying to scare anybody, but that's a fact. Some of you are going to get hit tomorrow like you haven't been hit all year. Now think about it.

"And then think about yakking it up in the shower room and fooling around on the field. When I taught fifth grade we had better attention than we had from you people out on that field today. We going down there for a party tomorrow or what? You can win the ballgame, but that's up to you. Coach Branahan and I right now are not satisfied.

"Boys, how does four and three sound to you? I think it *stinks*. Or do you like five and two better? I don't believe what I saw today on that field. Now you *think* about it. Think back right now, about all the hot days we had in August, the mile you ran, all the times you hung on the bars, the first time you ran the hill, the tires, the blisters you started to get. And then you put shoulder pads on and you hit. Remember the aches and pains, all the bruises you went home with, how thirsty you were. Think about the price you paid.

"You've only got two more chances, gentlemen, two more opportunities. We're down to *five more* practices. Let's think about the Gorton Wolves."

The team sat penitently as Coach Fowles erased the English words from the blackboard and wrote out the offensive and defensive alignments for review.

"First play of the game will be the wishbone, fullback at four," Coach Branahan said. "We'll run that until Ben gets tired or it stops going. Four or five times if we can."

Concluding the review, Coach Branahan said, "Hey, guys, they are a dirty, dirty football team. They will throw dirt in linemen's eyes. They have thrown lime from the yard-line stripes. Nobody lives up here like they do down at Gorton, in Yonkers. It's a rough city neighborhood."

"They are a lot of tough city kids," Coach Fowles said, "that's all I can say about them. Last year we were physically exhausted, beat up. And so were they. If somebody starts sticking fingers in your eyes or something, let your captain know, and he will very politely inform the official.

"Boys, they are calling for a hot day tomorrow. Let's get some salt in your diets tonight. Ted O'Neill, *salt!* And boys, I want your shoes shined tomorrow."

He rubbed a hand across his chin and down his throat. "You know, people come up to me and say, 'Coach, when that football team gets hot and breaks it open you're really going to have something.' And you know what? I agree with them. But we haven't done it yet."

16

SATURDAY, *October 30*

It was sunny, breezy, and mild, like a cool summer day. The players dressed and walked out to the bus for the hour's trip to Gorton.

Equipment continued to deteriorate. The zipper broke on Jonny's pants. He wrestled to rethread it outside the bus, and continued after he got on.

Coach Fowles arrived and went down the list of equipment. "Everybody got all their pads? Helmets? Make sure your helmet screws are tight . . ."

The team was aboard except for Clifford Albert. He came running up, signaled his arrival to Coach Fowles, then ran into the locker room and quickly returned carrying all his equipment.

On its way to the drab city of Yonkers, the bus wound through the hills which were covered with beautiful autumn woods, and across bridges that spanned the several necks of the reservoirs. "People all over the country should get a chance to see this," Coach Fowles said, looking out the window, "right here where we live."

"*Got* it," Jonny said, proudly zipping up his pants.

We arrived at the school, a large, dingy, several-storied red-brick building, and went down to the field. Close to the school on two sides ran cluttered, busy traffic arteries. Heavy road-construction equipment roared and clanked over one of them. Apartment buildings shadowed the field from the side opposite the school. The area outside the school reeked with the acrid odor of sour milk.

Permanent bleachers were built into the hill between the school and the field. The field itself was dirt, with rocks and glass. There was a gully at one five-yard line near the sideline. The top section of one metal goal post was missing, and had been replaced with a wooden stick.

I and several of the players were quick to cluck over the conditions, but Coach Fowles marched straight for the locker room, ignoring our observations. "I don't want the boys to get concerned with Mickey Mouse stuff," he said. "We're here to play football."

The team put on its shoulder pads and came out to warm up. Coach Fowles stopped one of the reserves who had unpolished shoes. "You better do something about those shoes, or you're not dressing," he said, "It's that simple." The boy retreated to the locker room.

Gorton was late, and Coach Fowles advised the officials of that.

"I'd really rather officiate up-county," one of them told me. "There are so many fewer problems, better conditions, better control of the game and the crowd. . . ."

The Gorton squad finally arrived, dressed in white jerseys and green pants, and began warming up. There were only twenty-three of them. The squad had been decimated, I had heard, by injuries and drop-outs.

The Harvesters went into the locker room to psyche-up.

". . . You know why we're gonna win?" Jonny said. "Because I don't want to work that hard on Monday. I want just a regular Monday, so if we bust ours now, we won't have to bust ours on Monday."

"You backs better hold onto the ball," Jim Marshall said. "If you saw the way the JVs were getting cracked, and you saw how many fumbles there were. . . ."

"Who won?"

"We did, nine nothin."

"They were hittin *hard* in that game. Can you imagine what the *varsity's* gonna do?"

The team was quieter than usual, but serious, thoughtful. Words were spoken rather than screamed.

"This is the day we gotta put it together," Rich Schenkle said.

"If we can get a couple quick touchdowns," Stan Beronski said, "their *morale* will shoot down. It did that before."

"We haven't come into our *own* yet," Jim Marshall said.

"We haven't shown no one *nothin,* what *we* can do," Jim said.

"Why don't all you guys just set a goal," Rich said, "that you're gonna come off the field beatin your man, that's all."

"All right, anything else anybody wants to say in here," Coach Fowles asked, looking around the room. "Coach Branahan?"

"Let's not give a team like this an easy touchdown, all right?" Coach Branahan said. "Secondary, make *sure* you are *keying,* make sure you are back off that ball. Al Stacey and Ken Furst, we want you *at least* eight yards off that ball. And let's *talk* back there. You four people back there, you got probably the biggest responsibility to make sure that no one gets beyond you. Let's talk to each other, make it a *team* on defense. Let's really hold this team down today, give the offense a real good chance to work."

"Boys," Coach Fowles said, "if you want respect—and there is not one human being in this whole world who does not want respect—if you *want* respect, you have to *earn* it. You don't go out and say, 'Hey, give me *respect!* It doesn't *work* that way. Doesn't work that way on the football field, doesn't work that way in life. You have to earn it.

"Now, we've played these people for four years, and they *still* don't respect us. Last year we beat them bad, and they thought it was a freak. This year we're a different team, a different family, a different *attitude.* If you want respect, you've got forty-eight minutes to earn it."

An official poked his head in the door. "Excuse me, Coach, but it's time...."

"Yes sir. Okay boys, who we gonna beat? ..."

The 10-yard chain was brought to the Laketown sideline. One of the boys manning the measuring chain wore a Gorton jacket, and had a cast on his arm. "Excuse me," Coach Fowles said, "but are you a member of the Gorton varsity?"

"Yes," the boy said.

Coach Fowles brought that to the official's attention, and the boy was replaced with a more neutral man.

The Harvesters both on the field and on the bench slapped their thigh pads rhythmically as Jim Marshall kicked off to start the game. Gorton returned to the 32.

Bob Mills was in Bradford McClure's defensive tackle spot—Bradford was dressed but on the bench—and Gorton ran through that hole twice, for a first down on the 43. Bob was yanked, yelled at, and put back in.

Jim Petrowski was kicked in the head. He staggered to the sideline to breathe some smelling salts.

Gorton drove powerfully and steadily on the ground to the Laketown 29. On fourth down and four, Rich Schenkle stunted from his linebacker spot and dropped the runner for a four-yard loss. Laketown took over.

Jonny opened up as planned, lining up in the wishbone and giving to Ben Schenkle on a quick-hitter behind Jack Forrest. He gained four the first time, and then five. But flags were thrown. Jonny had not put his mouthpiece in. That would have been a 15-yard penalty, but Gorton was offside on the same play. The two penalties nullified each other, and Ben's run.

Bruce Stacey swung wide right on a stomp for a first down on the 36. Then Jonny called the bomb to Don Heidner. He dropped back behind good protection. Don cut deep across the middle. But the cornerback was right with him, and broke up the pass.

Ben hit twice off the wishbone for a first down. Then Jonny, hit just as he threw, got the ball to Rich Schenkle on the sideline at the Gorton 38.

Keith Allen was put in to run the wide stomp he had been impressively running all week in practice. Tom Kase pulled quickly from right tackle and led the play, with Keith right on his heels. Danny made his block, Keith turned the corner, and only the last man in the secondary pulled Keith down after an 18-yard gain to the 20.

Ben dove straight ahead to the 17. Then Jonny faked a hand-off to his left, spun and gave to Ben on a fullback counter to the right. Ben burst through a hole made by the blocks of Tom Kase and Ted O'Neill, cut outside, and went in untouched for the score.

As rehearsed, the extra-point kick was faked. Jonny, who had lined up as the holder, threw to the far corner of the end zone to Ted O'Neill, who made a fine diving catch for the extra points. It was 8–0.

"My man's playing a yard and a half off me," right guard Jack Forrest said as he came to the sideline, "and he's tough. I can get to him, but I can't *move* him. If we can counter the other way...."

"All right, tell Jonny."

Gorton returned the kickoff to the 37. Barry Brill and Stan Beronski threw the passer for successive losses back to the 23. The first quarter ended.

With third and long yardage, Gorton quick-kicked. Ray Meister wheeled and dashed back and waited under the high kick at the Laketown 40. "Please catch the ball, Ray," Coach Fowles moaned as the ball hung in the air, "please, please. . . ." Ray did, put his head down, and banged five yards ahead to the 45.

Tailback Al Stacey twice sliced over left tackle behind John Curtis to the Gorton 34.

"Right now," Coach Fowles said to Coach Branahan, "he ought to call the fullback counter."

Having set it up with Al's tailback runs, that was just what Jonny called. Bruce Stacey ripped up the right side on the delay, breaking five tackles and dragging the last man hanging onto his shirt to the six-yard line.

Ben Schenkle replaced Bruce and dove to the four. Then Jonny rolled out to his right, looking for Don Heidner. Don had slanted out to the right sideline covered closely, and then, just as Jonny liked him to do, had abruptly doubled back toward the middle. Jonny drilled it to him on the run for the touchdown.

Ben kicked the extra point right through the middle, and Laketown led 15–0.

The indications of a rout were there, but with the Brushland game still fresh in their minds, players and coaches restrained their anticipation. Coach Fowles wanted the ball again. He called for an onside kick.

Ben cut in front of Jim Marshall and looped the ball, but not deep enough. The Gorton tackle caught it and fell to his knees on his own 45.

"Ben Schenkle, you gotta get it over their HEADS!" Coach Fowles shouted at his fullback, who had been called "pocket-size" in the papers that week. "The whole idea, from the scouting report, was that we knew that the end was back on the 28-yard line. You had all that *room* in there. What were you doing?"

"I wuff thrying to kick ith offa woof," Ben said around his mouthpiece.

"NO, NO! You gotta kick it OVER! It went right to the kid. It only went 12 yards. Okay, get your head up. Next time you'll do it right, okay?"

The pass-rush was ferocious. Rich Schenkle batted down two right off the quarterback's hands. Two draw plays up the middle gained big yardage to the Laketown 27.

Again the quarterback was rushed. Twice his hurried passes went short into the dirt. On third down he threw for the end zone. The receiver was behind safetyman Ken Furst, but the ball went off his fingertips.

"They're coming RIGHT BACK AT YOU, Ken!" Coach Branahan shouted to his safetyman. "Be READY!"

"Hey, Stu Rosenman," Coach Fowles called. "Let's get to that PASSER!"

On fourth down, the quarterback did come back with the same pass, but this time both Ken and Ray Meister were there to knock it down. Laketown took over.

"Jonny, let's *run* the ball," Coach Branahan said.

Al Stacey and Ben Schenkle alternated carrying to within a foot of a first down on the 37. With the running game showing such power, the coaches decided to go for it on fourth down. Bruce Stacey, in at fullback, went straight ahead for five and the first down. Then Bruce exploded through the middle for ten more.

Coach Fowles sent in a substitution for Rich Schenkle. "Rich, I just wanna give you a break. Take your hat off."

The coaches wanted the ball kept on the ground. Again and again Bruce Stacey was called upon. Finally, with the ball on the Gorton 32, Coach Fowles sent Ben in to relieve him. Bruce came wearily to the sideline.

With Ben fresh, Jonny faded back as if to pass, then handed off to Ben on a draw. Ben feinted, ducked, and slid to the 22.

"Good CALL, Jonny, BEAUTIFUL!" Coach Fowles yelled.

Ben took the hand-off again, weasled to the 15, but fumbled. Gorton recovered.

"Hey, Stu Rosenman, find out how much time is left."

Stu asked the official. "Minute and a half, Coach," he called back.

"Hey, QUAKER DEFENSE, BRUCE, WHITE!" The secondary responded by dropping back 10 yards farther than normal.

Ken Furst leaped to knock away a long pass in front of the Laketown bench. Rich Schenkle came to the sideline, holding his one damaged hand with the other.

"Jack Forrest, get in there for Rich Schenkle. Rich, you all right?"

"Yeah, Coach, just hurts."

Rich grabbed a plastic cold pack, broke the seal to allow the chilling chemicals to mix, and held it on his bandaged thumb. "Hey ROGER," he called to the manager, "get me another cold pack." Roger brought one over, but couldn't break the seal. Rich fretted as Roger strained. Finally Rich's little brother, Ben, came over and yanked it out of the manager's hands, ripped the seal, and gently laid it beside the other on Rich's hand.

Laketown took over on downs on the Gorton 47 and called time-out.

"Jonny, flanker around," Coach Branahan said. Jonny nodded. He stationed Don Heidner out to the right, took the snap, faked into the line, and handed off to Don circling wide to the left. Don followed Clifford Albert's downfield blocking around the end all the way to the 16. Again Jonny called time-out to stop the clock with just a few seconds left.

"How about Ted O'Neill delaying in the flat on the right, and slanting Don Heidner in real hard from the left?" Coach Fowles said.

"Yeah, *quick*," Coach Branahan said.

"Seventy quick?" Jonny asked. "To the flanker?"

"No, to Ted O'Neill," Coach Branahan said. "Have Don go deeper."

Jonny hit Ted off to the right at the six-yard line, where he quickly stepped out of bounds.

Jonny motioned a T with his hands to the official. "NO, NO JONNY! DON'T CALL TIME-OUT!" Coach Fowles hollered.

But Jonny, not realizing Ted had stepped out of bounds to stop the clock, mistakenly called Laketown's last time-out. Now they would not be able to stop the clock again. They would have to pass for the touchdown.

Jonny tried to arc one far to the left, over the defenders, for Don Heidner in the corner of the end zone. But the ball dropped short and was picked off by the cornerback—the fastest man on the Gorton team. The back turned quickly up the sideline and had only Jonny to beat. Jonny set an angle for midfield, ignoring the head-fake the runner gave him to the inside, and rammed him into the Laketown bench. The half ended.

The girls' locker room where the visiting teams dressed was small, so the Harvesters stayed outside at half time, wrapped in the sour-milk stench that enveloped the area. They sat on the ground. Rich Schenkle handed me a roll of tape and I began rewrapping his thumb with more padding.

"What's the score?" Jack Forrest asked.

"Fifteen nothin."

"Hey, get me one of those bottles?" Bruce Stacey asked.

"You can have it after this. Shake it first. Here you go, Bruce."

"Defense," Coach Fowles said, "after that first drive of theirs you really came alive and looked pretty good. Our pass defense is getting *better* and *better*. What are you in most of the time, Bruce?"

"Quaker."

"Quaker's good. Jonny, Don wasn't really open in the end zone . . ."

"I *saw* him open."

"Okay, okay. Now, they should be throwing the ball a little bit in the second half. I say we'll probably use both the laura and the quaker. We'll play that by ear."

"In the laura," Stan Beronski said, "it's hard for me to rush him when we're worried about a screen. I'd rather stay in a quaker."

"Yeah, we gotta watch that screen pass, Bruce," Coach Fowles said. "All right, offense. Boys, we are doing a real good job running the football, especially inside. How many times have we called the fullback counter?"

"We been calling the tailback counter," Jack Forrest said. "They don't take the fake on the fullback counter at all."

"Hey, the fullback counter got us the *touchdown*," Ted O'Neill said.

"But the linebackers aren't reacting well to it," Jack insisted.

"Jack, the end rushes out so when he goes downfield he knocks the linebacker *in*," Ted argued. "That's how we *scored*."

"Hey, Coach," Jim Marshall said, "I been pushing this kid, the middle linebacker, all over the field from the beginning. And the last few plays he's been grabbing for my eyes, and I told the referee and he doesn't do nothin about it."

"All right, Jim, there's nothing we can do about that right now . . ."

"I know, I just wanted to tell you."

"Okay, you told the umpire? All right."

"Can't we *pass* more?" Ted O'Neill asked.

"Why pass," Rich Schenkle said, "it's fun runnin."

"We don't want to *stop* passing completely," Coach Branahan said. "We can pass if it's absolutely necessary."

"Let's not do what we did *last* week," Stan said.

"We almost blew a twenty-two-point lead *last* week," Jonny said.

"Hey boys, as far as I'm concerned, the score is zero–zero, and we're in a ballgame up to our *ears*."

"That kid is playing bump-and-run on me, Coach," Don Heidner said.

"Then we oughta throw a *long* one to you, Don. Are you telling Jonny?"

"I told him I can beat him."

"Well then let's *do* it."

"Also, if I take my man short . . ."

"And Rich takes him deep . . ." Jonny said.

"Hey, Rich has a thumb *that* big," Coach Fowles said. "What's Rich gonna do? He might not even *play* the second half."

"Coach, one of their backs keys the quarterback."

"I know. We should run the outside belly, not the bootleg."

"But Coach," Jonny said, "everytime I stand there and fake, somebody gets in between the back and . . ."

"It'll work, Jonny, but *quick*, not much of a fake."

An official walked up. "Coach, you got one minute to go before warm-up, okay?"

"Okay, thank you."

"Coach," Jim Marshall said, "instead of hitting me in the helmet, he's grabbing my eyes. . . ."

"All right, I'll mention it . . . all right, let's go. Walk down. . . ."

"GET PSYCHED, LAKETOWN," Rich yelled into the huddle on the sideline.

"Zero–zero, Laketown," Jonny said.

"All right, boys, there's no score in this game. We've always been a second-half team. You *always* get stronger as the game goes on. And today's no exception. It's our kind of day, this is our kind of a game. Who's got more pride? . . ."

Don Heidner broke tackles on the kickoff return and brought it to the 39. Eddie McArthur went in with the offense to start in Rich Schenkle's left-end position.

From the wishbone, Ben Schenkle went up the middle twice on quick-openers for a first down on the 50.

"WAY TO BLOCK, JIM MARSHALL, DOIN THE JOB!"

Bruce Stacey replaced Ben and ran the fullback counter for another first down across the Gorton 40.

An official walked over and handed a piece of broken glass to Coach Fowles.

Ben got another first down on the 28. But then Al Stacey fumbled, and Gorton got it on the 25.

Rich Schenkle went in on defense. On the first play he stunted and rammed the quarterback head-on, driving him over backward for a loss to the 17. A screen pass got the first down. Then Gorton began penetrating the Laketown defensive line over their right side, driving into Laketown territory. Tom Kase was sent in to replace Bob Mills. Coach Fowles called Bradford McClure over. "You okay?" he asked.

"Yeah, I'm fine," Bradford said smiling, waiting to go in.

A pass over the middle was tipped up in the air by Jim Petrowski and came down in the arms of John Finch, who was tackled immediately. Rich Schenkle gave the intended Gorton receiver a playful tap in the belly, then turned and trotted off.

Again from the wishbone, Ben Schenkle hit quick for a first down on the Laketown 46. Laketown was held there, and Ted O'Neill punted to the Gorton 28.

Bob Mills came up to Coach Fowles. "Who's in on defense?"

"Okay, *you*, Bob. But don't go for the *counter*. Play your *area*. Hey, Stan Beronski, watch for the screen pass on the back side."

Laketown held, and Gorton punted to the Laketown 47 as the third quarter ended.

"LET'S TAKE IT IN, JONNY, COME ON!"

Ben Schenkle and Bruce Stacey blasted through the tackles to the Gorton 25, where it was fourth and one.

John Curtis asked the official for a time-out, showing him a broken strap on his shoulder pads. At the same time, a Gorton player asked for time-out for the same reason. "What's this?" the official asked, smiling and waving his arms over his head to signal the time-out. "Two guys at once?"

"Planned obsolescence," Jonny called back to him, raising a finger in the air as he came to the sideline.

On the fourth-down play, center Jim Marshall and guard Jack Forrest wedged open a big hole and Bruce Stacey shot up the middle all the way for the touchdown.

Jonny tried another fake kick, but couldn't find Ted O'Neill open, and the try failed. The score was 21–0.

Gorton took the kickoff back to their 47. Bradford McClure went in at right tackle, his thumb heavily bandaged. Players cheered for him.

"Hey, Brad!" Jonny yelled. "THUMBS UP!"

On the first play, Ray Meister came up from cornerback and hit the ball carrier, popping the ball free. It squirted away from Bradford, but John Finch finally fell on it.

"Right now, Jonny, right now," Coach Fowles said on the sideline. "Don Heidner, hey, Don. We're going for it right now."

Jonny threw deep down the middle for Don, who was all alone. The ball was a bit short and Don had to come back a step. He caught it and was dropped on the eight.

Bruce Stacey hit the middle to the five, then to the three.

The officials gave the four-minute warning to both benches.

Bruce drove to the goal line. Fourth down.

"Where's the ball exactly?" Coach Fowles called out.

"Six inches," Jonny said, coming to the sideline. He spaced his words between deep breaths. "Flanker right," he suggested, "wishbone right, and—set up Bruce—over there and—dive Ben back at six."

"You mean a counter?" Coach Fowles asked.

"No, just flanker right, wishbone right, and dive Ben straight ahead."

"Jonny, all we need is six inches. Why not just give it to Bruce straight ahead?"

"Cause they're gonna be stacked where Bruce is."

"Sandy, what do you think?"

"From the wishbone," Coach Branahan said, "dive Bruce from the wishbone. And have Ben in there too, at tailback."

"Dive Bruce at six?"

"Yeah. Hey, Ben, you're *tailback*, Ben."

Bruce went in for the score easily behind Clifford Albert's block at left guard.

Ben kicked the extra point, making the score 28–0.

"This game is boring," Stan Beronski said on the sideline.

Coach Fowles began substituting on defense. He sent in Cary Grimes and Freddie Delaney at ends, Vince Carradino and big Harry Wallace at tackles.

Gorton ran the kickoff back over midfield. They passed to the 33, then to the 24. More reserves went in for Laketown, some wearing old green jerseys with ragged, hand-stitched white numerals. Cary Grimes called defensive signals.

Gorton had fourth and five on the 17. The regulars now on the bench cheered loudly for the reserves.

"LET'S HOLD 'EM, LAKETOWN! HEY, LAKETOWN, HOLD 'EM!"

Little Jerry Spitz went in at tackle.

Gorton swept wide to the left for a first down on the eight. The reserves scrambled hard in their unfamiliar positions, but Gorton scored on a pass over the middle. They passed again for the extra points, making it 28–8 with one minute and fifteen seconds left.

The second-string offense went in, led by Ted O'Neill, now at quarterback. But Keith Allen lost the ball on a fumble on the first play. Gorton used up its time-outs to stop the clock, but lost the ball on downs on its 46. Laketown immediately called time-out with fourteen seconds left, to allow the Harvesters one final play.

Coach Fowles turned to Ted O'Neill on the sideline. "Well, what do you wanna do, Ted?"

"What do you *think!*" Ted said, smiling devilishly.

He went in and threw the bomb to end Dan Miranda, who took it all alone and crossed the goal line as the final whistle blew. Ted overthrew

Dan on the extra-point try. But Laketown had finally busted loose, 34–8.

The players ran off the field, pausing to exchange compliments with the weary, short-manned Gorton team. "That guy that played opposite me was the best I ever played in my life," Jack Forrest said.

"Those linebackers could *hit*," somebody else said.

I went over to congratulate one of the Gorton linebackers, a strong but tired black boy who had played the entire game, and had been all over the field making bruising tackles. "You tell that number 51," he said, smiling, "you tell him he can really *block*, man. Tell him for me? He was *tough!*"

I passed on the compliment to Jim Marshall as he boarded the bus. "Really?" Jim said. "That was a nice thing for him to say."

For a few moments Coach Fowles stood outside the bus, watching the Gorton team head toward its own bus. "Some day I would like to coach a team with a lot of black kids on it, poor kids," he said. "They want to do more than anybody. They want to win, and they want a sense of identity and pride."

He boarded the bus. "HEY, QUIET DOWN A MINUTE, BOYS! Sit down. I'm on my way to scout the last quarter of the Sleepy Hollow game against Greeley, so I'm not going back on the bus with you. We're proud of you. You played a good football game. And you know what? We've just begun. And next Saturday, who we gonna beat?"

"SLEEPY! . . . SLEEPY! . . . SLEEPY!"

The bus pulled onto the highway. Jerry Spitz was hoisted aloft and passed to the rear over the heads of the players. Then he was returned to the front, in the process losing his pants.

"They refused delivery in the rear," somebody yelled.

"Way to be tough, Jerry!"

The team savored its victory on the Petrowskis' patio, eating goulash and hard rolls, and drinking soda. Some of the players sat in the living room with girls on their laps. Some played pool in the cellar. Jonny sat on the floor by the stereo with earphones on, grooving.

Later, in the dark, a few of the players went skinny-dipping in the frigid reservoir.

The team seemed truly to relax for the first time since August 25, nine and a half weeks ago. Undefeated Sleepy Hollow, their toughest test of the season and their final opponent, was a week away. There would be time to gather strength.

17

SUNDAY, *October 31*

It was Halloween, and the doorbell rang constantly upstairs at the Fowleses' house as little children came begging for treats. Squeegy was out, so for a while Buddy answered the door to pass out candy bars. Then he went downstairs to meet with his team.

The Gorton film was run with few stops and little commentary. The fact was, the team had made few mistakes. Bruce Stacey had carried the ball twenty-one times and gained 116 yards, a season high for the team. Ben Schenkle carried sixteen times for 73 yards, his own personal high for the year.

But already the Gorton game seemed years past. Sleepy Hollow was on everybody's mind. Not only was Sleepy undefeated this year, but Laketown had never beaten them. A victory next Saturday would give the team a six-and-two record, which would equal the best ever under Coach Fowles. And this with a team, that at the start of the season was supposed to lose most, if not all, of its games. Because of its unique personality and spunk, and because these boys were the first of his earlier fifth graders to play for him, it had become Coach Fowles's favorite team of his coaching career. And the final week was at hand.

"They run from a box," Coach Fowles said, sketching on the blackboard, "similar to Horace Greeley. They will not try to be too fancy, they will run right at you. This end here they like to send on deep patterns, and the quarterback can throw the football. They are quick. They will counter. And when they do counter, they give it away because they pull their guard on the side they're going to counter. So we're going to key him.

"Bruce Stacey, if that guard pulls, you will follow him, because that's where the play is going. Don't worry about false keys. The Green Bay Packers will false key; Sleepy Hollow High School will not. When that guard pulls, they are *not* going to give it to the man through that hole, believe me. They will *fake* to him, so we can ignore him. Let *their* guards tell you where the play is going. Also, when they counter, the quarterback likes to swing the ball high first, as if he were going to pass.

"They like to quick-pitch to the outside just like we do, and when they do that they'll pull their guard *and* their tackle. They run their quarterback sneak many times on short-yardage situations—now pay attention to this—from a *two-point stance.* They will go without shifting down, trying to run that quarterback sneak before we're ready.

"But usually they like to get the ball centered pretty much on the same count every time, and from a three-point stance, so occasionally gamble with them. We're going to use the laura and the quaker against them.

"Now, defensively we feel that they're going to run a four-four. This is *my* guess, but who knows? But I'll tell you the truth: Nobody has pushed Peekskill around like *we* did a couple of weeks ago, and they used a four-four against us. So that doesn't bother us at all. It doesn't really matter what they use, we're going to push them around anyway. But expect to see the four-four.

"They will *switch* defenses, however, you can be sure. They'll use a five-three, which basically is what we call an Oklahoma front with three linebackers. They *will* stunt those linebackers. They will stunt two linebackers on second and long yardage. But they *show* it. You just remember that every time a team stunts they are giving you a weakness *someplace.* And we are very quick off the football. I can't believe the way our guards have picked up stunters all year. Our whole line is quick."

He left the alignments on the board and turned to face the team. "Now, their kicking game. They run punts back so well that some teams have actually tried to punt *out of bounds* on them so they could not run them back. I don't think we will have to do that. They like to run their punt return to the right—that's to our *left*. So you people on our left-hand side get down there *quick*. And *keep your eyes open*, because they have *great* downfield blocking.

"They will quick-kick, and they also have a good field-goal kicker. On kickoff returns, they like to come up the right side, so you people over there will have something to look forward to. Tom Kase, your job will be to go right for the man with the ball and cause a fumble.

"All right, it is a *beautiful* day for practice, and we will do things differently today. Let's get outside."

It was pouring rain. Coach Fowles told me he had been thinking of ways to psyche up the team for Sleepy Hollow—not wanting to go too far, but hoping to find some new idea.

The team went through calisthenics, then he called them together. They stood bunched in a crescent around him. The rain beat crisply on their helmets and shoulder pads.

"Boys, I'll tell you, this team is tough. They are the toughest team we have played. They are like the bullies of the block. This team has scouted us *six times*. They have cards on every play we have run. And they are un-defeated. This is a chance of a lifetime to play an undefeated team our last game. Boys, it's not too late for any of you to back out now."

He looked soberly around at the faces which were partially obscured behind the plastic-covered steel face guards.

"This team we're playing is *so* tough, I guess I can't really ask any-body to play against them. Everybody who wants to *volunteer* for this game, let's get on the field and play football."

The players spun around and took off for the game field.

"Was that bad?" he asked. "Too corny?"

"I was relieved it didn't get worse," I said.

He looked relieved too. "I had thought of asking each volunteer to take a step forward, but, you know. . . ."

The low-lying field was in the worst shape of the season, soggy grass floating on a palette of mud. The short soccer-style cleats were nearly useless.

At five o'clock he called them together. Their uniforms were now perhaps doubled in weight from the goo. "Boys," he said, "we have three things to do before we go in: run the hill, run the tires, and do sixteen sprints, all without a break. Right now. Let's go. Last chance to practice on a Monday night."

The team seemed momentarily stunned by the announcement of the task before them, but turned and ran over to the manbuilder. For eight minutes they churned up the hill, with Jonny and Ted O'Neill calling signals.

Coach Fowles was amused. "Watch how they're using every device to squeeze out the time," he said softly, "calling complicated plays, high counts. . . ."

Despite such mild chicaneries on the hill, the team drove itself. With no break, they ran over and pranced back and forth through the tires. Still with no break, they lined up for the 40-yard sprints. The coaches watched with mixed awe and pride as the Harvesters neither faltered nor complained through this concentrated period of torturous exercise.

Keith Allen was lagging, and I thought sulking. But the coaches said nothing. When I asked Coach Fowles what was wrong he said he didn't know.

After practice I went to Jonny's house and sat listening to him play the guitar and sing some songs. Jonny had been getting letters from prominent colleges; he had received another today.

"It would be a good place to study medicine," he said, "which is what I plan to do. But what they're really interested in me for is lacrosse." He put his guitar aside for a moment and twisted his wrists as if cradling a lacrosse stick. "You watch," he said, "in three years I'm going to be an All-American."

"You still seemed dissatisfied today with your throwing," I said, "with the spiral. I thought Coach Fowles's suggestion about spreading your fingers more solved that."

"Naw, I just can't throw that ball. I don't know why, it's just different. The game ball we started with, we lost that after the Mamaroneck game. That one just went better. That's why I been underthrowing Don on those deep patterns, you know? At the beginning of the season I didn't do that. This ball's just a tiny bit different. It *feels* different."

The team had started the season with two Wilson TD rubber game balls. Laketown used rubber because in wet weather it didn't get as slippery as leather. Most of the teams they played used leather balls. The one ball that was lost had long been Jonny's favorite. Now on the remaining game ball even the laces were worn out, and the ends had to be tucked in for games. The prospect of going into the climactic game without Jonny's favorite ball disturbed me, seemed wrong.

"Can't you get another one?" I asked.

"Uh, I don't know," he said, continuing to strum, unconcerned.

"But Jonny, I'm sure Coach Fowles would buy you one. Have you asked him?"

"Naw."

"Jonny, *I'll* get you one," I announced, pleased with an opportunity to contribute to the team.

"You don't haveta."

"Tomorrow, before practice, we'll drive to some stores, okay?"

He shrugged. " 'Kay."

Coach Fowles showed the Gorton film to the parents. Mr. Schenkle asked, "You were ahead only 15–0 in the third quarter. Remembering what happened the week before, against Brushland, why didn't you throw more?"

"We felt we were moving on the ground, and also using up the clock. We *could* have thrown more."

"On the third touchdown, why did you go for the second two-point conversion instead of kicking?"

"I don't know. We didn't call for that pass. There was a missed signal. I thought the kids played awfully well. They worked hard. But I still feel we haven't quite put it all together. Not quite yet. The kids had a good workout today, and I'm sure the mothers will love me all the more for the dirty clothes they brought home. You *know* it never rains on our football field. I wish we had a film to show you how hard the kids worked today. Because they love it. Because they want to beat Sleepy Hollow."

He smiled ironically and looked around the room. "Anybody want to take an Alka-Seltzer before I tell you about Sleepy Hollow?"

There were some chuckles. "You know a high-powered offense really impresses me. But the teams that really concern me are the teams with a fine *defense*, and *they* have a fine defense. In fact, they do *everything* well." He went to the blackboard and diagramed the Sleepy offense. "They aren't big, but they are quick and strong. They have the best weight program in the area. Their middle linebacker is a major-college football prospect. I would guess he bench-presses over 300 pounds now. . . ."

Somebody said, "Wow."

"They've scouted us six times. They have cards on over 300 plays on us. It's interesting about their scouting system. With *our* system, we normally know what a team does on first down, on second down, and so on. One of our former assistant coaches learned that system here. And then he took a job at Sleepy Hollow, and now they use our scouting system. And you know what? We're going to beat them anyway. . . ."

He mused for a moment. "If kids studied as hard as they practiced . . . but they are *motivated* to practice. . . . We need to motivate them to do other things. . . ."

Then he caught his thread. "Now, Sleepy beat Horace Greeley, and *we* beat Horace Greeley. Horace Greeley beat Fox Lane and we *lost* to Fox Lane. And Fox Lane hasn't won a game since. You know what the moral of *that* story is. . . . "

Clifford Albert's father, sitting behind his son, dressed in a dark suit, said gruffly, "You beat *yourselves*."

"That's right," Coach Fowles said, nodding, unsmiling. "Back up one step further. State of mind. After we beat Greeley, we thought we were all-universe for a while. The sad thing is, you can't turn the clock back. Any other questions?"

"What kind of defense are you going to use?"

"We have the laura and the Penn State quaker ready. Clifford Albert, you think this year went fast compared with last year when you were a junior?" Coach Fowles often directed gentle questions to players whose parents were present.

"It went quite fast," Clifford said, smiling demurely.

"We have three real practices left," Coach Fowles said. "I keep repeating, *have no regrets*. It's going to be a good football game. You will see bleachers all the way down one side of the field. They even have a press-box area. . . .

"One more thing before you leave. Collecting equipment is a real chore. Each boy is wearing about a hundred dollars' worth of equipment. Gee, I'd like to have everybody's cooperation. It costs a lot of money if we send the equipment away for reconditioning, so we clean the stuff ourselves. . . ."

"You need new zippers," Keith Allen's mother said.

Coach Fowles smiled. "Yeah, we need new *uniforms*. Uh, there's the matter of jerseys. There isn't a boy who ever played football who doesn't look at the green varsity jerseys with big numbers on them and say, 'Gee, I'd like one of those to keep.' "

Several parents laughed.

"But we don't give them away. So if you hear a boy around the house say, 'Oh, they're letting us keep them this year.' "

More parents laughed.

Heavy rain for the second straight day, dark and warm. Jonny finished classes at noon, and we drove to a nearby town to shop for a football. They had expensive leather footballs, and cheap rubber footballs. But they didn't have the twenty-five dollar rubber TD. Jonny handled a few of the balls, snapping his hand forward in a throwing motion. Then he put them back and thanked the salesman.

We were going to be late returning to practice. "Sorry about that," I said.

"I don't care about being late," he said. "To me, practicing football is practicing *football*, not all that other shit at the beginning."

"It's obvious you guys don't take calisthenics very seriously," I said.

"Naw. But see, that's the difference between last year's team and this year's. Last year they really did it, you know, *one, two, three*—calisthenics, everything. If we took it seriously, it just wouldn't be the same. We're just different, the guys are just different. Like Rich Schenkle—change just a little bit of him and he's not the same Sugarbear. Can you dig that?"

I nodded. Jonny was a curious mix of clown and prince, every day coming out late twenty minutes or so for practice, dancing gaily and waving his fingers in peace signs on his way to joining his teammates—and then the only one to do valid push-ups, all the way up and down; running all out in every sprint—while at the same time comically switching groups, running once with the fastest group, then the slowest; faking injuries from mock-punting, hiding true injuries during practices and games; joking during hard scrimmages, cracking the leadership whip during drills.

Once he had become volubly impatient with his backs and ends during a passing drill. The coaches were away for a few minutes. I had asked him about that, and he said, "See, I never joke around when the coaches *aren't* there. That's bush. If I'm going to mess around, I don't hide it."

Several schools, especially those in the prestigious Ivy League, were interested in having Jonny, because of his academic record and activities, and for his lacrosse and football ability. Once Coach Fowles told him, "If you want to play Ivy League football, I predict that not only will you play, you will *start*, and not only will you start, you will *star*."

Now, on the way back to school, I asked him if he would play football in college.

"Aw, I don't think I really want to play football anymore after this year," he said, propping his leather boots up on the dashboard, "cause I can't imagine it would be much fun at one of those colleges where the football program is—where you get so uptight about winning and losing. Where I can't, you know, sort of come out late for practice and sort of jag around and have fun and joke with the coach. That's how we've been *raised* on it here. And if it's not like that, I don't think I would enjoy it. See, the thing is, here we *love* to play football. . . ."

The sun came out for practice. Jack Forrest was suspected of having cracked ribs, so he was off getting x-rayed. The flu list grew; Ben Schenkle, Don Heidner, Ted O'Neill, Bradford McClure, Jerry Spitz, Brian Purcell, and Bob Mills were all out sick. Keith Allen was missing too, but was said to have been in school today. In all, only thirty of the forty-four Harvesters were dressed for practice.

Some of the team wandered out to start calisthenics. Others still hung around outside the locker room. Stan Beronski, leading the cals, was uncharacteristically angry. "What the hell are you doing up there!" he yelled to the laggards up by the locker room.

Appalled by this inattention during the last, fateful, dramatic week, I stalked up to the locker room and hollered for Coach Fowles. He came out of the coaches' room.

"Hey, hey," he said smiling, "I've never seen you so upset. What's up?"

"Boy, you better do something with this team cause they're just fucking around down there and nobody gives a shit and Sleepy Hollow is going to . . ."

"Hey," he said, smiling even more broadly and laying a hand on my shoulder, "it's good to see you so *involved*. We're going to be fine."

I left huffily, fuming now at *his* unconcern.

The team again skipped the bars and tires and went right into the scrimmage. On the first play Stu Rosenman twisted his ankle and limped off to dress, thereby joining the ranks of the missing.

"What about all these guys sick?" I asked Coach Fowles.

"Well, the mind does wonderful things," he said. "Now, I wouldn't want them sick the last two days before the game, but they'll be all right."

"Well what about the *attitude?*"

"In a sense this week is our whole season. Today represents the Port Chester scrimmage. Tomorrow will be better, Thursday even better." He walked away, laughing to me over his shoulder. "*Everything* will be all right."

For the second straight day, they ran the hill, the tires, and the sprints without a break. The coaches glowed with pride at their prime condition.

"Feel my heart," Jim Marshall said seriously. "Is it supposed to beat like that?"

I felt it and thought it beat too heavily. Coach Branahan felt it and said it was fine.

Coach Fowles asked about absences. "Where's Keith Allen, anybody know? All right, I want legal excuses from everybody absent today. If Keith doesn't have a legal excuse, I'm going to pull his equipment. Same goes for everybody else. That's it. Pass the word."

The team filed into the classroom for the meeting, damp and clean from the showers. Jack Forrest returned from his x-rays, fairly bubbled into the room with joy.

"They called me last night about the x-ray they took on Sunday," he said breathlessly, "and they said to come in again because it looked like a break. I was scared to death, shitting bricks. Then they x-rayed it again today, *and said it was okay!* They said maybe a blood vessel had got in the way last time, and it looked like a break. *They made a mistake!* I almost kissed the technician, I was so happy."

Coach Fowles ran the film of last year's Sleepy Hollow game. He stopped the film, reversed it, stopped it—all rapidly, accompanied by his incessant stream of advice and finger-shadows.

"*Look at their line,*" Jonny said. "They're not supermen. You know what, Coach? If we score on 'em quick, they're not going to understand what happened. They're not ready. They're going to wonder. . . ."

"They'll wonder for about two seconds," Stan said, scoffing, "that doesn't mean they're going to *quit.*"

". . . Our linebacker will scrape inside the end," Coach Fowles went on, "the defensive ends line up on inside shoulder. . . ."

Finally at 6:10, ten minutes after the custodial deadline for vacating classrooms, Coach Fowles finished the film.

"Makes me dizzy how he runs those films," somebody said.

WEDNESDAY, November 3

Rain was back for the third day, but it stopped before practice, leaving the air dark and cool. Keith Allen quit today. He told Coach Fowles he felt it was hopeless, to work all week for one play on Saturday.

"I figure he hasn't told his mother yet," Coach Fowles said, "because she hasn't called me."

"Did anybody tell Keith that if he'd quit a couple of weeks ago we wouldn't have lost to Peekskill?" Coach Branahan said.

Coach Fowles ignored the remark.

Stu Rosenman was back today, jogging with a limp around the track. "He'll be all right," Coach Branahan said.

"The pain threshold is very different on people," Coach Fowles said. "Stu has a low pain threshold, but I think he'll play."

In Stu's place at defensive end, Freddie Delaney was impressive. He penetrated fiercely. Fakes into the middle of the line never lured him away. Twice he stopped Jonny on bootlegs.

"Those fakes never fool you?" I asked.

"What fakes?" Freddie said.

The team ran the hill and the tires in quick succession. Coach Fowles looked admiringly on. "What do you think of the team's attitude?" he asked.

I shrugged. "It's okay."

"I think it's exactly right for Wednesday," he said, "perfect. Yesterday they were joking around, today a little more serious. And they are in *fine* shape—watch them on the tires."

"It's amazing to me that there hasn't been a single real game injury all year," I said.

"You think that's an accident?" he said. "We prevent injuries right here, on the tires, on the hill, in the sprints. These boys are in *excellent* shape, better than anybody we play."

I had never been fast, but never unconscionably slow either. Today I ran the sprints with the team, and finished last.

As they went in, Coach Fowles said, "You know, I have a feeling there's one more bad practice in this team. Today was a good practice. Either tomorrow or Friday will be bad. But that's okay. It will be normal."

After the showers, a few of the boys—Jim Marshall, Bruce Stacey, Bradford McClure, Rich Schenkle, Jonny—were standing outside talking about the prospects of a season-ending party after the Sleepy Hollow game. Last year the concluding party was a drunken affair to which the police were finally summoned. This year nothing firm seemed to be shaping up. Nobody was anxious to host. "I'm not having it at *my* house," one of them said, "cause I can't get drunk there."

"Should *I* give a party?" I asked.

"I wouldn't," Jonny said. "My advice to you is not to invite *anybody* to your place that night. You never can tell. I don't even know if I'll go to a party."

"No? Why not?"

He turned to speak more privately. "I might just go to church, with my girl," he said.

"You don't go to church," I said.

"I know. But it's something different, you know? It might be nice." He laughed. "You think I'm crazy."

"Not necessarily."

"Just probably?"

"Not even."

Tonight I had a few drinks, then I called Keith Allen. I made a speech. It went like this:

"Hey, listen. I just heard today you were trying to quit the team. From the coach. True? I figured something was wrong on Monday, because toward the end of practice you weren't doing anything. Can you tell me about it? Were the guys on you? Yeah, but that happens from time to time, and it never bothered you before. I never heard anything, just noticed you didn't run the hill and stuff.

"When you talked to Coach Fowles, what did he say? Well, you knew he wouldn't want you to quit.

"This will probably surprise you, but several weeks ago Coach Fowles asked me who I most admired as football players, and who I most identified with. I told him the guys I most admired were guys like Rich Schenkle and Jonny and Brad and Jack Forrest. But I told him that the guy I most identified with on the team was Keith Allen. Because I think I have a sense of a guy who is sort of on the outside and gets shit on a little. I always felt when I was on sports teams I was one of the outs, even though that may not have been true. I had a sense coaches were always down on me. In terms of just feeling the pains, I identified with you most. But I have never known a couple of coaches like these who showed so little favoritism. I wanted to add my voice to Coach Fowles's about persuading you to stay.

"We were talking about fumbling today. I suppose one of the things people ride you about is fumbling the ball a lot. In the Gorton game at the end, you were tackled and fumbled, and before you ever hit the ground you were slapping the front of your helmet in sort of disgust—remember that?—and to me that suggested a guy who was almost ready to fumble before he hit the line. I figure it's a psychological thing. You agree?

"You really *are* a fast runner. I was really pleased with the run you made against Gorton. You go in on one play and take the pitchout and almost break it. And the game wasn't a runaway at that point. The coaches sent you in because they thought you might go all the way on it, and you didn't disappoint them. That's pretty good testimony.

"Still I know what the weeks have been like for you. And I *also* was surprised when they put you in for that run. When Coach Fowles told me about your quitting today, he asked me for a prediction on what you would do. Now, this is just between you and me, Keith, because my own rules are that I wouldn't run stuff back and forth. But I said to him, 'Okay, I have a prediction. I don't think he'll come back, because I just identify with the situation—the guy who's downhearted to start with, faces two, three more days in the season, then would come back and maybe some guys would joke about it, put him through some more humiliation. And then maybe he wouldn't play anyway. I just don't see why he'd come back.' That's what I told him.

"But I've been thinking about it, trying to see how I would look at it in your position. I guess what I'm reacting to now is a challenge. It has to do with your own pride, and with mine too. I have been so impressed at how the team has hung together all season long. I would feel very proud just personally if you came back and finished this season.

"It could be that you still wouldn't play at all on Saturday. But a week from Saturday or a year from Saturday it could mean an awful lot. Because to leave the team now could mean the same thing as leaving it last August 30. Keith, will you be there tomorrow?"

Keith said, "I don't know. I been thinking about it the last two days. Probably won't get me anything. But I've decided to go back."

After a pause, he said, "Hey, Rich? Thanks a lot."

THURSDAY, *November 4*

Jonny and I drove to yet another town on our quest for a football. The store didn't have the TD rubber ball, but it had some fine leather balls which Jonny liked. He fondly cradled one expensive professional-quality leather ball in his hand, and tested it with his throwing motion.

"Now this is really a good ball," he said. "Like, compare it with *this* one." He handed me another at about the same price. I couldn't tell the difference. "Really, that one I wouldn't want to throw, but *this* one. . . ."

He handled several balls, spun them, exchanged one for another in his hand.

"Any one you want, Jonny," I said.

"I don't know. A leather ball for just one game. . . ."

"Jonny, it's my gift to you—to the team. This game is important."

He thought for a moment, then put all the balls back in their boxes. "I guess I'll stick with the old ball," he said. "It's good enough."

"But Jonny, even the laces. . . ."

"I *want* to. There's something about using that ball. I just like the idea, you know?"

The sun came out for the final day of uniformed practice. There were fluffy clouds, and it was cold and windy.

In the locker room there were carefully hand-lettered posters, rumored to have been provided by a mother: "Laketown Always Gives 110%— Others 100%"; "Have no regrets." The Sleepy Hollow roster was pinned up beside them.

Several of the flu victims were back. So was Keith Allen. The team's spirit was loud, gay. Calisthenics were enthusiastic. At their conclusion, at 3:20, Jonny came prancing out, waving his hands in a double peace sign.

"Isn't this *terrific?*" Coach Fowles said, chuckling merrily. "This is why I like the last week best of all. But I'm really going to hate to see it end."

The team scrimmaged hard in the crisp air. Several players wore sweat shirts for the first time. Players not in the scrimmage stuck their hands into the tops of their pants to keep them warm.

They went to hang on the bars. For the last ten seconds of that, Coach Fowles directed the juniors to stand aside. "All right, last time *ever* on the bars, seniors. Juniors, let's hear it for the seniors. Last time *ever*, seniors." The juniors cheered their older teammates who hung on the bars for the last time.

Then they went up to hit the seven-man sled. "Good day to work," Coach Fowles said. "Freddie Delaney's birthday, good day to work. We've came a long way since August 25 . . . okay, just the seniors on the sled. Last time, seniors."

They lined up behind Rich Schenkle to bounce the row of dummies one at a time. They hit like demons as the juniors cheered them on. They

:296:

slammed off each of the seven dummies in turn, kicking up the hardened mud behind them. Even Bradford McClure, who had smiled sarcastically at the call for this sentimental drill, rammed the sled viciously, as if it mattered.

The team went to the manbuilder. The seniors ran it for the last minute. "Is that a tear I see, Stan?" Jonny said sardonically to his friend. Stan chuckled.

Then the seniors ran the tires, fast, sharp, and proud. And they ran the last sprint alone. The team retired happily to the locker room to shower before the meeting.

On Keith Allen's locker there were some scrawled messages. One said, "QUITTER." Another said, "the only regret Allen should have is that he didn't quit sooner." The writing was there when he went into the shower, but when he came out it was gone.

As Freddie Delaney came down the hall toward the classroom, players sang "Happy Birthday." He responded by giving them the finger and holding it through the entire verse.

". . . Okay, hey, pay attention," Coach Fowles said as the meeting came to order. "We're gonna have squad pictures taken tomorrow. If you wanna be in it, you make sure you're there. It's a one-shot deal. We'll start practice at three o'clock, work out for maybe an hour and fifteen or twenty minutes. Then shower, have a meeting until maybe 5:30 or so. Then change into your green jerseys and white game pants, shoulder pads, preferably game shoes with clean white laces. Now don't walk up to me at the last minute and say, 'Coach, I forgot my stuff.' There's nothing I can do about it. You want to be in the picture you'll have to stand there without your uniform."

"In your *Bermudas*," Jonny said, brushing his long, wet hair.

"I'll tell you, last year's picture was the most beautiful photograph of any athletic team I've ever seen, I can't believe the clarity. He's coming over here with a *thousand-dollar camera*. The pictures cost $2.35, but we'll pay some of that. You're going to have to pay maybe $1.00 or $1.50. I'll let you know later."

"When do we have to have the money in?"

"It depends on how it looks," Jonny said.

"We'll talk about that later," Coach Fowles said, "don't worry about that."

"Same time you had to have your mouthguard money in," Bruce Stacey said.

"Hey Brad," Jonny said, "how many mouthpieces do you owe for, four? five?"

"All right, let's listen up now. . . ."

"Seventeen?"

". . . They have cards on about 350 of our plays, but it doesn't matter. Nobody over there knows what Jonny is going to call on Saturday. Remember, the first time we played them they beat us 13–6, second time 42–0, last year 8–6."

He paused and examined his fingernails, then looked back up. "At the beginning of the year, out of twenty-two starters last year we had only *two* starters back, and there were a lot of *unbelievers*. Unbelievers not only in this very room, but in the community. People who thought, 'Aw, they aren't going to win a ballgame.' Then after the Port Chester scrimmage they were *sure* we weren't going to win a ballgame."

As he spoke, Coach Branahan wrote on the blackboard, "1–7." Then he said, "You know how many coaches and teachers said *that* was going to be our record this year?"

"Who were we supposed to beat?" somebody asked. The room laughed.

"We were going to win the intrasquad game," Jonny said.

"Gorton," Coach Branahan said, "that was the only game that a lot of people gave us a chance to win."

"I'll tell you what," Coach Fowles said, "we have a *real* football team. We threw one game away with our mental attitude, and another game with two blocked punts—which will *never* happen again. You know what we should be right now? We should be *undefeated*. And this team is *so close* to being undefeated.

"I'll tell you something else. Since I've been here this is the best football team Laketown has ever had, offensively—the best offense Laketown has ever had. Right here. I know what I'm talking about. Sure, we've had some great kids in the past, but they did not work as hard as *you* have worked. That is a fact. They were not in as good a shape as *you* are. That, too, is a fact. I'm not knocking those teams, I'm complimenting *you*.

"Boys, we've got everything going for us, including a tremendous mental attitude. And this is a chance of a lifetime to go down and play an undefeated team the first Saturday in November—that's *fabulous*. I don't know if *you* do what I did as a kid, but I always used to imagine myself being in on that *key* play, you know. Like in baseball I *always* imagined two outs, bases loaded, and I'm up. And perhaps you've felt the same way.

This is the *dream* of a lifetime, to play Sleepy Hollow, an undefeated team, for our last game together.

"Now there's still a lot of people that think, 'Well, Laketown's got a pretty good team, but they can't beat Sleepy Hollow.' There's still a lot of people that think that. And we're just gonna take that whole idea and turn it around on Saturday."

"Can you imagine if we *beat* them?" somebody said.

"Definitely," Coach Fowles said, "we will beat them. This team, right here."

FRIDAY, *November 5*

The last day of practice for the 1971 Harvesters was cold and clear. The practice reflected a paradox. On the one hand, the practice season had been wound down, all that was to be learned was learned already, jockeying for positions on the team was over, practice pants had been taken home to wash for the final time. On the other hand, what would be the most important game of the season was yet to be played. So the team, in shorts, went cursorily through some plays and passes and punts as if they weren't important, while within their individual moods there was a seriousness, a reserve, a reflectiveness.

"This is a bad practice," Coach Fowles said to me, relating more a fact than an emotion. He did not seem disturbed.

Then he told the seniors to take the last lap around the sandy track they had run for four years.

Seniors poured onto the track lustily, bumping for position as if it were a roller derby. Then as they ended the first straightaway and headed round the curve at the far end, they began to spread out, each running more alone. Juniors watched silently from where I was, the school end of the football field.

Coming down the last straightaway, Bradford McClure surged from back in the pack to take the lead, cheered on by other seniors. As he chugged around the turn toward the finish, he yelled between gasps, "Nobody—wants practice—to end—more than ME!"

The seniors finished and bunched up to walk to the sidewalk just outside the locker room where the juniors formed a line by which they would pass to shake hands. Bruce Stacey was the first one there. He passed briskly down the line, eyes lowered like the rest. Most of the juniors gave the seniors the *power* handshake, grasping each other's thumbs, and they muttered words of football endearment: "Good job. . . . Nice season, Bruce, Brad, Stan. . . . Luck tomorrow. . . . Thanks for the family. . . . Keep it together. . . . Be tough tomorrow. . . . Way to work. . . . Take it all, Jonny. . . . Thanks guys, good year. . . ."

Next to last in the line was Coach Branahan who also gave the thumb handshake. Last was Coach Fowles who, unlike the rest, grasped right hands firmly in his strong right hand, covered the grips with his left, stared straight into the eyes of his seniors, and thanked each by name.

There were an uncomfortable few moments just as it was over; players were embarrassed by the intimacy. Then Rich Schenkle, massaging his injured right thumb, broke the silence. "All those handshakes hurt," he said, smiling shyly.

Then they went into the locker room to shower before the meeting. There was enough spirit left for players to dance around Stan Beronski and tease him about his leopard-skin silk underwear—which appeared this last day inexplicably, and for which he offered not the least explanation.

I wandered outside. The sun had disappeared behind the hill, leaving the football field dull and distant in the haze, as lonely as an empty stage.

Jim Marshall stood a bit away from the door, gazing across at the field, and crying softly. "I never really believed it would end," he said. "I just thought I'd be playing on that field next year. It's a part of you, you know? I thought it wouldn't end, even though I knew. . . ."

Bruce Stacey came out and sat down, straddling an old yellow kitchen chair a few yards away. He cried silently too. "It's all over. Regrets? Sure I have. Four years of them. . . ."

". . . There were days when my ankle and my knee bothered me like you can't believe," Coach Fowles said, "and yet I just can't tell you how much fun this has been for me, to spend every single day with you people. It's been a real pleasure. And I'll tell you, you're a great group of people. Don't ever forget that. I said this last Monday and I'm gonna say it again right now: No matter what happens tomorrow, I know I can be proud of you. It's been really *beautiful* for me, and I mean that from the bottom of my heart.

"I don't know how you feel about teachers, and I don't know how you feel about coaches, but there's something that I think I gotta say. I think the greatest profession in the world is teaching. And I say that because no matter what you plan to do in life—think about it right now—you have to depend on good teaching. A teacher is not necessarily somebody in a classroom. There are many fine teachers who are not in classrooms.

"One of the basic needs that you people have, whether you want to admit this or not, is to help other people—the need to be needed. At some time in your life you make sure you take a little bit of your time and spend it with some kids. Try to help them, be a good listener. And if you're lucky, you might even try coaching a bit. Not necessarily on the high school varsity level. It can even be with those little kids that you see around."

He stopped and looked at the floor, then up around the room. He said softly, "And if you're real *real* lucky, just maybe you might find a group of people like we have right here. I don't know if you'll ever be that lucky. That's why I say it's been beautiful for me. Really and truly—and this is a very selfish thing for me to say—I hate to see this season come to an end. I really do."

He turned abruptly away from the team and faced the blackboard. He cleared his throat. "Okay, let's talk about Sleepy Hollow *one more time.* They are very quick off the football. . . ."

Rich Schenkle came up to me, sheepishly. "I forgot my stuff. Can I use your van to go home?"

Moments after he left, his brother Ben came up. "I forgot my stuff. . . ."

"Rich's got my van."

"Uh, well, when he comes back?"

"Will there be time?"

"I can try."

Rich came back and I took Ben to get his game uniform. When we returned, the team was already packed together on the gym bleachers, and the photographer was arranging his lights and his Hasselblat. Ben scampered to the locker room.

Coach Fowles rearranged the players, removed items from the background, asked detailed, admiring questions about the camera.

I whispered to him, "If you can stall just a minute, Ben can make it."

"What do you think I'm doing?" he whispered back.

Finally Ben appeared, was wedged between the third and fourth rows, and had his picture snapped, along with the manager, two coaches, and forty-three other Harvesters.

18

SATURDAY, *November 6*

When we arrived at Sleepy Hollow, no one met the bus to take us to the locker room. Coach Fowles irritably ordered his team to stay aboard and went in search of the host coach. After a wait of about fifteen minutes, someone was found who could direct the now disgruntled team and coaches to their dressing quarters.

The coaches taped hands and ankles and tattered shoes, and sent the Harvesters out to the field.

It was a fitting scene for the climax of ten weeks of football. It was cool, and the first frost blanket of the season left the field sparkling in the sun. It was the best turf the team had seen all year, lush green, no bare spots. The field was on a plateau, with a grassy slope leading down from the visitors' side to the parking lot, and a steep wooded hill rising behind the bleachers across the way. Sleepy Hollow had an elevated press box where their spotters would be posted with telephones linked to the bench.

Laketown had no such telephones. But the hosts had provided a modicum of equity by having a flatbed truck back up to the snow fence on the Laketown side. From that modest height, the JV coaches would spot for Laketown and sing out information on situations they read on the field.

The Sleepy Hollow team had not yet appeared, and Laketown spread over the field to loosen up. At one end, Ben Schenkle practiced extra points. In the center, Jim Marshall practiced kickoffs. On one side, Jonny threw to his backs and ends. The linemen went through blocking exercises, slamming into each other to rid their stomachs and muscles of those butterflies which circulate until the first hard contact is made.

Occasionally, Harvesters would look at the large crowd, perhaps 5,000 fans, which was filling the stands that ran along the Sleepy Hollow side from one 10-yard line to the other.

Sleepy Hollow came out, but not onto the field. They were dressed in red jerseys and silvery white pants. They went through crisp calisthenics, accompanied by psyching screams, outside the fence at the end near the school. They would not come onto the field until game time—a bit of psychology (perhaps, I thought darkly, related to there being nobody present to greet the team when it arrived) of the type to which Coach Fowles was always alert.

The Harvesters finished their drills and retired to the sidelines, but players continued to stalk back and forth. Jonny had stopped throwing on the field, but soon resumed on the sideline, lobbing 10-yard passes to anybody who wanted to catch. Jerry Spitz, the seldom-used lineman, caught the return throws for Jonny so the quarterback wouldn't risk jamming a finger. Bruce Stacey and Jim Petrowski as usual seemed most tense, clenching their fists and working their mouths while they paced silent, solitary, near the bench.

Coach Fowles said privately to me, "I don't even know if I want to say anything to the boys about this. But I heard some comments from some of the opposing players, comments about long hair on our kids."

An official came over to Coach Fowles. "Ready for the coin toss," he said, "out there." He gestured toward where the Sleepy Hollow team was gathered, outside the fence beyond the end zone.

"Hunh-unh," Coach Fowles said, "nope. I'm not sending my boys out there. They can come over here."

The official turned away to deliver the message, and soon came back with the expected compromise. "How about down there at the goal posts?"

"Okay, fine. CAPTAINS, LET'S GO, COIN TOSS." Stan Beronski, Jim Marshall, and Rich Schenkle started out. Coach Fowles stopped them. "If we lose the toss," he said, "kick off *with the wind,* from the school end of the field."

The officials introduced themselves, and then the three Laketown captains were quickly presented to their two Sleepy Hollow counterparts. They all shook hands coolly and grunted greetings. The referee flipped a JFK half-dollar into the air, and Rich Schenkle called heads. It was tails, Laketown would kick off with the wind.

"Why don't we ever win the toss?" Rich grumbled as they headed back toward their bench.

"Kicking off sucks," Stan said.

"Why?" I asked. "You guys will hold and get it right back."

"Cause I get killed on the kickoffs," Stan said.

"We kick, coach," Rich said.

"All right boys, that's *exactly* what we want, because we will hold them in their territory and get the ball back in good field position. Okay, everybody, get together, down there . . ." he pointed to the end of the field opposite the school, "get the family together by yourselves and then we'll play football."

The team trotted down through the end zone and gathered on the small grassy slopes in the shade of the adjacent woods. Then there erupted throughout the team the rawest show of emotions I had seen this season. Tears rolled down Jonny Penchak's face.

"I'M NOT ABOUT TO LOSE THIS FUCKING GAME!" he cried. "I LOVE EVERY-ONE OF YOU GUYS ON THE TEAM, EVERYONE OF YOU GUYS. AND WE'VE WORKED TOO HARD AND COME TOO FUCKING FAR. . . ."

Bruce Stacey was crying too, so were Jim Marshall and many others. "We're too much of a FAMILY!" Bruce shouted, "we're too CLOSE to lose!"

"WE AIN'T GONNA LOSE, THERE AIN'T NO WAY WE CAN LOSE TO THESE MOTHERFUCKERS. . . ."

"This is LAKETOWN. They better BELIEVE THEY ARE GONNA GET HIT. . . ."

"PLEASE, PLEASE, LAKETOWN, EVERYBODY. . . ."

The words came furiously, with pride and fear and unity. It was a display that caught me dumbly by surprise, made me feel a distinct outsider, an interloper. For in those moments I was struck aware that I didn't really belong, that I had never been hit, would not *be* hit today, with them, out on the field. Neither victory nor defeat would include me as it did all of them. Their uninhibited words and tears made me inch slightly away on the grass.

Bradford McClure spoke with his customary clarity and reserve. "We're ONE FAMILY, guys, and we always play together and work together. We are ALL together today. And the defense will get the ball and the offense will score, because we will all do our jobs. . . ."

"I AIN'T GONNA LOSE THIS FUCKING GAME!" Jonny screamed, wedging his way to the center of the tightening cluster. "NOT THIS ONE!"

"WE GOT EVERYBODY READY, EVERYBODY TOGETHER!"

"THEY AREN'T OUR BROTHERS, BRUCE!" Jonny yelled to the linebacker-fullback. "STOMP ON THEIR HEADS. THEY'LL DO IT TO US. . . ."

"THEM FUCKERS ARE GONNA LEARN SO MUCH TODAY IT'S UNBELIEVABLE. . . ."

Players groaned and shuffled with tension. They slapped each other on the backs and helmets, grabbed each other's arms in wordless communion. Coach Fowles stepped into the group.

"We're one family, boys," he said gently, "one team, one family. Every single one of us is going to take part in what we do today out there on the field, against Sleepy Hollow. Coach Branahan, anything you want to say?"

The breeze ruffled Sandy's hair as he opened his mouth, then closed it and shook his head. He glanced skyward, and the sun twinkled off his glasses. He offered no technical admonitions to the team.

"Guys, I am just really choked up," he said, shaking his head again. "I just want to say . . ." He cleared his throat. "This team is really so special to me that I will hate to see you go. I really, I just, I can't tell you what a beautiful team this is, what you guys have meant to me. . . ."

On the field behind them, the band struck up the National Anthem.

"Boys," Coach Fowles said, "I heard some comments coming out of the locker room, from some of your opponents, about something I don't even *see*. All I see when I look around me right now is *beautiful people*. I don't ever want any comments about hair or anything else on this football team. I know you will never make any. Because we are together to play a football game. And it is our LAST football game together. Boys, who's got more pride?"

"LAKETOWN!"

"We've got so much pride on this team I can't believe it. And you've earned your pride. Who works harder?"

"LAKETOWN!"

"Nobody I have ever seen has worked harder than you people. And because of that, and your pride, and our FAMILY, right now, on this football field, RIGHT NOW, who are we gonna beat?"

"SLEEPY!"

"WHO are we gonna beat?"

"SLEEPY!"

"SLEEPY!"

The team wheeled and broke into a run back to the bench.

All the Laketown seniors lined up on the hashmarks facing the center of the field as the mock coin-toss took place. Tears were still on the faces of many of them. Then they came to the bench and formed the human tulip that was their pregame huddle. They reached their hands to the middle, toward their coach, and leaned in silently.

"Last time ever as a family," Jonny said softly.

"Okay, guys, okay."

Coach Fowles waited until all voices were stilled. Then he said in a low voice, "Today is going to be beautiful." He gripped the many hands even more firmly. He closed his eyes for a few seconds. Then he said, "Who we gonna beat? . . ."

The players slapped their thigh pads rapidly as Jim Marshall approached the ball for the kickoff. He met it squarely and it sailed high end-over-end, into the end zone where it was downed.

"ALL RIGHT, JIM!" Coach Fowles yelled. The Laketown defense took the field.

Sleepy Hollow's new football was placed with its nose against the 20. They came out of the huddle and lined up surprisingly in the I, with three running backs in a tight row behind the quarterback. Then they shifted into the box to the right. Blockers opened a big hole and jammed the linebacker, Rich Schenkle, to the inside. The running back picked his way outside Rich for eight yards.

"Hey, RICH!" Coach Fowles yelled.

The second play was a duplicate, but Laketown had already adjusted, and the back was hit behind the line by Rich, then Barry Brill, then Al Stacey, then Bradford McClure, for a loss of two to the 26.

On third down they went left, but the runner slipped, recovered, and doubled back far around to his right, where virtually the entire quick line trapped him and dropped him for another five-yard loss.

They punted to Don Heidner, who took it on a bounce on his 45, ran to his right, and was thrown out of bounds in front of the home-team bench, on the Sleepy 46.

"ALL RIGHT, DEFENSE!"

"WAY TO HIT, RICH!"

Jonny immediately went to the air, hitting Ted O'Neill on a quick slant-out to the right. Ted stiff-armed one man and got near a first down, just outside the 36. A Sleepy Hollow offside penalty on the next play moved the ball to the 31 and gave Laketown its initial first down.

"They're rotating to Don Heidner," Coach Fowles said to Coach Branahan. The defensive secondary was moving around to whichever side Don flanked on, to give him added coverage.

Bruce Stacey got a tough three yards. On the way back to the huddle, Ted O'Neill put his arm on Jonny's shoulder and whispered to him. On the next play Jonny sprinted to his right, and threw on the run for Ted on the ten. The pass was short, Ted dove back for it, but the Sleepy defender he had beaten was now in perfect position and intercepted on the 12.

The defense took the field.

"OFFENSE," Coach Fowles called, "OFFENSE, RIGHT HERE. Okay, gentlemen, down on one knee. This is what they're in. They're in a *four front*. Our guards are covered, their ends are on the outside shoulder of our ends, the linebackers are up on our tackles. A four-three-four with man-and-a-half coverage on Don Heidner. Okay, Jonny?"

"Coach," Jack Forrest said, "when we come out wishbone left they take my man and stick him in the gap between the tackle and the end. They stick a linebacker on me."

"Okay, Jack, good."

Sleepy countered to the right for seven yards. They came back to the left side, and the runner was gang-tackled for no gain. On third and three, they called the counter again on the right side, but the quarterback gave it away just as Laketown had anticipated, by first hoisting the ball high as if to pass. Bruce Stacey blasted the runner head-on for no gain.

They punted to the 50. Brian Purcell let it bounce and it almost hit him before it rolled dead.

"That ball came awfully close to you," Coach Fowles told Brian as he came off.

Al Stacey dove left for one, then countered to the right side for two. The Sleepy line was tough and stingy. Jonny tried to hit Rich Schenkle on a quick slant-in from the left, but Rich was rammed hard just as the ball arrived, and it squibbed off his fingertips incomplete.

Ted O'Neill's punt rolled into the end zone—just beyond the diving grasp of Al Stacey who tried to down it near the goal line.

Moving from its own 20, Sleepy went to work on its left side, at Bradford McClure. They gained four, another four, then only one. Bradford, Stan, and Jim Petrowski finally shut them off.

On fourth and one, Coach Fowles hollered out, "PLAY IT SAFE, BRUCE, PLAY IT SAFE!"

But they punted. Don Heidner took it on his 38, and was pulled down on the 41.

Ben Schenkle slipped through the right side for five. Jonny faked into the line and pitched out right to Ben, but the fullback was hit as he took it for a five-yard loss. On third down, Jonny had good protection, but overthrew Ted O'Neill slanting out on the Sleepy 45.

The punting team went in. Ted O'Neill got away a good kick. The Sleepy runner took it on his 20 and cut to his right behind a full wall of blockers. Down went Al Stacey, Barry Brill, and others, as the man ran up the sideline in front of the Laketown bench all the way to the Laketown 43.

A clipping penalty brought the ball back to the Sleepy 14, but that didn't save Al Stacey from Coach Fowles's wrath. "What are you DOIN, Al? YOU WENT DOWN LIKE A DUMMY! IF YOU DON'T WANNA PLAY FOOTBALL, SIT DOWN!"

Punting center Rich Merrill came dizzily to the bench and slumped down. He had been kicked in the head. The manager brought him an ammonia capsule to inhale.

"LET'S GET IT BACK NOW, DEFENSE!"

Sleepy tried a screen pass to the right, but the receiver didn't look up in time, and the ball fell harmlessly. The quarterback sprinted right and threw to that flat, but Ray Meister knocked it away. Then the quarterback faked to his right and threw back to the left flat. Karl Walsh was not with his man, and the pass was complete to the 25 for a first down. John Finch was sent in for Karl at cornerback.

"Hey, KARL!" Coach Fowles shouted. "What are you DOIN! Karl, third down and long yardage, don't you play a *zone*? What were you doin?"

Karl shook his head and looked at the ground.

"Come on Karl, I want to hear some WORDS!"

"I was just playing a little too deep."

"Yeah, DEEP, but you go deep OUT, to the OUTSIDE. You gave him the whole SIDELINE. Karl, that's a MENTAL mistake. . . ."

Two passes to the right were incomplete, but scarily close. Coach Fowles adjusted to this surprise passing game by instructing left end Stu Rosenman now to go inside, and Rich Schenkle, the linebacker behind him, to swing to the outside.

Sleepy faked a pass and pulled a draw, a delayed hand-off to their quick halfback.

"DRAW! DRAW!" screamed the bench.

He slipped through to his left, inside Bradford McClure who was pushed out, for 15 yards and the first down.

The ball was just short of the 40 as the first quarter ended. Sleepy had not yet been out of its own territory.

As the second quarter began, Coach Fowles yelled out to his corner-back, "HEY, RAY MEISTER, HEADS UP! WATCH THE LONG ONE!"

A pass over the middle fell incomplete. Then the quarterback worked to his left, passing complete in the flat. Al Stacey slipped off the tackle, and the receiver got loose to the Laketown 35.

The quarterback tried a draw, but Barry Brill was stunting on the play and dropped the fullback for a loss of three. A jump-pass to the left flat got seven, making it third and six on the Laketown 31.

"WATCH THE SCREEN PASSES NOW," Coach Fowles shouted.

The quarterback faked a draw, skillfully hiding the ball in his belly with his back to the line, and threw a screen pass to the right. But Rich Schenkle had read it, and leveled the receiver with a mighty swat of his forearms for no gain.

On fourth down, the quarterback rolled to his left, jumped, and threw. The receiver made a one-handed catch on the 25, cut back in and then out, and was finally thrown out of bounds on the five. First down and goal to go.

Again the quarterback rolled left, but Bradford shot through to drill him back to the 11. A substitute came in from the Sleepy bench, and whispered in the quarterback's ear.

"HEY, AL STACEY, HEADS UP! JOHN FINCH, MAN-TO-MAN ON THIS SIDE!"

The quarterback dropped back, looking to his left. What he saw was Stan Beronski barreling in. He whirled back to his right and, just as Stan drove him off his feet, threw hurriedly incomplete. Third down.

"HEY, STAN, HIT THAT END, SLOW HIM UP, STAN!"

As Sleepy lined up, Stan rocked back and forth, swinging his padded arms and staring at the end. Whacking the end en route, Stan again fired in and hit the quarterback as he threw. The pass floated over the middle, almost far enough for Ken Furst who dove and just missed the interception as the ball bounced on the goal line.

On fourth down, Sleepy sent in its field-goal unit. The kicking tee was put on the Laketown 17. The Harvester line dug in to rush the kick. The snapback was fast, Bradford McClure was flipped upsidedown at the line, and the kick was perfect. But Sleepy was called offside. One of their players yelled at the official, but the five-yard penalty was marked off. Now the kick would be from the 22.

"WATCH A FAKE! WATCH A FAKE!"

Sleepy intended no fake, but the snap from center bounced in front of the holder. He picked it up and tried to run to his left, but Rich Schenkle was after him, and caught him on the 23. Laketown had held and took over.

Coach Fowles again went at Al Stacey. "Al, I've never seen you like this. What's the matter? You all right? I saw a kid knock you DOWN, that's never happened before. Are you sick, Al?"

Al shook his head.

Ben Schenkle gained two up the middle.

"CHINSTRAP, ANYBODY GOT A CHINSTRAP?" Somebody threw one out to tackle John Curtis.

Jonny hit Ted O'Neill in the right flat, but it only gained a yard. Bruce Stacey got to the 30, three yards short, and the punting team went on.

Ted O'Neill got off a dismally short punt, but got a good roll to the Sleepy 48.

"I was open," Don Heidner told Jonny on the sideline. "All the 70 quicks. If you'd roll to the right. . . ."

Sleepy went to the air, and again to the flats, getting a first down on a pass to the left on the Laketown 43. Then they tried a sweep to the left. Bradford had penetrated and forced the runner deep, but he got by the Laketown tackle and gained four yards to the 39.

"TOO MUCH, LAKETOWN, TOO MUCH!"

A plunge got four to the 35.

The officials gave the four-minute warning.

The quarterback rolled right and threw a jump-pass, but Bruce Stacey batted it down. On fourth down and two, Sleepy would go for it.

"JOHN FINCH, PLAY YOUR AREA. RICH, JUST PLAY YOUR AREA, DON'T GET SUCKED IN!"

The quarterback rolled to his right and threw for the sideline—right into the arms of Rich Schenkle who took it on the 30 and banged straight ahead until he was wrestled down on the Laketown 40.

The Laketown bench, and the Laketown end of the stands across the field, were ecstatic.

On a counter, Ben Schenkle got five, to the 45. Jonny pitched out to the right to Bruce Stacey on a stomp. Tom Kase and Ted O'Neill were out ahead of him, but Bruce cut back in and ran into a crowd, gaining only three when it looked like a good path had been cleared to the outside. Third and two on the 47. Jonny called the bomb.

He dropped straight back, set up, waited a second, then threw perfectly. Don Heidner had split two defenders, took the ball over his shoulder on the Sleepy 40 without breaking stride, and raced the rest of the way for the first touchdown of the day.

The bench waved its arms and hopped in wild jubilation. Coach Fowles hugged Jonny as he came off. "Let's kick it," he said, motioning Ben to stay in.

The snap from Rich Merrill was high, forcing Ted O'Neill, the holder, to stand up to grab it. Ben immediately stepped in front of him to pass-block, and Ted threw for Bruce Stacey who had alertly slipped into the end zone. Bruce was knocked down, interference was called. The ball was moved from the three to the one-and-a-half-yard line, and now Coach Fowles decided to run it.

Jonny took the snap, kept it himself, and, behind clean straight-ahead blocks from Tom Kase, Jack Forrest, and Ted O'Neill on the right side, scooted into the end zone.

Sleepy Hollow was behind for the first time this season. With one minute and twenty seconds left in the half, the bench screamed and yelped its pleasure.

"They're going to be throwing now," Coach Fowles said.

Jim Marshall again kicked deep, to the seven. The return came back up the middle to the 36.

The quarterback dropped back to throw. His left end took a few medium-speed steps straight ahead, faked to the outside, and then turned back and sprinted upfield. The quarterback pump-faked to him on the early move, then dropped two steps farther back and heaved. The end's fake had drawn cornerback John Finch and safetyman Ken Furst in, and now he was several strides behind them. The end took the pass—as perfectly thrown as had been Jonny's moments before—and dashed the remaining 30 yards with nobody near him, for the touchdown.

The bench was stunned, the coaches were calm. "They been catching square-out passes," Coach Fowles said, "and then the kid turned upfield and broke it. It was *this*, you know, down, out, and down. They had the fake and the touchdown."

"Very fast man, too," Coach Branahan said.

"But the point is this: We gotta tell Ken to *give up* the short pass, don't worry about that . . ."

"We *did*, Buddy, that's what we *did* . . ."

"But that time he tried to come up, he took the fake, and the kid was gone."

Sleepy elected to try to tie the game with two extra points. But the quarterback was rushed and overthrew his man on the right side. The score stayed 8–6.

"It was *Ken's* fault," Ray Meister said on the sideline as he came off.

"I know it's not *your* fault," Coach Branahan said to his left corner-back. "Gotta have John Finch get on him, play him bump-and-run like he did. But Ken should be outside."

Sleepy tried a short onside kick, but Tom Kase fell on it on the Laketown 47.

"Jonny, HEY, JONNY!" Coach Fowles called, "one minute left. Use up your time-outs now."

But Jonny wanted more right away. He dropped back and threw deep for Ted O'Neill, but too far. The defender behind Ted took it over his shoulder, and turned back upfield to the Sleepy 30. A clipping penalty moved it back to the Sleepy seven.

"HEY, BRUCE, LAURA WHITE!" Coach Fowles shouted. The team went into its spread-out deep defense, willing to give up short yardage to protect against the touchdown play.

"KEN!" Coach Branahan yelled. "TELL 'EM HEADS UP FOR THE DRAW!"

"WATCH A DRAW!" Coach Fowles echoed.

A draw it was, up the middle to the 20. The half ended.

The team ran off toward the end of the field where they'd had their pre-game meeting. Several of the players looked back over their shoulders at some kind of disturbance near the stands behind the Sleepy bench.

". . . We don't HAVE any tomorrow, LAKETOWN!" Rich Schenkle yelled.

"TWENTY-FOUR MORE MINUTES, LAKETOWN!"

"DEFENSE!" said Bradford McClure. "We're playin FOOTBALL and NOTHIN ELSE! None of that SHIT!"

"YOU GUYS TACKLE HIM AND HE STARTS PUNCHIN YA," Jim Petrowski shouted in a near hysterical voice, "THAT'S A 15-YARD PENALTY!"

"We're gonna beat 'em on the SCOREBOARD!" Bradford said. "If they wanna get all mad they forget about playing football, they forget to COVER THEIR MAN. . . ."

"We can't fight," Jim said, "WE ADMIT IT! WE PLAY FOOTBALL!"

"Hey, give that Gatorade to the guys that PLAYED first. . . ."

"If no one's open, don't THROW it," Bradford said. "Man, we're just screwing OURSELVES. Just EAT it. . . ."

"Jonny, we can run at SEVEN. Jonny, Jonny, we can run at SEVEN."

"Boys, let's get together, everybody listen." The team quieted and heads turned to face Coach Fowles who stood on the downslope and looked up at them.

"This is it, this is the one we want. Let's bring it in a little closer, and everybody get down." The players huddled together, and sat on the grass.

"All right, let's start with defense, the most important thing of all. From now on, when that fast end splits five or six yards, we want the cornerman to his side—that'll be John Finch—to come back off the football at a forty-five degree angle *before* the ball is snapped. Your first move will be back and out. Your number one job then is going to be, if that end is in front of you, you start dropping back as he comes off the ball. Because they throw that thing—the quarterback doesn't even look, the ball is on its way when the kid turns around. You'll pick it off, John. So we want you at least eight yards back and at an angle toward the sideline. Now the first time they throw it they will not expect that. And if the kid goes ahead and throws it, John Finch is going to get it and we might get a touchdown.

"All right, defensively and every other place you're doing a good job, boys. I'll tell you what, and I know I can speak for Coach Branahan, we are *so proud* of the way you played this first half. But we're *better*. We've always been a *second-half* team. . . ."

"Let's GO, Laketown!" Bradford said.

". . . You know that as well as I do. All right, offensively. Instead of trying to move your people *laterally* as much, just hit the man and try to drive him back off the line of scrimmage. Our backs have done a good job running on daylight all year. Listen, we are so *explosive*, we can score on any play, *any time*. They're gonna kick off to us and we will have the football. Let's show all these people down here what a real offense *is*.

"Our kicking game has been good. Jim Marshall, you're doin a tremendous job on kickoffs. Punting's not bad. We're playing *errorless* football. Only one mistake and we gave up that touchdown. But you guys came back on that extra point like champions and stopped them. Yes?"

"What was goin on at the sidelines at the end?"

"Some people were complaining at the officials, and the officials walked toward the bleachers and uh, well, the crowd reacted to the officials. And you know what that is? That's *bush*. I mean we are above that sort of thing like you can't believe. We've got too much class. Now, any comments, little tips or anything?"

Cary Grimes, the reserve end, raised his hand tentatively. "Coach, I think that back, number 2, when they're gonna pass he gets down in the set with both hands on the ground. When they're gonna run he's only got one hand down."

"All right. Cary Grimes feels that number 2 for Sleepy Hollow, when he's got both hands on the ground they're passing."

"They're centering on *one* every time."

"Hey, did everybody hear that? They're centering the ball on GO, ONE. Look, you know what you did when you came out for football? You took a *gamble*. You are gambling with your body in one of the roughest games that we have on the face of this earth. *Gamble on defense* a little bit. Gamble like Bradford did, down near the goal line. Bradford was into the backfield like *wow!* Jack Forrest?"

"When we line up on offense, their linebacker yells either *in* or *out*, and that's the way their defensive line is gonna shoot."

"All right, everybody hear that? That tells us if they're going inside or outside. That's a definite advantage to our offensive linemen."

"They don't wanna play football with us," Jack Forrest said.

"They wanna *fight*," Bradford said, "but we're gonna play *football*."

"They're all *hotheads*."

"We're gonna beat them in the *worst way possible*," Coach Fowles said, "and that is on the *scoreboard*. That's what they *don't want*. You know, gentlemen, they thought they were just going to throw their jocks on the field today and beat us. Well guess *what* the little people from Laketown are doing. *This* is a football team, right here. And you know what? We haven't even started yet. Because in every single game we are a second-half team. This is a game of hit and be hit, and we are *hitting*. That is so beautiful to watch. Coach Branahan, anything else?"

"Just the same old thing: Secondary, you guys can't make a mistake out there, you just *can't*. We've been controlling their ground game, right? Ends, make sure you give a good crack at any end before you go in. And let's really put some pressure on that quarterback. He's been sprinting out to the box side."

"Coach, can we use the five-four a little more?" Ray Meister asked. "We used it like *once* the whole first half."

"The laura? For what advantage?"

"I think it's easier to cover passes."

"Well, we could, the only thing . . ."

An official walked up. "Coach, you got two minutes. You want the choice of which goal to defend, or you want to receive?"

"We want the *football*, sir."

"Fine, okay."

"*Yes sir*, we want the football. Hey, take care of that knee."

The official smiled and waved.

"Okay, now, Ray. If it's an obvious passing situation maybe we *could* stunt a little bit on that laura someplace. The only thing I don't like about it, Ray, is that it's weak against those bounce-offs and screens.

"All right boys, listen to me: You know how many more minutes we have together in football? Twenty-four. But you know what? They're gonna be twenty-four of the most precious minutes we've ever spent together. Boys, who we gonna *upset?*"

"SLEEPY! SLEEPY! SLEEPY!"

"Let's go boys, get out there and warm up."

It had become more cloudy and windy. The Sleepy Hollow cheerleaders had strung a huge sheet of paper between the goal posts at the opposite end of the field. The wind whipped the paper. The Sleepy Hollow team came through the snow fence and approached the paper in somber procession, walking. Their captain burst through the paper and continued walking, and the team followed in single file, silently, not looking over at the Laketown team. But Laketown was watching them.

"LOOK AT 'EM WALK!"

"Hey you guys, they can't run, they gotta WALK!"

I watched the Sleepy team gather slowly at its bench. "Is that a team ready to play football?" I asked Coach Fowles.

"*This* team is," he said.

Laketown took the kickoff to its 28 and got its second first down of the day. Bruce Stacey dove for three, Ben Schenkle ran from tailback for five. Bruce was stopped for no gain. Jonny gambled on fourth down, sending Ben behind Tom Kase and Ted O'Neill for three yards and a first down on the 39.

Jonny threw a quick slant-out to Ted O'Neill on the right to the 42. Ben gained a yard on the right side. On third and six Jonny called a stomp-left, intending to pitch out to Bruce Stacey around left end. That meant that the left guard and tackle were to pull and lead the play as blockers.

The play had been a consistent gainer all season, but was usually run to the right, to make use of right tackle Tom Kase's great speed as a blocker. This time Jonny took the snap, left guard Clifford Albert pulled smartly and was headed away. Jonny turned and pitched underhand toward Bruce, but the ball glanced off Clifford's left arm and bounced loose in the backfield. The lineman coming through Clifford's vacated spot beat Jonny to the ball, and Sleepy took over on the 36.

It was a crucial play. Jonny didn't know what had gone wrong. Perhaps Clifford had taken a slightly bigger step backward to pull; perhaps by pitching to the left side, Jonny's right arm was closer to the pulling guard than when pitching to the other side. In any case, Sleepy seized the momentum just when it seemed Laketown was moving, and now the defense would have to hang on.

Sleepy began running between the tackles and the ends, to both sides. They went right for five, driving Stu Rosenman outside. They went right again, pushing Stu inside this time and going outside for a first down on the 25. Coach Fowles took Stu out and put Freddie Delaney in.

"You're not going back in until you're *tougher!*" Coach Fowles barked at Stu.

They came back at the left side for a yard. Stu went back in. They hit the right side for four, to the 20. Then they swept the other way, chopping down the right side of the defensive line, to the 11. Finally they came back to their right, their line wiped out the entire left defensive side, and the back ran wide and untouched into the end zone.

They faked the kick, and ran right again for the extra points. The score was 14-8, and the Harvesters seemed tired and dispirited, as if the whole cliff-hanging season were suddenly on their backs.

"Let's go, Laketown, *huh?*" Bradford whined.

Ben Schenkle took the kickoff on the 20 back to the 30. Jonny bootlegged to the left, but was stopped for no gain. Bruce Stacey hit the right side for two. Jonny sent Don Heidner deep for the bomb. Three defenders were on him to knock it away. Laketown was forced to punt.

"It was supposed to be a bounce-pass to Bruce," Jonny explained as he angrily snapped off his chinstrap, "but I don't know where the hell he was. . . ."

Ted O'Neill's punt wobbled low only to the Sleepy 39, where it rolled dead.

"HOW MUCH PRIDE DO WE HAVE?" Coach Fowles yelled along the bench, clapping his hands. "LET'S GO!"

The Sleepy quarterback kept around right end for four. Freddie Delaney was now in, looking around at Jim Petrowski and Bruce Stacey for instructions on how to line up for every play.

"LAURA! LAURA, BRUCE!" Coach Fowles yelled, calling for the adjustment to shut off the powerful running game.

Sleepy came out in the I and didn't shift. The quarterback handed to the third man through. He was hit and the ball squirted free and was found under a swarm of Laketown defenders. Laketown ball on its 48.

Jonny had good field position, and there was plenty of time. It was a matter of momentum now.

He hit Ted O'Neill on a quick slant-in for five, but Laketown was offside. A draw to Bruce Stacey gained nothing. A pass to the right flat went off Ted O'Neill's usually sure fingers; one to the left went through Rich Schenkle's usually reliable arms.

Bruce Stacey complained to an official that somebody took a punch at him, and he yelled the same thing to the bench.

"WHAT NUMBER?" Coach Fowles called.

Ted O'Neill punted the ball away, but immediately a flag was thrown at the line of scrimmage. Rich Merrill had not had his mouthpiece in. Laketown was pushed back another 15 yards. Ted kicked again, to the Sleepy 33.

John Curtis complained of being punched. "MR. REFEREE, MR. REFEREE, SIR!" The referee came over to Coach Fowles. "Sir, you know I don't complain, and my kids don't usually complain. But my kids *are* complaining now that they are being poked in the eyes and slugged. Would you tell the umpire to watch for it please?"

The official nodded.

Sleepy ran with power into the left side for six, to the 39.

The third quarter ended. "OKAY, TWELVE MINUTES," Coach Fowles yelled, "LET'S GO, LAKETOWN!"

"STAY LOW, BRADFORD, STAY LOW!"

Again the power, Sleepy drove the whole left side of the line straight back for a first down on the 46.

"BRUCE! BRUCE! GET IN THE LAURA!"

The defense again moved out of the quaker into the five-four laura. Two straight-ahead power plays gained six. On third and four they countered, but Freddie Delaney was in and dropped the runner for a yard loss, on the Laketown 49.

The punter boomed it deep. Don Heidner took it over his shoulder on the 10, faked one tackler away, spun from another, and brought it back to the 21.

Ben dove for one, then countered the other way for three more. On third and six, Coach Branahan sent in instructions for Jonny to try the bootleg.

"I don't think so, Sandy," Coach Fowles said, but he didn't overrule his assistant.

Jonny ran the bootleg to his right, and was stopped for no gain.

Ted O'Neill's punt bounced on the Sleepy 46 and rolled on to the 34 where it was downed.

Sleepy swept to the right for three, and to the left for two. A 15-yard penalty was called on Sleepy for a personal foul.

"WATCH THE DRAW! HEY, BARRY BRILL, WATCH THE DRAW!"

They passed complete to the left flat, but cornerback Ray Meister was there to make a resounding head-on tackle. A pass over the middle was complete. Barry Brill slipped off the man, and Al Stacey finally brought him down on the 49, where it was a first down.

Ray Meister was staggering. "Ray, Ray come on out," Coach Fowles called. Ray didn't respond. "Get somebody in for him, Coach."

Ray was steered to the bench. Somebody threw a cape around his shoulders, and he was given an ammonia capsule to hold under his nose.

Two more personal fouls were called on Sleepy, and the ball was now moved back to the 15. On third down, the quarterback took the snap and pitched quickly behind him. It was a quick-kick, and a magnificent one. It soared over the heads of the Laketown secondary, hit on the Laketown 40 and continued rolling. The closest man to it, Karl Walsh, had no choice but to let it go, and it rolled dead on the Laketown 21.

"That was a beautiful football call," Coach Fowles said softly, "a really fine call by their coach, and one of the best executed quick-kicks I have ever seen."

Jonny threw incomplete twice, then on third down was smothered back on the nine-yard line.

". . . GIVE HIM A WARNING. . . ."

"MR. REFEREE! MR. REFEREE, SIR!"

The head linesman came over.

"Sir," Coach Fowles said, "would it be possible for me to have a rules discussion with the referee about a case. . . ."

"Maybe I can explain it, Coach," the official said. "He didn't *see* him do it, he only was *accused* of slugging. The umpire said if he had *seen* him do it, he would have thrown him out."

"Uh, okay. I thought maybe he was, uh, okay, you better get back to the game."

"The point is," Coach Fowles said to me, "the umpire is right there, and he is *supposed* to see things. His *job* is to see it if the linemen are slugging."

Ted O'Neill stood in the end zone to punt. The snap was low and Ted hurried the kick, barely getting it away. It reached only the Laketown 25. Three minutes were left.

John Curtis again complained to an official, and the official waggled a finger at one of the Sleepy linesmen.

Sleepy gained seven on two power plays. On third down, the quarterback rolled out to his right, stopped and looked, then was forced to run. Bradford McClure, coming all the way from the other side of the field, caught him from behind at the 16.

With fourth and one, Sleepy lined up for a field goal. The kicking tee was placed on the 23. With the high school goal posts on the rear line of the end zone, the kick would have to travel 33 yards.

"WATCH OUT FOR A FAKE!" Coach Fowles hollered.

But there was no fake. The kick was perfect, with yards to spare. With one minute and fifty-six seconds left in the game, the score was 17–8.

Laketown lined up to receive the kickoff.

"HEY, BEN SCHENKLE," Coach Fowles shouted, "I WANT DON HEIDNER TO CATCH THE BALL. LET DON HEIDNER RETURN IT."

The short kick was fielded by Ken Furst on the 25, and he brought it back to the 32.

"Jonny," Coach Fowles said as his quarterback started in, "use your time-outs now, watch the clock. . . ."

Jonny dropped back, was forced to roll out to his right, tripped, and threw off balance and short, right into the arms of a defender on the 42.

Sleepy ran twice into the line and the game was over.

The season was gone, like a thunderstorm, leaving only echos of all its power and violence. The band played the Notre Dame victory march as the opposing teams congratulated each other on the field.

The Harvesters walked off toward the bus. Coach Fowles ran off the other way, to talk to the Sleepy coach. The team gathered at the bus and waited impatiently for their coach.

"Come on, let's *go*," Bradford whined.

"Where the hell is Coach Fowles?"

"Sleepy Hollow's a bunch of fucks," Bruce Stacey said.

Finally Coach Fowles arrived, climbed aboard, and faced his team down the aisle.

"Boys, we did not quit, we never gave up. We made a couple mistakes, but nobody's perfect."

The busdriver closed the door and got underway. Coach Fowles swayed as the bus lurched over bumps.

". . . We came out of *nowhere* this year. The real optimists said we'd win *one* game. Five and three is not bad. *We can't go back and undo that.* We can't undo that no matter how we want to. We've won together and we've lost together. But in a sense I don't think we've ever really lost. Remember some of the things you learned about yourself this season. You people have class, and you always *will* have. When I say I'm proud of you, I'm not just talking about football. I'm talking about a lot of things in a lot of ways. We played a good football team today. But in many ways, gentlemen, they'll never touch us, *never*."

The bus growled onto the highway. Coach Fowles raised his voice above the noise of the engine.

"Seniors, it's been out of this world. Juniors, start thinking about our first football game next year and get yourself ready for a great season. I think the seniors really set some kind of example for you juniors this year, and don't forget it.

"Now Monday we'll collect equipment. Take it home, clean it up, take care of it. Because we need it for next year. Because the family never actually stops. It just continues. It goes on."

He sat down and stared out the front window. Behind him now there were tears, on the faces of Jonny, Don Heidner, Bruce Stacey. Other heads were down on the seatbacks, so I couldn't see. . . .

The bus clanked and groaned in its own mechanical anguish up and down the hills. The season was over. Suddenly all those boring days of practice, all those exciting days of games, were compressed into a melancholy memory of everything having happened too quickly. My tape recorder, hanging at my side, was my buffer against tears, a professional reminder that I was an adult at work, not a kid football player. But I was not too far removed from the team to sense their private thoughts, that so much had happened so fast, that ten weeks of ordinary high school football was like a lifetime in some ways. The family goes on. Nothing would ever be exactly the same, but the pain and joy of this year were no more intense than they had been last year, or would be next year.

Was it all then no more than a parade of similar practices and games, repetitious wins and losses, season after season? Was the broiling intensity I had felt in these ten weeks of no further significance beyond the memories stored, and regrets?

"We're gonna do both."

Coach Fowles's words broke my reverie.

"What?"

He smiled and looked directly into my eyes. "The day is coming, Richard, when we're gonna do both. We're going to help kids understand important things about their own lives, and we're going to win our football games. We're gonna do both. I know that as sure as I know the sun's coming up tomorrow morning. And when it happens—maybe next year, maybe the year after—people won't believe it."

AFTERWORD

In a sense, the season died hard, as if jealous of its hold on the partici-
pants. Already by Monday the players and coaches were talking about
other things in their lives. Players would move on to basketball, wrestling,
swimming, lacrosse, baseball. . . .

But there were the formalities. There was the meeting on Monday.
Coach Fowles went casually over the Sleepy Hollow game with the team,
passed on praise from the opposing coach, apologized for not getting all
the seniors in for the final few plays.

There was the sluggish collection of equipment.

There were the awards and dinners. Mothers catered a buffet dinner
for the team, and the players came dressed casually in sport jackets, ties,
and dungarees. Coach Fowles presented to each of the players tiny
trophies with golden footballs and their names engraved.

Jonny Penchak, Rich Schenkle, and Bruce Stacey were named to the
all-league team, with Stan Beronski and Jack Forrest getting honorable
mention. Jonny was named all-county.

The all-county banquet, to celebrate the forty-four players chosen,
was held in a large restaurant. Jonny was the only one in attendance with
truly long hair. Before the roast beef, there was an opening prayer, a
football metaphor, which concluded with:

> "O God, help us keep our eyes on the ball
> as we acknowledge our forgetfulness
> that You are the author of life
> and life's games.

Remind us to line up everything
with You and then allow us to
carry our heads high as we head
towards the end zone. You,
Above all, keep running interference for us.
We need it in these troubled times."

The main speech was given by a coach from Harvard, who talked about motivating boys to become men. He said that courage, leadership, and teamwork were the most valuable things we could teach young people, and that these things were not taught in the classroom, but by high school coaches. "You find this only in sports," he said. "If we lose sports, this country is vulnerable. . . . Gentlemen, good luck, Godspeed."

The master-of-ceremonies concluded by saying, "Tonight, boys, whether you like it or not, you've all become part of the establishment."

"Right on," Jonny said softly, raising a fist, and looking down at the citation on which his name was spelled wrong.

Bradford McClure's father died suddenly just before Christmas. "All the shit that's around us all the time," Bradford told me in a halting voice, "all the bullshit. I know my father was alive yesterday, and he's dead today. That's what's important. I loved him. Why do we have to spend so much time on stuff that doesn't mean anything?"

Jim Petrowski's father died, too, less than a month later, before getting a chance to see Jim in the wrestling championships. "It's hard to believe," Jim said, "like it's not real."

We stood in the silent funeral parlor. Jim looked frail in a blue jacket too large for him. His hair, combed, swept down over the tops of his eyes. He stood with his mother and his older brother.

"We'll be all right," he said, "we're all going to get along okay."

The family, then, would go on.